THE LIFE

OF

SIR JOHN FRANKLIN, R.N.

By H. D. TRAILL

AUTHOR OF 'THE NEW LUCIAN' 'WILLIAM III' 'THE MARQUIS OF SALISBURY'
'LORD STRAFFORD' ETC.

WITH MAPS, PORTRAITS, AND FACSIMILES

LONDON
JOHN MURRAY, ALBEMARLE STREET
1896

R.ᵗ Admiral Sir John Franklin, Kᵗ
K.C.H., K.R.G., D.C.L., F.R.S., etc.
from a drawing by Negelin.

PREFACE

THE exploits of SIR JOHN FRANKLIN are written so large across the map of the Arctic Ocean and its coasts; the circumstances of his tragic end have rendered his name and achievements familiar to so many Englishmen not otherwise specially conversant with the subject of Polar exploration; the story of his voyages and discoveries has so often been related as a part of the general history of English adventure, that the appearance of this biography, nearly half a century after his death, may seem to require a few explanatory words.

It has been felt by his surviving relatives, as it was felt by his devoted wife and widow, that to the records, ample and appreciative as many of them have been, of the career of the explorer there needed the addition of some personal memoir of the man. What Franklin *did* may be sufficiently well known to his countrymen already. What he *was*—how kindly and affectionate, how modest and magnanimous, how loyal in his friendships, how faithful in his allegiance to duty, how deeply and unaffectedly religious—has never been and never could be known to any but his intimates. But that knowledge ought not to be confined to them. The character of such men as Franklin is, in truth, as much a national possession as their fame and work. Its influence may be as potent and its example as inspiring; and it has been felt by those responsible for the production of this volume that some attempt should at last be made to present it to his fellow-countrymen.

It was the long-cherished desire of Miss Sophia Cracroft, niece of Sir John Franklin, and constant and attached companion of Lady Franklin, to perform this labour of love herself, and it supplied the animating motive of her unwearied industry in collecting the mass of documents hitherto unpublished which have been employed in the preparation of this work. Failing health and almost total loss of sight, however, prevented the accomplishment of her purpose, and eventually her executors, Mr. and Mrs. G. B. Austen Lefroy, have entrusted the work to the present writer.

Both to them and to him it is a source of much satisfaction that this Biography should issue from the house of Mr. John Murray, whose father was the publisher of Franklin's two Narratives of his Arctic Explorations and the personal friend of their author and Lady Franklin, and who has himself taken a warm interest in the present undertaking.

In dealing with Franklin's achievements as an

explorer ample assistance was accessible to me in already published works. The story of his first two Arctic expeditions—the former a tale of unexampled toil and sufferings heroically endured—has been told with admirable clearness, simplicity, and modesty by Franklin himself. In 1860, after the return of the Fox from her famous and successful voyage, the late Admiral Sherard Osborn, himself an active and distinguished member of one of the earlier search expeditions, published a little volume of a hundred pages, entitled ' The Career, Last Voyage, and Fate of Franklin,' containing a condensed but masterly sketch of his hero's earlier discoveries and a most graphic and moving description of his last ill-starred adventure. The particulars of Sir Leopold McClintock's search for and discovery of the sole extant record of the crews of the Erebus and Terror have been gathered from that gallant officer's painfully interesting narrative of his voyage. But still more important and indeed invaluable help has been derived by me from the able and exhaustive monograph on Franklin contributed to the ' World's Great Explorers ' series by Admiral A. H. Markham, himself an Arctic officer of distinction, whose ready kindness, moreover, in advising me on an obscure point in the history of Franklin's closing hours and in perusing the proofs of the chapters dealing with his last expedition I desire most gratefully to acknowledge.

Nor can I close this record of my obligations without expressing my thanks to Miss Jessie Lefroy for such a lightening of my labours by the methodical arrangement of documents as only those who have suffered from the lack of such assistance in examining and digesting voluminous masses of manuscript material can fully appreciate.

H. D. T.

LONDON, 1895.

CONTENTS

LIST OF ILLUSTRATIONS

LIFE

OF

SIR JOHN FRANKLIN

——◦————

CHAPTER I

EARLY YEARS AFLOAT

1786-1807

THE name of Franklin has none of that obscurity of origin which sometimes perplexes a biographer at the very threshold of his work. Its blood and history unmistakably proclaim themselves. The 'franklin' was the old English freeholder— the man who held direct of the Crown, and was frank, or free from any services to a feudal lord. He was, in fact, the original type of the small independent country squire, and so continued to be until, at any rate, the time of Chaucer, whose delightful description of the 'Frankeleyn' pilgrim in the Prologue to the 'Canterbury Tales' distinctly stamps him as of this rank. By Shakespeare's day, however, it is clear that his status had somewhat declined. More than one reference to a 'franklin' and a 'franklin's wife' in the Shakespearian drama shows clearly enough that the word no longer designated any one of sufficient importance to have it written of him that 'at sessions ther was he lord and sire;' still less that 'ful ofte tyme he was knight of the schire.' We may take it as certain, in fact, that before the Elizabethan period the title of 'franklin' had become identified with the order of well-to-do substantial yeomen; and though by that time of course the process of converting the description of men's rank or calling into their surnames had long since completed itself,

B

there were in continuing existence, no doubt, many English families whose surname still represented their status. There were still Franklins by name who had originally been franklins by position. The famous American statesman and natural philosopher claimed descent from 'a family which had been settled for four centuries at Ecton, in Northamptonshire;' and it was from this same sturdy order of Englishmen, for many an age the pillar of the country's prosperity in peace and its right arm in war, that John Franklin, the famous Arctic explorer, sprang.

The family had been East Anglian from as far back as it was possible to trace it. A sister of John Franklin's, who had been at pains to investigate its history, states that her forbears came originally from the county of Norfolk. Her inquiries were not successful enough to enable her to fix the period of migration, but there is evidence dating from the early years of the eighteenth century that the family was at that time settled at Sibsey, near Boston, in Lincolnshire, on an estate which had even then been in their possession for several generations. The wealthier yeomanry of those flourishing times took rank almost as a small local squirearchy, whose members were not always among the most provident of men ; and at least two generations of the Sibsey Franklins seem to have lived up to this position with an only too dramatic success. The family tradition, at any rate, is, that John Franklin, the grandfather of the explorer, following paternal example, so greatly reduced the ancestral patrimony as to leave little more at his death than 'a moderate subsistence for his widow;' and, forced to rebuild their fortunes, the Franklins passed, as many a good English house has done before and since, from the ranks of the country gentry into those of trade. John Franklin's widow, 'a woman,' writes one of her descendants, 'of masculine capacity and great resolution of character,' rose to the occasion. She apprenticed her eldest son Willingham to a grocer and draper in Lincoln, and as soon as he was out of his indentures removed with him to the market town of Spilsby, where she opened a little shop, and, 'not content with acting as housekeeper for her son, superintended the business in every department which admitted of female supervision with the utmost activity and success.' Thanks to her assistance and to his own energy, Willingham prospered in his trade, added to it in due time a banking business, married the daughter of a substantial farmer in 1773, and, six years later, had accumulated sufficient capital to acquire the freehold of his house and shop in the town, and to purchase a small property a few miles off as a place of retreat for his old age. It was in the house at Spilsby, on April 15, 1786, that John Franklin first saw the light.

He was the fifth and youngest son and the ninth child of a patriarchal family of twelve. The second and third of his four elder brothers (the fourth died in infancy) rose, like himself, to distinction in the public service. Willingham Franklin, the second son, who was seven years John's senior, was sent to Westminster and Oxford, becoming scholar of Corpus, and afterwards Fellow of Oriel. He was called to the Bar from the Inner Temple, and was in 1822 appointed Puisne Judge of the Supreme Court at Madras, where, two years later, his career was prematurely cut short by cholera. James Franklin, the third son, entered the East India Company's service as a cadet in 1805, served with credit in the Pindari war, and singled himself out as an officer of considerable scientific attainments. He was employed on important Indian surveys, and after his retirement from the service was elected a Fellow of the Royal Society. He died in 1834 at the age of fifty-one.

Of Franklin's seven sisters, two died unmarried: one of them in comparatively early years, the other, Miss Elizabeth Franklin, at an advanced age. Of the five married sisters, two also died before attaining their thirtieth year. Sarah Franklin, the younger of them, had become the wife of Mr. Selwood, and was the mother of the two ladies who married two brothers of a name destined to become illustrious throughout the English-speaking world, and the younger of whom still survives as the Dowager Lady Tennyson, widow of the late Poet Laureate.

A third sister, Hannah, married Mr. John Booth, and their daughter Mary became the wife of Franklin's staunch comrade and friend, Sir John Richardson.

It was, perhaps, with his sister Isabella, the sixth daughter of the family, that John Franklin was the most closely linked in after life. She married Mr. Thomas Robert Cracroft, and it is to the pious labours of her daughter Miss Sophia Cracroft, seconding and prolonging those of Lady Franklin, whose devoted friend and lifelong companion she was, that I am indebted for the copious materials on which this memoir is based.

Henrietta, the youngest daughter, married the Rev. Richard Wright, and died some ten years ago in extreme old age, leaving a son, the present Canon Wright, Rector of Coningsby, Lincolnshire.

The early life of a boy with half a dozen elder brothers and sisters is in most families much the same. He becomes the fag of the one, the pet of the other, and by turns the pride and the plague of their common parents. In John Franklin's case the fagging may have been remitted; but there is distinct evidence of the petting, which, moreover, was no doubt encouraged and justified by the fact that, like many children destined to a vigorous manhood, he was a singularly weak and ailing infant, whose prospect of being reared at all was during the first two or three years of his life considered extremely doubtful. Though undoubtedly of an affectionate and generally docile disposition, John, his brother-in-law Mr. Booth records, was 'not noted, like his brothers and sisters, for neatness and orderliness;' and the combination of this not uncommon failing with a certain harmless propensity—which indeed may even have been the germ of a virtue—led to unpleasant consequences. It was, in fact, the cause of at least one incident which was without precedent in the family, and which is spoken of even in the records of a later generation almost with bated breath. On the landing of the staircase in the house at Spilsby, as probably in many a similar spot in many another English household of that Spartan age, there hung a whip; 'but such was the dutiful

obedience at all times paid by the children to their parents'
that from an instrument of correction it had declined into a
mere emblem of authority. It was reserved, however, for the
future explorer to show that, like the sword of the magistrate,
it was not borne in vain. Opposite to the Franklins' house
stood that of the Rev. Mr. Walls, the owner of Boothby
Hall, a gentleman of 'ample private fortune,' at whose door
the carriages of callers were constantly to be seen. Upon
the youngest son of the Franklin family the sight of these
arriving and departing visitors exercised an irresistible
fascination. Naturally, however, his parents, having regard
to that unfortunate want of ' neatness and orderliness ' above
mentioned, were unwilling to exhibit John as a sample of the
Franklin household, and he was 'strictly forbidden to go
over the way and stare at this daily spectacle.' But the
child ' seemed utterly incapable of putting a curb on his
curiosity.' The conclusion of the painful story is almost
visible already. A boy of untidy appearance, intensely
interested in the fashionable arrivals at the house of a
neighbour, and, in defiance of parental injunctions, determined
to assist at them : we have here the plot of a domestic
tragedy ready made. After repeated commands, repeatedly
disobeyed, the emblem of authority became once more an
instrument of correction ; the whip which hung on the
landing was taken down—and used. But, ' though the boy
was in no way rebellious on any other point, neither entreaty
nor whipping could prevent his punctual attendance at the
opposite door whenever a carriage drew up.' It was not
exactly the explorer's thirst for discovery, yet perhaps it may
have had its latent affinities with that passion. It was
certainly gratified with all an explorer's determination. With
his mind intently directed towards his childish object, and
his will resolutely bent on attaining it, it seems clear that
John Franklin accepted his punishment as a mere unpleasant incident of the enterprise, an experience to be submitted
to and disregarded, like the Polar cold, or the winter darkness
of the Arctic Circle.

But, indeed, there is evidence enough that he was a lad

full of adventurous aspirations. There was almost as much of earnest as of jest in the endeavour to outdo the projects of his playfellows, which an anecdote of his boyish years records. The family story goes that, after each of them had specified the particular feat of strength or heroism which he intended to perform on attaining manhood, nothing less ambitious would satisfy young Franklin than the construction of a ladder whereby to ' climb up to heaven.' Gravitation and statical laws were possibly recognised even then as obstacles ; but obstacles only existed to be overcome.

To a lad possessed by so early and extravagant a longing to do battle with the forces of Nature, it is a critical moment when he is first confronted with that mighty adversary in its most impressive and defiant form. The turning-point of his career is usually reached on the day when he receives his first challenge from the sea.

To Franklin it was not long in coming. At the age of ten he was sent to school at St. Ives, whence he was shortly afterwards transferred to that nursery of Lincoln-shire worthies, at which Charles and Alfred Tennyson were many years after also educated, the Grammar School at Louth ; and one day, during his earlier time at this school, he started off with a playmate to pay his first visit to the coast. His native town of Spilsby, though but a few miles inland, had no connections, by trade or otherwise, with any East Anglian port, and there had been nothing therefore in his surroundings to inspire him with curiosity as to maritime matters or with interest in a seafaring life. But that drop of brine which is in the blood of every Eng-lishman, and which has driven many a youth from the very heart of the Midlands to make his lifelong home upon the ocean, must have stirred in young Franklin's veins. Setting out from Louth one holiday with this young companion, he made his way to Saltfleet, a little watering-place some ten miles off, and there looked for the first time on that world of waters on which he was to play so memorable a part.

That one look was enough. The boy returned home as irrevocably vowed to a sailor's life as though he had

been dedicated by some rite of antiquity to the god of the
Sea. His father—like nine English fathers out of ten—
objected. That curious spirit of parental resistance to what
ever has been, and, it is to be hoped, ever will be, the
natural and irresistible vocation of so many thousands of
English sons, was strong within him. John was his
youngest—how often it is the youngest!—the Benjamin of
the flock ; and it would be a hard matter to part with him,
for all his 'want of neatness' and his undue curiosity
about the visitors over the way.

Mr. Franklin's attitude, in fact, towards his son's maritime aspirations was simply that adopted before and no doubt
since his time by innumerable British fathers similarly situated. It seems only to have differed from the traditional
paternal posture in that it was taken up with more intensity
of conviction and maintained with more persistency than in
the average case. Not many a father, that is to say, would
go so far perhaps as to declare, with the elder Franklin, that
'he would rather follow his son to the grave than to the
sea ;' though many, no doubt, have resorted to the means
adopted by him for testing the reality and seriousness of
the boy's inclinations. John, after all, was but twelve years
old. How many lads of that age, especially during the
school term—a very important point—had been seized with
what they imagined to be a passion for a seafaring life,
but what was in reality only a distaste for the restraints of
the class-room or a want of sympathy with the usher! Mr.
Franklin accordingly had recourse to a test which fathers in
like case have not infrequently applied, with, from their own
point of view, complete success. After two years' resistance
to his son's importunities he sent him for a cruise on board a
merchantman trading between Hull and Lisbon, no doubt in
the expectation that from that most efficient of hospitals for
the treatment of the sea-fever from which John was supposed
to be suffering, he would be able to report himself as 'discharged cured.' But, so far from yielding to this rough remedy
—even rougher in those days than in these—the malady
became more acute. The boy returned from his voyage

confirmed in his longing for a sailor's life ; and, this fact once
ascertained, Mr. Franklin, like a wise man, gave way. A
berth was soon obtained for him as a 'first-class volunteer'
on board the Polyphemus, Captain Lawford, and in the
autumn of 1800 his eldest brother Thomas was sent up to
London with him to procure his outfit and see him off. Duties
of this kind are not always dear to the heart of an elder brother, and when he is a young man of twenty-seven, actively
engaged in business, and full, as was the case here, of grave
business anxieties, some little impatience with the delays of
his mission is perhaps excusable. This, at any rate, seems the
probable explanation of Thomas's curious proposal to 'place
John at school' while awaiting the return of the Polyphemus, then engaged in 'demonstrating' off Elsinore, to Yarmouth Roads. 'I fear,' he writes to his father, 'that it will be
impossible for me to save Monday'—that is, to return by
that day. 'If it is possible I shall do it, for never was I
so tired of doing nothing, yet continually running after
this nasty cloaths-buying business, which to-morrow I shall
compleat.' Still, he speaks with a proper fraternal pride of
the result of his labours, and admits that 'the dirk and
cocked hat, which are certainly very formidable, are among
the most attractive parts of his dress.'

It was not till the end of October that the Polyphemus
arrived in port, and that Mr. Allenby, the friend with whom
John had been placed in London, was able to tell his father,
'I have just seen your delightful boy off in the Yarmouth
coach, inside ; paid all for him and gave him ten pounds in
his pocket. This I thought necessary, as he has his bedding,
&c., to buy at Yarmouth, and if he is admitted to a mess with
the officers he will have to subscribe to it.' He adds, with
what reads like a mild sidelong rebuke of the impatient
Thomas : 'I hope that Mr. T. Franklin is gone to Yarmouth
to meet him. If not, I hope he will go, as he will not have
to attend him again on the same business. In future I have
no doubt but he will fight his own way.' The first letter
written by the lad as an officer in His Majesty's service
gave every indication that he would. For this is the

bright, boyish, spirited fashion in which the young middy writes :—

H.M.S. Polyphemus, Yarmouth Roads : March 11, 1801.

Dear Parents,—I take this opportunity to inform you that we were yesterday put under sailing orders for the Baltic, and it is expected that we shall certainly sail this week. It is thought we are going to Elsineur to attempt to take the castle, but some think we cannot succeed. I think they will turn their tale when they consider we have thirty-five sail of the line, exclusive of bombs, frigates, and sloops, and on a moderate consideration there will be one thousand double-shotted guns to be fired as a salute to poor Elsineur Castle at first sight.

Then follows a passage which is interesting as showing that exploration was more in the boy's thoughts even then than the excitement of war :—

I am afraid I shall not have the felicity of going out with Captain Flinders [who was preparing a vessel for a survey of the Australasian coast], for which I am truly sorry, as we in all probability will be out above four months ; but if we do return before the Investigator sails, I will thank you to use your interest for me to go. You cannot hesitate asking Captain Lawford to part with me when you consider the advantages of it. Look at Samuel Flinders, who has the promise of getting his commission to go out with his brother. . . . [whereas, in our present service], if we take any ships or make any prize money, it will be two years before we receive it, and very little will fall to my share.

I will thank you when you write to Anne and Willingham to tell them of our expedition up the Baltic, by which some of us will 'lose a fin' or 'the number of our mess,' which are sailor's terms.

I will give you the names of the ships which are going with us, and of those which remain in Yarmouth under the command of Admiral Dickson. [Here follows a list of Sir Hyde Parker's fleet.] I think we shall play pretty well among the Russians and Danes if they go to war with us.

Please to remember me to my brothers and sisters.

I remain your affectionate son,

JOHN FRANKLIN.

Excuse my bad writing, as we expect it is the last boat. The ships that remain in Yarmouth are the Princess of Orange, the Texill (54), the Leyden (68), and two or three others for a guard.

Remember me to dear Henrietta, and tell her when I get a ship she shall be my housekeeper. Also to Isabella.

The youthful prophet was right. The 'salute to poor Elsineur Castle' shook Europe, and echoes through our history to the present hour. In less than three weeks after these words were written young Franklin was bearing a part in what the greatest of our naval heroes pronounced 'the most terrible' of the hundred battles he had fought.

The British fleet sailed from Yarmouth on March 12, under Sir Hyde Parker, with Nelson as his second in command, and arrived off Zealand on the 27th. Entering the Sound, in spite of the opposition of the Governor of Cronenberg, who, after protesting against their entrance, opened fire upon them from his batteries as they sailed through that channel on March 30 with a fair wind from the N.W., our vessels bore up towards the harbour of Copenhagen. Menacing indeed was the armament upon which the lad's eyes rested when, after a four hours' sail up the Sound, the Polyphemus came to anchor with the rest of the squadron opposite this famous and formidable port. The garrison of the city consisted of ten thousand men, with whom was combined a still stronger force of volunteers. All that was possible had been done to strengthen the sea-defences, and the array of forts, ramparts, ships of the line, fireships, gunboats, and floating batteries, was such as might well have deterred any other assailant but the hero of the Nile. Six line-of-battle ships and eleven floating batteries, with a large number of smaller vessels, were moored in an external line to protect the entrance to a harbour flanked on either side by two islands, on the smaller of which fifty-six, and on the larger sixty-eight heavy guns were mounted. Four other sail of the line were moored within, across the harbour mouth, while a fort mounting thirty-six powerful pieces of ordnance had been constructed on a shoal, supported by piles. These were so disposed that their fire would cross that of the batteries in the citadel of Copenhagen and on the island of Amager. It seemed hardly possible that any ships could pass over the centre of the deadly circle and live.

Nor were these armaments the only obstacles which confronted the British fleet. The channel, by which alone the harbour could be approached, was little known and extremely intricate ; all the buoys had been removed, and the sea on either side abounded with shoals and sandbanks, on which if any of the vessels grounded they would instantly be torn to pieces by the fire from the Danish batteries. The Danes themselves considered this particular barrier insurmountable, and Nelson himself was fully aware of the difficulty of surmounting it ; for a day and a night were incessantly occupied by the boats of the fleet, under his orders, in making the necessary soundings and replacing by new buoys those which had been taken away. Despite these precautions, however, and despite all that British seamanship could do in the way of skilled navigation, the harbour shoals proved formidable antagonists when the actual attack was made on the morning of April 2. Of the twelve line-of-battle ships which made fearlessly for the entrance of the harbour, amid the joyous cheers of their crews, on that memorable day, no fewer than three went aground and stuck immovable, exposed to the withering fire of the Tre Kroner batteries and unable to render any effective aid in the attack.

The Polyphemus was in Nelson's division, and was one of those which escaped this untoward mishap. The Edgar, under Captain Murray, led the division, and it was the Agamemnon, the ship immediately behind her, which was the first to go aground. The Polyphemus, which had been the last but three of the line, was signalled to advance out of her turn. Then followed the Monarch, the Ardent, and other vessels. The two that shared the fate of the second vessel in the division were the ships which had been in the immediate rear of Franklin's, the Bellona and the Russell. Nelson followed in the Elephant, and only saved his vessel and the remainder of his division by a swiftly conceived and executed change of course.

Pressing onward, however, with the rest of his force, which had been warned by the fate of the Agamemnon to alter their course, and pass inside instead of, as had been intended, outside the line taken by their leading vessels, the nine remaining vessels reached their stations, and at forty-five minutes past ten the action commenced, becoming general by half-past eleven.

The Polyphemus was soon at it hammer and tongs; and was among the vessels which, during those four furious hours, had the hottest work. Here is an extract from her official log :—

At 10.45 the Danes opened fire upon our leading ships, which was returned as they led in. We led in at 11.20. We anchored by the stern abreast of two of the enemy's ships moored in the channel, the Isis next ahead of us. The force that engaged us was two ships, one of 74, the other of 64 guns. At half-past eleven the action became general, and a continual fire was kept up between us and the enemy's ships and batteries. At noon a very heavy and constant fire was kept up between us and the enemy, and this was continued without intermission until forty-five minutes past two, when the 74 abreast of us ceased firing; but not being able to discern whether she had struck, our fire was kept up fifteen minutes longer, when we could perceive their people making their escape to the shore in boats. We ceased firing and boarded both ships and took possession of them. Several others were also taken possession of by the rest of our ships; one blown up in action, two sunk. Mustered ship's company and found we had six men killed and twenty-four wounded, and two lower-deck guns disabled.

Such was the result of the triple duel between the Polyphemus and the Danish block-ships Wagner and Provestien, assisted by the Tre Kroner battery. The cannonade all round was tremendous, nearly two thousand guns on both sides concentrating their fire upon a space not exceeding a mile and a half in breadth. For three hours had the engagement continued without showing any signs of slackening in its firing; when Sir Hyde Parker signalled to Nelson a permissive order to retire, and there occurred the often related, but recently questioned,[1] incident of Nelson's putting his telescope to his blind eye. Sir Hyde's motive was a generous one. He had seen with concern the grounding of the three ships, and their almost helpless exposure to the Danish cannonade. ‘ The fire,’ Southey reports him as saying, ‘ is too hot for Nelson; a retreat must be made. I am aware

[1] See Professor J. K. Laughton's *Nelson*. ‘Men of Action Series.’ (Macmillan.)

of the consequences to my own personal reputation, but it would be cowardly in me to leave Nelson to bear the whole shame of the failure, if failure it should be deemed.' Doubtless, too, he knew his man well enough to feel confident that if Nelson saw the slightest chance of continuing the contest with success—and the chance must have been slight indeed which did not satisfy Nelson—he would disobey the order. Figuratively in fact, if not literally speaking, he foresaw the legendary application of the telescope to the blind eye, and his foresight proved accurate. Nelson failed to 'see' the signal, and, nailing his own colours to the mast, prolonged the desperate fight for another hour, until, the rapidity and precision of the British fire having at last proved irresistible, the Danish replies began at two o'clock in the afternoon to abate sensibly in vigour. Ship after ship struck amid the cheers of our sailors, and before three the whole force of the six line-of-battle ships and the eleven floating batteries which had formed the front line of defence were either taken, sunk, burnt, or otherwise destroyed. Finally, the resistance of the enemy having now been completely broken down, Nelson sent proposals for an armistice, which were accepted, and the attacking squadron drew off to rejoin Sir Hyde Parker's ships in the centre of the Straits. The loss on board the British fleet was very severe. It was no less than 1,200 killed and wounded, a larger proportion to the number of seamen engaged than in any other general action during the whole war. On the side of the Danes, however, it was much greater, the total number of killed, wounded, and prisoners amounting to 6,000.

The condition indeed of the enemy at the close of the action presented a heart-rending spectacle. White flags were flying from every mast that was yet erect, and guns of distress booming from every hull that was still afloat. The sea was thickly covered with the floating spars, and lurid with the light of flaming wrecks. English boats thronged the waters endeavouring to render all the assistance in their power to their wounded and drowning enemies, who as fast as they could be rescued were sent ashore ; but great numbers perished.   It was not till daybreak on the following morning that Nelson's flag-ship, the Elephant, which had gone aground in returning to Sir Hyde Parker's squadron, was got afloat and the prizes carried off.

Thus ended this murderous battle, one of the most obstinately contested in the annals of the British Navy.   For the boy Franklin it was a baptism of fire indeed ; and even in those days of the Great War, when Englishmen thought nothing of sending their children almost from the nursery to the cockpit, the case of this lad of fifteen who passed with such startling abruptness from the sleepy peace of a Lincolnshire country town to the thunder and slaughter of the dreadful day of Copenhagen can hardly have had many parallels.   There could, at any rate, have been no more dramatically appropriate opening to a life of peril and adventure destined to be crowned by a tragic death.

The horrors of the scene produced, as well as they might, a deep impression on young Franklin's mind ; and a kinsman records having been told by him in later years that ' he saw a prodigious number of the slain at the bottom of the remarkably clear water of that harbour, men who had perished on both sides in that most sanguinary action.'   But exultation over the victory and pride at having borne a part in it were, of course, more enduring sentiments in the young midshipman's mind.   He was genuinely attached to his profession and happy in its pursuit ; and even from the few written records which have been preserved of this early period of his career one can gather details which shape themselves into an attractive, if imperfect, picture of the lad.   The weakliness from which, as already mentioned, he had suffered in his infancy had long since disappeared.   Even in his school days he was remarkable, relates a reminiscent of that time, Mr. Tennyson d'Eyncourt, ' for his manly figure and bravery,' and his ' flowing hair ;' and both then and afterwards he appears to have struck observers by a peculiar earnestness and animation of countenance.   The characteristic which had impressed Mr. Tennyson d'Eyncourt in the face of the school-boy is noted, curiously enough, almost in the same words, by

an officer who met him when on the verge of manhood, and
who subsequently testified to the accuracy of the observation
by at once recognising him again after a lapse of forty years.
This witness also speaks of him as a youth 'with a most
animated face.' It was doubtless the immature and unde-
veloped form of that fine expression of energy and daring
which distinguishes his later portraits. In other physical
respects, too, the boy appears to have been 'the father of the
man;' for 'the round-faced, round-headed' lad with an
evident tendency to 'put on flesh' who is described elsewhere
in the last-quoted of these accounts might very well ripen
into the portly and full-bodied Franklin of middle age.

His ways and disposition were evidently full of charm.
From many slight but sufficient indications, traceable even in
the scanty reminiscences of this far-off time, one can plainly
discern those winning qualities which afterwards endeared
him, beyond all leaders that one has ever heard of, to his
companions in adventure. There is the same frankness of
speech and bearing, the same open and affectionate disposition, and no doubt, too, the same hot but generous temper,
which in after years made him at once so quick to resent a
slight and so ready to forgive it.

His fear lest the despatch of the Polyphemus to the
Baltic should make him lose the chance of joining the
exploring expedition to the South Seas proved fortunately
groundless. Had he been too late to join it, the whole course
of his career might have been altered. He might quite
possibly have settled down into the life of the ordinary naval
officer and never have acquired that passion for geographical
discovery which afterwards bore such brilliant fruits. But
the hope expressed by him in the letter above quoted was
realised. The Polyphemus was ordered home with the rest
of the Baltic fleet in the summer of 1801 ; and a berth was
obtained for Franklin on board the Investigator, which started
for the Southern Hemisphere on July 7 of that year. Her
commander, Captain Matthew Flinders, who had married an
aunt of Franklin's, was a sailor of first-rate capacity, and had
already won high distinction as an explorer in the seas to

which he had now been despatched on no less ambitious an enterprise than that of effecting a survey of the entire seaboard of Australia. There could have been no better school or schoolmaster for a youth of John Franklin's bent and aspirations. He was proud of his commander's achievements, and attached to him both by relationship and regard. The character of his duties was in many respects novel, and his voyage, he was aware, would procure him an amount of training in navigation and practical seamanship which he could not have acquired with anything like the same expedition in the regular service of the navy. Of the spirit in which he entered on his duties we may judge by the following extract from a letter of Captain Flinders to the elder Franklin :—

It is with great pleasure that I tell you of the good conduct of John. He is a very fine youth, and there is every probability of his doing credit to the Investigator and himself. Mr. Crossley has begun with him, and in a few months he will be sufficient of an astronomer to be my right-hand man in that way. His attention to his duty has gained him the esteem of the first lieutenant, who scarcely knows how to talk enough in his praise. He is rated midshipman, and I sincerely hope that an early opportunity after his time is served will enable me to show the regard I have for your family and his merit.

By October of 1801 the Investigator had reached the Cape of Good Hope, and from that station Franklin wrote his father a letter describing the incidents of the voyage. They had touched at Madeira on the way out, and the lad's account of that island and its people abounds in evidences of an observant faculty beyond his years. Now, as always, he was studying more than the mere routine of his profession, in the scientific branches of which, however, he was obviously making good progress. He was, indeed, acquiring a proficiency for which he did not obtain quite his fair amount of recognition ; for it would seem that Sam Flinders, his captain's brother, was in the habit of entrusting to him a considerable share of the duty of taking observations without being equally careful in distributing the credit of the results. To this 'exploitation' of himself young Franklin thought it wise to submit, though not without privately recorded protests ; and it is with some natural feelings of resentful relief that later on he chronicles the fact of Sam's having exchanged his berth on the Investigator for a post which his brother had succeeded in obtaining for him on board another vessel.

The elder Flinders did much, however, to atone for the unsatisfactory conduct of the younger. He instructed his nephew pretty steadily in navigation and relieved him when at sea of day watches, Franklin reports, in order to enable him to attend his captain 'in working his timepieces, lunars, &c. ;' so that, on the whole, the eager young sailor had no reason to be dissatisfied with his opportunities of self-improvement. The example of the fine seaman and enthusiastic explorer under whom he served must indeed, for a lad of Franklin's ardent temperament, have been an education in itself. Throughout his whole life he cherished the warmest admiration for the character of Matthew Flinders, and in later years he gladly welcomed the opportunity of paying an enduring tribute to his old commander's memory in that very region of the world which his discoveries had done so much to conquer for civilisation.

In the summer of 1802, when, after having surveyed the whole of the southern coast of the Australian continent from King George's Sound in Western Australia to Port Jackson, the Investigator was refitting in that harbour, Franklin wrote his mother a letter full of that dutiful simplicity of filial affection which was so marked a feature in his character. ' I take this opportunity,' he says, in the quaintly ceremonious manner of the time,

of returning my most sincere thanks to my worthy parents for their care of me in my younger days, for my education, and lastly for the genteel and expensive outfit for this long voyage ; and if a due application to my duty and anxiety to push forward in my profession will repay them, they may rely on it as far as I'm able. . . . My father, I trust and hope, is more easy about the situation in life I have chosen. He sees it was not either the youthful whim of the moment, or the attractive uniform, or the hopes of getting rid of school that drew me to think of it. No ! I pictured to myself both the hardships and pleasures of a sailor's life (even to the extreme) before ever it was told to me ; which I find in a great measure to

C

agree. My mind was then so steadfastly bent on going to sea, that to settle to business would be merely impossible. Probably my father, like many others who are unacquainted with the sea, thinks that sailors are a careless, swearing, reprobate, and good-for-nothing set of men. Do not let that idea possess you, or condemn all for some. Believe me, there are good and bad men sailors. It is natural for a person who has been living on salt junk for several months when he gets on shore to swag about. Picture to yourself a man debarred from all sorts of comfortables such as mutton, beef, vegetables, wine, and beer. Would he not after that bar was broke begin with double vigour? But I have said enough on this subject. A line in answer to this would satisfy me.

Later on in the letter he reverts to a matter which was seldom absent from his mind—the necessity of steady endeavour to perfect himself in his profession :—

Thank you for that good and genuine advice in your letter. . . The first thing which demands immediate attention is the learning perfectly my duty as an officer and seaman. It would be an unpardonable shame if after serving two years I was ignorant of it. The next, the taking and working of astronomical observations which (thank God !) by the assistance of Captain Flinders I am now nearly able to do. Then French: many is the time I have envied the hours spent in play instead of learning. Now I feel the want of a knowledge of French, for there are two ships of that nation engaged in discovery here and I'm not able to converse with them in French, but am obliged to refer to unfamiliar Latin.

Writing a few months later to his sister Elizabeth, he gives a detailed account of his reading, interspersed with criticisms, amusing in their youthful air of profundity, on the subjects of his study :—

The following are the books which I read in my leisure hours (inform me, do you approve of them ?) :—' Junius's Letters.' What astonishing criticisms ! What a knowledge of the State affairs at that time ! But he was at last mastered by Horne Tooke, who had a right cause to handle. ' Shakespeare's Works.'—How well must that man have been acquainted with man and nature ! The beautiful sympathetic speeches he makes them use ! Of comedies, the ' Taming of the Shrew ' and the ' Merry Wives of Windsor ' are his masterpieces. Of tragedy, ' Macbeth ' and ' King John.' History of Scotland, from the Encyclopædia, ' Naval Tactics,' ' Roderick Random,' ' Peregrine Pickle,' sometimes Pope's Works. And, exclusive of navigation books and Latin and French, geography sometimes employs a good deal of my time, as was the request of my brother Thomas in his last letter.

He winds up with a piece of information most interesting to a sister—

I am grown very much indeed, and a little thinner, so that I shall be a spruce and genteel young man, and sail within three points of the wind, and run nine knots under close-reefed topsails, which is good sailing—

and also admirably well adapted to bewilder the female mind, as was no doubt its intention, with its shower of unfamiliar nautical expressions.

The pursuit of literature, however, could only have been the occupation of a not very abundant leisure; for it is certain that Franklin was kept pretty fully employed during his stay at Sydney in assisting to promote the scientific objects of the voyage. An observatory was set up on shore, to which all the chronometers were removed, and where all the necessary observations were taken. It was placed under the charge of Samuel Flinders, to whom Franklin was attached as assistant; and his services in that capacity were thought at least sufficiently worthy of recognition by the local authorities to have earned for him the humorous appellation of 'Mr Tycho Brahé' from Governor King, then presiding over the colony of New South Wales.

A few days after the letter last quoted was written, the vessel resumed its voyage, which, however, was destined to be cut short by unforeseen causes before its object was fully attained. Unfortunately, it turned out that the scientific curiosity of the Admiralty had not, like charity, begun at home. Before commissioning the Investigator to survey the coast of New Holland it would have been better to more carefully survey the Investigator. After rounding the north-east point of the continent and entering the Gulf of Carpentaria, the extensive coast-line of which was examined and duly delineated on the chart, the old vessel began to 'exhibit unmistakable signs of decay;' and it was discovered on examination that her timbers were in so rotten a condition that it was not considered likely that she would hold together in ordinary weather for more than six months, while in the event of her being caught in a gale she would in all probability founder.   Her commander, it is true, was not unprepared for this discovery.   Evidence of her general unseaworthiness had come to light, indeed, before she had reached Madeira on her outward voyage ; but, as Captain Flinders characteristically put it, he had been 'given to understand that the exigencies of the Navy were such that no better ship could be spared from the service, and his anxiety to complete the investigation of the coasts of Terra Australis did not admit of his refusing the one offered.'   Admirable, however, as is the spirit of a naval officer whose ardour in adventure will not permit him to decline the offer of a rotten ship if a sound one is not to be had, one cannot feel equally impressed with the conduct of naval authorities who send him out in such a vessel to explore the entire seaboard of Australia, with an injunction 'not to return to England until that work is satisfactorily accomplished.'   As it was, Captain Flinders had all his work cut out for him to return, not to England, but to Sydney, which port he succeeded in reaching in June 1803, after an anxious and perilous voyage round the west coast of Australia.   At Sydney the Investigator was again examined, and the experts by whom she was examined having reported her ' not worth repairing in any country,' she was ultimately converted into a storehouse hulk, and it was arranged that Flinders, with a portion of his officers and crew, should return home in the Porpoise, in order to report the facts of the case to the Admiralty and endeavour to obtain another vessel in which to continue the work of Australian exploration.

The breakdown of the Investigator was, however, but the first of the series of misadventures which Franklin was destined to meet with in this his maiden cruise as an explorer. Six days out of Sydney the Porpoise, making for the newly discovered Torres Strait with two merchant vessels under its pilotage, struck upon a reef—a fate which was shared by one of its consorts—the other making off, one regrets to record, without rendering any assistance. The disaster occurred towards nightfall, and, the ships fortunately holding together until the morning, their crews managed to effect a landing, with such of the provisions and stores of the two vessels as they were able to save, on a sandbank some nine hundred feet by fifty, about half a mile from the wreck. Their position here, however, was sufficiently critical. The nearest known land was two hundred miles off, and Sydney, the only place from which assistance was to be hoped for, they had left nearly four times that distance behind them. It is needless to say that they faced the situation with the cheerful pluck and resourcefulness of their nation and calling. Tents were erected with the salvaged sails; a blue ensign with the union-jack down was hoisted on a tall spar as a signal of distress; an inventory of stores was taken and found sufficient to last the ninety-four castaways, if properly husbanded, for a period of three months. A council of officers was then called, and it was decided that one of the six-oared cutters should be despatched to Sydney, under the command of the indomitable Flinders, to obtain relief. Accordingly, on August 27, accompanied by the commander of the lost merchant ship and twelve men, and having stored his small boat with provisions and water for three weeks, that officer set out on his doubtful and hazardous voyage of seven hundred and fifty miles. Week after week passed, and at length, on October 7, when their stores were beginning to run low and the castaways were within measurable distance of the date at which it had been resolved that if no help came they would themselves make a desperate dash for the mainland of Australia in two boats which they had constructed out of materials saved from the wreck, they caught the welcome sight of a sail. It was Flinders returning from Sydney in the Rolla, bound for Canton, accompanied by the two Government schooners Cumberland and Francis. Franklin, with the bulk of the shipwrecked crew, embarked on board the first-named vessel; his captain, anxious to get home as soon as possible to report his discoveries and prepare his charts for publication, preferred to return to England at once in the Cumberland. It was a fatal choice. The vessel touched at the Mauritius on its way home, and there, by one of those many acts of downright brigandage which disgraced the name of France at the rupture of the Treaty of Amiens, he was made a prisoner by the French Governor of the island and detained for no less than six and a half years. He lived, this much-enduring Ulysses, to return to England and to write an account of his memorable voyage ; but the volume and the charts accompanying it, which he had lost his liberty in hurrying home to publish, only issued from the press, by a truly tragic coincidence, on the very day of his death.

Franklin had gone to Canton in the Rolla to await a homeward-bound ship, but there were yet further adventures in store for him before reaching England. A squadron of sixteen Indiamen was on the point of sailing, under the command of Commodore Nathaniel Dance, of the H.E.I.C.S. ; and the officers and men of the Investigator were distributed among its vessels, Franklin's berth falling to him on board the Earl Camden, which flew the commodore's flag. They carried arms, did these merchantmen of John Company, as indeed such vessels mostly did in those troublous times ; but their guns, from thirty to thirty-six in number, were of light calibre, and the gallant vessels relied rather upon the 'brag' of their appearance than on their real fighting power ; for their hulls were painted in imitation of line-of-battle ships and frigates, the more easily to deceive the enemy's cruisers and privateers. They could hardly hope, however, to escape the attentions of a powerful French squadron by devices of this kind ; and it was with such a squadron that they were fated to fall in. Its commander, Admiral Linois, was not otherwise than a brave and capable officer, and the five vessels under his command, consisting of the Marengo, a line-of-battle ship of 84 guns, La Belle Poule, 48, two other vessels of 36 and 24 guns respectively, and an eighteen-gun brig under Dutch colours, were no doubt considerably more than a match in fighting power for the fleet of Indiamen. Yet this did not prevent the Admiral and his squadron from getting quite comically the worst of one of the most singular encounters in the whole of our naval history. Linois, having received news

of the sailing of the Indiamen from Canton, put to sea at once
from Batavia, and came across his intended captures as they
were entering the Straits of Malacca. Their behaviour,
however, was contrary to all maritime precedent. A witty
countryman of the Admiral has in two often-quoted lines
expressed the scandalised astonishment with which the hunter
would naturally regard resistance on the part of a usually
fugitive quarry—

> Cet animal est très méchant :
> Lorsqu'on attaque, il se défend—

and Linois found to his surprise that these particular
merchantmen were animals of just this vicious temper.
Instead of making all sail to escape their pursuers, they
formed in order of battle, and showed every sign of preparing
for a regular engagement. It was late in the afternoon ; and
the phenomenon was so perplexing that the French Admiral
not unnaturally thought he might as well take a night
to consider it, and decided to postpone the attack till the
following morning. Under cover of the darkness the English
ships might, no doubt, have made their escape without difficulty,
but Commodore Dance had no intention of thus spoiling so
pretty a quarrel. His ships lay to for the night ; and Linois
finding them in the same position next day began to suspect
that they must consist partly of men-of-war, and continued
to hold aloof. Thereupon Dance gave orders for his ships to
continue their course under easy sail. The French Admiral,
encouraged by this movement, pressed forward with the
design of cutting off some of the rearward ships. Upon
this, however, the English Commodore instantly faced about,
and young Franklin, who was acting as signal-midshipman,
was ordered to run up the signal : 'Tack in succession, bear
down in line ahead, and engage the enemy.'

Whether in the King's uniform or out of it, Jack in
all ages of our history has asked nothing better ; and as
quickly as this manœuvre could be executed the two squadrons
engaged. The action was short and sharp, if not exactly
decisive. After three-quarters of an hour of it the French

ceased firing and drew off, whereupon the insatiable Dance actually gave the signal for a 'general chase,' and the astonished seas beheld the unique spectacle of sixteen English merchantmen in hot pursuit of a French squadron of war. The Commodore gave chase for 'upwards of two hours,' and then, rightly concluding that he had done enough for honour, recalled his pursuing ships, proceeded on his homeward course, and duly arrived in England to be rewarded with a well-merited knighthood. It was one of the most dashing feats of 'bounce' on record, and deserves to rank with that other and better known exploit of heroic impudence which has for generations been celebrated in many a gruff forecastle chorus to the refrain of the 'Saucy Arethusa.'

How Franklin's services on this occasion were appreciated by his commander the following extract from a letter, written by Sir Nathaniel Dance a year later, will show. Addressing Mr. William Ramsay, an official of the East India Company, he says :

I beg leave to present to the notice of the Hon. Court, Mr. Franklin and Mr. Olive, midshipmen in His Majesty's Navy, who were cast away with Lieut. Fowler in the Porpoise, and who were, as well as that gentleman, passengers for England on board the Earl Camden. Whatever may have been the merits of others, theirs in their station were equally conspicuous, and I should find it difficult in the ship's company to name any one who for zeal and alacrity of service and for general good conduct could advance a stronger claim to approbation and reward.

On August 6 the Earl Camden arrived in the English Channel, and for the first time after a prolonged interval of enforced silence the young sailor was able to communicate with his family. His prolonged cruise had been full of trials and not free from disaster, but he dwells in his usual mood of cheery contentment on its compensating gains :—

Although mishaps seem to attend every companion of the voyage —viz. a rotten ship, being wrecked, the worthy commander detained, and the great expense of twice fitting out—yet do we cheer ourselves with a well-founded idea that we have gained some knowledge and experience, both professional and general, even while visiting the dreary and uncultivated regions of New Holland.

His father had in the meantime retired from business to the retreat which he had provided for himself many years before, and thus the son overwhelms him with inquiries :—

I have formed many and various conjectures concerning the Enderby House and enjoyments, and of the residences and situation of my dear brothers and sisters, particularly of Willingham, not having heard of or from him since 1801, nor from Spilsby since June 1802. Sensible of the pleasure the receipt of letters will afford, particularly from home, I trust some kind person will not fail answering this by return, and mention how every member of the family is—whether any of the Spilsby friends are dead, whether the old town looks gay, whether you have received Captain Palmer's account of the Porpoise's wreck, dated January 10, 1804, and how my old acquaintances in and about Spilsby are. Some of them have, I expect, paid the debt of Nature.

A truly characteristic midshipman's account of information-arrears.

On August 7, 1804, Franklin was discharged from the Earl Camden, and on the following day he was appointed to H.M.S. Bellerophon, Captain Loring, which now historic vessel, after a six weeks' leave spent with his family and friends, he joined on September 20. And, just as he had left home for the first time to fight in the great battle of Copenhagen, so now, at the end of his first short leave of absence, he quitted England to take part, after only a few months' longer interval, in the still more memorable struggle of Trafalgar.

The winter of 1804 was spent in blockading the French fleet in the harbour of Brest, a new experience for Franklin in naval operations. In April of the following year Captain Loring was succeeded in the command of the Bellerophon by Captain James Cooke, whom the midshipman, in that tone of kindly patronage which not infrequently marks the gun-room's criticism of the commanding officer, describes to his mother as seeming 'very gentlemanly and active;' adding, 'I like his appearance much.' The weary blockade was still continuing, though spring was ripening into summer; and Franklin, seizing an opportunity at Cawsand Bay for an 'epistolary conversation with my relatives previous to our departure to resume this station,' goes on to say :—

We have victualled and stored our ship for six months, for the purpose of being in perfect preparation to chase the Brest fleet, should any of them think of moving this summer.   There are twelve sail of us which have fitted for foreign service ; but I believe for no better reason than the above.   Some rumours have sent us out to the West Indies, others off Cadiz, and some to the East Indies ; but certainly without foundation.

Then his thoughts reverting to his father's newly adopted country life, the young sailor continues in youth's diverting vein of didactic reflection :—

I trust my father keeps his health and spirits.   The farm at this season of the year must afford him much amusement.   The green fields, the approaching harvest, all tend to gladden the heart of the farmer, who measures, as it were, every ray of sun and drop of rain, and is able to tell that this does good and that harm.

Later on in the letter he adds :—

The Devonshire fields promise good crops.   I hope Lincolnshire does likewise.   Days begin to grow long and the shore very pleasant. I have been on shore once and enjoyed a long walk.   To us Channel-gropers, believe me, a walk on shore, even in the detestable borders of the seaport, is charming.

Cadiz proved, after all, to be the destination of the Bellerophon.   She sailed in the summer for that port, and remained there for some time under Lord Collingwood's orders, when she was detached with three other ships to convoy the transports and troops despatched from England to Malta with secret orders, supposed, as Franklin says, to be ' for landing in Egypt should Bonaparte endeavour to march any force towards our Indian settlements.'   Returning from this duty, the squadron was ordered to blockade the port and harbour of Carthagena, wherein lay six line-of-battle ships which by some accident had been prevented from joining the combined fleets of France and Spain, then in the West Indies, with Nelson hunting for them in vain.

Events meanwhile were rapidly working up to the dramatic climax of Trafalgar.   From the same letter, concluded three days later, Franklin reports the great Admiral's return to Cadiz after the final abandonment of his West Indian chase ; and a little later Collingwood's command was taken over from him by Nelson, and the British fleet, consisting of twenty-seven sail of the line and three frigates, was concentrated off the Spanish coast. Yet another month, and on the ever-memorable October 21 it closed with those of France and Spain in that tremendous conflict which was to shatter Napoleon's hopes of conquest and leave the British flag supreme on every sea.

The Bellerophon, as all the world knows, was in the thick of the battle, and Franklin, again appointed to the post of signal midshipman, was in the hottest of the fire that swept her decks. The following account of one of the most dramatic incidents of the action was afterwards given by him to his brother-in-law, Mr. Booth :—

Very early in the engagement the Bellerophon's masts became entangled with and caught fast hold of a French line-of-battle ship [apparently L'Aigle]. Though the masts were pretty close together at the top, there was a space between them below, but not so great as to prevent the French sailors from trying to board the Bellerophon. In the attempt their hands received severe blows, as they laid hold of the side of the ship, from whatever the English sailors could lay their hands on. In this way hundreds of Frenchmen fell between the ships and were drowned. While the Bellerophon was fastened to the enemy on one side, another French man-of-war was at liberty to turn round and fire first one broadside and then another into the English ship. In consequence 300 men were killed on board the Bellerophon. At last, after a very sharp contest, the French ship which was at liberty received such a severe handling that she veered about and sailed away ; but still a desultory yet destructive warfare was carried on between the two entangled ships, until out of forty-seven men upon the quarter-deck, of whom Franklin was one, all were either killed or wounded but seven. Towards the end of the action only a very few guns could be fired on either of the ships, the sailors were so disabled. But there remained a man in the foretop of the enemy's ship, wearing a cocked hat, who had during the engagement taken off with his rifle several of the officers and men. [It was a shot from one of these sharpshooters in the rigging of the Redoutable, it will be remembered, that struck Nelson down.] Franklin was standing close by, and speaking to a midshipman, his most esteemed friend, when the fellow above shot him and

he fell dead at his comrade's feet. Soon after, Franklin and a
sergeant of Marines were carrying down a black seaman to have his
wounds dressed, when a ball from the rifleman entered his breast
and killed the poor fellow as they carried him along. Franklin said
to the sergeant, 'He'll have you next;' but the sergeant swore he
should not, and said that he would go below to a quarter of the ship
from which he could command the French rifleman, and would never
cease firing at him till he had killed him. As Franklin was going
back on the deck, keeping his eye on the rifleman, he saw the fellow
lift his rifle to his shoulder and aim at him; but with an elasticity
very common in his family he bounded behind a mast. Rapid as
the movement was, the ball from the rifle entered the deck of the
ship a few feet behind him. Meantime, so few guns were being discharged that he could hear the sergeant firing away with his musket
from below, and, looking out from behind the mast, he saw the rifleman, whose features he vowed he should never forget so long as he
lived, fall over headforemost into the sea. Upon the sergeant coming
up, he asked him how many times he fired: 'I killed him,' said the
sergeant, 'at the seventh shot.'

Franklin himself escaped without a wound. Throughout
the greater part of the fight he had been stationed on the poop,
and he was one out of only four or five in that quarter of the
ship who emerged unscathed from the struggle. But even
upon him it left its mark in an injury invisible indeed but
not unfelt. 'After Trafalgar,' says one of his relatives, 'he
was always a little deaf.' To the last day of his life he bore
about with him this troublesome reminder of that furious
cannonade.

The Bellerophon returned to England in December of
1805, Franklin carrying with him a certificate from Lieutenant
Cumby, who had succeeded to Captain Cooke's command when
that gallant officer fell, to the effect that he had performed the
duties of signal-midshipman 'with very conspicuous zeal and
ability.' His stay in England, however, was destined to be
only a short one. The Bellerophon remained at Plymouth
no longer than was necessary to refit, and make good the
injuries sustained in the action; after which she put to sea
again, and for the next eighteen months was employed in
cruising between Finisterre and Ushant. Franklin's connection
with the famous vessel was soon to come to an end. On

October 27, 1807, he begins a letter to one of his sisters with the remark that she will probably be surprised at the new address from which he writes. Two days before he had been drafted from the Bellerophon on to the Bedford, 'commanded by Captain Walker, a smart, active officer, and the ship, I judge, will be a fine ship. Report says she is going foreign, but it must receive some authentication before I can believe it. Indeed, I hope she may.'

His hopes were realised ; but the foreign service on which he was despatched turned out to be in disappointing contrast with the exciting experiences of the recent past. He could hardly expect, however, that these would be indefinitely prolonged. The pace, indeed, had been too good to last ; and there could not have been many midshipmen in His Majesty's service who had, even in those stirring times, come in for so large a share of adventure in so short a period as had fallen to the lot of John Franklin. It was but six years since he had entered the Navy, a lad of fifteen, and before completing his twenty-first year he had smelt powder in two of the greatest naval battles of our history, explored a continent, suffered shipwreck, and played his part in one of the most singular and, in its almost comical way, most brilliant exploits in the annals of our maritime warfare. Thus his courage and fighting quality had been splendidly tested ; he had had his training in seamanship on half the waters of the globe ; he had learnt energy and resource in the stern school of disaster ; and he had had admirable opportunities for studying navigation and the scientific branches of his profession in general under one of the most capable and painstaking of commanding officers. Fortune had favoured him with many advantages, but to have made the most of them was his own merit. His passionate love of his calling had never abated, and his ambition to perfect himself in all its duties had never flagged. There is no doubt that, thanks in part to his favouring stars, but still more to his own great gifts as a seaman, he had even at this early period of his career already qualified himself for a position of command. By the time he attained his majority he was 'fit to go anywhere and do anything.' But the good luck

which had hitherto attended him was now about to bid him
adieu for some time to come. Some years were to pass before
he again escaped from the dull routine of duty into the
field of warlike adventure, and yet a good many more years
before he found his way to that special sphere of maritime
enterprise in which his true vocation lay.

CHAPTER II

IN the concluding chapter of Southey's 'Life of Nelson' the
author of that classic biography, by way of illustrating the
fame of his hero and the confidence reposed in him by
his countrymen, ventures upon the daring hyperbole that
'the destruction of the French and Spanish fleets, and the
total prostration of the maritime schemes of Napoleon, hardly
appeared to add to our security or strength, for, while Nelson
was living to watch the combined squadrons of the enemy,
we felt ourselves secure as now, when they were no longer in
existence.' Still, after all, 'stone dead hath no fellow,' and
we can hardly doubt that the annihilation of the French fleet,
saddened though our glorious victory was by the death of
Nelson, was generally regarded by the English nation as
preferable to any other arrangement.

The only class among them who might conceivably have
preferred a less complete triumph were the officers of the
British Navy. For the last quarter of a century, with few
and brief intermissions, they had been as well supplied with
opportunities for the practical study of their profession, both
in seamanship and in fighting, as any sailors could desire.
But Nelson had made such a 'clean job' of it at Trafalgar as
to cut off the main source of these opportunities at a stroke.
By sweeping the enemies of Great Britain off the face of the
sea he left her defenders for many years to come without any
efficient training school in naval warfare.

It was Franklin's good fortune to have joined the British
Navy in time to share its last five years of glorious activity;
had he entered it in 1806 instead of 1801, he would have

been condemned to commence, as he was now to continue, his career by undergoing as long or a longer spell of uneventful and monotonous duty. The record of his service afloat from the end of 1807 to the beginning of 1813 is in effect the history of a continuous patrol. The first mission of the Bedford after Franklin joined her as master's mate—a rank, however, from which he was promoted in a couple of months to that of acting lieutenant—was to convoy the fugitive royal family of Portugal, driven from Lisbon by the French invasion, to Rio Janeiro, and for no less than two years the vessel remained stationed in South American waters. She returned to England in the summer of 1810, but for only a very brief period, for the unlucky Walcheren expedition was on foot, and for the next two years she was employed in the not much more exciting duty of blockading Flushing and the entrance of the Texel.

During this period, therefore, the external and public side of the young sailor's life claims but little of a biographer's attention, which may be devoted mainly to such details of his private history and domestic relations as serve to illustrate his personal character. To the Franklin family circle the years which we are now approaching were far from being unmarked by important events. One at least of these events had all the memorable qualities of disaster. Early in the century the commercial affairs of the bank in which Thomas Franklin had embarked much of his own capital, and in which a good deal of his father's savings were also invested, took an unfortunate turn. Thomas became involved in business transactions with one Walker, whose honesty seems to have been open to something more than suspicion; and the consequent pecuniary difficulties in which he found himself entangled led ultimately to the failure of the Spilsby Bank. The shock of this calamity brought the son to the grave in 1807 at the early age of thirty-four, besides hastening the death of his mother a few years later; and it communicated itself in a sufficiently perceptible fashion even to John himself overseas. During the twelve or thirteen years of embarrassment due to these misfortunes, Franklin received no money whatever from home. His scanty pay was all he had to subsist on, and his position in such circumstances must have been one of no little difficulty and discomfort. But the adversity of the family only served to bring into stronger relief the fine qualities of the youngest son. His letters of this period are full of cheerful courage, and testify throughout to a deep filial affection, which was further illustrated in the touching little incident, recorded by his brother-in-law, of his laboriously saving the sum of 5*l.* out of his midshipman's pittance and remitting it to his parents as his mite of relief to their embarrassed finances.

Most tiresome, perhaps, of all the duties of this monotonous period were those of the squadron detailed to dance attendance upon the exiled Prince Regent of Portugal and his Court. They were as dull as the manœuvres of a blockade, without any of its sustaining hopes of a possible engagement. In a letter to his sister from the Bedford, cruising off Rio Janeiro, in December 1808, one sees how eagerly he caught at any piece of political news from home which might seem to promise an earlier close of his distasteful commission :—

By a corvette from Lisbon despatched purposely to the Prince we learn that the capitulation entered into by General Dalrymple [the Convention of Cintra] is done away, and that a considerable number of the French army are prisoners. This, we hope, may excite the Prince to a desire of return, an event we all anticipate. There, again, I think I hear you say : 'Sailors are always dissatisfied : for instance, my brother and his companions, when living in one of the most luxuriant countries under heaven's canopy, where the least exertion in husbandry or agriculture is overpaid by superabundant return, and whose very bowels contain the richest mines of gold and silver.' This remark as to the characteristic of sailors may be true, yet I assure you in this case it is excusable in those obliged to remain among perhaps the most ungrateful inhabitants of the earth, for whom it is impossible to have the slightest esteem or respect, subject to their bigotry, and observers of their lethargy and indecision, with the greater considerations of a dear, expensive market, and unhealthy crowded towns.

Still, there were occasional diversions, and one such adventure of Franklin's on the island of Madeira, whither he

D

had been sent to reclaim two deserters from the Bedford who
had been captured by the Portuguese authorities, is so well
and graphically told by him in his despatch to his commanding officer, Captain Mackenzie, that the amusing story had
best be given in his own words :—

In obedience to your directions (he writes) I herein state the
conduct of Sergeant Joachim Francisco Uramão, who had possession
of the two deserters from H.M.S. Bedford, whom you sent me to
claim on the 25th August, 1809.

After leaving the ship with the person who gave the information
of these men being taken, I went to the captain of the regiment by
whom the informer was despatched, and begged he would give orders
that the men might be delivered to me.   He sent a guide with the
necessary instructions for the sergeant, whom [the guide] we took on
the boat and proceeded to the spot.

Immediately on entering the village we saw the deserters, apparently unguarded.   One was assisting in thatching the sergeant's
house, the other drunk.   I inquired for the sergeant, but it was some
time before I saw him, and then he was just rising from his bed, and
drunk also.   I desired my interpreter to say those men had deserted
from the Bedford, that I was a lieutenant of the ship, and sent to
claim them by my captain, having also got the necessary orders for
their discharge from his captain.   He arose, and very insolently told
me I could not have them, that he had an order from his colonel to
take them on board, as well as a letter from Captain Mackenzie, and
that he meant to carry them the next day.   Seeing the facility there
was for their escaping in the night, I pointed out that I had full power
to give any receipt he wished, and that, having come far from the ship,
I did not wish to return without the men.   He then grew more
violent, and said : 'Your commander may command his ship but not
the shore,' still persisting in not giving them up to me.   Finding all
remonstrance vain on my part, I begged the guide to repeat the
orders he had received from his captain respecting the release of the
two men, and at that repetition he waxed furious, and told him he
did not care for the captain, that he ought not to have acquainted
the English of the two men being in his possession, and that he
would put both the captain and the guide to death.

(Sergeant Joachim Francesco Uramão must evidently have
been very drunk indeed.)

After these expressions I thought it necessary to remind the
sergeant that I should inform you of his conduct, and was assured of
your forwarding the complaint to his superiors.   He then cooled

down, and promised to let the men go if I would permit him to accompany them.   This being my original intention, I of course assented.   He prepared himself, and ordered a canoe to follow him. That, I suppose, was about three o'clock.   He afterwards went to another part of the village and stayed a considerable time.   Being far distant from the ship, and night coming on, I became impatient, and requested his companions would hasten him and point out the necessity of our going immediately.   After two or three messages he returned, and positively refused either to let the men go or accompany them himself, using the strange language that 'the English did not command there, and that he did not care for his captain,' &c., which was expressed with such gestures as greatly to irritate my feelings as well as those of the men whom I had ordered up.   I desired the interpreter to request that he would give me a decisive answer whether he meant to release the men to me or not, and also impress again on his mind that I was fully empowered to give a receipt, and at the same time to assure him of my firm determination to acquaint you with every circumstance.

After this explanation he resigned the deserters up to me (by the advice of many of his neighbours), under the idea of accompanying them.   On our passage over the hill he told me that I might take him to the Prince, but that he did not care for that.   The Prince did not pay him, and he was under no obligation to serve him, with many other incoherent expressions, which I did not attend to. I took him in the boat and left him with the captain, whom I called on to acknowledge the receipt of the men.   I beg leave to mention that this happened in the presence of Mr. St. Quintin, and of some men whom I took over the hill to guard the prisoners back, and they can testify to the prisoners' violent conduct.

As a specimen of quiet tenacity combined with judgment, temper, and self-command, the successful taming of this intoxicated Portuguese sergeant must be admitted to be a pretty creditable performance for a young naval officer of two-and-twenty.

The records, however, of these tedious years of patrol-work abound in evidences of Franklin's impatience with the life of inaction to which he was condemned. With the despatch of the Bedford on the Walcheren expedition he was visited by a delusive gleam of hope ; and his letters from the Texel throughout the twenty-four months of the blockade bear amusing witness to his eagerness to come to blows. Surely, surely the enemy must be 'spoiling for a fight' as much as himself. 'Our fleet consists of fifteen of the line, but two are kept off the mouth of the Texel, and two are always in the Downs; the enemy have seventeen in readiness and two more about to join. It is generally supposed they will push for Brest. Surely such a force will not be kept stationary and useless in the Scheldt.' No, they would come out and give their enemy a chance at them. But then again occurs the depressing thought that there is yet a third possibility. They might come out only to give the blockaders the slip and sneak away. ' I fear they will wait for longer nights, and, by taking advantage '—a mean advantage Franklin evidently thinks it—'of a stiff breeze, run along shore and give us a running chase, and perhaps avoid a general action. However, let us hope for the best and wait with patience.'

This virtue, as we all know, was not rewarded. The inactivity of the French naval commanders at sea was as masterly as that displayed, according to the famous epigram, by Lord Chatham and Sir Richard Strahan on land; and long before his two years of blockading duty had expired Franklin had probably given up all hopes of coming to close quarters with the enemy's fleet. In 1812 we find him drawing up memorials of his services for transmission to the Admiralty, and endeavouring to procure his exchange into another ship, the frigate Nymphe, with the desire, as he puts it, of ' seeing the varieties of the service.' His efforts, however, were in vain; he was fated to remain in the Bedford until the return of that vessel to England.

With the commencement of 1813, however, a welcome change occurred. The war with America had broken out, and orders were received for the Bedford to convoy a fleet of merchant vessels to the West Indies. This duty discharged, she was given another nine months' spell of blockading duty off the Texel and Scheveningen; but in September of 1814 she was again sent with a convoy to the West Indies, whence she was ordered to New Orleans to assist in the operations about to be undertaken against the Americans. The attack on New Orleans had been decided on, and Franklin, doubtless to his great delight, was one of the party sent out to execute the preliminary operation of clearing Lake Borgne of the American gunboats which had assembled there in force for the protection of the port.

The operations of our military forces before New Orleans are not among the most brilliantly successful exploits of the British arms; but the part played therein by the naval contingent can be recalled perhaps with less dissatisfaction than any others of their incidents. This is especially true of the attack delivered upon the gunboats at Lake Borgne, which, whatever may be thought of it from the strategical point of view, was certainly executed with a dash and determination highly creditable to the arm to which it was entrusted.

But a word or two should first be said on the strategical position of New Orleans itself, a port and town in which, for reasons best known to our commanders, we gave ourselves about as hard a nut to crack as could have been picked up anywhere along the whole eastern seaboard of North America. The first of the causes which contributed to its safety from attack was the shallowness of the river at its mouth and the extreme rapidity of its current. After flowing on in a vast sheet of water varying in depth from one hundred to thirty fathoms, the Mississippi divides, before entering the Gulf of Mexico, into four or five mouths, the most considerable of which is, or was in those days, obstructed by a sandbank continually liable to shift. Over this bank no vessel drawing more than seventeen feet of water could pass; once across, there was no longer any difficulty in floating, but it was dangerous to anchor on account of the huge logs which were constantly carried down the stream, some on its surface, others sunken, and borne along by the undercurrent within a few feet of the bottom.

In addition to these formidable natural obstacles to invasion, the mouth of the river was defended by a fort which, from its position, might well have been deemed impregnable. It was built upon an artificial causeway, and surrounded on all sides by impassable swamps extending on either bank of the river to a place called the *Détour des Anglais* some twenty miles from the city. Here two other forts were erected, one on each bank, and, like that at the river's mouth, encircled by a marsh traversable for the garrison only by a single narrow path from the firm ground beyond. If, therefore, an enemy should contrive to pass both the bar and the first fort, he would inevitably be stopped here ; to land being impossible because of the nature of the ground, and further ascent of the river being prevented by its here taking so sharp a curve that vessels were in those days compelled to await a change of wind before they could make any further way. Moreover, from *Détour des Anglais* onward to the city the ground, though broken here and there to some extent by arable land, was still swampy, and, even where there was foothold, containing no broken ground or any other cover for military movements.

To attack New Orleans, then, from the river was out of the question, and the only mode of approaching it was by way of the lake, or rather gulf, for it was a salt-water inlet, which deeply indented the shore to the east of the Mississippi mouths. Even this mode of assault, however, had its difficulties. The shores of the lake were themselves so swampy as hardly to supply footing for infantry, far less for the disembarkation and transport of artillery. To effect a landing it would be necessary for an attacking force to avail itself of the creeks or bayous which run up from the lake towards the city, but of these there were not more than one or two that could be so used. The Bayou of St. John was one, but was too well defended ; another, the Bayou Calatan, was afterwards actually employed for the purpose. The idea of the British commander was to effect a landing somewhere on the bank of the lake after a rapid and, it was hoped, an unperceived transit of its waters, and thence to push on and seize the town before any effectual preparation could be made for its defence. With this view the troops were transferred from the larger into the lighter vessels, and these, under convoy of such gun-brigs as the shallow water would float, began on December 13, 1814, to enter Lake Borgne. They had not proceeded far, however, before it became apparent that the Americans were aware of their intentions and were fully prepared to meet the attack. Five large cutters, armed with six heavy guns each, were seen at anchor in the distance, and, as all endeavours to land till these were captured or driven away would have been useless, the transports and the largest of the gun-brigs cast anchor, while the smaller craft gave chase to the enemy. The American cutters, however, were specially built for operations on the lake, and quickly 'got the heels' of their pursuers, whose draught of water rendered effective pursuit impossible. Yet to leave these pests to hover round the British force in a position to cut off any boats which attempted to cross the lake would have been fatal. It was, therefore, determined to capture them at all costs, and, since our lightest craft could not float where they sailed, a flotilla of launches and ships' barges was got ready for the purpose. It consisted of fifty open boats manned with a force of one thousand officers and men, and most of them armed with carronades. The command of this force was given to Captain Nicholas Lockyer, and Lieutenant Franklin probably led a division or subdivision of the attack. About noon of December 13, writes a chronicler of the campaign, the late venerable Chaplain-General of the Forces and well-known author of 'The Subaltern,' the Rev. G. R. Gleig, who was himself attached to the British expeditionary force before New Orleans, and therefore describes the scene with almost the authority of an eye-witness, Captain Lockyer came in sight of the enemy moored fore and aft, with their broadsides pointing towards him.

Having pulled a considerable distance, he resolved to refresh his men before hurrying them into action ; and, therefore, letting fall grapplings just beyond reach of the enemy's guns, the crews of the different boats coolly ate their dinners. As soon as that meal was finished and an hour spent in resting, the boats again got ready to advance. But unfortunately a light breeze which had hitherto favoured them now ceased to blow, and they were accordingly compelled to make way only with the oars. The tide also ran strong against them, at once increasing their labour and retarding their progress ; but all these difficulties appeared trifling to British sailors, and, giving a hearty cheer, they moved steadily onward in one extended line.

It was not long before the enemy's guns opened upon them, and a tremendous shower of balls saluted their approach. Some boats were sunk, others disabled, and many men were killed and wounded ; but the rest, pulling with all their might, and occasionally returning the discharges from their carronades, succeeded after an hour's labour in closing with the Americans. The Marines now began a deadly discharge of musketry ; while the seamen, sword in hand, sprang up the vessels' sides in spite of all opposition, and, sabreing every man that stood in the way, hauled down the American ensign and hoisted the British flag in its place.

One cutter, however, which bore the commodore's broad pennant, was not so easily subdued. Having noted its pre-eminence, Captain Lockyer directed his own boat against it, and, happening to have placed himself in one of the lightest and fastest sailing barges in the flotilla, he found himself alongside of the enemy before any of the others were near enough to render him the slightest support. But, nothing dismayed by odds so fearful, the gallant crew of this small bark, following their leader, instantly leaped on board the American. A desperate conflict now ensued, in which Captain Lockyer received several severe wounds ; but after fighting from the bow to the stern, the enemy was at length overpowered, and, other barges coming up to the assistance of their commander, the commodore's flag shared the same fate with the others.

In this warm little affair Franklin was himself wounded ; and, indeed, though the victory was complete and gave the British forces undisputed command of the lake throughout the rest of the campaign, it had to be pretty heavily paid for. Three midshipmen and fourteen men were killed, while the captain, three other lieutenants besides Franklin, three master's mates, one lieutenant of Marines, seven midshipmen (two mortally), and sixty-one men were wounded. The American loss was slight by comparison. For his share in this action Franklin received a medal and was honourably mentioned in despatches.

Would that the later operations of this disastrous campaign had been more worthy of its brilliant beginning, and that its military chiefs had performed their part with as much skill and success, instead of only with as much bravery, as their naval supporters ! The expedition against the cutters had

carried our boats many leagues up Lake Borgne. Another
day passed before the crews could get back to their ships,
and it was not till the 15th that the fleet again weighed
anchor and stood up the lake.   It was soon found, however,
that not even by the lake route was it possible to carry the
troops up to a point at which a landing could be with any
advantage effected.   Ship after ship ran aground ; those
which still floated became more and more overloaded with
the men transferred to them, till at last even vessels of the
lightest draught stuck fast, and boats of necessity had to be
lowered to carry the troops a distance of more than thirty
miles.   The distresses of such a method of transport were
greatly enhanced by an unlucky change of the weather, heavy
rains having set in, and finally, after an exposure of ten hours
in their new and confined transports, each division was landed
at a small uninhabited island in the lake, where it was
determined to collect the whole force preliminary to its
debarkation on the main land.   Pine Island, as it was called,
apparently from its growing a few stunted firs near the
water's edge, consisted principally of swamp, with a comparatively small piece of firm land at one end, on which the
troops were collected.   With the exception of alligators,
which abounded in its pools and creeks, it contained no living
creatures but water-fowl, too shy to be shot.   It did not even
yield fuel sufficient to supply its wretched tenants with fires.

In these miserable quarters the British army was assembled without tents, huts, or any sort of shelter from the
inclemency of the weather, which, though rainy in the day-
time, became sharply frosty after sunset, so that the saturated
uniforms of the soldiers were frozen hard at night, an experience naturally fatal to the negroes attached to the service
of the expedition, who perished in considerable numbers in
their sleep.   The only food which could be supplied to the
force in the gameless condition of the island was salt meat
and ship biscuit moistened with a little rum.   For Franklin
and his comrades these hardships were in one sense aggravated,
if in another sense perhaps relieved, by the severest physical
toil.   Night and day boats were pulling from the fleet to the

island and from the island to the fleet. It was not till the
21st that the last of the troops were got on shore, and, as
there was little time to inquire into 'turns' of labour, many
seamen were four or five days continually at the oar.

On the 22nd General Keane, the commander of the expedition, reviewed his forces, and formed an advance guard
of 1,600 men to start on the morrow for the mainland. Their
destination was Bayou Calatan, the creek already spoken of,
which lay at no less a distance than eighty miles from Pine
Island. Nothing, indeed, is more surprising or, though it
compels admiration, more calculated to suggest Marshal
Canrobert's historic utterance than the vastness of the space
which, with no base to speak of and hardly any transport
worthy of the name, our forces had to cover in this remarkable
expedition before they could even get within striking distance
of the enemy. One cannot but suspect that, however
'magnificent' were these operations considered as feats of
human resource and endurance, they could not possibly be
'war.' As in the later case, however, which called forth the
French general's criticism, the British soldier and sailor never
'reasoned why.' There were not boats enough to transport
more than one-third of the army at a time, so that the
advance guard had to take its chance of being attacked in
detail and cut off before its supports could arrive. Chancing
this, however, as they were bound to do, the force started off
on the 23rd under a sky of lowering clouds, soon to descend
in torrents of rain, and to be followed by the usual frost at
night; and, after a voyage of some twenty-four hours, pursued
under the exhausting and depressing conditions to which
they had become habituated, they reached the mouth of
Bayou Calatan, where they surprised and easily captured the
small and unsuspicious picket posted there, and by nine o'clock
on the morning of the 24th they at last set foot on the mainland of America.

Bayou Calatan emerges from the lake about ten miles
below New Orleans; and, as the nature of the ground on
which the advance guard had landed afforded good cover,
they naturally proposed to lie concealed until they could be

joined by the remainder of the force. Encouraged, however, by the reports of deserters who came in, assuring them that there were not more than five thousand men under arms throughout the State, among whom not more than twelve hundred were regular soldiers, and that the whole force was at present several miles on the opposite side of the town, expecting an attack on that quarter and apprehending no danger on this, General Keane resolved to push on into the open. His forces accordingly made a march of several miles in the direction of New Orleans, hit off the main road leading to the city, and finally halted on the neck of land on which it is built, and which at that point was not more than a mile broad, having a marsh on the right hand and the Mississippi on the left, with the New Orleans road running parallel, and a lofty dyke between river and highway. Into a more complete death-trap this unlucky advance guard could hardly have been led. About seven o'clock in the evening a large schooner stole up the river and opened a deadly fire of grape upon them from eighteen guns. There is a grim mixture of the comic and the tragic in Gleig's account of what followed :

Against this dreadful fire we had nothing whatever to oppose. The artillery which we had landed was too light to bring into competition with an adversary so powerful ; and, as she had anchored within a short distance of the opposite bank, no musketry could reach her with any precision or effect. A few rockets were discharged, *which made a beautiful appearance in the air* ; but the rocket is an uncertain weapon, and these deviated too far from their object to produce even terror among those against whom they were directed. Under these circumstances, as nothing could be done aggressively, our sole object was to shelter the men as much as possible from the iron hail. With this view they were commanded to leave the camp-fires and to hasten under the dyke. Thither all accordingly repaired without much regard to order and regularity, and, laying ourselves along wherever we could find room, we listened in painful silence to the pattering of grape-shot among our huts, and to the shrieks and groans of those who lay wounded beside them.

Worse still, the attack of the schooner, as they were soon to discover, was only one part of the enemy's concerted plan. After lying for almost an hour in this condition, a straggling fire from their piquets attracted their attention, and, while each man was speculating as to what these new sounds might portend, they were 'succeeded by a fearful yell and the heavens were illuminated on all sides by a semi-circular blaze of musketry.'

It was now clear that we were surrounded, and that by a very superior force ; and, therefore, no alternative remained but either to surrender at discretion or to beat back the assailants. The first of these plans was never for an instant thought of, and the second was immediately put into force. Rushing from under the bank, the 85th and 95th flew to support the piquets ; while the 4th, stealing to the rear of the encampment, formed close column and remained as a reserve. But to describe this action is altogether out of the question, for it was such a battle as the annals of modern warfare can hardly match. All order, all discipline, was lost. Each officer, as he was able to collect twenty or thirty men round him, advanced into the middle of the enemy, when it was fought hand to hand, bayonet to bayonet, and sword to sword, with the tumult and ferocity of one of Homer's combats.

Unfortunately, there was no Olympian god to interfere in their behalf. They had to hold their ground by sheer desperate fighting, and they succeeded in doing so. The Americans ultimately drew off, leaving them in possession of the field. 'Our loss, however, was enormous. Not less than 500 men (nearly a third of the force) had fallen, many of whom were our finest soldiers and best officers, and yet we could not but consider ourselves fortunate in escaping from the toils even at the expense of so great a sacrifice.' That the toils which it required so great a sacrifice to escape from need never have been entered at all is, of course, but too unhappily evident. On the arrival of General Keane's supports on the following day with artillery of sufficient strength, the obnoxious schooner was attacked and blown up, the river cleared of the enemy, and the position generally made good ; all which, but for the precipitate forward march of the advanced guard, would certainly have been accomplished at a far smaller loss than that of 500 men.

With the arrival of the main body came a new commander, General Sir Edward Pakenham, of Peninsular fame,

just despatched from England to succeed General Ross, who
had fallen at Baltimore, and under his command the army
advanced in two columns to within six miles of New Orleans,
where again preparations for defence had been made. The
American army, under General Jackson, an officer destined
both to military and to political celebrity in the later history
of his country, was posted behind an entrenchment, having
the left bank of the Mississippi for its right extremity and
stretching to a dense and impassable forest on the left. The
line was strengthened by a ditch about four feet deep which
ran along its front, and was defended by flank bastions, which
enfiladed its whole extent, and on which a formidable array
of heavy ordnance was placed. On the right bank of the
Mississippi, which is there nearly half a mile broad, a battery
of twenty guns had been constructed.

This formidable line of entrenchments being evidently
much too strong to be carried by a *coup de main*, several
attempts were made to approach it in strict scientific
fashion. But it was soon found that the enemy's guns were
so superior in weight and numbers that nothing was to be
expected from this species of attack. The position on the
right bank of the Mississippi was evidently the point on which
to direct their efforts, but how to approach it? There was
only one way of doing so—a most ambitious and laborious
method; but those blundering heroes shrank from nothing.
Again the services of the naval arm, to which they already
owed so much, were called in, and the task committed to
them was no less a one than that of cutting through the
entire neck of land from the Bayou Calatan to the river, and
constructing a canal of sufficient width and depth to admit
of boats being brought up from the lake in order to convey
an attacking force across the Mississippi. This Roman work
was executed with a spirit worthy of the legions of Cæsar.
The men were divided into four companies, and toiled night
and day at their appointed task. It was not till after a sharp
but indecisive engagement with the enemy on January 1 that
the order was given, and by the 6th the work was completed.
A general attack on the American position was then planned

for five o'clock on the morning of the 8th. Colonel Thornton, with a force of 1,400 men, was to cross the Mississippi during the previous night, capture the right bank battery, and turn its guns against the enemy on the other side of the river. In this forlorn hope—for the singularly imperfect dispositions of the adventure almost entitle it to that name—the young lieutenant of the Bedford bore a gallant part.

On the night of the 7th, Colonel Thornton, with a force of 1,400 men, moved stealthily down to the bank of the river; but there were no boats awaiting him. Hour after hour passed before they came, and only a portion of them arrived at last. The soft banks of the canal had given way, choking up the channel and impassably obstructing the passage of the heavier boats. Instead of a flotilla for 1,400 men, the Colonel found himself provided with transport for only 350. But what did that matter? Three hundred and fifty men are not fourteen hundred, but they are three hundred and fifty. The Colonel had undertaken to cross the river and carry the enemy's position on the opposite side, and it was absolutely necessary that this part of the plan should be carried into execution. Accordingly, dismissing 1,050 of his force, the Colonel put himself at the head of 250 men of his own regiment (the 85th), a division of fifty sailors, of whom Franklin was one, under Captain Rowland Money, and as many Marines, and crossed the river.

Instead of reaching it, however, at midnight, dawn was already breaking when, as they set foot on the landing-place, a rocket soared into the air from the opposite bank and added wings to their speed. Pakenham had already begun the attack. He had either not received intelligence of Thornton's enforced delay or had disregarded it. With an impatience which proved fatal to the enterprise, he had determined to advance without awaiting the concert of his comrade on the other shore. Scaling-ladders and fascines, however, are no less desirable appliances in an attack on parapeted works than boats for the transit of rivers; and Pakenham was without the one, as Thornton had been without the other. The troops actually had to be halted under the enemy's guns while the scaling-ladders were sent for; but the fire was soon so terrible that the head of the column, riddled through and through, fell back in disorder.

The remainder of this shocking—and splendid—story may be told in the words of Alison :—

Pakenham, whose buoyant courage ever led him to the scene of danger, thinking they were now fairly in for it, and must go on, rode to the front, rallied the troops again, led them to the slope of the glacis, and was in the act, with his hat off, of cheering on his fol-lowers, when he fell mortally wounded, pierced at the same moment by two balls. General Gibbs also was soon struck down. Keane, who led on the reserve, headed by the 93rd, shared the same fate ; but that noble regiment, composed entirely of Sutherland High-landers, a thousand strong, instead of being daunted by the carnage, rushed with frantic valour through the throng, and with such fury pressed the leading files on that, without either fascines or ladders, they fairly found their way by mounting upon each other's shoulders into the works. So close and deadly, however, was the fire of the riflemen when they got in, that the successful assailants were cut off to a man.

At last, General Lambert, to whom the death of Pakenham and the disablement of Gibbs and Keane had transferred the command, finding that it was impossible to carry the work and that the slaughter was tremendous, drew off the remnant of his shattered troops.

Meanwhile, the attack on the right bank battery had been brilliantly successful. The enemy on that side outnumbered Thornton's force by three to one and was strongly entrenched. The assailants had not a single piece of artillery nor any means but such as Nature provided of scaling the rampart ; but they prepared without a moment's hesitation for an assault. The 85th extended its files across the entire line of the enemy, the Marines formed in rear of the centre as a reserve, and at the sound of the bugle Money's little band of sailors rushed forward with a shout upon the guns. For an instant they wavered under the heavy discharge of grape and canister which met them, but, recovering themselves, they pushed on, and, the 85th dashing forward to their aid, the whole force swept into and over the works like a wave. The

Americans broke and fled, leaving the British in possession of their tents and of their eighteen pieces of artillery. Just at the moment, however, when they were about to turn these guns against the enemy, news reached them of the repulse of Pakenham's attack, and with it the disappointing order to abandon a captured position which Lambert's forces were not strong enough to hold. Deeply dispirited, we may imagine, by these evil tidings, the winners of this barren victory rejoined their defeated comrades on the opposite bank of the river. The whole force retreated on the night of the 18th, and in another ten days they were re-embarked.

Franklin's share in this sharp engagement, in which his commander, Captain Money, was desperately wounded, though he himself escaped without a scratch, was an important addition to the young officer's list of services, and he was in consequence of it recommended officially and very warmly, though in the result, as will be seen, ineffectually, for promotion. The Bedford, which does not seem to have taken part in the subsequent and more successful operations against Fort Boyer, near Mobile, in February 1815, set sail for home in March of that year, and reached Spithead on May 30. She was paid off on July 5 following, and, though Franklin had served on board of her uninterruptedly for five years, he was reappointed to another ship two days afterwards. He joined the Forth as first lieutenant, under Captain Sir William Bolton, and remained until she also was paid off in the following September; the only incident worth recording of this short period of service being the employment of the vessel to convey the Duchesse d'Angoulême to France on her return to her native country at the Restoration.

CHAPTER III

THE DOROTHEA AND THE TRENT

1815–1818

IT is noteworthy, as showing the natural bent of the born explorer, that during these years of inaction it was upon maritime discovery rather than naval warfare that Franklin's mind was fixed. It was not to Copenhagen and Trafalgar, but to the shores of Australia and the waters of the Southern Ocean, that his thoughts reverted. His heart was evidently with the crazy old Investigator, mouldering ingloriously as a storehouse hulk at Port Jackson, rather than with the Polyphemus and the Bellerophon, 'twin thunderbolts of war' though they were. He longed for fresh employment in the work of exploration ; yet, while all his inquiring and adventurous instincts urged him in this direction, his legitimate professional ambitions acted to some extent as an opposing influence. The difficulty of his position is strikingly brought out in an interesting letter, written in August 1814, in which one sees his shrewd common-sense almost amusingly at odds with his enthusiasm. He had previously written to Mr. Robert Brown, who had sailed with him as naturalist in the Investigator, deploring the fact that Captain Flinders's narrative of his voyage had not reached the public till the very day of its author's death, and reflecting in a somewhat depressed tone on the unlikelihood of any official recognition being given to the services of the younger officers under Flinders's command. Mr. Brown had remarked in his reply on the possibility, and even probability, that another voyage of discovery would soon be thought of, and had intimated that he might have an opportunity of suggesting the employment of his correspondent thereon, 'provided I were certain

E

that you would have no objection, or rather that you would prefer, to embark again in this line of the service.' To this Franklin answers :—

I am extremely obliged also for your communication that it is possible another voyage may be thought of, and particularly grateful for the kindness you have evinced by requesting my views on the subject of being employed therein. I have no hesitation in assuring you they are decidedly in favour of that service ; but I should hope, were an offer ever made to me, it would be accompanied by promotion. To embark on an expedition of that nature without some grounds for sanguine expectation, when an absence of five or six years may be calculated upon, and a total separation from any chance of improving your interest, is a most serious consideration ; and perhaps on return, with a constitution much shattered, you may find the patrons and friends of the voyage either removed or unable to procure you the appointment you have anxiously sought. These, my dear sir, are objections, you will readily admit, I think, which ought to have some weight, and even might be used (without the imputation of being inclined to cavil) as an argument why they should give me promotion previous to starting.

In the end, however, disinterested enthusiasm wins.

I will, however, confess these disadvantages would not discourage me, so interested do I feel in that service ; and could I suppose it probable that a responsible office in such a voyage would be offered me, I should think it my duty to devote my greatest attention to those studies which would fit me for the better performance of it.

Again, it was but a few weeks since he had forwarded to the Admiralty a statement of his services and testimonials from his various commanding officers in support of an application for promotion, and he feared to appear importunate by applying again so soon.

By December 1814 he had added to these services and strengthened their resulting claim by his share in the brilliant dash at the gunboats of New Orleans and in the subsequent attack on the forts. But in the next year, unfortunately for all young ambitions in either service, came the Peace of Vienna ; and then to Franklin's renewed application for promotion came the curt official answer from Lord Melville that, 'having read the petition of Lieutenant John Franklin,' he was sorry he could not hold out any expectation of his advancement at an early period. 'As the Navy,' added the First Lord, 'is now placed on a peace establishment, all promotion must in consequence cease, excepting in the few cases that may occur on the foreign stations.'

Neither promotion nor renewal of active service seemed in prospect, and there was nothing for the young officer but to submit as patiently as might be to that which his restless spirit always found it hardest to bear—inaction. The next three years were spent principally with members of his family in Lincolnshire and elsewhere; and though, no doubt, he was continually on the look-out for any signs of change in the official horizon, there is no trace among the correspondence of these years of any renewed application to the Admiralty. The opportunity which at last came to him, and by which his future career was practically determined, came, as far as can be ascertained, unsought.

It is not very easy to discover why at this particular moment the spirit of Arctic exploration should suddenly have taken possession of the Ministerial mind. The then Secretary of the Admiralty, Sir John Barrow, was, it is true, an ardent geographer, and specially interested in the subject of Polar research. He had carefully collected all the reports bearing on its conditions and possibilities, as affected mainly by the state and situation of the ice in high northern latitudes; and with this information as a basis he drew up an elaborate scheme for the exploration of the Arctic regions. This, warmly supported by the President and Council of the Royal Society, was submitted to the Lords of the Admiralty, by whom it was also approved. But many a Secretary might have piped to a Government as inspiritingly without inducing that Government to dance. The three years of inaction may have begun to bore even Whitehall itself; or the favour with which Sir John Barrow's idea was received by the public may have insensibly influenced the official mind; or some other unknown or now forgotten impulse may have been in operation. This only is certain, that an interest in Arctic discovery, which had slept for nearly half a century in Ministerial bosoms, suddenly awakened. It was five-and-forty years since the Racehorse, under Captain Phipps, and the Carcass, under Commander Lutwidge, bearing the young Horatio Nelson and his fortunes, set sail from Sheerness with orders to proceed to the North Pole, or as close to it as ice and other obstructions would permit, and reached a latitude of 80° 48', returning three months later in the same year, 1773. And now, in 1818, a British Government had again made up its mind to another attack on the same problem, and had even indeed resolved to combine it with another project. The Admiralty now contemplated the despatch of two expeditions—one with the object of endeavouring to discover a passage round the northern and north-western coasts of America from the Atlantic to the Pacific; the other for the purpose of attempting to reach the North Pole. What is more, they proceeded to give what to the English mind has always seemed the best, perhaps the only, proof that a man or a Government means business. Where the private citizen 'backs his opinion' with a bet, the State is expected to support the undertaking which it patronises by the offer of a reward.

So many, moreover, of our national enterprises leave their mark in some form or other on the Statute Book, that the history of this revival of English interest in Arctic exploration would not have been complete unless it had included an Act of Parliament in its records. The recitals of this enactment bear ample witness to the fact that the impulse which gave birth to it was no new one in our history. Among the references to past legislation which are to be found in 58 George III. c. 20, 'An Act for more effectually discovering the longitude at sea and encouraging attempts to find a Northern Passage between the Atlantic and Pacific Oceans, and to approach the Northern Pole,' is one from which it will be seen, to the surprise perhaps of most people, that the last-mentioned project had engaged the attention of the Imperial Legislature more than seventy years before. As far back as 1745 an Act had been passed offering a reward of 20,000*l.* to the owner or owners of any ship or vessel which should first find out and navigate a 'North-West Passage through Hudson's Straights to the Western and Southern Oceans of

America;' and thirty-one years later 'a sum of 5,000*l.* was offered to any person who should approach by sea within one degree of the Northern Pole.'

This last provision was extended in the Act of 1818 by a clause providing that ' for the encouragement of persons who may attempt the said passage or approach the Northern Pole, but not wholly accomplish the same,' it should be competent for certain commissioners appointed under the Act to propose, by memorial to the King in Council, ' to direct and establish proportionate rewards to be paid to such person as aforesaid who shall first accomplish certain proportions of the said Passage or Approach.' In pursuance of this, a scale of reward was subsequently fixed by Order in Council according to which any vessel that first succeeded in reaching the 83rd parallel of latitude would be entitled to a reward of 1,000*l.* ; double that sum would be granted for crossing the 85th parallel ; 3,000*l.* to any vessel that should reach 87° N. ; 4,000*l.* for attaining the 88th parallel, and 5,000*l.* for the Pole.

It was apparently regarded in official as well as unofficial circles as not at all improbable that the largest of these rewards would be actually earned. Indeed, one cannot resist a slight feeling of amusement at noting, after a lapse of nearly eighty years, the tone of easy familiarity with which the Admiralty of that period spoke of the North Pole—a tone which almost recalls the well-known pleasantry about a certain famous critic's attitude towards the Equator. ' Should you reach the Pole, your future course must mainly depend,' &c. ' If . . . the weather should prove favourable, you are to remain in the vicinity of the Pole for a few days, in order to the more accurately making the observations which it is to be expected your interesting and unexampled situation may furnish you with.' Interesting and unexampled indeed ! ' On leaving the Pole you will endeavour,' &c. ' Should you, either by passing over or near the Pole or by any lateral direction, make your way to Behring Straits, you are,' &c. Such are the constantly recurring phrases of the instructions issued by the Admiralty, and probably framed by Sir John Barrow himself, for the conduct of this expedition ; and their confident handling of their obscure subject is to be attributed not only to the imperfect acquaintance even of the best geographers of that day with the terraqueous conditions of the Polar regions, but also no doubt to the glorious belief then prevalent, a survival from the great war, that there was no exploit under heaven which the British Navy and its sailors could not perform, in all probability at the first attempt.

The Admiralty, it must be admitted, set about the work in a spirit of thoroughness. Though their Lordships spoke familiarly of the object of their attack, they did not actually expect that they could, so to speak, stroll into the Arctic citadel at any point they might choose to select. They deemed it advisable, as we have seen, to organise two distinct plans of assault and to approach the stronghold from two different sides. Four vessels were accordingly prepared for the service, two of which, the Isabella and the Alexander, under the command respectively of Captain Ross and Lieutenant Parry, were to proceed by the western route through Baffin's Bay; while the other two, the Dorothea and the Trent, were to take what is called the Spitzbergen route due northwards. For the command of the second expedition the Admiralty selected Captain David Buchan, R.N., who had a short time previously distinguished himself in charge of an expedition into the interior of Newfoundland. The vessel on which he hoisted his pennant was the Dorothea, a ship of 370 tons burden, and Lieutenant Franklin was placed under his orders in command of the smaller Trent, a brig of 250 tons. Both these vessels were hired into the service for the occasion, and were taken into dock, where they were rendered—or, unfortunately, supposed to have been rendered —as strong as wood and iron could make them. Captain Buchan's instructions were to make the best of his way into the Spitzbergen seas, and thence to endeavour to force his ships northward between Spitzbergen and Greenland. If successful in reaching the Pole—a contingency which, in the then state of knowledge as to the condition of the seas in the highest latitudes, was evidently quite within official contemplation—the commander of the expedition was, if the weather was favourable, to remain, as we have seen, for a few days in the vicinity of the Pole for the purpose of making observations. On 'leaving the Pole' they were to shape their course for Behring Strait, or, if this proved impracticable, to sail round the north end of Greenland and return home by Baffin's Bay and Davis Straits. If the Dorothea and the Trent were unable to reach the Pole, but if it seemed possible, without accomplishing that feat, to hit off a course affording any prospect of reaching Behring Strait, Buchan and Franklin were directed to take it, 'recollecting that, although it is highly desirable in the interests of science and the extension of natural knowledge that you should reach the Pole, yet that the passage between the Atlantic and the Pacific is the main object of your mission.' And this elaborately framed document goes on to give minute instructions for the conduct of the two commanders in the event of their discovering and navigating the North-West Passage. They are then to make the best of their way to Kamschatka, call on the Russian Governor for the purpose of delivering to him duplicates of all the journals and other documents which the voyage may have produced, for immediate transmission overland to London, proceed thence to the Sandwich Islands or New Albion or some other place in the Pacific Ocean to refit and to refresh their crews, winter there, and in the spring repass Behring Strait once more, and return home to England by the way they had come. It is true, a discretion is allowed them as to the attempt of this last-mentioned feat. They are maturely to consider and weigh the prudence of making it. 'If your original passages should be made with facility, and you see reason to believe that your success was not owing to circumstances merely accidental or temporary, and that there is a probability that you may be able, also, to accomplish the passage back, it would be undoubtedly of great importance that you should endeavour to make it; but if, on the other hand, it shall have been attended with circumstances of danger or difficulty so great as to persuade you that the attempt to return would risk the safety of the ships and the lives of the crews, you in this case are to abandon all thought of returning by the northern passage, and are to make the best of your way homeward by Cape Horn.' And this portion of a tolerably comprehensive, not to say ambitious, itinerary concludes with certain orders as to concerted action between the two expeditions of which the cardinal injunction is to 'fix with Captain Ross, to whom the other expedition is entrusted, upon a rendezvous in the Pacific

One more extract must, however, be made from it by the quotation of a passage having reference to a contingency which was in fact realised :—

In the event of any irreparable accident happening to either of the ships, you are to cause the officers and crew of the disabled ship to be removed into the other, and with her singly to proceed in prosecution of the voyage or return to England according as circumstances shall appear to require. Should, unfortunately, your own ship be the one disabled, you are in that case to take command of the Trent ; and in the event of your inability, by sickness or otherwise, to carry these instructions into execution, you are to transfer them to the lieutenant next in command, who is hereby required to execute them in the best manner he can for the attainment of the several objects in view.

On April 25 the two vessels sailed out of the Thames, after an experience of the popular feeling in the matter which shows in how lively a fashion the enterprise had impressed itself on the public imagination of that day. Thus, writing to Mrs. Cracroft on April 6, Franklin says :—

I hope we shall have left the Nore by this day week. We all go in the highest spirits, and indeed it would be ungrateful to feel otherwise, encouraged as we have been by the kind interest and attention of all ranks of society. It would be quite impossible for me to convey to you the amazing interest our little squadron has excited. Deptford has been covered with carriages and the ships with visitors every day since they were in a state to be seen. Indeed, their coming in such shoals has greatly retarded our equipment. We have, in fact, moved further down the river to prevent that general influx, and shall now, I hope, be enabled to get our ships in tolerable order before sailing further.

It was not, however, mere vulgar curiosity alone which drew so many visitors to the Dorothea and Trent.

You would be surprised to hear the number of persons this voyage has led me to become personally known to, some of them persons of considerable rank and all men of scientific eminence. They have most of them submitted some queries to be solved by us, or suggestions for us to be guided by, and all have expressed earnest wishes for our success. . . . It really seems quite ridiculous to find myself placed among these parties, when I consider how little I know of the matters which usually form the subject of their conversations. At present, however, the bare circumstance of going to the North Pole is a sufficient passport anywhere. What a fortunate person must I, therefore, consider myself to be to have it, and thankful indeed to my good friends who procured it for me ! I only hope I may have the opportunity of evincing my gratitude by an ardent exertion of earnest endeavours in the cause they have so much at heart.

And the letter concludes, as was Franklin's affectionate wont, with much kindly and playful talk of his little nieces Sophy and Isabella :—

I hope you will endeavour to keep upon their minds the remembrance of Uncle John, or rather make them familiar with my name ; and I trust it will not be long ere they may have an opportunity of becoming familiar with my countenance also ; which, if they see me after it has been reddened and hardened by a Polar winter, they will not, I think, at the age they will then be, easily forget.

He then goes on to give a lively description of his Arctic outfit, which included, we learn, ' a beautiful mask for the face in the most severe weather and noses for the more mild.'

The only first-hand account of this voyage is contained in a volume published five-and-twenty years later by Captain Beechey, who sailed as Franklin's first lieutenant in the Trent. It is a most spirited narrative of a voyage the interest of which as a series of maritime adventures considerably exceeded its scientific results. The Dorothea and Trent failed to get any nearer to the Pole than between the 80th and 81st parallels of latitude, at which point their progress was arrested by an impenetrable barrier of ice ; and a subsequent attempt to force a passage westward, in pursuance no doubt of the alternative plan prescribed in their instructions, was equally unsuccessful.

But, considered as a record of manifold dangers and difficulties encountered with unflinching courage and overcome by brilliant seamanship, the story of their voyage must always hold a high place in the history of Arctic adventure. The Admiralty, as it turned out, had made a contribution of its own to the trials of the voyagers by providing them with one unseaworthy ship. Even before leaving Lerwick a leak was discovered in the sides of the Trent, and it was with difficulty that the vessel was sufficiently patched up to proceed on her journey. Twice were they beset in the pack, the first time for thirteen days, and the second for three weeks ; and on the former occasion it was discovered that a workman, of a type better known perhaps in these days than in those, had also, though with a guilt more deliberate than that of his superiors, lent a hand to their destruction. A dockyard shipwright had murderously left out a bolt in the process of construction and concealed the defect by smearing the hole with pitch.

This, however, is somewhat to anticipate the history of a voyage which, short as it was, abounded in incidents. The two vessels made Magdalena Bay, on the north-west coast of Spitzbergen—not without having experienced some very rough weather on their northward voyage—by the beginning of June, and resolved to wait for a few days in order to give time to the loosened 'pack' of the previous winter to complete the process of its dispersal. But in the course of the survey and exploration of the Spitzbergen coast—an experience which first inspired Franklin with his henceforth insatiable passion for Arctic travel—the commander of the Trent had a narrow escape of his life, from a danger which the explorers had probably not included in their calculations before starting. Icebergs they knew of as a source of Arctic peril, but they had no doubt mentally contemplated them only as in actual existence and not as in process of creation ; nor had it occurred to them that to assist at the birth of an iceberg from its mother glacier was so hazardous an undertaking as they found it. Twice did they witness this act of Titanic parturition, a picturesque and animated account of which is given by Captain Beechey in his 'Voyage of Discovery towards the North Pole :'—

On two occasions we witnessed avalanches on the most magnificent scale. The first was occasioned by the discharge of a musket at about half a mile distance from the glacier. Immediately after the report of the gun a noise resembling thunder was heard in the direction of the iceberg, and in a few seconds more an immense piece broke away and fell headlong into the sea. The crew of the launch, supposing themselves to be beyond the reach of its influence, quietly looked upon the scene, when presently a sea rose and rolled towards the shore with such rapidity that the crew had not time to take any precaution, and the boat was in consequence washed up on the beach and completely filled by the succeeding wave. As soon as their astonishment had subsided they examined the boat, and found her so badly stove that it became necessary to repair her in order to return to the ship. They had also the curiosity to measure the distance the boat had been carried by the wave, and found it ninety-six feet.

On the second occasion they were much nearer the scene of the convulsion, and might easily have been overwhelmed by the avalanche in its descent:—

Lieutenant Franklin and myself had approached one of these stupendous walls of ice, and were endeavouring to search into the innermost recess of a deep cavern that was near the foot of the glacier, when we heard a report as of a cannon, and, turning to the quarter whence it proceeded, we perceived an immense piece of the front of the berg sliding down from a height of two hundred feet at least into the sea, and dispersing the water in every direction, accompanied by a loud grinding noise, and followed by a quantity of water, which, being previously lodged in the fissures, now made its escape in numberless small cataracts over the front of the glacier. We kept the boat's head in the direction of the sea, and thus escaped the disaster which had befallen the other boat, for the disturbance occasioned by the plunge of this enormous fragment caused a succession of rollers, which swept over the surface of the bay, making its shores resound as it travelled along it, and at a distance of four miles was so considerable that it became necessary to right the Dorothea, which was then careening, by immediately releasing the tackles which confined her.

The piece that had been disengaged at first wholly disappeared under water, and nothing was seen but a violent boiling of the sea and a shooting-up of clouds of spray like that which occurs at the foot of a great cataract. After a short time, it raised its head full a hundred feet above the surface, with water pouring down from all parts of it, and then labouring as if doubtful which way it should fall over, and, after rocking about some minutes, it at length became settled.

We now approached it, and found it nearly a quarter of a mile in circumference and sixty feet out of the water. Knowing its specific gravity, and making a fair allowance for its inequalities, we computed its weight at 421,660 tons.

On June 7 the expedition quitted Magdalena Bay after five days' stay, but found the ice outside in much the same condition as when they had left it. They stood along its margin searching for an opening, but in vain, and soon afterwards they were driven by the wind into the pack. Here they remained beset for several days, and in a position at times of no little danger.

On one occasion, the Trent, though she appeared to be so closely wedged up that it did not seem possible for her to be moved, was suddenly lifted four feet by an enormous mass of ice getting under her keel; at another time the fragments of the crumbling floe were piled up under her bows, to the great danger of her bowsprit. Nor was the Dorothea in less imminent peril. The point of a floe came in contact with her side, where it remained a short time, and then, glancing off, impinged upon the larger mass of ice to which the vessel was moored. The terrible pressure to which she had been subjected was then demonstrated by the rending asunder of the larger mass; while the point of the floe was broken into fragments, which were speedily heaped up in a pyramid thirty-five feet in height, upon the very summit of which there appeared a huge mass bearing the impression of the planks and bolts of the vessel's bottom. And all this time, while the roaring of the sea upon the edge of the pack and the stormy sky showed plainly that it was blowing a gale at sea, 'the ships were so perfectly becalmed that the vane at the masthead was scarcely agitated.' The silent tightening of the fearful grasp in which the vessels were held was the only sign of the elemental war outside.

The summer being now pretty well advanced, the explorers began to perceive that if any progress northward was to be made that year it must be begun at once. Captain Buchan

accordingly resorted to the laborious experiment of dragging
the vessels through the ice wherever the smallest opening was
to be found. Iron hooks having been driven into the ice, large
ropes were attached to them, and by dint of working these
with the windlass and removing obstructions in the channels
with the ice-saws, they succeeded, after several hours of labour,
in reaching a tolerably clear lane of water, where, with the aid
of their sails, they ran a few miles to the northward. The
following two days were spent in the same toilsome work,
after which they found, to their cruel mortification, that they
had all the time been contending against a current flowing
from the north so strongly as to carry the pack in a southward direction at a greater rate of speed than that of their
own northward advance over its surface. At the end of two
long days of toil they found that they were actually eleven or
twelve miles lower in latitude than they had been at the beginning of the period.

On July 19, Captain Buchan came definitely to the conclusion that it was vain to attempt further progress to the
northward. The only course open to them was to abandon
the endeavour to reach the Pole, and, regaining the open sea
as quickly as possible, to try a westward course. They were
now, however, about thirty miles distant from the open sea,
and it was only after nine days' incessant labour in warping
the ships in the required direction that they had at last
the satisfaction of finding themselves in clear water, and were
able to turn their ships' heads to the west. But here the
gravest peril which they encountered, and the one which put
their courage and the resources of their seamanship to the
severest test, assailed them. Hardly had they entered on
their new course when a furious gale sprang up, and to escape
immediate destruction they were driven to the unusual and
almost desperate expedient of taking shelter in the pack.
One of the largest hemp cables was cut up into lengths of
about thirty feet, and with these pieces, together with some
walrus hides and iron plates, a sort of shield was constructed
round the hull of the ship to protect it against damage from
the huge blocks of ice with which it would have to come into

contact. While still a few fathoms from the ice, they searched with anxiety for a place that was more open than the general line of the pack, but in vain ; all parts appeared to be equally impenetrable, and to present one unbroken line of breakers, on which immense pieces of ice were heaving and subsiding with the waves, and dashing together with a violence which nothing apparently but a solid body could withstand. To continue in the stirring words of Beechey's narrative :—

No language, I am convinced, can convey an adequate idea of the terrific grandeur of the effect now produced by the collision of the ice and the tempestuous ocean. The sea violently agitated, and rolling its mountainous waves against an opposing body, is at all times a sublime and awful sight ; but when, in addition, it encounters immense masses of ice which it has set in motion with a violence equal to its own, its effect is prodigiously increased. At one moment it bursts upon these icy fragments, and buries them many feet beneath the wave, and the next, as the buoyancy of the depressed body struggles for reascendency, the water rushes in foaming cataracts over its edges, while every individual mass, rocking and labouring in its bed, grinds against and contends with its opponent until one is either split with the shock or upheaved upon the surface of the other. Nor is this collision confined to any particular spot ; it is going on as far as the sight can reach ; and when from the convulsive scene below the eye is turned to the extraordinary appearance of the 'ice blink' in the sky above, where the unnatural clearness of a calm and silvery atmosphere presents itself, bounded by a dark, hard line of stormy clouds—such as at this moment lowered over our masts, as if to mark the confines within which the efforts of man would be of no avail—the reader may imagine the sensation of awe which must accompany that of grandeur in the mind of the beholder.

Then follows a striking piece of testimony to the unshaken nerve, or, one might better say, to the buoyant bravery of Franklin, on whom the mere imminence of deadly peril seems always to have produced an exhilarating effect :—

At the instant when we were about to put the strength of our little vessel in competition with that of the great icy continent, and when it seemed almost presumption to reckon on the possibility of her surviving the unequal conflict, it was gratifying in the extreme to observe in all our crew the greatest calmness and resolution. If ever the fortitude of seamen was fairly tried, it was assuredly on this occasion ; and I will not conceal the pride I felt in witnessing the bold and decisive tone in which the orders were issued by the commander of our little vessel, and the promptitude and steadiness with which they were executed by the crew.

A few minutes more and they were within a few yards of the tossing, jostling herd of icebergs into which they were about to plunge :—

Each person instinctively secured his own hold, and, with his eyes fixed upon the masts, awaited in breathless anxiety the moment of concussion. It soon arrived ; the brig, cutting her way through the light ice, came in violent contact with the main body. In an instant we all lost our footing, the masts bent with the impetus, and the cracking timbers from below bespoke a pressure which was calculated to awaken our serious apprehensions. The vessel staggered under the shock, and for a moment seemed to recoil ; but the next wave, curling up under her counter, drove her about her own length within the margin of the ice, where she gave one roll, and was immediately thrown broadside to the wind by the succeeding wave, which beat furiously against her stern, and brought her lee side in contact with the main body, leaving her weather side exposed at the same time to a piece of ice about twice her own dimensions. . . . Literally tossed from piece to piece, we had nothing left but patiently to abide the issue, for we could scarcely keep our feet, much less render any assistance to the vessel. The motion was so great that the ship's bell, which in the heaviest gale of wind had never struck by itself, now tolled so continually that it was ordered to be muffled, for the purpose of escaping the unpleasant association it was calculated to produce.

By dint of crowding on more sail, Franklin succeeded in forcing the Trent further into the pack, where its masses of ice were less violently agitated, and in a few hours the gale subsided. Open water was reached on the following morning, and the two vessels, for the Trent's consort had also weathered the storm, sought refuge in Fair Haven, a bay on the northern shore of Spitzbergen. Franklin and Buchan then proceeded to examine their wounded ships. They proved, as might have been expected, to have sustained fearful injuries in this glacial tournament. The Trent was much mauled, but the Dorothea was the worse sufferer of the two. She was indeed so desperately damaged on her port side that it was a wonder she had been able to keep afloat.

Exploring was obviously at an end for her ; it was felt

that she must either at once return to England or be abandoned. Franklin tried hard to persuade his superior officer
that the Trent was still fit for service, and pleaded earnestly
for permission to pursue their enterprise ; but Captain Buchan,
no doubt wisely, declined to listen to his impetuous comrade.
His official instructions, indeed, hardly permitted him to
accede to Franklin's request. These instructions, it may
be remembered, expressly enjoined him, in the event of his
own ship being disabled, to take command of the Trent ; but
in that case what was to be done with the Dorothea ? Had
any 'irreparable accident' happened to her, it would, it is true,
have been his duty to 'cause her officers and crew to be removed' to her companion vessel, and either to proceed with
that vessel 'singly in prosecution of the voyage, or to return
to England as circumstances should appear to require.'. But
the Dorothea was not irreparably damaged ; she was perhaps
sufficiently seaworthy to accomplish the return journey to
England, though not to face new dangers in the Arctic seas ;
and he did not, therefore, feel justified in abandoning her. If,
however, he had taken command of the Trent and sent his
own vessel home in charge of her first lieutenant, he felt that
'he would incur the appearance of wishing to escape the
danger to which his crew would be exposed.' Nor, it seems,
was he even prepared to take the responsibility of separating
the two ships in order to allow Franklin to continue the
expedition alone in the Trent, the condition of the Dorothea
being, in his opinion, so dangerous as to render it unadvisable
for her to undertake the homeward voyage unaccompanied
by her consort. He finally determined, therefore, that both
ships should desist from the prosecution of their enterprise
and return home together.

There remained only the question whether something more
might not yet be accomplished by a boat journey over the
ice ; but upon consulting with Franklin, and examining into
the resources of the ships for such an undertaking, they were
found so inadequate that the project was speedily given up.
Captain Buchan was, therefore, reluctantly compelled to
abandon all further attempts at discovery, and to proceed to

England as soon as the necessary repairs of the Dorothea should be completed. Franklin no less reluctantly yielded, and, after employing the remainder of their time at the anchorage in magnetic observations and a thorough survey of the neighbouring coast of Spitzbergen, the commanders of the Dorothea and Trent put to sea on August 30, and arrived at Deptford on October 22, after an absence of almost exactly six months.

CHAPTER IV

FIRST ARCTIC EXPEDITION

1818–1821

IT is difficult for us of the present age—an age which has, so to speak, grown almost *blasé* of Polar exploration, and which has moreover seen even this romantic form of adventure partially vulgarised by association with the tactics of the advertiser—to realise the admiring interest which Arctic voyages aroused in the minds of our countrymen of the early nineteenth century. Nor is it easy to frame any adequate conception of the strength of that spell which they cast over the adventurous spirits of the British Navy, restless as they were with the excitements, and fired rather than satiated with the triumphs, of a long and glorious war. The Arctic Ocean had for some of them taken the place of the Spanish Main for the sailors of Elizabeth, and the Pole seemed to them like that fabled El Dorado that so bewitched the contemporaries of Drake and Raleigh. To Franklin, exploration had always appealed more powerfully than even war itself, and the stimulating yet not wholly satisfactory experiences of his voyage with Buchan had inflamed his passion for Arctic discovery to a still higher pitch of ardour. It was with intense satisfaction that he now found even the chilly atmosphere of the Admiralty warming gradually to the work. The reports of the leaders of the two expeditions were considered and discussed in official quarters, and ere long it was decided by the Government to continue the work of exploration to the westward by Baffin's Bay, while a party was to be sent overland to explore the northern coast of Arctic America. The command of the former expedition was entrusted to Lieutenant Parry, who had already seen service as

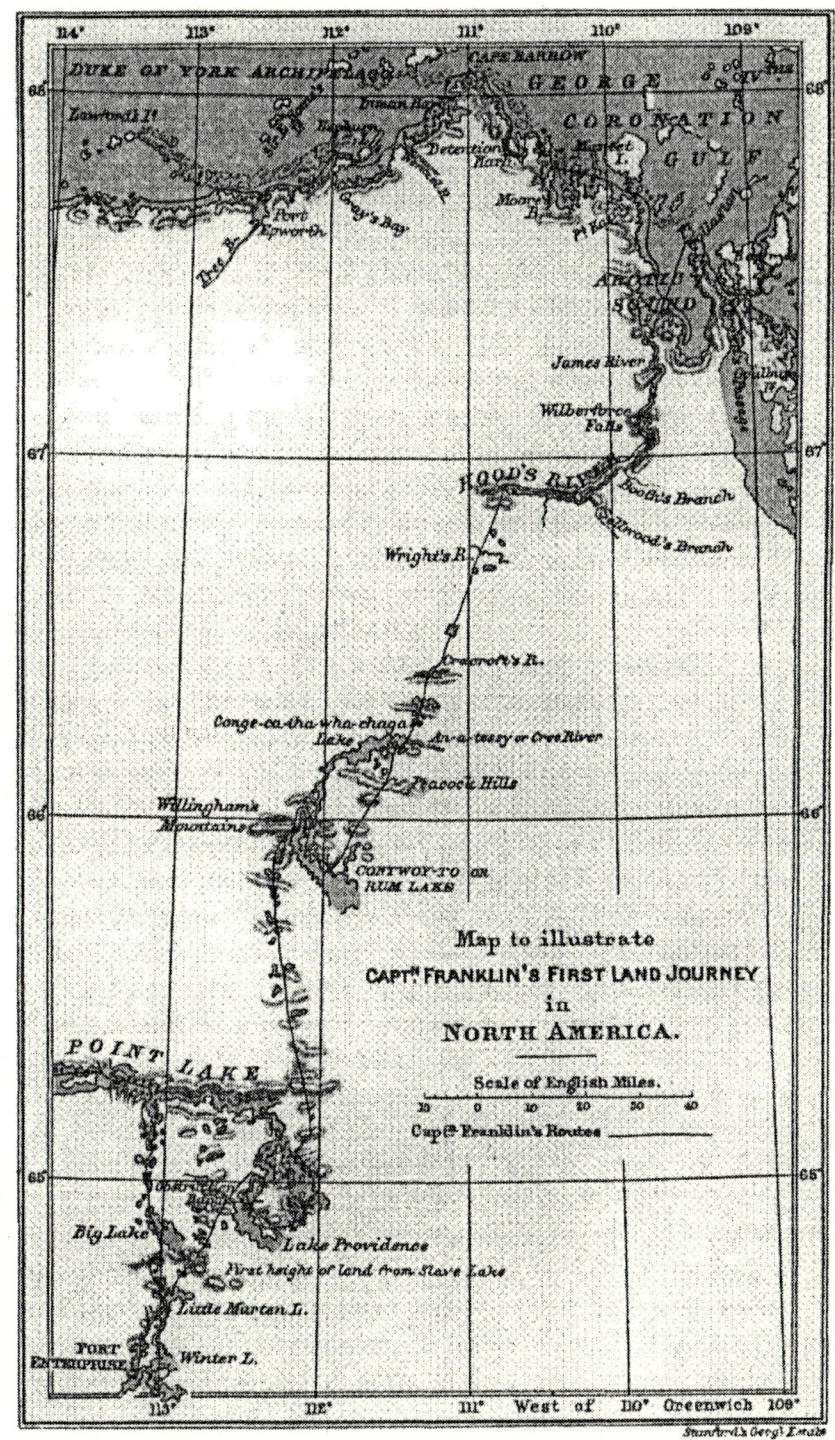

Map to illustrate

CAPT^N. FRANKLIN'S FIRST LAND JOURNEY

in

NORTH AMERICA.

Scale of English Miles.

Captⁿ Franklin's Routes

London: John Murray, Albemarle St.

second in command of the earlier expedition under Captain Ross. The vessels selected for the service, the Hecla and the Griper, sailed on May 11, 1819, with instructions to proceed up Baffin's Bay, and to endeavour to reach the Pacific through any channel that might be discovered to the westward.

The other expedition, which, it will be observed, was an entirely new departure in point of method, was placed under the command of Franklin. Its instructions were to proceed by land from the north-western shore of Hudson's Bay, across the vast tract of country lying between that bay and the shores of the Arctic Sea, to a point at or near the mouth of the Coppermine River. Thence the explorers were to endeavour to make their way in an easterly direction along the north coast of the continent, and if possible to effect a junction with Parry as he voyaged westward from the northern extremity of Baffin's Bay.

It was a service well calculated to kindle Franklin's ready enthusiasm. The land journey lay through a country in those days blank upon our maps, save where it was threaded by a couple of thin lines traced in the previous century—the routes of Hearne and Mackenzie, two adventurous servants of the Hudson's Bay Company, who, one in 1770 and the other in 1789, had succeeded in making their way across it to the sea. It was along the route taken or supposed to have been taken by the former of these pioneers that Franklin was directed to advance ; but Hearne was a very inaccurate observer, and the correctness of his surveys had been much questioned ; some even doubted whether he had ever reached the sea at all. None knew, in fact, what might be the difficulties and dangers of the shadowy track that the expedition was to follow, through what inhospitable regions the travellers might have to pass on their way to the Arctic Ocean, or what obstacles might oppose themselves to the progress of the expedition in the attempt to continue their journey by water when that ocean was reached. Above all, it was impossible —as the event only too terribly showed—to know how far it would be found practicable to retrace their steps to their base of operations or to measure the risk which in the attempt to do so they would incur of perishing from cold, hunger, and fatigue. The enterprise, in fact, on which Franklin was then setting out, though it is nowadays perhaps the least known, was yet undoubtedly the greatest of his achievements. Its geographical gains are apt to be forgotten ; and in the now well-filled maps of Arctic America the strip of coast line which he reclaimed from the region of the unknown by this expedition cuts no very great figure. Yet is the history of this adventure in reality as much more glorious than that of many explorations more fruitful in discoveries of importance, as heroism is more glorious than material success. For it is a tale of indomitable courage, and of unflinching endurance, than which none more splendid and inspiring is to be found in all the long and illustrious record of the great things done and suffered by the men of our race.

How deeply sensible was Franklin himself of the uncertainty of its issue, we may judge by the following extract from a letter to his sister, Mrs. Cracroft, which characteristically reflects the simple piety of his nature, and that temper of trust in the Divine guidance and of resignation to the Divine will in which he entered upon any important undertaking of life. After detailing the instructions which he had received from the Admiralty, and estimating his probable period of absence at about two years and a half, by which time, he thinks, 'we shall either have ascertained the practicability or impracticability of reaching northwards,' he continues :—

Experience, however, has taught me never to indulge in too superior hopes either of success or reward ; but I will hope and pray, through the assistance of an Almighty Providence, that each individual among us may be enabled to do his utmost with cheerfulness and zeal, having his mind anxiously devoted to the cause. . . . May that Almighty power protect and guide us, Who alone can order all things, and doth as seemeth best to His infinite wisdom ! May we trust in Him, and endeavour to do our utmost ! This must be our prayer, and, I trust, will be that of all our friends.

Franklin's companions on this adventurous expedition were, fortunately for its prospects, resolute and trusty men,

Foremost among them was Dr. John Richardson, a Navy surgeon and a keen and well-trained scientific inquirer. Another was George Back, who himself subsequently rose to fame and honours as an independent Arctic explorer. He had served with Franklin in the Trent, and had so well acquitted himself that he was at once selected by his former commander to accompany him on this new venture. Robert Hood, destined to a tragic end, was another; and in a lower grade John Hepburn, an old man-of-war's man, to whose staunch fidelity and heroic self-sacrifice some members of the expedition were indebted for the actual preservation of their lives. The plan which Franklin was commissioned to carry out was of a comprehensive nature. After reaching Hudson's Bay he was to travel northward with the object of astronomically determining the position of all capes, headlands, bays, harbours, and rivers, and also to sketch the trend of the coast-line of North America between the eastern extremity of that continent and the mouth of the Coppermine River, with liberty to select, according to circumstances, the best route to enable him to reach the shores of the Arctic Sea in the shortest possible time.

Whether the departure of this expedition excited as much popular interest as that of its forerunner in the previous year we do not learn; but, having regard to the circumstances of its despatch, and the higher expectations entertained of its result, the public feeling on the subject is hardly likely to have been less pronounced. Some enterprising caterer for the amusement of the metropolis had, it seems, conceived the idea of presenting the incidents of the previous voyage for the instruction and entertainment of his fellow-citizens in the form of a panorama—an exhibition which Franklin, still embarrassed, like most of the distinguished men of his time, by a species of modesty which many of the celebrities of our own day have successfully overcome, regarded, it is evident, with mixed feelings. Writing to his sister some six weeks before his departure, he says :—

The panorama opens for public exhibition this day. There can have been but few visitors, for it has rained unceasingly. I have not seen it for some weeks, when it was about half finished. I do not expect to see it again, since my likeness is said to be strong. I shall not venture to approach very near Leicester Square, for fear the passers-by should say, 'There goes the fellow in the panorama.' I have just learnt that Sir Joseph Banks has seen it, and approves of it highly.

On May 23, 1819, the expedition set sail from Gravesend in the Hudson's Bay Company's ship Prince of Wales ; but bad weather and adverse winds rendered their progress slow, and it was not till June 3 that they reached Stromness, in the Orkney Islands. Here Franklin endeavoured to engage an adequate crew of boatmen to assist him in ascending the rivers of the Hudson's Bay Territory ; but owing (he says in a letter to his father from this port) to 'the great demand for them at home, which at this time affords them full occupation,' the recruits whom he was able to obtain were only four in number.

Here Franklin again reviewed the prospects of his enterprise, and, as can easily be perceived, with growing doubts of its feasibility :—

I have read a copy of Hearne's original journal. The details are somewhat similar to his printed book, but given in an embellished style ; and, though I am not prepared to go the length of some persons and doubt his statements altogether, I yet think he has left a tolerably wide field for observation, and if we are so fortunate as to search beyond him, I hope we may add something to the geography and natural history of that unknown part of the globe. Though we do not permit ourselves to indulge in sanguine hopes of success, our fervent prayers, I hope, will be offered up for the blessing and assistance of an Almighty Parent on our humble endeavours. From every estimate I can at present form I think the service in any case will occupy near three years. By October 1821 I shall calculate on bending my steps homeward ; but long before that period, and indeed by every opportunity that offers, you may rely on my informing you of our proceedings.

On the 16th the Prince of Wales again put to sea for what was to prove its eventful and perilous voyage to the shores of Hudson's Bay. 'We had,' writes its commander,

a very narrow escape from shipwreck on the outward passage, and actually struck thrice on dangerous rocks, and once against an iceberg of great height and extent. The blows caused the ship to leak so much that we were apprehensive of the vessel keeping afloat, and, indeed, in this state of uncertainty, pumping and baling to the utmost, we remained for six-and-thirty hours. Then the carpenters were enabled to stop the leak.

Despite these mishaps, however, their voyage does not seem to have been prolonged much beyond its estimated time. On August 30 the Prince of Wales anchored off York Factory, where the members of the expedition landed. Here they made a stay of over a week collecting stores, and therewith equipping one of the large transport boats of the Hudson's Bay Company, in which they were to continue their journey. On September 19 they resumed it, and after a weary march of from seven to eight hundred miles they reached Cumberland House, on the Saskatchewan River, on the 23rd of the following month. Some three weeks previously Franklin had had a narrow escape from drowning. He lost his footing on a rock on which he was standing engaged in an attempt to force the boat up a rapid, and was carried some distance down the swirling torrent before he was able to stay his helpless descent by grasping the branch of a willow, to which he held fast until rescued from his hazardous position by his companions.

Franklin, as we know, was not disposed to underrate the difficulties of his task, yet the event proved that even his carefully considered and liberal estimate of the amount of time which would be required for its completion fell short of the mark. He had spoken, we have seen in his last letter, of nearly three years as representing its probable duration, but, as a matter of fact, it exceeded that period by nearly five months. More than two whole years had, in fact, expired, and two dreary winters had been passed, before they reached the shores of the Arctic Ocean and could begin their attempt to survey the coast. Nor was this due to material difficulties alone, though these, it is true, were enormous. Their commodious but unwieldy transport boat, heavily laden with stores, made naturally slow progress, and though it was possible by unloading to traverse rapids of a not too impetuous and precipitous character, it was, of course, necessary to circumvent actual falls by way of 'portage.' Twenty-one statute miles is Admiral Markham's computation of the united length of all the portages crossed by them in less than one-third of their journey, and, as each portage had to be traversed seven times in order to transfer their goods across, this involved nearly one hundred and fifty miles of walking.

But the difficulties, it must be repeated, were not material alone. The voluminous letter-books of correspondence relating to the earlier stages of the expedition are somewhat weary reading, and would be wearier still were it not that Franklin's dogged pertinacity and immovable self-control rebuke the reader's impatience; but one gathers from it distinctly enough that the leader of the expedition had to contend not only with Nature, but with human nature also. The local authorities of the Hudson's Bay Company were well affected enough towards the undertaking; and there is no positive ground for affirming anything else of the officials of the other great trading body, the North-Western Company, which in those days divided jurisdiction with it over this vast and wild region of the world. But, unfortunately, the two companies, or some of their officers, were by no means well affected towards each other; and, inasmuch as supplies had often to be ordered through the servants of one company to be supplied by those of its rival, their mutual jealousies were a constant source of inconvenience, not to say a continual menace of disaster.

It cannot perhaps be affirmed that either association, or indeed that anybody in particular, was responsible for the first serious disappointment which awaited Franklin at Fort Cumberland, where he found, to his extreme concern, that the guides, hunters, interpreters, and others whose services he had hoped to obtain, were not to be had on any terms. Still, it is pretty evident that he must have relied upon expert assurances on this point, and that 'some one had blundered.' And the blunder was the more serious because it appeared to Franklin to be only remediable by undertaking a journey of nearly a thousand miles in the dead of winter in order to reach a station at which this indispensable assistance could be secured. Accordingly, on January 18, 1820, leaving Dr. Richardson and Hood to pass the remainder of the winter at Fort Cumberland and bring on the stores and provisions as soon as the rivers were open for navigation, Franklin, Back, and Hepburn set out in a couple of dog sledges, and with only fifteen days' supplies, for Fort Chipewyan. Travelling in a temperature that froze the mercury in the thermometer and 'the tea in our teapots before we could drink it,' they reached Carlton House, an intermediate post, by February 1, and, after remaining there a week to recruit, resumed and completed their daring journey to Fort Chipewyan on March 26.

Here they remained during the rest of the long, lingering winter, making such endeavours as they could to complete their preparations for a forward movement as soon as the year was sufficiently advanced. But their efforts met with but partial success. For again the wretched rivalry between the two trading companies which disputed the country intervened. They were rejoined by Hood and Dr. Richardson as soon as the state of the rivers permitted the transport of the stores in their keeping, but it was in vain that Franklin strove to supplement them adequately with additional supplies ; and when the expedition at last resumed its northward march, it was with but a scanty supply of powder and little more than one day's provisions. Franklin coldly reports the fact in one of his periodical despatches to Mr. Goulburn, Under-Secretary of State for the Colonies, with what seems a merely formal expression of regret. Writing on July 17, the day before starting, he records the arrival of Dr. Richardson and Hood three days before, and observes that the additional supply of men they brought with them had enabled him to make a selection of 'active, good men for our service, and to complete the arrangements for leaving this place to-morrow morning for Fort Providence.' But he adds : 'Our progress thither, I regret to say, will be slower than I at first apprehended, from the necessity we shall be under of hunting and fishing on the way, as we have been unable to procure any provisions from either of the forts here.'

Hunting and fishing on the way! This, indeed, was to 'make adventure support adventure.' But 'the necessity' of so doing—as, indeed, the fact itself of starting on a journey of many hundred miles unprovided, or practically unprovided, with anything to eat on the way—is here referred to quite in the matter-of-fact manner of a man reporting an untoward but not at all unnatural circumstance. The truth probably was that no mishap of this kind, however serious, was any longer regarded by the members of the expedition as otherwise than in the natural order of affairs. They had already had a year's experience of the sort of thing that was to be expected. But they did not yet know, nor were they to experience until a good deal later, the worst of its consequences. Accommodating themselves, however, in the meantime with their usual cheerful stoicism to the situation, they proceeded to hunt and fish their way along the chain of lakes and rivers which lay between them and the Coppermine River. The Great Slave Lake was reached in a few days, and by the 29th of the month they arrived at Fort Providence, a station at its north end. After a stay here of three or four days they resumed their journey, and were joined on August 3 by a band of Indians with their canoes, who had arranged to meet them at that point and accompany them northward, hunting game for them on the way. Their services in this capacity may have slightly expedited the progress of the explorers ; but it was not till the 20th of the month that the next lake in this seemingly interminable chain was reached, and then, to his intense mortification, Franklin found that it was impossible to proceed further that year. The first days after their arrival were spent in constructing winter quarters on the south-west side of Winter Lake ; log huts were erected to house the officers and men of the expedition and their stores, and the name of Fort Enterprise was given to the new post. But while thus providing for a winter sojourn Franklin had not at first abandoned the hope of proceeding on his journey, and even of reaching the sea, before the year was out ; and the persistence with which he endeavoured to convert his Indian companions to his views in the matter is so characteristic that his report thereon to Mr. Goulburn should perhaps be transcribed entire :—

I sent for the Indians, who had been despatched on hunting excursions, and communicated my intentions to them. You can judge, sir, of the extreme mortification and disappointment which all the officers experienced to find the leader and the party were not only opposed to the proposal, but positively refused to accompany us. They represented the very attempt as an act of madness, and insisted that the winter had already commenced, because the weather was then stormy and there had been a sudden change in the temperature. From this determination no argument or persuasion, which you may be assured were plentifully applied, could turn them. But I will transcribe the leader's own words on this occasion, as the best means of conveying his sentiments. The attempt, he said, would be highly imprudent and dangerous. The winter season had already commenced, as we saw, which would soon be followed by severe weather, and that in consequence the lives of those who embarked on such an undertaking would be forfeited.

It would require six days to get to the Coppermine River, and five more to where wood would be found ; until the expiration of which time we could not expect to have fires, since there are no trees whatever after leaving this lake. They only travelled the road in summer when the moss is dry, which could not be expected during the frequent rains of this season ; and, in fact, he concluded the discouraging recital by maintaining that it would require forty days to get to the sea, and that under those circumstances neither he nor the hunters would accompany us. It was then mentioned to him that all these sentiments differed widely from his former account given at Fort Providence and along the route, and that up to this time we had been encouraged in the expectation that the party not only could go towards the sea, but should be accompanied by himself and the hunters. But this speech had no effect in altering his opinion or determination, nor those of the rest of the hunters, who are entirely under his guidance. It was then pointed out to him that even the sight of the river would be desirable, and he was informed that we were provided with instruments which would infallibly point out when the cold set in, and faithful promise was made to return on the first warning of a change. But to this he answered that the cold weather had already commenced, and repeated that in this part of the country the transition from such weather to great severity was immediate, and that in this respect it was unlike countries more to the southward.

It was then communicated to him that the sun would in a few

days be darkened (alluding to the eclipse expected on September 17), and that it was desirable to observe the phenomenon as far north as possible. He now began to feel hurt at our persisting to urge him, and added with great warmth : ' I have said everything I can to dissuade you from making such a rash attempt. It appears as if you wished to lose your own lives and those Indians who might accompany you. However, if you are determined to go, since we have brought you hither, it shall not be said that we permitted you to die alone. Some of my young men shall also go, but the moment they embark we shall suppose them all gone, and begin to deplore their loss as dead men.' I could only answer to this forcible appeal by assuring him that I looked with the utmost solicitude to the safety of my men, Indians as well as Canadians, and that it was far from my wish to expose the life of a single man, and repeated the promise to return on seeing the river, if the weather should then prove too cold. These sentiments appeased his warmth, but he then produced another reason which, I confess, had weight—that this is the season when the reindeer skins are in the best condition for clothing, and that his party must prepare their underdresses, and also some skins for the Canadians, who could not live here without them ; and he justly remarked that if the opportunity was now lost it could not be regained, and that the consequence might be that some men would be starved to death, especially the Indians, who were not strong or capable of bearing severity of weather if slightly clothed, like Canadians or Europeans. Perceiving that all efforts were in vain to make him waive his objection, I left him for the night without declaring any resolution, and I learnt the next morning that after I was gone he spoke of returning back to Fort Providence when he had collected provisions for our winter consumption, thinking, since his advice was not followed, that he was useless here. I deemed this information more important than any other, considering the uncertainty of the Indian character, because it is certain that his going would cause the whole tribe to remove, and thereby be destructive to the prospect of our getting pemmican made in the spring, which is indispensable for our future proceedings. Therefore, with great reluctance and concern, I thought it proper to relinquish the plan of proceeding towards the sea, and instead proposed that a party should go to see the [Coppermine River, and] find out the shortest path for the conveyance of our stores to its banks in the spring, and gather other information that might facilitate our progress at that time.

This reduced programme was successfully fulfilled. A party was sent out on August 29, under the direction of Hood and Back, who succeeded in reaching its banks in three days, just half the time estimated by the Indian chief, and, after travelling down its course for one day and in the reverse direction for four days, returned to Fort Enterprise, which they regained on September 12, a fortnight from the date of their departure.

After this the party settled down with such patience as they could muster to their long confinement in the prison of a northern winter. This trial is, it is well known, the hardest to be borne by the Arctic explorer ; it is the one which most searchingly tests the inward resources of his nature. Upon a man of Franklin's deeply religious temperament its effect may be easily anticipated. During these long hours of enforced inaction his mind naturally turned inward, and in a letter of this period to his sister, Mrs. Wright, he makes her the confidant of his pious and prayerful meditations. The language in which he expresses himself belongs essentially to a bygone age of religious thought ; for, though the spirit of devotion be eternal and unchangeable in the heart of man, its modes of expression are as transient as all human inventions. It is the habit of our own day for even the most devout souls to maintain a reserve in their communications on spiritual concerns with those nearest and dearest to them which would have been unintelligible, which would even perhaps have seemed reprehensible, to religious men and women of the early nineteenth century. Even in these sacred matters there are changing fashions of human speech ; and, just as our later language of piety would have seemed to Franklin cold and lifeless in its restraint, so his own utterances would be apt in their effusiveness to convey to a reader of these days an impression of the extravagant and unreal. But no one who makes due allowance for such differences in the form of expression can doubt that these outpourings came from the very depth of Franklin's heart :—

I shall not enter at any length (he writes) into the subject of our pursuits and proceedings here, but rather devote this sheet to the more interesting communication respecting my present sentiments on religion, which I think will be equally, if not more, gratifying to you, my dear sister ; and before I enter upon them I would humbly offer my grateful thanks to Almighty God that the peculiar circumstances of my situation, arising from want of society and full occupation, have led me to seek that consolation from the perusal of religious books, which I have found—especially in the Holy Bible—abundantly supplied. To this sacred volume I have applied for grounds of hope, comfort, and support, and never in vain ; and I am fully convinced that therein, and therein only, can be found the treasures of heavenly love and mercy. I have been amazed at the state of ignorance under which I laboured with respect to its blessed contents. Neither the order, connection, or regularity of God's mercies to the Jews were known to me. Consequently, His goodness and the grandeur of the deliverances vouchsafed to them were not duly appreciated by me. But an attentive perusal of His Holy Word, with fervent application for His assistance, will open all these mysteries to the inquiring mind, and lead you through them to see the mighty work of redemption by the death of His Blessed Son for all mankind. Truly rich and valuable are the precepts and doctrines our Blessed Saviour taught, and amazing His love for all mankind. Surely that heart must be awfully impenitent which can read the recital of His sufferings unmoved or without feeling a sincere desire to repent and pray fervently for that heavenly grace which He faithfully promised to all who firmly believe on Him and seek to do His will. Serious reflection will soon convince the sinner of his guilt and of his inability to do anything of himself: for every day's experience proclaims to him with a powerful voice that he is weak, irresolute, and unprofitable, and constantly exposed to the attacks of sin and Satan. If, haply, under this conviction he should inquire, How, then, can I be saved ? would it not be joy unspeakable for him to find that the Gospel points out the way ? Christ, who died for the salvation of sinners, is the way, the truth, and the life. Whoso cometh unto Him in full purpose of heart shall in no wise be cast out. Can anything be more cheering than these assurances, or better calculated to fill the mind with heavenly impressions, and lift up the heart in grateful adoration to God ? This is the commencement of the Christian joy which, if it beget a live faith that worketh by love, producing the fruits of obedience, will lead to everlasting life. But he should remember that our Blessed Lord's example hath shown, and every portion of His Holy Word declareth, that the Christian's life must be a continual warfare against the world, the flesh, and the devil ; he must never relax his efforts, but strive continually against his evil passions and propensities, and pray constantly that he may be strengthened by the power of grace to surmount them.

Very interesting, too, is it to find that among the religious works by which Franklin was most impressed in these hours of lonely meditation was the book which is understood to have first awakened the religious emotion in the mind of Dr. Johnson, and from which men of the most diverse temperaments have derived spiritual support and stimulus—Law's ' Serious Call to a Holy Life.' Of this and of Doddridge's ' Rise and Progress of Religion,' he writes :—

I admire their systematic manners of devotion, and by their arguments am convinced of the necessity and advantage of more method and regularity in meditation and prayer than is usually observed. . . . How different are my sentiments on these books to what they were on first reading them ! Then I could find neither beauty nor force in their language or reasoning ; but now I think they abound in both, and, if read with a serious desire to gain information on the most important subjects of life, much fruit may be gathered from them. I would recommend them most earnestly to all my dear relations, and I doubt not they would derive benefit and instruction.

So the long and dreary winter wore on ; but it had not half run its course before the little party were threatened with a more formidable foe than either cold or solitude. The reindeer, which had at first been plentiful enough to supply them with food, unexpectedly shifted their ground shortly after the establishment of the expedition in its winter quarters, and some considerable time before the end of the year the explorers found themselves threatened with the exhaustion of their supplies. Their stock of provisions fell so low that at last it became absolutely necessary to communicate with Fort Chipewyan, with a view to the replenishment of their stores. For this arduous and perilous service Mr. Back volunteered. He was accordingly despatched in the month of November, and, after unexampled labours and privations—he travelled more than 1,100 miles on snow-shoes, protected at night by only a single blanket and a deerskin against a temperature frequently down to —40°, and on one occasion as low as —57°, and sometimes without food for two or three consecutive days—the gallant young officer returned on March 15, having successfully executed his commission.

Nor at this, any more than at other stages of its course, were the difficulties of the enterprise due solely to the opposition of Nature. The letters exchanged between Franklin

and the 'partners' of the North-Western Company at Fort
Chipewyan are somewhat painful reading.   The correspondence starts with an official despatch from Back at Fort
Providence, complaining of the non-arrival of stores entrusted
to the Company's servants for transport, and containing the
strong statement that he has discovered through other channels
a great lukewarmness on the part of the North-Western
Company absolutely amounting to ' a denial of further services to the expedition.'   This naturally drew indignant re-
monstrances from Franklin, addressed respectively to Mr.
Smith and Mr. Keith, the two agents, and provoking from the
latter a rejoinder in the same tone.   Mr. Keith, in fact, roundly
lectures him on the impropriety of imputing to the Company
any want of goodwill towards the expedition.   It betrays,
says he, ' an unguarded precipitation and want of discernment
little corresponding with your experience and high station
and character in life.'   Franklin, it seems evident, had been
a little hasty, and in his subsequent letters he shows himself
anxious to disclaim the injurious construction placed upon
his words.   Much allowance should in any case be made for
a man in want of supplies in the depth of an Arctic winter,
and chafing under the vexatious delays and miscarriages of
many months.

There is an end to everything, however, even to an Arctic
winter ; and at 2 P.M. on June 14, 1821, the expedition was
at last able to leave Fort Enterprise behind it and set out
for the sea.   The party consisted of Franklin and his four
English officers, a couple of Eskimo interpreters, who had
been respectively christened Augustus and Junius by some
unknown humourist, and about a dozen Indians and half-
breed Canadian *voyageurs*.   Their means of travel and transport consisted of two large canoes and several sledges.   Before
their departure arrangements were made by Franklin with
one of the Indian chiefs, named Akaitcho, probably the chief
with whom he had held the discussion above quoted, for
depositing a supply of provisions at Fort Enterprise during
their absence, with a view to the contingency of their having
to pass another winter at the station.   Little did they suspect

at the time what terrible and wellnigh fatal issues were dependent on the due execution of that order.

The progress of the party was at the outset tediously slow, as they had to cross many stretches of barren land and several high and rugged hills, each man having to carry or drag a weight of some 180 pounds ; and it was not till July 1, or seventeen days after their departure, that they at last reached the long-desired waters of the Coppermine River. For another fortnight they made their way down its stream, their course often obstructed and their safety sometimes endangered by large masses of floating ice, until, on June 14, Franklin had the high satisfaction of recording in his journal : 'To-day Dr. Richardson ascended a lofty hill about three miles from the encampment, and from its summit obtained a distant view of the sea from NNE. to NE. by E. A large promontory bore NNE. The surface appeared to be covered with ice. He saw the sun set a few minutes before midnight from the same elevated situation.' Another week's voyaging brought them to the mouth of the river, and on June 21 the adventurous explorers found themselves afloat upon the Arctic Sea.

The remaining history of their outward voyage belongs to those records of geographical discovery to which it contributed so interesting, and for those days so important, a chapter ; and it does not fall within the scope of this memoir to relate it in any detail. It may suffice to quote the lucid and succinct account which has been given of it by Admiral Markham : 'The coast along which the explorers sailed in their small and frail barks was a sterile and inhospitable one ; cliff succeeded cliff in tiresome and monotonous uniformity, the valleys that intervened being covered with the *débris* that fell from the cliffs, to the exclusion of any kind of herbage. Occasionally their progress was temporarily impeded by ice, while a strong " ice-blink " was invariably seen to seaward. It must not be forgotten that the expedition was navigating a rock-bound coast fringed with heavy masses of solid ice, that rose and fell with every motion of a rough tempestuous sea, threatening momentarily to crush the light,

G

frail canoes, fit only for lake or river navigation, in which Franklin and his party were embarked. This voyage along the shores of the Arctic Sea must always take rank as one of the most daring and hazardous exploits that has ever been accomplished in the interest of geographical research. Following all the tortuous sinuosities of the coast-line, and accurately delineating the northern shore of North America as they pushed onwards in an easterly direction, naming all the principal headlands, sounds, bays, and islands that were discovered, the expedition reached a point on August 18, in latitude 68° 19' N. and longitude 110° 5' W., on the coast of North America, where Franklin reluctantly came to the conclusion that they had reached the end of their journey, and must return from the interesting work on which they were engaged, and for the following reasons. In the first place, they had only three days' pemmican left, and the Canadian *voyageurs* had consequently manifested a very decided reluctance to continue the work of exploration, believing, and not unnaturally, that great difficulty would be experienced at that time in replenishing their fast decreasing store of provisions. In the second place, the gales of wind which were so prevalent, were, they thought, sure indications of the break-up of the travelling season, and, therefore, that in itself appeared sufficient reason for them to be thinking of wending their way in a southerly direction. The absence of all traces of Eskimo, from whom they had calculated on obtaining supplies of food, was also discouraging; while the amount of time that had already been occupied in exploring the various bays and sounds that lay in their route was so great that it entirely precluded all hopes of reaching Repulse Bay before the winter.

' Although on the chart the position reached by the expedition, which was very appropriately named Point Turnagain, was only six and a half degrees of longitude to the eastward of the mouth of the Coppermine River, so tortuous and winding was the contour of the newly discovered coast that they were actually obliged to sail and paddle in their canoes a distance of 555 geographical miles in order to accomplish the journey ; this would be about equal to the direct distance between the Coppermine River and Repulse Bay. It was, therefore, obvious that the only prudent course that could be pursued was to return as soon as possible, in order to reach the Indians, who had been directed to procure a supply of provisions for the expedition before the next winter should set in.

'From their researches up to this point, Franklin had arrived at the conclusion (subsequently proved to be a well-founded one), that a navigable passage for ships along the coast by which they had travelled was practicable, and, although he was disappointed in not meeting his friend Captain Parry and his vessels, he felt convinced that they stood an excellent chance of satisfactorily clearing up the long-unsolved problem of a North-West Passage.'

CHAPTER V

THE FIGHT WITH FAMINE

1821-1822

WITH the commencement of the return journey we resume a more detailed narrative; for, if the outward voyage belongs rather to the province of geographical history, and has, as such, been dealt with in the fullest detail by other writers on this subject, the story of the awful struggle back to Fort Enterprise is in a more emphatic sense the property of a biographer of Franklin, and has never, perhaps, been circumstantially related, save by one whom his own modesty forbade to do full justice to the splendid heroism of the exploit.

It is natural to inquire why Franklin took that decision to return to Fort Enterprise by a different route, which was fraught with such disastrous and wellnigh fatal consequences for the expedition; but it appears from his journal that he had no choice. His original intention had been to return as he had come, by way of the Coppermine River, but his very scanty stock of provisions, and the length of the voyage to the mouth of that river, in the very forward state of the season, 'rendered it necessary,' he says, ' to proceed to a nearer place; and it was determined that we should go hence to Arctic Sound, where we had found animals very abundant, and entering Hood's River,' so named, of course, after Franklin's young officer, ' to advance up the stream as far as it was navigable, and there construct small canoes out of the longer ones. We had already experienced that the country between Cape Barrow and the Coppermine River was inadequate to supply our party, and it seemed probable that it would be still more impracticable now. Besides, we must expect the frequent recurrence of gales, which would cause much detention, if not danger, in proceeding along this very rocky part of the coast.'

So, then, it was resolved, and so done. The fateful decision to return by way of Hood River was taken, it seems, on August 23, and two days later the explorers reached the mouth of the stream to which they had determined to commit themselves and their fortunes. 'Our pemmican,' writes Franklin, 'was now reduced so low that we could only issue a few mouthfuls to each person.' Already, indeed, the grave apprehension seems to have occurred to them that they might not live to tell the tale of their adventures. In crossing Riley's Bay 'a tin case was thrown overboard, containing an outline of our proceedings hitherto, and the latitude of the part we turned back from, with a request that it might be forwarded to the Admiralty if picked up.' For another ten days they pursued their way up the Hood River, but on September 3 it became evident that they must abandon it. It was bearing far too much to the westward, and their observations told them that to follow its course would lead them away from the direct route to Fort Enterprise, their destination. Accordingly, on the day named, they definitely resolved to quit its banks, and to strike across the country in a south-westerly direction. Henceforth their journey had to be performed almost entirely on foot over a stony and barren country, but they carried their canoes with them against the event of having to cross any lakes or rivers that might lie on the route, or that flowed in the right direction. And at this point begins a story of unexampled sufferings and of unrivalled fortitude—an ordeal extending with rare and brief intermissions over a period of more than two months.

'We sat down to breakfast at 10.30 on September 4,' writes Franklin in his manuscript journal ; 'and this,' he adds quietly, ' finished the remainder of our meat.' Henceforth, and until they should arrive at the distant station where they hoped to find provisions stored for them, they were to be dependent on what they could find in that inhospitable region for their daily food ; and they did not find much. Later in the day the hunters 'saw several reindeer, principally males, going to the southward, but could not get them.' To add to their discomforts, a violent storm of wind and rain set in and lasted for the better part of three days. The party, while it was at its height, remained in their tents, but on the third day they determined to push on. They feared from this sudden and totally unexpected change in the weather that winter had begun in earnest, and thought that by delay they would be exposed to increased difficulties, which they would be less able to combat when reduced to a more weakly state by the pangs of hunger. Orders were accordingly given for a start, but it was no easy matter to carry them out. 'The tents and bedclothes were frozen, and even our garments were stiffened by frost and exposure to the keen wind, which blew so piercingly that no one could keep his hands long out of his mittens, and the men, therefore, had great difficulty in arranging their packages. We had no means of making a fire, the moss, at all times difficult to kindle, being covered by the ice and snow. On being exposed to the air I became quite faint with hunger, but on eating a small piece of portable soup I was soon sufficiently recovered to move on with the party. We commenced our cheerless march at 10 A.M. The ground was covered with snow a foot in depth, and we had to pass across swamps and marshy places, sometimes stepping up to the knee in water, and at others on the side of a slippery stone which often brought us down. The men who carried the canoes had a most laborious task. They even frequently fell down, either prostrated by the violence of the wind or by the insecurity of their steps.' One of these accidents had a very serious result. 'The best canoe was so damaged as to be rendered wholly useless. This was indeed a serious misfortune to us, as the remaining canoe had been made through mishap too small, and we were doubtful whether it would be sufficient to transport the party across any river.' But it is an ill wind that blows nobody any good. 'As the accident could not now be remedied, we determined on turning the materials to the best account. We made a fire of the bark and timbers, and cooked the remainder of the soup and arrowroot.' The meal, though scanty enough for men who had been three days fasting, seemed to allay their hunger and refresh them. 'We proceeded in the afternoon over some gravelly hills and across small marshy meadows, and encamped at 6 P.M. A few partridges were killed, and half a one was issued to each person. This, boiled with a small quantity of *tripe de roche*, formed our supper. A few willows were collected from under the snow, which served to cook our meal and thaw our frozen shoes so that they could be changed.'

As the Arctic delicacy above referred to is destined to play a very prominent though not very agreeable part in the subsequent narrative, it may be as well to pause at this first mention of it to give a brief account of its character and properties.

Tripe de roche, then, is simply a lichen peculiar to these latitudes, and known to botanists, by reason of its circular form and the surface of the leaf being marked with curved lines, as *Gyrophora*. It is described, with some excess of scientific politeness, as 'edible;' the fact being that it can be eaten, though with extreme difficulty and distaste, by most people, and by others not at all. Hood, as will appear later, belonged to the latter class. Dr. Richardson's account of its qualities and effects is highly unfavourable. 'We used it,' he says, 'as an article of food, but, not having the means of extracting the bitter principle from it, it proved nauseous to all, and noxious to several of the party, producing severe bowel complaints.'

On this wretched stuff and what remained to them of their 'bag' of partridges they subsisted for the next three days; and on the 10th, when matters were again becoming serious, they espied, to their great joy, a herd of musk-oxen grazing in a neighbouring valley.

The party instantly halted, and all the hunters were sent out. We beheld their proceedings with the utmost anxiety from the brow of a hill for nearly two hours, and many, I have no doubt, offered fervent prayers for their success. At length they fired, and, to our infinite satisfaction and relief, we beheld an animal fall to the ground, and a second badly wounded, which escaped from them and fled with the rest of the herd. This success infused spirit into our breasts, and animated every countenance. We hastily proceeded to join the hunters, but before our arrival the animal was skinned and cut up. Our appetites were so keen that the raw intestines were eaten on the spot, and pronounced to be excellent. The men requested we might encamp. The tents were quickly pitched ; some willows which peeped above the snow were speedily gathered, a fire made, and supper cooked, which was eaten with avidity, the first hearty meal we had had since the morning of September 4. Two of the hunters went after the herd after supper, but could not come up with them.

The flesh of the musk-ox lasted them for three days ; and on the fourth they were reduced to their fungoid diet once more. Their journey, too, was now interrupted by discouraging obstacles. On the 13th they found their way barred by a vast lake, and were compelled to coast its rocky shores all that day and part of the next, in the vain endeavour to find a suitable crossing-place. Finding at length that it appeared to terminate in a river at a few miles from their last night's encampment, they resolved on proceeding thither. ' Here,' writes Franklin, ' I cannot forbear mentioning an act of kindness performed by Perrault, one of our Canadian *voyageurs*, which won the deepest gratitude from every officer. When they were assembled round a small fire, and on the point of starting, he presented each of us with a small piece of meat which he had saved from his own allowance. This act of generosity, so totally unexpected, and coming at such a seasonable time, drew forth tears.'

Hardly had this touching incident occurred, when gunshots were heard in the direction the party were proposing to advance, and soon afterwards the *voyageur* Crédit appeared with the welcome intelligence that he had killed two deer. Once again, then, they had been rescued from starvation ; but it was, on the whole, a day of more disaster than good fortune. The canoe in which Franklin attempted to cross the river was upset, and, although he himself escaped and made his way with difficulty to the opposite bank, the portfolio containing the greater part of his astronomical and meteorological observations was irrecoverably lost. The fate of the canoe itself was for some time in doubt, and ' I cannot,' records Franklin, ' express my sentiment on viewing the melancholy scene. Standing, as I did, perfectly alone, unprovided either with gun or ammunition, separated from my companions by the fatal stream, and conscious that if the canoe should be destroyed or rendered so ineffective as to be unable to carry the party across, I never could regain them, my relief and joy can easily be imagined when I perceived the canoe was safe. The officers were so kind as to embark a person to make a fire for me by the first conveyance.' They afterwards moved a little higher up, and the whole party, with their baggage, effected a crossing in safety, though the canoe filled with water at every traverse.

This was September 14, and for another week they struggled slowly on, subsisting mainly on *tripe de roche*, with the occasional addition of a chance partridge or two, though they were reduced on one day of exceptional straits to devouring some fragments of deer skin and bones, the leavings of the wolves that had killed the animals in the previous spring. So they fared till the 26th, when again they were lucky enough to shoot five small deer, and to fill their bellies for the first time for many days with a substantial meal. But the leader of the party could have found little in these chance strokes of good fortune to relieve the anxiety which his ever-darkening prospects must have inspired. A new cause of disquietude had now presented itself in the demoralisation of the Canadian *voyageurs*. Peltier, who had received several severe falls in carrying the remaining canoe, refused to be burdened with it any longer, and it was handed over to Vaillant, one of his comrades. The man seemed at first to be managing it so well that Franklin left him a little in the rear, and went on to join the party in advance; but some time afterwards, on going back to search for the men, who were long in coming up, Franklin found to his horror that they had left the canoe behind them. It had been, they alleged, so completely broken by another fall as to be rendered incapable of repair and entirely useless. 'The anguish this intelligence occasioned may be conceived,' he writes, 'but it is beyond my power to describe it. Impressed, however, with the necessity of taking it forward, even in the state in which these men represented it to be, we urgently desired them to fetch it;

but they declined going, and the strength of the officers was inadequate to the task. To their infatuated obstinacy on this occasion a great portion of the melancholy circumstances which attended our subsequent progress may perhaps be attributed.' But the wretched *voyageurs* had, it is evident, got completely out of hand. 'The men now seemed to have lost all hope of being preserved ; and all the arguments we could use failed in stimulating them to the least exertion.'

On the 26th of the month they at last struck the Coppermine River, and, as their shortest way to Fort Enterprise was to cross to the opposite bank as soon as possible, the loss of the canoe was now severely felt ; for, though the current was swift and there were two rapids in this part of its course, it could have been crossed in a canoe with ease and safety. The river was carefully examined for a ford, but in vain. Then it was suggested that a raft might be made of the willows growing in the neighbourhood, or even that the framework of a boat might be constructed with them and covered with the canvas of the tents ; but both those schemes had to be abandoned through the obstinacy of the interpreters and the most experienced *voyageurs*, who declared that neither raft nor boat would prove adequate to the conveyance of the party, and that they would only be losing valuable time in making the attempt. The fact was that the men did not believe they had reached the Coppermine River, and it needed all the repeated and confident assurance of their officers that they were within forty miles of Fort Enterprise to rouse them from their despondency. They at last began to look more favourably on the boat-building scheme, but it was found that there were no willows tall enough to form the frame of a sufficiently large canoe. The alternative of the raft had to be definitely adopted, and a search was made along the border of Point Lake, which they had reached by this time, for timber suitable to the purpose. The search was fruitless. It led them only to an arm of the lake stretching so far away to the north-east that the idea of rounding it and travelling over so barren a country was 'dreadful,' the more so as it was to be feared that other arms equally large might

obstruct their path, and that the strength of the party would
fail long before they could reach the only part where they
were certain of finding pine wood, a point twenty-five miles
distant in a direct line.

'While we halted to consider of this subject and to collect
our party, the carcase of a deer was discovered in the cleft of
a rock into which it had fallen in the spring. It was putrid,
but it was little less acceptable to us on that account in our
present circumstances, and, a fire being kindled, it was devoured
on the spot.' Refreshed by this horrible meal, the *voyageurs*
took a more favourable view of the willow considered as a
raft-building material, and declared their belief that it would
be quite possible to cross the stream on a willow-built raft.
The party accordingly having returned about a mile towards
the rapid, encamped in a willow copse, and the work of construction was at once set about.

The day following (September 29) was signalised by an act
of such splendid and indeed reckless devotion, that, though
Franklin himself was not the hero of it, the course of this
narrative must be arrested for a moment in order to record it
in his own words :—

The men commenced at an early hour to bind up the willows in
faggots for the construction of the raft, which was completed by
seven o'clock, but as the sticks were green the raft was not sufficiently
buoyant to support more than one man. We hoped, however, that if
a line could be carried across by this person, the whole party might
be transported over the river by hauling the raft backwards and forwards. Several attempts were made by Belanger and Bénoit to
convey the raft across, but ineffectually for want of oars. Whenever
they had got a short distance from the shore they could not reach
bottom with the longest pole we could construct (by tying all the tent-
poles together), and then their paddle, which was the only substitute
for an oar we had, was inefficient to prevent the raft from being driven
into the shore again by the current and a strong breeze, which blew
from the opposite side of the river. During these trials all the men
had suffered extremely from the coldness of the water (the temperature being 38°), in which they were necessarily immersed, and having
witnessed these repeated failures we began to consider the scheme as
hopeless. At this time, Dr. Richardson, prompted by a noble and
humane desire to relieve his suffering companions, proposed to swim
across the river with a line, and when landed to haul the raft over ; but

this service had near cost his valuable life. He launched into the stream with the line round his middle, but when he had got a short distance from the land his arms became benumbed with the cold and he lost the power of moving them. Still he persevered, and, turning on his back, had nearly gained the opposite shore, when to our infinite alarm we beheld him sink. Happily, the direction he had previously given to haul upon the line was understood, and by our doing so he again appeared upon the surface and was then gently dragged to the shore. He could just articulate when landed. We placed him between blankets, which were arranged before a fire near the spot, and fortunately he was in a state to give some general directions respecting the manner of treating him, and by the blessing of God, and to our great relief, he recovered strength gradually, and after a few hours could converse. We regretted then to learn that the skin of the left side of his body was deprived of feeling owing to the too great heat of the fire, and I am sorry to add he suffered from that inconvenience some months. When he was about to step first into the water he placed his foot on a large dagger-like stone, and received a gash to the bone, but this misfortune did not prevent him from attempting to execute his generous undertaking.

Then follows this piteously graphic detail :—

I cannot forbear to mention how shocked every one was at seeing his debilitated frame when he had undressed, a perfect skeleton of skin and bone. The sight drew from each person an involuntary sigh, and from many of our Canadian *voyageurs* the pathetic exclamation, ' *Ah ! que nous sommes maigres !* '

A new and more efficient raft was constructed, but the wind, which had been rising, was now too high to allow of their using it. To add to their discomfort, heavy snowfalls set in, and for three days they were detained in their foodless condition, living on scraps of leather and *tripe de roche*, and unable to cross the river which lay between them and their homeward route. At last the gradual conversion of the *voyageurs* advanced a further stage. They had risen from the conception of a pinewood to that of a willow raft, and one of them now went further and ' proposed to make a canoe of the fragments of painted canvas in which we wrapped our bedding. The proposal met with an eager assent, and after two days spent upon it the work was pronounced finished. The canoe was brought to the beach, where all the party were assembled in anxious expectation. St. Germain embarked in it amid the heartfelt prayers of his comrades for his success, and contrived to reach the opposite shore. The canoe was then drawn back again by the rope attached to it, and another person transported ; and in this manner, by drawing it back- wards and forwards, the whole party were conveyed over without any serious accident.'

On their reaching the southern bank of the Coppermine River, which at this part of its course flows nearly east and west, the variable spirits of the *voyageurs* revived in an extra- ordinary manner. Each of them shook the officers by the hand, declaring that they now considered the worst of their difficulties over, and they did not doubt of reaching Fort Enterprise in a few days even in their feeble condition. Franklin, however, as he was not liable to their fits of pro- found depression, so did not share their excessive elation. Judging it to be impossible that the entire party could hold out against famine for the long period of time it would take them to reach Fort Enterprise in their debilitated state, he despatched Back, who was the youngest and most robust of the party, to the Fort with three of the *voyageurs* to bring back supplies with all possible speed from the store which he had engaged the Indians to deposit at that station. He himself, with Richardson, Hood, Hepburn, the eight remain- ing *voyageurs*, and an Iroquois named Michel, struggled on in the rear. Snow had been falling heavily and lay deep on the ground, making their progress distressingly slow.

Mr. Hood, who was now very feeble, and Dr. Richardson, who attached himself to him, walked together at a gentle pace in the rear of the party. I kept with the foremost men, to cause them to halt occasionally until the stragglers came up.

They supped that night off *tripe de roche* and some scraps of roasted leather. The distance completed by them had been only six miles. In the course of the next day two of the Canadians, Crédit and Vaillant, fell out of the party, and one of their companions came up with the main body bringing the sad tidings that they were unable to proceed further.

Some willows being discovered in a valley near to us, I proposed to halt the party there while Dr. Richardson went back to visit them. I hoped, too, that when the sufferers received the information of a fire being kindled at so short a distance they would be cheered, and use their utmost efforts to reach it ; but this proved a vain hope. The Doctor found Vaillant about a mile and a half in the rear, much exhausted with cold and fatigue. Having encouraged him to advance to the fire, after repeated solicitations he made the attempt, but fell down in the deep snow at every step. Leaving him in this situation, the Doctor went about half a mile further back to the spot where Crédit was said to have halted, but, the track being nearly obliterated, it became unsafe for him to go further. Returning, he passed Vaillant, who, having moved only a few yards during his absence, had fallen down, was unable to rise, and could scarcely answer his questions. Being unable to afford him any effectual assistance, he hastened on to inform us of his situation.

Another of the *voyageurs*, J. B. Belanger, then volunteered to go back to Vaillant and bring up his burden. On his return with it he stated that he had found the poor fellow lying on his back, benumbed with cold and incapable of being roused. The stoutest men of the party were earnestly entreated to bring him to the fire, but they declared themselves, as indeed might well be the case, unequal to the task.

A consultation was now held among the officers. Franklin felt that the time had come when the resolution which all no doubt had foreseen and all dreaded must at last be definitely taken. It had become only too clear that the remnant of the little party which had dared and suffered so much together must separate. The Canadians were too weak to bear their burdens further. They begged that they might be allowed to throw them down in order that they might make their way to Fort Enterprise before their strength failed them altogether. Franklin could not but feel that their prayer was irresistible, and that they must be relieved of their loads if their lives were to be saved. Hood, moreover, was now almost too feeble to advance further, and Dr. Richardson offered to remain behind with him and a single attendant, together with any other member of the party who might wish to halt, at the first place at which sufficient wood could be found and enough *tripe de roche* for ten days' consumption. Franklin in the meantime was to proceed as expeditiously as possible with the other men to the Fort, and send back to them an immediate supply of provisions. The greater part of the ammunition was also to be left behind with Richardson and Hood, as it was hoped that this deposit might be an inducement to the Indians to venture across the Barren Lands to their relief. 'This proposal,' writes Franklin, 'was acceded to on my part, though the idea of even a temporary separation from my friends in affliction was extremely distressing to my feelings ; but this would be the only arrangement which could contribute to the safety of the party.'

The morning of the next day was mild, with a light breeze from the south, a change of temperature encouraging to the minds of men who contemplated encamping ; and on arriving at a cluster of pines a few miles from their last night's resting-place, a tent was pitched, and Dr. Richardson, Hood, and Hepburn prepared to take up their quarters in it. The offer was again repeated that any of the men who felt themselves too weak to proceed at a quick pace should remain behind, but none accepted it. Franklin accordingly set off with seven of the *voyageurs*, and the party toiled painfully on through deep snow for about four miles and a half, when they were obliged to encamp ; but by this time two of his companions were utterly exhausted. Belanger, one of the *voyageurs*, burst into tears and, declaring he could go no further, begged to be permitted to go back and join the officers in the rear on the following day. The Iroquois Michel soon afterwards joined in the request. Franklin consented to their returning if they felt as weak the next morning, but endeavoured, with that cheery and indomitable pluck which seems never to have failed him for a moment throughout the whole awful ordeal, to dispel the gloom which this incident had thrown over the party by assuring them that it was but a short distance from the Fort, and that in all probability they would reach it in a few days. No *tripe de roche* was to be found, and supper consisted of a so-called tea made of herbs. The next morning, Belanger and Michel, not having recovered any of their strength, were sent back again with a letter from Franklin to Dr. Richardson informing him of a more eligible encampment in a pine wood a little further on than the halting-place which had been selected. Perrault was the next to give in and to be sent back, and later in the day Antonio Fontano broke down, and begged, and was permitted, to return. The number of Franklin's companions was now reduced to four—Peltier, Semandré, Benoit, and Adam. With them he walked on about a mile further, and then encamped for the night under a rocky hill whereon some *tripe de roche* was seen growing; but the weed was frozen so hard upon the rock that the men could not gather it, and were obliged to sup again on the 'country tea' and some pieces of fried leather.

Next day, however, they were enabled to collect some of the lichen, and to enjoy the first meal they had had for four days past. On October 10 the famine-stricken men were mocked by the appearance on a neighbouring hill of a herd of reindeer, which they were too feeble and too cold to follow. Again no *tripe de roche* could be found, and once more the country tea and a few strips of fried leather had to serve them for supper.

At last, on October 11, five days after quitting the companions they had left behind them, Fort Enterprise came in sight, and as fast as their exhaustion would permit they hurried forward to enter it. But here the most cruel of all their disappointments awaited the starving wanderers. They staggered into the Fort to find it entirely empty! There was no store of food; no trace of the Indians who had been so straitly charged, and had so repeatedly promised, to provide it; no letter from Mr. Wentzel, the official of the North-Western Company, who had travelled part of the way with them, to direct them to any spot where provisions might be found. Even at this appalling moment, however, Franklin's first thought was for others. 'Under these distressing circumstances,' he says, 'my mind was instantly filled with a fearful anxiety for our suffering companions who had been left in the rear, whose safety entirely depended on our sending speedy relief from this place. The whole party shed tears, for it was impossible to divest our minds of the melancholy apprehension that the lives of our companions would in all probability be forfeited.' For their sole comfort they found a letter from Mr. Back, dated the same day, and informing them that he was going to search for the Indians, but was of course doubtful whether he should meet them, as he had no direction to follow, and that, if he failed, he intended to proceed to Fort Providence, should the strength of his party permit, and thence send succour to us. It was evident, however, that any relief from Fort Providence would not only be long in reaching Franklin's party, but could not be sufficiently ample to afford succour to their companions behind.

The first thing, however, was to replenish, however scantily, their own fast-waning fuel of life. Food, if food it could be called, was sought and found, but they were now to partake of the poorest, not to say the foulest, of all their many miserable meals. They lighted in an outhouse on some rotting deer skins, the refuse of their last winter's sojourn at the Fort; they grubbed up some old bones from an ash-heap, and these, with *tripe de roche*, 'we considered would support us tolerably well for a time.' The bones, though quite acrid from decomposition, were 'pounded and boiled with the *tripe de roche* and made a very palatable mess.' It was devoured in a temperature ranging from 15° to 20° below zero. Their bodily condition was now truly distressing. They were so weak and emaciated as to be unable to move except for a few yards at a time; they were afflicted with swellings in their joints, limbs, and other parts of their bodies; their eye-balls were dilated; they spoke in hollow, sepulchral tones and their mouths were raw and excoriated, as a result of the fare on which they had subsisted. Adam in particular was suffering terribly, and grew daily worse.

After nine more days spent under these fearful privations, Franklin resolved to set out, with the *voyageur* Benoit and the Eskimo Augustus, in search of the Indians, and, equipped with snow-shoes, they started forth on the 20th. On the day after his departure, however, he was unfortunate enough to

H

break one of his snow-shoes, and, fearing lest the accident should retard the progress of the party, Franklin returned to Fort Enterprise after giving Benoit careful instructions as to the course he was to pursue.　Another week dragged on its course under the same wretched conditions.　Adam and Semandré were now unable to rise from their beds, and Peltier was often too weak to assist his leader in gathering *tripe de roche* and in searching for bones, which were now becoming more and more hard to find.　Nothing, however, could shake Franklin's invincible fortitude or provoke from him a single word of complaint.　On the 27th he writes in his journal :—

I have this day been *twenty-one years* in H.M. service, and exposed to many hardships in my professional career, but was never placed in such a melancholy and affecting situation as the present. However, with sincere praises to Almighty God for His past goodness and protection, I will humbly confide in His gracious mercy and hope for deliverance from this severe trial.

Two days afterwards, to the great surprise and, for a moment, the unmixed joy of the leader, who had almost given them up for lost, Dr. Richardson and Hepburn crawled painfully into the Fort.　But Franklin's gratification at their safety was soon to be dashed by the tale of horror which they had to unfold.　Poor Hood was dead, murdered, it was supposed, and it was Richardson's own hand that had executed justice on his murderer.　Of the whole party that had remained behind and had been reinforced by those of Franklin's detachment whose strength had failed them, and who had been compelled to return, but these two now survived. Perrault and Belanger, the *voyageurs* who had fallen out of the advance party, were the first to be missed.　They were never again heard of, and, though the manner of their death was never conclusively ascertained, there is the strongest ground for suspicion that they were killed by Michel in order that the wretched man might appease the pangs of famine by devouring their bodies.　Before, however, their absence had given much anxiety, a more sinister cause for suspecting Michel had arisen.　On the morning of Sunday, October 20, Richardson, who had gone out on an expedition to gather lichen, leaving Hood 'sitting before the tent at the fireside arguing with Michel,' and Hepburn employed in cutting down a tree for firewood at a short distance off, heard the report of a gun, and shortly afterwards the voice of Hepburn calling to him in tones of great alarm, to 'come quickly.' Hastening back to the camp, he found Hood lying lifeless, shot through the head. Michel, who was standing near him, being questioned as to how it had happened, declared that he had not been present at the moment, and that Hood, whether intentionally or by mischance, had shot himself. But the character alike of the wound and of the weapon entirely precluded belief in the story. The shot had entered the back part of the dead man's head, and passed out at the forehead, and the muzzle of the gun had been applied so close as to set fire to the nightcap behind. The gun itself was of the longest kind supplied to the Indians, and could not have possibly been placed by Hood himself in a position to inflict such a wound. Hepburn, moreover, averred positively that Michel was not absent when the gunshot was discharged, but, on the contrary, was standing on the precise spot from which the fatal shot could have been fired. According to Hepburn's statement, Hood and Michel were speaking to each other in an elevated, angry tone, the former being then seated at the fireside and hidden from him by intervening willows; but on hearing the report he looked up and saw Michel 'rising up from before the tent-door, or just behind where Mr. Hood was seated, and then going into the tent. Thinking that the gun had been discharged for the purpose of cleaning it, he did not go to the fire at first, and when Michel called to him that Mr. Hood was dead a considerable time had elapsed.'

This last circumstance in itself sufficed to demonstrate the falsehood of Michel's account of the matter; for his explanation of his alleged absence was that Hood had 'sent him into the tent for the short gun,' an errand which would only have taken a few minutes to execute, so that he must, on his own showing, have for some considerable time withheld the fact of Hood's death from his companions. Strong, however, as were their suspicions, they dared not at the moment openly evince them, and not a word was said to Michel to reveal their belief that he was guilty of the deed. The man, how- ever, 'accused himself by excuse,' repeatedly protesting that he was incapable of such a crime, and at the same time taking great care to prevent Richardson and Hepburn from being left alone together. But inasmuch as this chapter of tragic incidents was closed by an act of stern justice and self-pro- tective necessity, which did not, however, escape the censures of the 'armchair critic' at home, it is desirable to let Dr. Richardson himself complete the narrative in his own words. Resolved to push on to the Fort at all hazards, he and his party had struck their camp on the morning of the 23rd, 'thick snowy weather and a head wind' having delayed their departure till that day. Hepburn and Michel had each a gun. Richardson carried a small pistol, which Hepburn had loaded for him :—

In the course of the march Michel alarmed us by his gestures and conduct, was constantly muttering to himself, expressed an un- willingness to go to the Fort, and tried to persuade me to go south- ward to the woods, where he said he could maintain himself all the winter by killing deer. In consequence of this behaviour and the expression of his countenance, I requested him to leave and to go to the southward by himself. The proposal increased his ill-nature ; he threw out some obscure hints of freeing himself from all restraint on the morrow ; and I overheard him muttering threats against Hepburn, whom he openly accused of having told stories against him. He also for the first time assumed such a tone of superiority in addressing me as evinced that he considered us to be completely in his power, and he gave vent to several expressions of hatred towards the white people, or, as he termed us in the idiom of the *voyageurs*, the French, some of whom he said had killed and eaten his uncle and two of his relations. In short, taking every circumstance into consideration, I came to the conclusion that he would attempt to destroy us on the first opportunity that offered, and that he had hitherto abstained from doing so from his ignorance of the way to the Fort, but that he would never suffer us to go thither in company with him. In the course of the day he had several times remarked that we were pursuing the same course that Mr. Franklin was doing when he left him, and that by keeping towards the setting sun he could find his way himself. Hepburn and I were not in a condition to resist even an open attack, nor could we

by any device escape from him.   Our united strength was far inferior
to his, and, beside his gun, he was armed with his pistols, an Indian
bayonet, and a knife.   In the afternoon, coming to a rock on which
there was some *tripe de roche*, he halted, and said he would gather it
whilst we went on, and that he would soon overtake us.   Hepburn
and I were now left together for the first time since Mr. Hood's death,
and he acquainted me with several circumstances which he had observed of Michel's behaviour, and which confirmed me in the opinion
that there was no safety for us except in his death, and he offered to
be the instrument of it.   I determined, however, as I was thoroughly
convinced of the necessity of the dreadful act, to take the whole
responsibility upon myself, and on Michel's coming up I put an end
to his life by shooting him through the head with a pistol.   Had my
own life alone been threatened, I would not have purchased it by
such a measure ; but I considered myself as entrusted also with the
protection of Hepburn's, a man who by his humane attention and
devotedness had so endeared himself to me that I felt more anxiety for
his safety than for my own.   Michel had gathered no *tripe de roche*, and
it was evident to me that he had halted for the purpose of putting his
gun in order with the intention of attacking us, perhaps while we were
in the act of encamping.   I have dwelt in the preceding narrative
on many circumstances of Michel's conduct, not for the purpose of
aggravating it, but to put the reader in possession of the reason that
influenced me in depriving a fellow-creature of life.

Nothing, of course, could have mitigated the painful shock
which Franklin received from the tidings of Hood's tragic
end.   It was the manner of his death rather than his loss
which was so agitating to his leader, who, as appeared afterwards, had already abandoned all hope that his young comrade's life would be preserved.   He seems to have been the
only one of the party whose digestive organs obstinately
revolted against the miserable food on which his companion
could just manage to keep body and soul together ; and discovering, as Franklin did when he reached Fort Enterprise,
that this would have for an indefinite period to be the sole
food of the party he had left behind him, he gave up Hood
for lost.   This, as will be seen hereafter, he brings out quite
clearly, though with much tenderness and delicacy, in his
reply to a subsequent communication from the bereaved
father.   But to return to our narrative.

Hepburn, just before reaching the Fort, had had the good

luck to shoot a partridge. The starving men hurriedly tore
the feathers from the bird, held it for a few minutes before the
fire, and then, dividing it into equal portions, greedily devoured
it. It was the first morsel of flesh they had tasted for thirty-
one days, unless 'the small gristly particles' occasionally found
adhering to the bones on which they had helped to support
their lives could be so described.

From what inward reserves of strength and spirit the three
Englishmen contrived to sustain themselves during the awful
week that followed must ever be a mystery to all who have read
the harrowing story. From the first, however, it was evident
that whatever it was possible to do for the preservation of the
party, by cutting wood for fires and preparing their scanty
meals of animal refuse, would have to be done by Franklin
and his two English companions. The three Canadians were
all of them too weak to move. Adam, the interpreter, had
been for some time disabled, and Peltier and Semandré were
now equally helpless. Both complained of sore throats, produced by the acridity of the bone soup, and Semandré had
the cramp in his fingers. The former felt the cold extremely
piercing in his reduced state of body, and half a blanket was
served out to him to repair his flannel shirt and drawers,
which occupation, observes Franklin quaintly, 'afforded some
amusement to him and Semandré in the evening and revived
their spirits.' But on November 2 the end came. On the
morning of that day both men were obviously at the point of
death. Peltier 'sat up with difficulty and looked piteously,
exclaiming frequently, "Je suis faible! Je suis faible!" and
spoke often of the increased soreness of his throat. At length
he slid down from the spot on which he was sitting on
to his bed, which was placed near the fire, as if to sleep, and
remained for two hours without our apprehending him to be
in immediate danger, until we were alarmed by hearing a
rattling noise in his throat. On Dr. Richardson examining
him he was found to be speechless.' It was the speechless-
ness of death. Semandré lingered through the day, complaining always of increasing cold and weakness, and expired at
daylight on the following morning. Dr. Richardson and

Hepburn removed the two men's bodies from the room, ' but were quite unable either to inter them or carry them down to the water.'

Still, they remained the strongest of the four men to whom the party was now reduced ; for Franklin, with his customary candour, admits that they had 'outstayed' him, and that during these last days the task of wood-cutting devolved wholly upon them, Franklin himself having only just strength enough to hunt for deerskins under the snow. After another two days, however, the strength even of the indefatigable pair began rapidly to decline. Yet, their leader adds, ' they were full of hope, and went to their labour of gathering wood cheerfully.' But on Tuesday, November 6, it became evident that they were on the verge of absolute exhaustion. ' To cut one log of wood is an occupation for half an hour to Hepburn, and to carry it into the house occupied Richardson almost the same time, though the distance does not exceed twenty yards. I endeavoured to render the men some assistance in this employment, but my aid was feeble. It is evident, however,' continues Franklin, with a rebound of his marvellously elastic spirits, ' that if their strength diminishes with the rapidity it has done for the last three days, I shall be the strongest in a day or two.'

With this last utterance of an inexhaustible courage this last manifestation of a pride of endurance which had no doubt been not a little wounded by his companions superiority in physical strength, the long-drawn tale of suffering fitly closes. On the following day relief came. The manner of its arrival is described in Franklin's published narrative of the expedition ; but an infinitely more touching record of it can just be deciphered on the soiled and dogs-eared page of the little paper-covered pocket journal that lies before me. Regularly, religiously, day by day throughout that grim struggle with death, its entries follow one another with methodical precision, and in the dim, blurred pencil-marks that record that heartfelt cry of thanksgiving on the page which has here been reproduced in facsimile one almost seems to be listening to the faint and broken utterances of the famine-stricken and almost dying man. On Sunday, November 4, he had written, so far as it is possible to decipher the entry :

May the devout prayers of the congregations on behalf of the afflicted find . . . before the Throne of Mercy.

Then follows, on the page which has been reproduced, an account of the incidents of the two following days—of their failure to discover any *tripe de roche* or bones ; of their meal off fried skins and tea ; of the increasing weakness of the Doctor and Hepburn : 'eats little, and was getting this day quite dispirited.' And then at the bottom of the page :

Wednesday, Nov. 7.—Praise be unto the Lord ! We were this day rejoiced by the appearance of Indians with supplies at noon.

The trembling hand that penned these now barely legible lines is long since dust ; and the dingy and crumpled little book that contains them would, but for the pious care which has preserved it, have perished years ago. But it was found among certain papers sealed and described in its owner's handwriting as 'The Original Notes of Capt. Franklin, written during the most distressing part of his last residence at Fort Enterprise in 1821—much defaced by being worn in his pocket ;' and it has, of course, been cherished as among the most sacred of their possessions by his relatives. Nor is it possible, even for those who can only claim the kinship with him of a common humanity, to look unmoved upon this silent companion and daily confidant of a hero throughout the long agony of his fight with famine.

> Sunt lacrymæ rerum et mentem mortalia tangunt.

Dull indeed must be the imagination that does not feel its pathos, and sluggish the sympathies that it fails to stir.

It was to the gallant and devoted Back that they owed their lives. His sufferings since he separated from the party on October 4 had been no less severe than theirs. For days together he and the three men with him had supported life 'on an old pair of leather trousers, a gun-cover, and a pair of old shoes, with a little *tripe de roche* that they succeeded in

FACSIMILE PAGES OF SIR JOHN FRANKLIN'S NOTE-BOOK.

scraping off the rocks.' On the 26th, one of his companions died of exhaustion; but the survivors, knowing that the lives of the party they had left behind them depended on their exertions, still pressed on. On November 4 they fell in with Akaitcho and his Indians, and at once despatched them to Fort Enterprise to Franklin's relief. The supplies they brought with them consisted of some dried deer's meat and a few tongues, on which the sufferers would have fallen like famished wolves had it not been for the warnings of Dr. Richardson. Yet never perhaps was the well-known admonition, 'Do as I say, but not as I do'—that soundest counsel of the professional adviser, alike in medicine and in morals— more amusingly illustrated; for Franklin admits in his official narrative that Richardson was himself 'unable to practise the caution he so judiciously recommended,' and there is evidence in their private journals that the Doctor suffered more severely from distension than any other member of the party.

The Indians, to do them justice, endeavoured to the best of their ability to atone for their so nearly fatal neglect. The interpreter Adam, who was undoubtedly within a few hours of death when the relief arrived, owed his speedy convalescence to their attentive care; and they did their utmost, by procuring game and fish, and in other ways, to minister to the wants of the whole of the exhausted party. In little more than another week, so wonderful is man's recuperative power, their energies were sufficiently restored to enable them to proceed. On November 16 they quitted the station which had been the scene of their miseries, and on the 11th of the following month they reached Fort Providence. Hence, after resting a few days, they went on to Moose Deer Island, where they passed the remainder of the winter. On May 26, 1822, they started homeward, and, reaching York Factory about the middle of July, took ship for England, where they arrived in October, after an absence of three years and a half and journeyings by land and water of more than 5,500 miles.

Very shortly after their arrival, Franklin, who had in his absence been promoted to the rank of commander, was advanced to that of post-captain, and was about the same time unanimously elected a Fellow of the Royal Society, in recognition of his services to the cause of geographical science. Those services, it is true, had been considerable, and well deserved the rewards, official and unofficial, which they had won. But the debt of the English nation—nay, of the whole human race—to the heroic explorers was far greater than that of the geographer ; and the shores of the Coppermine River, the Barren Lands of Arctic America, and the rude shelter of Fort Enterprise, are sacred and memorable in human history, not as the mere monuments of a scientific conquest, but as the scene of labours and sufferings which have inspired the world with a new conception of the powers of human endurance, a new glory in the unconquerable soul of man.

CHAPTER VI

HUSBAND AND WIDOWER

1822-1825

IN the first quarter of the present century the position of a
'lion' was not to be so cheaply won as it is now, nor, even
when recognised as such, was the noble animal pursued by
nearly as many hunters or with anything like the amount of
spirit as is the case to-day. Franklin's exploits, however, even
apart from their gallantry and hardihood, were of too novel
and picturesque a character not to create a sensation even
among the comparatively sedate public of 1822. There is
abundant evidence at this period of his life that he had become a conspicuous figure in London society, a welcome guest
at many dinner-tables, an object of interest and admiration
in many drawing-rooms. Doubtless he received notice and
courtship enough to have turned the head of any less
modest and simple-minded man; but Franklin was in no
danger of being thus spoilt. He was, indeed, protected from
any such danger, not only, as has been said, by his modesty,
but also by his ambition. There is, perhaps, no more
effectual safeguard against undue vanity over past achievements than an ardent desire to add greater exploits to
their number. The honourable discontent which such a
desire, until gratified, generates is essentially antagonistic to
that mood of mind in which alone complacency can flourish;
and the passion for Arctic discovery gave Franklin no rest.
Immediately on his arrival in England he set to work to
prepare that well-written and spirited narrative of his expedition which has been so frequently quoted above, and which
was, in fact, published by Mr. Murray in the following year.

It must have been while he was engaged in preparing this

volume for publication that he received the letter above referred to from the father of the unfortunate young man who had fallen a victim to the murderous impulse of the half-insane Indian, Michel ; and Franklin's reply to it is so eminently illustrative of his genuine kindness of heart that it deserves quotation almost in full. The elder Hood, in the postscript of a pathetic letter of thanks to Franklin for the terms in which he had spoken of his murdered comrade in the official despatch reporting the circumstances of his death, appends a question respecting ' what perhaps the dreadful circumstances of the moment scarcely permitted,' namely, the interment of his son's remains. ' May I trouble you,' he adds, ' to inform me what time he first began to be ill, and whether in your opinion, if that infernal villain had not perpetrated his shocking crime, he might probably have survived until the period of relief ? '

In his reply to this letter, Franklin, after dwelling upon the excellent qualities of the ill-fated young officer, proceeds :—

You will, therefore, readily imagine I looked with painful solicitude at the possibility of losing such a valuable member of our small society, which, I lament to say, was too awfully apparent at the time of my arrival at Fort Enterprise, when I experienced the indescribable disappointment of finding the house destitute of provisions. On my separation from your son, he remarked that he never should be able to move the distance of our house [from where he then was], about thirty-six miles, without being drawn on a sledge. I think, however, his strength was then sufficient to have gone two or three days further at an easy pace ; but then, in all probability, he must have halted, as by going on we advanced into a country where the soil was sandy and lichens—our only food at the time—were less abundant. This unpalatable nourishment, however, from which the others derived some degree of support, was seldom taken by him, save in the smallest quantity, on account of the constant irritation which the eating of it produced in his bowels. He might, too, as were others far stronger in appearance, have been completely exhausted in the following day's march by the increased exertions required to wade through the deeper snow we came to. He had been in a very weakly state upwards of a month preceding his death, and I am informed by Dr. Richardson and Hepburn that at the time when the ever-to-be-deplored crime was committed by Michel the afflicted sufferer was in such a perfectly debilitated state of body that he could scarcely walk twenty yards without support. Under such circumstances, it was to be feared that his earthly career would have terminated in a short time had not the awful event taken place—especially as it would have been totally out of my power to have sent relief immediately forward on its reaching me at Fort Enterprise on November 7, owing to the few persons with me at the house being almost in a similar deplorably weak condition.

To the other, the more difficult and distressing question put to him, Franklin replies, and doubtless could only reply very little ; but that little is put with much tact and good feeling :—

With respect to the interment of his body, I am certain the strength of the survivors was inadequate to the labour of opening a sufficient space of the perfectly frozen ground ; but I have little doubt of their having covered the body with snow and stones. Dr. Richardson, however, will be able to give you information on that point.

And the letter concludes with the following testimony to Franklin's affectionate regard for his lost comrade :—

Among the last conversations which I had with your excellent son Robert, he mentioned his brother to me, and particularly requested I would endeavour to find him out and cultivate his friendship. He spoke most highly of his talents and application, and he did me the kindness to request, if ever I should be employed on any other expedition, that he might accompany me. With this, his last request, I should feel it a peculiar pleasure in complying, providing it should meet your and his brother's wish. At least, I beg you to be assured that I shall seek the earliest opportunity of meeting your surviving son, and be desirous to show by every act in my power how sincerely I wish to extend to him the friendship I entertained for his departed brother.

Not much addition is needed to this picture : the young officer, at the point of death from starvation in the Arctic wilderness, anxiously soliciting employment for his brother in the same dangerous service, and his leader conveying the proposal of this opening for ' your surviving son' to the bereaved father, with perfect confidence in his assumption that the offer, whether accepted or not, will be welcome. They were a Spartan race, the Englishmen of those days. May their descendants prove worthy of them !

But the enthusiasm which Franklin thus confidently

attributed to the father of his murdered comrade was not more ardent, after all, than the passion which glowed within his own breast. If it did not occur to him that bereavement could discourage it in another, it was because he was conscious that the last extremities of danger and suffering had not one whit diminished it in himself. Less than a year had gone by since he was undergoing one of the most appalling trials of human fortitude that man has ever endured and survived. He had passed through experiences which would have seemed to many a man sufficient for a lifetime, nay, which may almost be said to have compressed the agonies of a lifetime into a few terrible weeks. Who could have wondered if his sole desire had been for long repose and for a gradual release from hideous recollections hovering around his pillow in nightmares of horror-haunted dream? Yet nothing could have been further from the actual fact. The man who, in the winter of 1821, had been starving upon acrid lichens and putrid offal in the Arctic wilds was actually again exploring those deadly regions in imagination in the summer of 1822. Such leisure as was left him by the preparation of the Narrative he employed, not in contemplating his past triumphs, but in planning future conquests. Even in this very year we find him making proposals to the Admiralty for a new expedition to the coasts of Arctic America by a somewhat different route.

Nevertheless, these pre-occupations of his were not so absorbing as to exclude another of a very important kind. Even the busiest of men contrive somehow to find the leisure necessary for falling in love, and still more for prosecuting the courtship which is the natural sequel to that incident. There are reasons for thinking that the first step— if a 'fall' can be so described—had been taken by Franklin several years before. It is, at any rate, highly significant that to a small group of islands discovered by his expedition in the Arctic Sea he should have given the name of the Porden Islands. Flinders, and Buchan, and Hood, who stood sponsors for the newly discovered capes, or bays, or rivers, of those latitudes, can at once be identified as former commanders or present comrades. But there was no member of the expedition bearing the name given to these islands, whereas there was a certain Miss Eleanor Anne Porden, the daughter of an eminent architect, and with some considerable reputation as a poetess, who had celebrated the earlier voyage of the Dorothea and Trent in an admiring sonnet. Not only so, but after making Franklin's acquaintance, probably in her capacity as the sonneteer, she addressed to him a short poem, the authorship of which was no doubt made known to him, though veiled from the public under the name of 'Green Stockings.' The lines are supposed to be addressed by an Eskimo girl to the adventurous Englishman, and begin as follows :—

Yes, yes, thou art gone to the climes of the East ;
　　Thou hast welcomed the sun as he springs from the sea,
And thou car'st not, though sorrow lie cold on my breast,
　　Though the night of the grave may be closing on me.
And though he may beam in those changeable skies,
Where he dawns but to set, and descends but to rise,
Though on wonders I dream not his lustre may shine,
Yet he warms not one bosom more constant than mine.
And what if the daughters of Albion be fair,
　　With their soft eyes of azure and tresses of gold ?
To the flow'rs of the meadows their charms I compare ;
　　They bloom in the sunshine, but shrink from the cold.
But I through the snow and the forest would guide thee,
On the smooth-frozen lake I would gambol beside thee ;
With thongs of the reindeer thy buskins would weave,
And dress thy light meal as thou slumber'st at eve.
But frown not ; thou knowest that such moments have been,
　　Though cruel and false, thou could'st calmly depart.
Thy comrade too truly has pictured the scene
　　And my form : but thine own, it is drawn on my heart.
Think not in thy green isle some fair one to view,
For with tempest and storm shall my vengeance pursue.
My bidding at noonday shall darken the air,
And the rage of my climate shall follow thee there.

And thus the love-smitten 'Green Stockings' concludes :—

Return ! and the ice shall be swept from thy path ;
　　I will breathe out my spells o'er the land and the sea.
Return ! and the tempest shall pause in his wrath,
　　Nor the winds nor the waves dare be rebels to thee.

Spread thy canvas once more, keep the Pole Star before thee,
'Tis constancy's type and the beacon of glory ;
By the lake, by the mountain, the forest and river,
In the wilds of the North, I am thine, and for ever !

As will be perceived, it is eminently in the taste of the time—a time, it need hardly be added, in which English minor poetry was not at its best. But Miss Porden's intellectual abilities would be unfairly measured by her power of expressing her thoughts and emotions in a language which but few, and they of the highest poetic genius, had at that time mastered, though it is in these days handled with comparative ease and fluency even by many who have neither thought nor emotion to express. One would prefer not to judge her even by her epic poem in two volumes entitled 'Cœur de Lion ;' though the fact that she wrote a 'scientific poem' called 'The Veils,' which procured her the unusual honour of being elected a member of the French Institute, is enough to prove that, whatever the form of her poetic utterances, she must have had considerable clearness of mental vision and even some vigour of mental grasp. A far better estimate, however, can be formed of her from the letters from which some extracts will be given hereafter, and which show her to have possessed a most alert intelligence, a keen eye for character and situation, and no inconsiderable fund of humour.

Franklin's wooing of this lady was no long business. They became engaged to each other in the summer of 1823, and in August 19 they were married. It was in every respect save one—but that unfortunately a most important respect—a happy union. Mrs. Franklin's health, always very delicate, began to fail rapidly within a year after the marriage. The fatal signs of pulmonary disease revealed themselves, and it soon became too sadly evident that the young wife's days were numbered. In the early months of their wedded life, however, the gravity of her case was not apparent. Franklin, writing to one of his sisters in December 1823, describes her merely as 'somewhat of an invalid,' and at that time, probably, her happiness was unclouded by any apprehensions. How thorough a sympathy existed between them he goes on to show; for, after speaking of the steps which he had then just taken to procure the despatch of another Arctic expedition, he continues: 'All my proceedings in this matter have been made with the entire concurrence and indeed assistance of my wife, who, you are aware, is as warm in the cause of Arctic discoveries as I can possibly be. Her mind, indeed, is so thoroughly English that she would cheerfully make any sacrifice to promote our national character, and more particularly where my professional fame is concerned.' Little could he have foreseen at that moment how great would be the sacrifice actually required of her, and with what fortitude and devotion it would be met.

The nature of his plans could not, he adds, be communicated to his correspondent at the present stage, but he promised her that she and the rest of his family should receive the earliest intelligence respecting them if they were sanctioned and likely to be adopted. The scheme proposed by him, which was as a matter of fact accepted by the authorities at the Admiralty, differed from that of the former expedition in that the projected route of approach to the Arctic Ocean was to be by way not of the Coppermine, but of the Mackenzie River. On reaching its mouth the party were to divide, one portion of it proceeding along the coast to the westward, while the remainder took an eastward course along it as far as the Coppermine River, so as to connect the new survey of the North American shore with the discoveries of the earlier exploration. Concurrently with the despatch of these two land parties it was decided, as in the former case, to send out a naval expedition also; but in this instance the programme of 1819 was to be reversed. The vessel commissioned for the service, H.M.S. Blossom, under the command of Captain Beechey, Franklin's old lieutenant on the Trent, was to enter the Arctic Ocean not as did Parry's vessel from the eastward by way of Baffin's Bay, but through Behring Strait on the west; and it was to aim at effecting a junction with Franklin's westward-bound coasting party at some point between that strait and the mouth of the Mackenzie River. In the event

I

of such junction being effected, the Blossom was to convey him and his party either to Canton or the Sandwich Islands, as might seem advisable, or to carry out any other instructions Franklin might think proper to issue.

Many months, however, had yet to elapse before the preparations for the departure of the two expeditions were completed. For Franklin of course they were months full of business, involving probably not a little separation from his young wife, whose health was already beginning to decline, and who in the spring of 1824 was expecting the birth of her first, and, as it proved to be, her only child. Several letters from her to her sisters-in-law during this period have been preserved—letters which testify abundantly to the bright liveliness of her temperament, yet are not without a pathetic interest of their own. Incidentally they show the keen public interest which the new project of Arctic exploration had aroused, and the more vigorous 'lionising' to which Franklin was being subjected in consequence. ' I am much better than I have been,' writes his wife to her sister-in-law, under the light of one of those delusive gleams of hope which so cruelly mock the victims of consumption, ' and begin to be a little more useful about the house ; but I do not get out yet either on my own legs or any other, and my cough is often extremely troublesome. I have been flattered from week to week with the promise of a wonderful change in me ; but hitherto it has been all flattery. I am not very ill, however, and I shall do very well with the help of a little patience. Your brother is very kind and takes great care of poor little me, so that I have not been dull after all, and my friends are now beginning to rally round me. I only wish they would suspend their invitations a little while till I am able to accept and enjoy them.'

The cheerful courage with which the frail and failing woman looks forward to a prospect which had evidently disturbed the composure of her correspondent comes out very strikingly in the following passage :—

I perceive the idea of your brother's engaging in another expedition has quite frightened you, and you will set me down as either having no feeling or not caring a straw for him because I cannot share in your fears. I am, however, better off than I had expected to be, for I always looked to his leaving me this spring, and now I shall have his society nearly a twelvemonth longer—time enough for us to get tired of each other according to some people's opinion, but I see no signs of such an event at present. I think I can venture to assure you that, so far as human calculation can extend or human prudence can provide, there is no danger of his again encountering the sufferings of his last journey. The fatigue and want of the comforts of civilised life which must be inseparable from all travels into uncolonised countries, he must of course be prepared to meet, but I trust that he is endowed with every mental and bodily requisite to surmount them ; and what would you think of any man who scrupled to encounter these inconveniences in the path of duty and honour ? . . . Let me beg of you, therefore, to dismiss your apprehensions. If evil should come, it will come soon enough. We have no occasion to cloud the present hour by anticipating it ; and should the enterprise be successful, I am sure you love your brother too well not to wish that he may have the happiness and honour of achieving it. At any rate, he is still under the care of the same Providence which has once so wonderfully sustained him, and, as I said before, every human precaution will be taken.

On June 3, 1824, Mrs. Franklin gave birth to a daughter, who was christened Eleanor, after her mother. The event, as so often happens in such cases, sensibly accelerated the progress of her malady, and from that date, no doubt, the probability if not the imminence of the fatal issue was no longer to be concealed from the sufferer's husband and her friends.

Her own hopefulness, however, was invincible, and a letter of hers of more than three months' later date from Tunbridge Wells is quite touching in its vivacity and high spirits :—

I am getting stout and well, and mean soon to be strong enough to look better after your brother, and try to keep him in some sort of order.

(In an earlier letter she had written : ' I suppose the newspapers have told you how the ladies pulled your brother to pieces at Captain Parry's ball. He was in such request that I wonder they left a bit of him for me.')

Such a flirt as he is ! The like was never known. Only think of his being one of a party to gallant sixteen young ladies (ladies are always young, you know), who, not contented with making a monopoly of the carriages in the neighbourhood (so that poor I, who was left at home, could hardly procure a wretched one), actually stormed the house of a gentleman whom they did not know, a few miles off, and insisted on eating their picnic meal in his dining-room ! John Bull grumbled a little at first, as might be expected ; but as John Bull is always good-natured at bottom, and, moreover, easily taken in, he yielded at last at the thought of these sixteen lovely damsels getting wet through in an impending shower, at the doleful picture of coughs and colds which was drawn by Lady Ellenborough's butler, for she was leader of the storming party. Well, as I said, the poor gouty old gentleman's heart was softened, and, what is more, his wife was neither angry nor jealous. The young ladies were allowed to do as they liked—namely, to make themselves quite at home on his terri-tory. So they wandered on the margin of his lake, which had been the original attraction, and sang songs in his sylvan avenues till the despairing nightingales dropped down dead with envy, and the moon rose a full hour before the time to look at what was going on. I understand your brother's sweetness of voice and delicacy of taste were particularly admired in a tender Italian duet with one of the Misses L. He has had a good deal of practice lately in singing to baby, and were it not for the approaching expedition I should expect to see him come out as a successor to Braham.

Then follows an amusing anecdote of another distinguished man :—

Mr. Chantrey, the sculptor, who has been residing here some time, came down from London last Saturday, and on Sunday discovered that he had left the keys of his cellar and strong box behind. Nothing remained but to go back to London for them. Monday morning came, all the coaches full, so what does he do but order a post-chaise and set off ! At Seven Oaks he finds a gentleman in despair at being able to procure no conveyance to town when he was summoned by earnest business ; so Mr. Chantrey in his generosity volunteers to take him on. So far, so good ; but half a mile further he found his keys in his breeches pocket, and, being ashamed to tell the tale of his own folly, actually went on to London for the sake of keeping faith with his travelling companion. Men of genius do strange things. . . . Not a word about baby yet ! Not a word of sober common-sense ! Well, I can't help it. I have dealt in dismals so long that I am deter-mined not to be serious again until after your brother is gone ; nor then, either, if I can help it.

No apology, it is to be hoped, is needed for these some-what lengthy extracts. The letters from which they are taken afford us our only glimpse into the inner life of the bright and hapless young creature over whom the grave was so soon to close. A situation more intensely tragic than that in which Franklin was placed at this moment it would be impossible to imagine. As the date of his departure drew nearer and nearer, so also did it become more and more evident that the hour was as fast approaching when his beloved wife must herself begin, in words destined years afterwards to be graven on his own cenotaph, her 'happier voyage, towards no earthly Pole.' It was plainly as much a question of days with one event as with the other; and in this grim race between Death and Duty the unhappy husband found himself almost longing for the victory of the former, in order that he might be with his wife to the end. The following letter to his brother-in-law, Mr. Sellwood, written less than a week before, reflects a state of feeling which would render it almost too painful for extract, were not the distressing situation so relieved and ennobled by the quiet heroism of the dying woman:—

Hannah's last letter to Mr. Booth will have apprised you of my dearest Eleanor being in a very alarming state. The disease has continued its rapid progress, and she is now to all appearance nearly at her last extremity; but such has been her muscular strength that she has rallied frequently, and it is not improbable she may linger even through this day. I seize an interval of repose to commence this letter to you in this room, where I have been watching all the night. You, my dearest friend, have experienced the awful trial I have got to witness, and can fully enter into my feelings and truly condole with my afflictions. Great as my loss must be, it is assuredly some alleviation to reflect that it is possible it may please the Almighty to remove her from this transitory scene before I take my departure, and, though short the time of my stay, I may have the opportunity of arranging for the care of our dear infant. . . . It is impossible to imagine any person more resigned than she has been, and is especially since the paroxysms have subsided. She has desired me to pray for her in express words during the night, and about three hours since asked me to read the chapter of Corinthians used for the funeral service. All her private arrangements have been made with perfect calmness and self-collection, and now her mind is perfectly at ease. She only says 'God's will be done!' It is, too, extremely satisfactory to me that she expressed before the whole party her decided wish that I should not delay in going on the expedition, that it has ever been her desire, and that she is not of opinion that the circumstance of my going has hastened the crisis of her complaint, which she now thinks has been long in progress, and certainly advancing by rapid strides since our return from Tunbridge Wells.

The end, however, was not nearly so close at hand as appeared. In a few hours the patient rallied. The doctors, Franklin reported later, 'saw symptoms of amendment. Other measures were immediately adopted. The medicine produced the effect looked for, and I thank God my dearest wife has been since improving, and that even now there are hopes of her recovery, faint as they may be and as I shall consider them. She said to-day, " It would be better for me that you were gone." It is delightful how happy the state of her mind is.'

By the middle of the month of February the expedition was at last ready to start. All the details connected with its equipment had been personally superintended by Franklin, who also made the necessary arrangements with the Hudson's Bay Company's officials for the conveyance of his people, stores, and provisions to Great Bear Lake. In accordance with his wishes, three boats were specially constructed in such a manner as to combine seaworthiness and stability with such lightness as should render them sufficiently easy of transport over the numerous portages and various rapids that would be met with before reaching the Arctic waters on which they were to be launched. The largest of these boats was twenty-six feet long, and was capable of carrying eight people ; the other two, each constructed to hold seven men, were twenty-four feet in length. The two companions who had played so gallant a part in Franklin's former adventure, Dr. Richardson and Lieutenant Back, were again associated with him, and Mr. Kendall, an officer who had served in Parry's last expedition, and was afterwards to become Franklin's nephew by marriage, was also of the party.

It is not necessary for the purpose of the present memoir to give so detailed an account of this second expedition as has been given of the first. Less dramatic in its incidents, and attended with far less formidable difficulties and dangers, it is proportionately less illustrative of the personal character

and qualities of its commander, and its results, though of high
scientific value, belong rather to the general history of geographical exploration.   Except, therefore, at those stages of
its course at which it is marked by occurrences bearing on
the history of Franklin's private life or throwing additional
light on his individuality, the narrative of it in these pages
will have to be more or less concisely summarised.

One such occurrence, however, and that of a tragic nature,
confronts us, as was indeed but too evidently and sadly pre-
destined, at its very outset.   The officers of the expedition, who
had been preceded by the men and stores, left England on
February 16, 1825, and on the 22nd, less than a week after,
Mrs. Franklin breathed her last.   It was not, however, until
near the end of April that the sorrowful news overtook her
husband ; and, grave as had been the apprehensions with
which he had left her, the tidings came upon him—as all such
tidings do, however men may think themselves prepared for
them—with an overwhelming shock.

It was the more severe since it would seem that that
pathetic power of self-deception which love bestows had actually been strong enough since Franklin's departure to revive
in him hopes of his wife's ultimate recovery.   He wrote letter
after letter to Mrs. Franklin, then, alas ! no more, which
breathe, in many passages at any rate, a spirit of confidence
and even of cheerfulness, which may of course have been
partly, but could not have been wholly, assumed.   It was in
this strain that he wrote to her during his outward passage, a
very pleasant and favourable one as he describes it, in the
American packet-ship Columbia.   ' I have every hope,' he
says, ' that it will please God to restore you to health, and
that we shall meet after the lapse of a few short years to
unite in thanksgiving and prayer to the Almighty, and to
enjoy each other's and our dear child's society.'

Again, on March 22, after his arrival at New York, he
writes describing the town in his usual lively fashion, and
incidentally gives us a glimpse of the interior of an American
theatre of those days.   ' It is a neat house and happened to
be well filled.   Some of the gentlemen, however, sat with their

hats on in the boxes by the side of the ladies.   So much for a
young country, and for liberty and independence!'   And the
letter ends: 'I often think how you and our little girl are
getting on, and am always so sanguine as to hope you are
well. . . . I long to hear from you, and it is unfortunate that
the next packet has not arrived, which will no doubt bear
letters from you or some one of the family.'   A third letter is
from Albany, full of travelling incidents and giving a description of the Falls of Niagara.   And then comes the last he
ever wrote to her before learning the fatal truth.   It was
written from Penentanguishene, a lonely outlying British station on Lake Huron, and is dated April 22 :—

I am sure you will be rejoiced to learn that we arrived safely at
this place, to which you may remember a part of our stores were forwarded from Montreal. The Canadian *voyageurs* had not reached York
Factory at the time of the departure from thence. I therefore left Mr.
Back to bring them up. Part of these men have already come up, Mr.
Back and the remainder we expect to-day, so that we shall probably
commence our voyage this evening or to-morrow. We are first to
cross Lake Huron and Lake Superior, and at Fort William, on the
north side of the latter lake, we embark in the proper travelling canoes,
which are of a smaller size than those we now use.

Penentanguishene is the most northerly of our naval stations, and
the key to Lake Huron. At the close of the war they were preparing to build a frigate of thirty-two guns, but its construction was
deferred when the peace was concluded, and the establishment was
then reduced. We have found, however, very comfortable quarters
in the house of the lieutenant commanding. There are a lieutenant
of the army with his wife, and a surgeon and his wife stationed here ;
these form a social party and cause the time to pass very pleasantly
. . . I do not think, however, that either you or I would relish such
a secluded life.   If we could convey our library, it would be the
very place for me to get through it.

I should have rejoiced at having you by my side on our journey
from New York. There were many scenes which you could have
described so well, and I am sure it would have given you sincere
pleasure to have witnessed the industry of the American character
evinced by the number of the towns and villages which have sprung
up within a few years, and where there was every appearance of prosperity and comfort. Many of the best-informed Americans whom we
met complain, and I think with justice, of the misstatements that
have been made of their country by English travellers, though they

comfort themselves with the reflection that the greater part of these men are persons who in their own country are considered as desperate adventurers, and who have in consequence been excluded from good society. I certainly have no partiality either for the Americans or for their Constitution, but it is impossible not to admire their industry. . . .

I was in hopes that before we left this place I should have received a letter to inform me that you continued to improve. The packet from Liverpool must have had a long passage to New York, or I should have had that gratification. I shall embark, however, with every hope that the Almighty has been pleased to restore you to health before this, and that you are now in the enjoyment of every comfort. I daily remember you and our dear little one in my prayers, and I have no doubt yours are offered up on my behalf. . . . She must be growing very entertaining, and I sincerely trust she will be a source of great comfort to us, especially to you in my absence. With what heartfelt pleasure shall I embrace you both on my return ! I suppose Captain Beechey has sailed before this time, and hope that he will be the bearer of a letter from you or from some of the family if you should have been unequal to writing. . . . Your flag is yet snug in the box, and will not be displayed till we get to a more northern region. Mr. Back and the men have arrived.

Here the letter breaks off abruptly, and then in an agitated handwriting are added the words :

Seven o'clock P.M. The distressing intelligence of my dearest wife's death has just reached me.

This was actually the second letter which he had written that very day in the same resolutely hopeful tone. Or, at any rate, there is a letter of his of the same date—though it may possibly have been penned by him in fact a day earlier, and left open, as was the fashion in that age of rare and costly communication, until the last moment before despatch, in order to make it carry the very latest news—in which, writing to his sister of his wife, then nearly two months in her grave, he dwells on her prospects of recovery in that tone of hopefulness to which fate and man's ignorance sometimes lend so terrible an irony :—

I had expected during our stay here to have received the letters which Mrs. Kay and Hannah promised to write for some days after my departure from London, to acquaint me as to the state of Eleanor ; but the packet appears to have had a long passage from Liverpool, as they have not come to hand. I cherish the hope that it hath pleased the Almighty to assist her with His protection, and that she is now restored to health. The last days of my stay at home were indeed sorrowful, and I thank the Almighty for enabling me to support them, and that the morning of my departure was brightened by the hope of my dear wife's recovery. . . . The struggle which my dear Eleanor then had convinced me that her health is very precarious, and that in consequence she needs all the care and attention that my family can give her during my absence.

And this letter, too, concludes with the same sad post-script :—

Seven P.M. I have just received through the newspaper an account of the death of my dearest Eleanor. You can imagine my distress, as I had hoped from the change which had taken place two days before my departure that her life might have been spared. But it hath pleased the Almighty in His wise dispensation to remove her from me, and I trust she is now associated with the spirits of the just made perfect. I feel deeply for my dearest child, though I know she will receive from Isabella (Mrs. Cracroft) a mother's anxious love, yet to a tender female a mother's loss is irreparable. I earnestly pray God to protect her, and that she may be brought up in His love.

CHAPTER VII

SECOND ARCTIC EXPEDITION

1825–1827

PENENTANGUISHENE, on Lake Huron, the place from which these sorrowful letters are dated, is some 1,500 miles as the crow flies from Fort Cumberland, the originally intended rendezvous of the expedition, and on the day after it was written Franklin and his party set off in two canoes which had been deposited at that place in the preceding autumn. Following the great north-westward-stretching chain of lakes—that is to say, up Rainy Lake, the Lake of the Woods, and Lake Winnipeg—and issuing thence into the Saskatchewan River, they made their way to Fort Cumberland, which was reached on June 15. Here they learned that their boats, which had arrived before them, had left on the 2nd of the month ; and, accordingly, after one night's stay at the fort, they proceeded on their voyage. On June 29 they overtook the boats and the remainder of the party, who had travelled *via* York Factory, and on July 15 they reached Fort Chipewyan, whence, after a stay of two days, they pursued their way to Fort Resolution, on the Great Slave Lake. At that station they remained a few days, making the necessary arrangements with the Indians for the supply of provisions for the winter, and August 2 saw them embarked in their canoes on the Mackenzie River. Two days' journey down its stream brought them to Fort Simpson, and yet another four days' travel to Fort Norman. Here, as there still remained a few weeks of the travelling season, the party, under Franklin's instructions, divided. Back, accompanied by an officer of the Hudson's Bay Company, was directed to proceed to Great Bear Lake, and there to construct winter quarters for the expedition. Dr. Richardson was despatched at his own request to explore the northern shore of the lake; while Franklin himself, taking with him Kendall, a crew of six Englishmen, a native guide, and his old friend the Eskimo interpreter, started in one of the boats for the mouth of the Mackenzie River, with the view of examining the condition of the ice in the Arctic Ocean, and forming an estimate of the prospects of a successful voyage along its shores in the following year.

The parties separated on August 9, and so well was Franklin served by the new English-built boat he had brought out with him, that by the 14th of that month they had reached the Polar Sea. Franklin had brought out with him a silk union-jack worked by his dying wife, which, according to her wish, was not to be displayed until her husband and his companions had gained the coast. That moment having now arrived, he unfolded the flag and planted it on the shore, and then that piquant mixture of qualities which goes to the making of the typical sailor's nature comes out in his characteristic comment on the incident. 'Here,' he writes, 'was first displayed the flag which my lamented Eleanor made, and you can imagine it was with heartfelt emotion I first saw it unfurled; but in a short time I derived great pleasure in looking at it.' All the affection of the husband speaks in one half of the sentence, all the buoyant spirit of the born adventurer in the other; while there is all the charm of Franklin's character in the perfect simplicity and candour with which he combines the revelation of the two. No one could have been less justly accused of levity or shallowness of feeling; but he was of those with whom sorrow, however profound and genuine, finds instant relief in the thought of action, and it is by these, and perhaps by these alone, that all the greater practical work of the world is done.

By September 5 all three exploring parties had returned and had established themselves in their winter quarters at Fort Franklin, the station constructed by Back on Great Bear Lake, and so named by him in compliment to his absent leader. The long Arctic winter passed after its usual tedious fashion, diversified by no incident of interest, but blessed for that very reason with a good fortune akin to that of the nation which 'has no history.' Despite the lowness of the temperature, which fell on one occasion to 49° below zero of Fahrenheit, or 81° of frost, they seemed to have suffered little from it, and the supplies of game and fish procured for them by their Indian hunters were fairly abundant. Writing to one of his sisters on November 8 from Fort Franklin, he says :—

We are snugly seated in our winter quarters, the name of which I am sure will please you. They form three sides of a square, the centre house being occupied by the officers, the buildings on its left by the men, and on its right is a store, the whole surrounded by wooden stockades, which serve to keep the drift away from the yard. Our house contains a spacious hall, and on each side of it are two apartments which are fitted up according to the taste and means of the occupiers. Dr. Richardson and myself are in one of these, which is neatly whitewashed and ornamented with books, instruments, clothes, and beds. The latter are the principal features of elegance—mine in particular, as Wilson, the piper, who is my servant, has fitted it up à la tente with the lining of our marquee, and, that no space may be lost, the interior is decorated with my dirk, pistol, glass, cap, writing-case, and sash. My limbs repose nightly on a well-stuffed bed, covered with leather, between good, warm blankets, and, as you may suppose, I sleep soundly. The season of darkness is daily advancing, and in the height of winter we must not expect to have more than five hours' light, so that we may have sleep to our hearts' content. We generally, however, sit up till midnight, reading or employed otherwise, and rise about eight o'clock, have our breakfast directly, dinner at half-past five, and tea at nine. The evening is passed away often in a game at chess or some sport, and the day devoted to business. We are about to establish a school for the instruction of the men ; and on Sundays Divine Service with sermons is held twice, and it is a real gratification to find the men joining on these occasions with great fervency and attention.

I sincerely pray, through the blessing of God, that these opportunities of offering praise and thanksgiving to the Almighty, and of hearing His Holy Word, may lead to our present and eternal benefit. I wish to have the impression deeply seated in my mind, as well as in those of my companions, that the Almighty can alone support and help us in our present pursuits, and that He ordereth each event of our lives. . . . You must not suppose, my dear sister, from my writing in this manner that I am gloomy ; for I assure you that I am more calm, cheerful, and happy than I have been for some time, and,

indeed, than I expected to have been under the severe trial I have
had to sustain.   I feel the dispensations of the Almighty to have been
appointed in infinite wisdom, and, therefore, I pray for power to bear
them with humble resignation and reverence.   Had my poor wife's
life been prolonged, I find it must have been attended with continual and very acute suffering.   Surely, then, the fondest desire of
the heart could not mourn beyond the first days of grief at her
removal from this weight of woe to a state of eternal rest.

To this same month of November 1825 belongs a letter
from Franklin to the eminent geologist, Mr. (afterwards Sir
Roderick) Murchison, in which he gives an interesting
account of the fare, occupations, and amusements, mental and
physical, of the imprisoned men :—

We have, as yet, had no severe weather, nor do I think we are
likely to have the temperature so low as at Fort Enterprise.   We are,
in fact, much less elevated in this secondary formation than when in
its vicinity, where the rocks are entirely granitic.   Until the day
before yesterday we had comparatively little snow, and this is the
first day that our dogs have been used in dragging sledges.   Four
trains of two dogs each were despatched for meat this morning.   We
endeavour to keep ourselves in good humour, health, and spirits by
an agreeable variety of useful occupation and amusement.   Till the
snow fell the game of hockey played on the ice was the morning's
sport.   At other times Wilson's pipes are put in request, and now
and then a game of blind man's buff; in fact, any recreation is encouraged to promote exercise and good feeling.   I wish you could
pop in and partake our fare.   You would be sure of a hearty welcome, and you should have your choice of either moose, or reindeer,
or trout weighing from forty to fifty pounds.   But you must bring
wine and bread if you wish either for more than one day.

Nor were intellectual occupations of a graver, not to say
of a severe discipline wanting to the party, as will be seen
from the following passages, in which one notices, not without amusement, that Franklin's criticisms of literary classics
were marked in his fortieth year by considerably more diffidence than he was wont to display at the age of sixteen :—

I have been delighted with Dante, and so have my companions ;
but I must confess there is frequently a depth of thought and reasoning to which my mind can hardly reach.   Perhaps these poets will
be better comprehended in perusal.   It seems clear that Milton, as
well as other poets, has borrowed ideas from his comprehensive
mind.

It was not till June 24, 1826, that they were able to start on their summer expedition, the plan of which was thus arranged:—Franklin and Back were to explore the coast to the westward of the mouth of the Mackenzie River, while Dr. Richardson, accompanied by Mr. Kendall, was to make an eastward journey from the same point to the mouth of the Coppermine River, returning to Fort Franklin before the next winter set in, Mr. Dease, an officer of the Hudson's Bay Company attached to the expedition, remaining at that station to look after the supplies. On July 3 the *Franklin* and *Richardson* parties separated at a bifurcation of the Mackenzie River, and on the 7th the former party reached its mouth. Here they met with what was perhaps the solitary incident of their journey—an attack on the boats, with a view to plunder, by a tribe of Eskimos some 300 strong. It was subsequently ascertained that this attempt at pillage was part of an organised plot to massacre the whole expedition; but it was foiled by the cool courage and steady self-control of Franklin and his men.

The affair seems, however, to have had at the outset a sufficiently unpremeditated appearance. On arriving at the mouth of the Mackenzie River, the expedition came somewhat unexpectedly upon an Eskimo encampment—a crowd of tents pitched on an island in the bay into which the river opened, and with many Eskimos strolling about among them. Franklin immediately prepared to open communications with them agreeably with his instructions. A selection of articles for presents and trade being made, the rest of the lading was closely covered up, the arms were inspected, and every man was directed to keep his gun ready for immediate use. Franklin had previously informed Back of his intention to open communication with the Eskimos by landing among them, accompanied only by Augustus, the interpreter; and Back was now instructed to keep the boats afloat, and the crews with their arms ready to support their leader in the event of the natives proving hostile, but on no account to fire until he was convinced that his safety could be secured in no other way. Having received an impression from the narra-

tives of different navigators that the sacrifices of life which
had occurred in these interviews with savages had been
generally occasioned by the crews mistaking noise and
violent gestures for decided hostility, Franklin thought it
advisable to explain his views on this point to all the men,
and peremptorily forbade their firing until he set the example or until they were ordered to do so by Back. They were
also forbidden to trade with the natives on any pretence,
and were ordered to leave everything of that kind to the
officers.

On approaching the island the water became shallow,
and the boats grounded about a mile from the beach. The
explorers shouted and made signs to the Eskimos to come off,
and then pulled back a little way to await their arrival in
deeper water. Three canoes at once put off from the shore,
and immediately afterwards others were launched in such
quick succession that the whole space between the island and
the boats was covered with them. Franklin had counted as
many as seventy-three, when the sea became so crowded
with them that he could proceed no further in his reckoning. The three foremost canoes were paddled by elderly
men, apparently selected to open the communications. As
soon as they were within hail Augustus explained to them
in detail the purport of the visit, and told them that if his
leader succeeded in finding a navigable channel for large
ships, a trade highly beneficial to them would be opened.
They were delighted with the intelligence and repeated it to
their countrymen, who testified their joy by tossing their
hands aloft and raising a deafening shout of applause.

After the first present, Franklin resolved to bestow no
more gratuitously, but always to exact something, however
small, in return. The three elderly men readily offered the
ornaments they wore in their cheeks, their arms, and their
knives in exchange for the articles given them. Up to this
time the first three canoes alone had ventured near the boats,
but the crowd soon increased to 250 or 300 persons, all
anxious to share in the lucrative trade they saw established,
and pressing eagerly forward to offer for sale their bows,

arrows, and spears, which they had hitherto kept concealed within the canoes. Franklin endeavoured in vain amid the clamour and bustle of barter to obtain some information respecting the coast, but, finding the natives becoming more and more importunate and troublesome, he determined to leave them, and therefore directed the boats' heads to be put to seaward.

Hitherto the Eskimos had shown no unfriendly disposition; but at this juncture an accident happened which, in a quite unforeseen fashion, altered the whole aspect of affairs. A canoe being accidentally upset by an oar of one of the boats, its owner was plunged into the water with his head in the mud, and apparently in danger of being drowned. He was extricated from his unpleasant position by the crew, and taken into the boat until the water could be baled out of his canoe, Augustus throwing his own great-coat over him, as he was shivering with cold. At first he was exceedingly angry, but soon became reconciled to the situation, and, looking about, discovered that the boat was full of what he regarded as concealed treasures. He soon began to ask for everything he saw, and expressed high displeasure at the refusal of his demands. He proceeded, moreover, so to excite the cupidity of his fellows by his account of the inexhaustible riches contained in the boats, that several of the younger men attempted to join him. While resisting the attempt, one of the crew observed that the man who had been rescued from the mud had a pistol under his shirt, and was about to take it from him, when Franklin ordered his follower to desist, thinking that the weapon might belong to him. It had, in fact, been stolen from Back, and the thief, perceiving the attention directed to it, jumped out of the boat and joined his countrymen, carrying with him Augustus's great-coat.

The water had now ebbed so far that it was not knee-deep at the boats, and the younger men wading in crowds around them attempted to steal everything within their reach; slyly, however, and with so much dexterity as almost to escape detection. This mode of procedure, however, being found unsatisfactory, they seized on the boat under Back's

K

command, the Reliance, and set to work to drag it ashore, upon which Franklin gave orders to his own boat, the Lion, to follow it. But the Lion had stuck fast aground and refused to move, on seeing which the Eskimos lent a friendly hand, and both boats were dragged ashore.

This was the signal for an organised attempt to plunder them. A numerous party stripped to the waist, and with drawn knives ran to the Reliance, and, having hauled her up as they could, began a regular pillage, handing the articles to the women, who, ranged in a row behind them, quickly conveyed the thefts out of sight. Back and his crew strenuously but good-humouredly resisted the attack, and rescued many things from their grasp; but they were overpowered by numbers, and had even some difficulty in preserving their arms. Franklin and his crew were also beset, though by smaller numbers, but by sitting tight on the covered cargo, and belabouring the natives with the butt-ends of their muskets, were able to prevent any article of importance from being carried away. 'In the whole of this unequal contest,' says Franklin, 'the self-possession of our men was not more conspicuous than the coolness with which the Eskimos received the blows dealt out to them with the butts of the muskets. But at length, being irritated by the repeated failure of their attempts, several of them jumped on board and forcibly endeavoured to take the daggers and shot-belts from about the men's persons.' Franklin himself was engaged with three of them who were trying to disarm him, and was only just in time to prevent one of his men from discharging the contents of his musket into the body of an Eskimo who had struck at him with a knife. In short, what had begun as a sort of half-friendly rough-and-tumble 'bear fight,' complicated with petty larceny, was now threatening to develop into a massacre, when suddenly the whole of the Eskimos took to flight and hid themselves behind the canoes and drift timber on the beach. It appeared that, the Reliance having been again got afloat, Back wisely judged that the moment had arrived for more active interference, and ordered his men to level their muskets, which had produced this sudden panic. Happily, the Lion floated soon after, and both were retiring from the beach when the Eskimos, having recovered from their consternation, launched their canoes and were preparing to follow, but Franklin desired Augustus to say that he would shoot the first man who came within range of his musket, upon which they halted.

The scuffle had lasted for several hours, but with such spirit had the contest been waged on Franklin's side that the only things of any importance which the natives succeeded in carrying off were the mess canteen and kettles, a tent, a box containing blankets and shoes, one of the men's bags, and the jibsails. The rest of their booty could well be spared, and the articles of which it consisted would in fact have been distributed among them if they had remained quiet. In concluding his account of the affair Franklin writes:—

I cannot sufficiently praise the fortitude and obedience of both boats' crews in abstaining from the use of their arms. In the first instance I had been influenced by the desire of preventing unnecessary bloodshed, and afterwards, when the critical situation of my party might well have warranted me in employing more decided means for their defence, I still endeavoured to temporise, being convinced that so long as the boats lay aground and we were beset by such numbers armed with long knives, bows and arrows, and spears, we could not use firearms to advantage. The howling of the women and the clamour of the men proved the high excitement to which they had wrought themselves ; and I am still of opinion that, mingled as we were with them, the first blood we had shed would have been instantly revenged by the sacrifice of all our lives.

His methods undoubtedly were very different from those of the modern explorer, who, even if he had hesitated from prudential motives to fire on the Eskimos while surrounded by them, would in all probability have returned the next morning and 'read them a lesson' from a safe distance with Remington rifles.

This episode at an end, the expedition was at last able on July 14 to take the sea, unobstructed at any rate by human obstacles. But icebergs now took the place of Eskimos, and for four or five days longer they were condemned to inaction. At the expiration of this time the ice

cleared sufficiently to permit a passage for their boats, and
they were able to push on.   But their progress was disap-
pointingly slow.   The favourable promise of navigation which
the Arctic Ocean had held out the previous year proved
wholly delusive.   Their way was continually being barred by
ice, sometimes for days together; they were frequently
delayed by gales and fogs, and their boats were sadly knocked
about by floating ice-blocks, from which they sustained considerable damage.   On July 27 they reached what Franklin
describes as the most westerly river in the British dominions,
as it was close to the (of course imaginary) line of demarca-
tion between Great Britain and Russia, in those days, it will
be remembered, mistress of Alaska.   This river Franklin
named the Clarence, 'in honour of His Royal Highness the
Lord High Admiral.   Under a pile of drift timber which we
erected on the most elevated point of the coast near its mouth
was deposited a tin box containing a royal silver medal, with
an account of the proceedings of the expedition, and the
Union flag was hoisted under three hearty cheers, the only
salute that we could afford.'

At this point they found more open water than they had
yet met with, and their spirits accordingly rose.   Not, however, for long, for their difficulties recommenced almost
immediately, and reached their climax at a spot which they
vindictively christened Foggy Island.   It is a question, indeed,
whether the partial failure of their enterprise was not more
due to fogs than ice; for the prevalence of the former
obstacle lost them many of the precious days in which they
might possibly have managed to overcome or rather circumvent the other.   Nothing was more remarkable than the
difference of conditions which had prevailed in this respect
between the present and Franklin's former expedition.   'We
were only,' he says, 'detained three times in navigating along
the coast in 1821 to the east of the Coppermine River; but
westward of the mouth of the Mackenzie hardly a day passed
that the atmosphere was not at some time or other so foggy
as to hide any object from view for a distance of four or five
miles.'   It was no doubt due, as Franklin suggests, not only to

the swampy character of the land, but to the Rocky Mountains preventing its moisture from being carried off.

Nevertheless, and in spite of all obstructions, whether of fog or ice, the expedition struggled gallantly on, until at length, on August 18, after having traced the coast line for 374 miles, Franklin came with much reluctance to the conclusion that it would be imprudent to pursue their journey further. The autumn was wearing on, and as yet they had only traversed half the distance between the mouth of the Mackenzie and Icy Cape. At the same rate of speed it would take them at least another six weeks to make that headland, and by that time the winter would be setting in and Captain Beechey, with whom Franklin was endeavouring to effect a junction, would in all likelihood have put the Blossom about and be sailing southward. Beechey, as it happened, was at this very moment off Icy Cape, the furthest point of his voyage, and had despatched a boat to the eastward to look out for Franklin's party. This boat arrived on August 25 within little more than 160 miles of the point at which Franklin a week before had resolved to turn back. Tantalising, however, as was this near approach which failed to become a meeting, it would not have been possible for the two parties to meet. Franklin could not have covered the intervening distance between August 18 and 25, and he and his men therefore could not have arrived at the 'furthest' of the Blossom's boat before it returned to the ship. As it was, he of course knew nothing of the despatch of this boat. He had simply to weigh the probability of his own expedition being able to effect a junction with the Blossom herself during the short remaining period of the travelling season. And this question he was, of course, bound to consider by the light of his previous and terrible experiences, and of the knowledge gained therefrom of the climate, the food supply, and the reasonable weather forecasts for the time of the year.

The decision which he arrived at was so important, and the abandonment of his hope of joining hands with Beechey and thus completing the exploration of the entire American coast from the Mackenzie westward to Behring Strait was so

bitter a disappointment, that it seems best to allow Franklin
to state his reasons for his resolution in the words of his own
' Narrative of a Second Expedition to the Shores of the Polar
Sea : '—

The preceding narrative shows the difficulties of navigating such a
coast even during the finest part of the summer ; if, indeed, any
portion of a season which had been marked by a constant succession
of gales and fogs could be called fine. No opportunity of advancing
had been let slip after the time of our arrival in the Arctic Sea ; and
the unwearied zeal and exertion of the crews had been required for
an entire month to explore the ten degrees of longitude between
Herschel Island and our present situation. I had, therefore, no
reason to suppose that the ten remaining degrees could be navigated
in much less time. The ice, it is true, was now broken up and the
sea around our present encampment was clear; but we had lately
seen how readily the drift ice was packed upon the shoals by every
breeze of wind blowing towards the land. The summer, bad as it
had been, was now nearly at an end. And on this point I had the
experience of the former voyage for a guide. At Point Turnagain, two
degrees to the south of our present situation, the comparatively warm
summer of 1821 terminated on August 17 by severe storms of wind
and snow ; and in the space of a fortnight afterwards winter set in
with all its severity. Last year, too, on the 18th and following days
of the month, we had a heavy gale at the mouth of the Mackenzie,
and appearances did not indicate that the present season would prove
more favourable. The mean temperature of the atmosphere had
decreased rapidly since the sun had begun to sink below the horizon,
and the thermometer had not lately shown a higher temperature than
37°. Ice of considerable thickness formed in the night, and the number of flocks of geese which were hourly seen pursuing their course to
the westward showed that their autumnal flight had commenced.

While a hope remained of reaching Behring Strait, I looked
upon the hazard to which we had on several occasions been exposed
of shipwreck on the flats or on the ice as inseparable from a
voyage of the nature of that which we had undertaken ; and if such
an accident had occurred, I should have hoped, with a sufficient
portion of the summer before me, to conduct my party in safety back
to the Mackenzie. But the loss of the boats, when we should have
been far advanced, and at the end of the season, would have been
fatal. The deer hasten from the coast as soon as the snow falls ; no
Eskimos had lately been seen, nor any winter houses to denote
that this part of the coast was much frequented ; and if we did meet
them under adverse circumstances we could not with safety trust to
their assistance for a supply of provisions ; nor do I believe that,

even if willing, they would have been able to support us for any length of time.

Till our tedious detention at Foggy Island we had had no doubt of ultimate success; and it was with no ordinary pain that I could now bring myself even to think of relinquishing the great object of my ambition, and of disappointing the flattering confidence that had been reposed in my exertions. But I had higher duties to perform than the gratification of my own feelings; and a mature consideration of all the above matters forced me to the conclusion that we had reached that point beyond which perseverance would be rashness and our best efforts must be fruitless. . . .

In the evening I communicated my determination to the whole party; they received it with the good feeling that had marked their conduct throughout the voyage, and they assured me of their cheerful acquiescence in any order I should give. The readiness with which they would have prosecuted the voyage was the more creditable because many of them had their legs swelled and inflamed from continually wading in ice-cold water while launching the boats. . . . Nor were these symptoms to be overlooked in coming to a determination; for though no one who knows the resolute disposition of the British sailor can be surprised at their more than willingness to proceed, I felt that it was my business to judge of their capability for so doing, and not to allow myself to be seduced by their ardour, however honourable to them and cheering to me.

Had Franklin known, he added, that a party from the Blossom had been at the distance of only 160 miles from him, 'no difficulties, dangers, or discouraging cirstances should have prevailed on him to return;' but, taking into account the uncertainty of all voyages in a sea obstructed by ice, he had no right to expect that the Blossom had got so far eastward from Behring Strait as the point which she had actually attained, still less that any party from her had got to a point which, as a matter of fact, in an attempt to repeat the feat the next summer, their boat failed to reach by 100 miles. Anyhow, the decision to return was taken and acted upon, and never in his life perhaps did Franklin display truer and finer moral courage than when, despite his burning zeal for discovery and his not unworthy thirst for fame as an explorer, he thus unhesitatingly laid aside his ambitions and quietly accepted disappointment.

They were back again at Fort Franklin by September 21

and were rejoiced to find that the eastward expedition had been perfectly successful, having traced nearly 900 miles of undiscovered coast-line between the Mackenzie and Coppermine Rivers, and regained the station on Great Bear Lake full three weeks before the return of Franklin's party. In the course of their exploration they had discovered a large bay, which they had named after their distinguished leader ; and it may not be out of place here to quote the warm eulogy which Dr. Richardson afterwards pronounced on his chief in his published narrative of the transaction :—

In bestowing the name of Franklin on this remarkable bay, I paid an appropriate compliment to the officer under whose orders and by whose arrangements the delineation of all that is known of the northern coast of the American continent has been effected, with the exception of the parts in the vicinity of Icy Cape discovered by Captain Beechey.

It would not be proper, nor is it my intention, to descant on the merits of my superior officer ; but, after having served under Captain Franklin for nearly seven years in two successive voyages of discovery, I trust I may be allowed to say that, however high his brother-officers may rate his courage and talents, either in the ordinary line of his professional duty or in the field of discovery, the hold he acquires upon the affections of those under his command by a continued series of the most conciliatory attentions to their feelings and a uniform and unremitting regard to their best interests, is not less conspicuous. I feel that the sentiments of my friends and companions, Captain Back and Lieutenant Kendall, are in unison with my own when I affirm that gratitude and attachment to our late commander will animate our breasts to the latest period of our lives.

This is only one among many similar tributes to the attractive personal qualities of this great explorer. The roll on which Franklin's name is inscribed has received many additions since that now distant day when these words were written, but of how few of those who have carried on his work of discovery could they have been written with equal truth ! In the gifts and attainments which go to the making of the successful explorer Franklin has had many rivals ; but in this remarkable power of enlisting the enthusiastic loyalty and devotion of his followers he has far excelled the majority of his successors, has been equalled by few of them, and surpassed by none.

The winter of 1826 had of course to be spent, like the preceding one, at Fort Franklin, and early in the following year preparations were made for a return to England. Leaving instructions for Back, now promoted to the rank of commander, to proceed to York Factory with the remainder of the party as soon as the ice should break up, Franklin left the Fort accompanied by five men.

Fort Simpson was reached on March 8, Fort Resolution on the 26th, Fort Chipewyan on April 12, and the party were at Fort Cumberland by June 18. Thence Franklin proceeded to Montreal and New York, whence he took ship to England, where he arrived on September 26, 1827, after an absence of over two years and seven months.

CHAPTER VIII

THREE YEARS OF REPOSE

1827–1830

THIS second Arctic voyage, though naturally enough it impressed itself less upon the popular imagination than the first, was felt in official no less than in scientific circles to have established Franklin's claim to more distinguished honours than had previously been bestowed upon him. It had, indeed, been rich in solid additions to our knowledge of the earth's surface. Its geographical result, taking Franklin's and Richardson's exploration together, was the discovery and exact delineation of more than 1,200 miles of the coast of the American continent up to that time absolutely unknown. The geological, magnetic, meteorological, and other scientific observations made by the various members of the expedition, and given in full in the appendix to Franklin's 'Narrative,' were also of the highest value and interest, and were so recognised by the Admiralty and the learned societies. Franklin himself believed, and with justice, that he had accomplished yet more, and that his inability to effect a junction with Beechey was rather a failure in form than in fact. Writing to his sister-in-law, Mrs. Kay, from Fort Franklin in September 1826, he had said :—

I have reason to think that the Government will be perfectly satisfied with our proceedings ; indeed, a great deal has been accomplished, and I think there will no longer be a doubt remaining in the mind of any reasonable man as to the existence of a North-West Passage, especially if Captain Beechey gets round Icy Cape.

Nevertheless, some delay of a not quite explicable character was interposed to the official recognition of Franklin's service ; and France, indeed, by presenting him with the

Jane, Lady Franklin
from a drawing in National Portrait Gallery
made in 1815 by Mad.lle Romily at Geneva.

Walker & Boutall Ph Sc

gold medal of the Paris Geographical Society, may be said to have recognised them before his native country. It was not till the spring of 1829 that he was knighted, nor till the summer of that year that, in company with Sir Edward Parry, he received the justly prized honour of the degree of D.C.L. at the hands of the University of Oxford.

The previous year, however, was marked by an incident of even greater interest, his engagement to the lady who became his second wife. In this, as in the former case, we may find the first shadow of this coming event projected on the map of the Arctic regions, and trace the name of the future bride in the nomenclature of Franklin's latest discoveries. It seems evident that the attractions of Miss Jane Griffin must have caught Franklin's observation at some time between his first and the second expedition, and have led to his commemorating her in the bestowal of the name of Point Griffin on a promontory discovered by him on the American coast to the west of the Mackenzie River. Never, at any rate, was conquest easier to understand. The portrait of this lady, taken only some few years before the date of her first acquaintance with Franklin, shows a countenance not only beautiful of feature, but alive with a vivacity and animation which add indescribably to its charm. The sweetness of nature, the bright intelligence, and the playful humour which were united in this remarkable woman, and which rendered her conversation and still renders her correspondence delightful, look forth unmistakably from this presentment of her by a skilled artistic hand. A man of a far less impressionable nature might not have been proof against her combined fascinations of person, temperament, and mind. No wonder the susceptible Franklin found them impossible to resist.

Nor is it at all extraordinary that the attraction should have been mutual. In point of age and social position they were equally matched; and as the hero of memorable and daring adventures Franklin was surrounded by an air of romance which was likely to prove captivating to a woman of imagination. That winning personality, too, which so much endeared him to his followers could hardly fail to impress itself on Miss Griffin. It was in the main, no doubt, a charm of spirit and address, and of what we are accustomed to describe indefinitely but expressively as 'ways ;' yet it is clear that it was not unassociated at this time of his life with the advantages of a pleasing exterior. 'His features and expression,' says one of his relations describing him at about this period, 'were grave and mild, and very benignant ; his stature rather below the middle height ; his look very kind and his manner very quiet, as of one accustomed to command others.' In a word, he was emphatically a man well calculated to win that mixture of respect and admiration which in women of intelligence and force of character who have left mere girlhood behind is always more or less likely under favouring circumstances to beget a warmer sentiment.

Miss Griffin was the second daughter of Mr. John Griffin, of Bedford Place, a solicitor of high standing in his profession. Her elder sister, to whom she was sincerely attached, and who was the recipient of many of her most interesting letters, became the wife of Mr. Simpkinson, a successful barrister, subsequently Q.C. and Bencher of his Inn. It was no doubt a special recommendation to Franklin's affections that Miss Griffin had been a personal friend of his first wife and took an almost motherly interest in his orphan daughter.

The engagement was one of but a few months' duration, but they were months of busiest occupation for the ever-active Franklin. It seems probable that the stimulating results of the last expedition—incompletely successful yet so tantalisingly near complete success—may have quickened the maritime instincts of the Duke of Clarence, then Lord High Admiral. It is, at any rate, certain that before Franklin had been a year in England we find him drafting, 'by His Royal Highness's command,' a plan for the 'completion of the survey of the northern coast of America.' Two, and only two, portions of coast, he pointed out, and those of no very great extent as compared with the amount already delineated, remained to be explored—one to the eastward, lying between the Fury and Hecla Strait of Parry and Cape Turnagain (Franklin's own furthest of 1821) ; the other within Russian territory, to the

westward, being in fact the 160 miles of coast which divided
Point Beechey (Franklin's furthest westward from the Mackenzie River in 1826) and the discoveries of Captain Beechey
to the eastward of Behring Strait.

As regards the former and, as he says, the most interesting
of these portions, Franklin's idea was to send two boat de-
tachments across Melville Peninsula from a ship stationed
in Repulse Bay, one to proceed westward to Point Turnagain,
and the other northward to the Fury and Hecla Strait,
Cockburn Island, and Prince Regent's Inlet in the same
season. The first part of this scheme would no doubt have
been impracticable. At the time when Franklin conceived it
it was not known that the American coast westward of
Melville Peninsula took an immense trend to the north-
westward, forming the promontory now known as Boothia
Felix, which, until the discovery of Bellot Strait, was supposed to be continuous with North Somerset Land, and to
survey which, therefore, by a boat expedition would have meant
coasting round some thousand miles of shore before the
explorers could get back even to the mere latitude of Cape
Turnagain.

But the interest of the plan lies in its supplemental
proposal, at once bold and ingenious, to send another party
under an experienced guide through the interior of America
to the eastern side of the Great Slave Lake. Of the prospects
of discovery which such a party would find before them
Franklin writes as follows :—

The Northern Indians have described a river which, passing near
the east end of this lake, flows into the Polar Sea. Though we could
not learn the exact position of its mouth, yet we found sufficient testimony to warrant the conclusion that it lies to the eastward of Point
Turnagain. The land party, being provided with two boats or canoes,
might descend this stream and trace the coast from its mouth westward to Point Turnagain. If the distance to that point proves inconsiderable, the party should return and continue eastward along the
coast until it met the party from Repulse Bay, or to such time as
would allow of their reaching their winter quarters. If the junction
did take place, the land party might accompany the others to the
ship.

Franklin then proceeds to set out his companion scheme for the exploration of the westerly portion of the unexplored coast, and concludes :—

I have thus endeavoured to state my opinions regarding these surveys as briefly as the objects would admit, reserving the details relative to the kind of boats to be used and the general equipment of the ships until it is your Royal Highness's pleasure to honour me with your further commands on these points. They are the result of the closest reflection and most mature consideration of the subject, and I humbly offer them under the full impression that, if these attempts were directed to be made, they would lead to a successful termination. I may further add that if the boats did succeed in passing along the shore, as I have proposed, the question of a North-West Passage would be satisfactorily determined, as the whole of the coast between Behring Strait and the outlet into the Atlantic would then have been traced and the sea actually navigated.

Should these suggestions meet the approbation of your Royal Highness, and be in consequence ordered to be put into execution, I hope your Royal Highness will permit me to solicit the honour of an appointment to one of them.

Whether they met the Duke's private approbation or not, there is nothing to show, but their official rejection could hardly have been more speedy and summary than it was. Franklin's memorandum is dated June 17, and within twenty-four hours he received a reply from an Admiralty official, who had been 'commanded by His Royal Highness to acknowledge the receipt of your letter of yesterday's date, and to acquaint you that His Royal Highness does not intend to recommend any more Northern expeditions to His Majesty's Government.'

For punctuality, directness, and decision, this letter left nothing to be desired, and Franklin was now free to make arrangements for a visit to a foreign State, his interest in which had possibly been quickened by his recent invasion of its most remote dominions. Accordingly, and within less than a fortnight after receiving the above-quoted communication from the Admiralty, he applied to that department in the usual form for permission to proceed to Russia, and a six months' leave having been granted him, subject to the customary restrictions as to not 'entering into the service of any foreign

Power or State,' he left England for what proved to be a very interesting visit to the Russian capital. The curiosity as to his personality which his achievements as an explorer had aroused throughout Europe was as strong in Courts and palaces as elsewhere ; and when Franklin, through our representative in St. Petersburg, solicited the honour of a presentation to the Empress of Russia, she graciously replied that she would in his case depart from the usual etiquette attending introductions to Her Majesty, and invited him to dine at the palace on ' the 19th of September at two o'clock,' and bestowed a further mark of her favour by including in the invitation a Russian Admiral of Franklin's acquaintance, in order that some one might be at hand to explain to her every point relative to the English explorer's recent voyage. Of this dinner-party he gives a minute and interesting account in his diary. The Emperor was greatly interested in his voyages, and plied him with many questions on the subject. After dinner he was introduced to the Grand Duke, destined to a troubled reign and a tragic end as the Czar Alexander II. At his departure the young heir-apparent, then about ten years old, took leave of him in the following stately fashion :—

'I am happy, Captain Franklin, in having had the pleasure of seeing you, and should I ever visit England it will afford me much pleasure to renew my acquaintance with you.' Finding as we were leaving the room that we were going into the library, he requested the permission of his tutor to accompany us, which was granted. A map of North America was spread out, and the librarian begged of me to point out our route from New York, and the discoveries along the coast, and put many other questions, to which the Grand Duke listened very attentively. It was evident, too, that many of these were put for his instruction, as they related to other parts besides the line of our voyage. A French translation of my first narrative was then brought out, and I was told that it was from this work, which she had read twice, that the Empress gained her information.

Then follows a pleasant ' touch of nature,' author's and explorer's :—

I confess I felt a regret that she had only read this voyage compressed in a small octavo—which was without plates—and I immediately said I would have the honour of forwarding a quarto edition of that as well as of the last narrative. The Grand Duke then drew forth a set of plates belonging to the voyage of Captain Ross, and begged me to explain them, which I of course did, dwelling, by the way, on the modes used to break the ice so as to admit the ships, on the killing of bears, and other subjects to which the pictures had reference.

After another brief interview with the Empress, who 'begged that if I returned to Russia I would give her the opportunity of seeing me again,' the visitor finally took his leave. In reviewing the incidents of the visit, he recalls only one question put to him bearing upon politics, which was when the Empress-Mother asked him how the Emperor was liked in England. For an 'only question,' it was a pretty awkward one for an Englishman to answer in 1828. Franklin does not record his reply. Nor does he refer further to the Czar Nicholas, except to relate of him a rather striking little anecdote. The Emperor himself seemed, he remarked, to be fond of the Navy,'especially of ship-building, from his having ordered many new ships to be built.' On his being told that the wood was green, and that his ships could not be expected to last if hastily put together, he made the somewhat ominous reply, ' Never mind ; if they will hold together five years they will answer my present purpose.' Before that period had passed Franklin was to find himself placed as an English naval officer in a situation in which it is not improbable that this Imperial utterance, with all the sinister import which might attach to it, recurred to his mind.

Meanwhile the future Lady Franklin, as might be expected from a woman of her energetic disposition, had not been content to remain inactive in England, to the neglect of such an opportunity as now presented itself of enjoying a foreign tour in the society of her intended husband. It had been Franklin's wish that she should accompany him to Russia, but for reasons which will appear below she had declined to do so ; and the letter in which she refers to this matter is through-out so pleasantly illustrative both of her own winning qualities and of her admiring affection for Franklin, that the following passages may well be extracted from it. As much may be learned of a man's personality from the character and depth of the sentiment with which he was able to inspire such a woman as Miss Griffin as could perhaps be gathered from any words or acts of his own. The letter is superscribed ' At sea, July 26.' It appears to have been written very shortly after quitting England for the shores of the Baltic :—

My dear Captain Franklin,—I give you early proof of thinking of you because I begin to feel very uncomfortable, and in a short time I may perhaps be fit for nothing during the remainder of the voyage. I know also that the post goes out from Hamburg on Tuesday, and that after our arrival at the hotel on Monday evening we shall have no more than just time enough to look after carriages and horses to convey ourselves and our baggage to Lübeck, particularly as we shall be obliged to leave Hamburg early on Tuesday morning. . . . Our condition is somewhat better than it was yesterday evening, for the captain has so far kept his promise as to remove one tier of boxes from behind the sailcloth, and the others have been lashed together, so that another tier of berths has been developed, though the stern windows remain invisible and closed. I care as little about these minor inconveniences as most people, or rather can submit to them as well, if they are necessary and inevitable, but not otherwise ; and whenever I think I am imposed upon my spirit rises, and I struggle harder to resist than perhaps is quite consistent with that meek and resigned spirit which men endeavour to teach us is not only becoming but obligatory, and which we poor women endowed with acute sensibilities, though with less energy and much less power than men, often find to be our surest and safest way to happiness.

Do not be alarmed at these moralising reflections drawn from the consideration of the boxes and the cabin windows. You are of a much more easy disposition than myself, in spite of that energy and firmness of mind which, when the occasion calls for it, you can display as well or better than most men, and without which you never could have won my regard. It must be my province, therefore, when we travel together in France or elsewhere, or even on our lengthened journey through life, to combat those things which excite my more sensitive temper ; while it must and shall be yours, as my beloved and most honoured husband, to control even this disposition whenever you think it improperly excited, and to exert over me in all things that influence, or, if it must be [substituted for, 'if you please,' as perhaps going less imprudently far in the way of concession], that authority which it will be your privilege to use and my duty to yield to. But do I speak of *duty*? You are of too

L

manly, too generous, too affectionate a disposition to like the word, and God forbid I should ever be the wretched wife who obeyed her husband from a sense of duty alone without finding her greatest delight in yielding to his wishes in all things. Do not fear, therefore, that as long as my respect and esteem for you remain unimpaired, and consequently my affection uninjured, so long will my conjugal yoke sit most lightly and easily upon me, and that ring of which I now bear the emblem on the *wrong* finger will be (as I sometimes fancy it looks like) not the badge of slavery, but the cherished link of the purest affection.

Need I call you *my dear* (again?) after this? I think you can afford that I should spare myself the use of all such epithets : or perhaps you might have liked an epithet or two the more, and my serious observations the less. If you are a very prudent man, however, you will put this letter by and turn it to account at some future time when I am in a rebellious mood ; and upon this consideration I think you ought to feel infinitely obliged to me for furnishing you with so valuable a document. How soon shall I repent of it myself? I cannot pretend to say, but at present my silly heart reminds me that I have given you some little cause for reproach against me by opposing your original inclination to be of our party throughout the journey, and I want you to feel that never, *never* more, after our bonds are tied, shall I wish to be separated from you, or to differ from or to thwart your strongly expressed inclinations. In the present case, however, my objection to your first proposal arose from a strong sense of impropriety in the arrangement, as well as from a conviction that we should all be placed in a number of awkward and disagreeable situations during long and rough voyages and journeys which it would be extremely unpleasant to me to partake in and impossible to avoid. . . . You yielded to my feelings with a forbearance which obliged me, and I thought to compromise matters a little, and to avoid many other inconveniences, by suggesting that the marriage could take place abroad—a circumstance perfectly natural, since there was not time enough between the time when you first explained yourself to me and the moment fixed for our departure for it to take place beforehand. . . . When we gave up this last arrangement, nothing remained for us but to be absent from one another till our return in October (for I was ill-behaved enough not to wish you to join us at all during our journey), or to delay our setting off and be united first.

Having recalled the reasons why this last plan was unacceptable, she continues :—

Besides, I do not now feel the same alarm as to the journey. By your disinterested zeal and kindness we are furnished with every

facility that can insure a safe and prosperous expedition, and, therefore, when I regret that you cannot now accompany us, and look
forward with pleasure to our meeting at Petersburg, it is not
altogether or alone from the want I feel of your present and future
services as because I grieve that you are disappointed now, and
rejoice that you are looking forward to something that will please
you hereafter. . . . Come, then, to St. Petersburg, and in the meantime do not suppose it possible that I can feel otherwise than *painfully*
your absence. I should rejoice to see with you the same things for
the first time, to help or be helped by you in every little difficulty, to
become acquainted together with the same people, to be the objects of
the same hospitality and kindness, and to witness with pride and
sympathy that your claims to interest and esteem are acknowledged
in a foreign land as well as in your own. I shall be far from wishing
you to give up going to Moscow, even should it involve your later
return to England and the consequent derangement of all our plans.
It would be a matter of great concern, and even compunction to me,
should you have any after regrets on the subject.

In another letter, written 'At sea, in the Gulf of Finland,'
in which the formality of her former commencement, 'My
dear Captain Franklin,' is exchanged with a view to 'local
colour' for 'My dear Ivan,' while for herself she adopts
the Russianised signature of 'Jane Ivanovna,' Miss Griffin
amusingly hits off one of Franklin's most characteristic traits :—

The only ground of anxiety I have that you should not be in
time is founded upon the possibility of your not learning at Hamburg the mistake in your further calculations. This would have been
highly improbable, since, though no German scholar, you would have
found means enough there of asking questions ; and since my visit
with you to the Elstree Reservoir I cannot doubt of your always
being inquisitive enough. You recollect that it was remarked of you
there that they should not have supposed it possible that any reservoir,
be it as deep or as wide as it might, could have afforded room for
such varied and innumerable interrogations.

Both Franklin and his future wife had returned from their
Russian tour by the early autumn of 1828, and in the month
of October of this year he paid a visit worth recording to his
old commander, Captain Cumby, who had retired from the
Navy and was living the life of a country squire at Hughing-
ton, near Darlington. Franklin arrived there on the ever-
memorable 21st, which it was his host's annual custom to cele-

brate, and in a letter of the following day to Miss Griffin, then staying for her health at Malvern, he gives the following interesting account of the rejoicings. After describing how all the young people of the village had been paraded and feasted in honour of the day, he continues :—

On the church steeple, the flag under which the old Bellerophon fought was waving, with many of its shot-holes still unclosed, and you can well conceive the delight it afforded to me, especially as the preservation of it in the hour of battle was one of the particular parts of my duty as signal officer on the occasion. Twice it was lowered by the enemy's shot, but again speedily re-hoisted in triumph ; and lest the enemy might suppose from its being even for a moment lowered that it was done intentionally, another flag was spread along the rigging by an intrepid seaman under the most galling fire, which was continued throughout the action in that position. With the exception of Mrs. and Miss Cumby, the Captain's eldest son, and the vicar and his brother, the party consisted of naval men. The most interesting person was the Rev. Dr. Scott, Lord Nelson's chaplain, in whose arms, I believe, our noble commander-in-chief breathed his last sigh. He gave us a variety of anecdotes of Nelson, ante-cedently to this battle, relating to the chase which he made after the enemy to the West Indies.

Franklin's wedding with Miss Griffin took place on November 5, 1828, at Stanmore Church, ' very prettily situated in one of the most picturesque villages near London,' and, it is to be gathered from a letter to his sister, under auspices as happy in every respect as became a marriage of such obviously mutual affection and esteem. The bride and bride-groom, who were married from the house of the former's sister, left it in the evening for Ascot Place, ' the mansion of a considerable estate belonging to the Manor of Ascot and the property of one of Mr. Franklin's cousins.' Here they re-mained for a week, and then quitted England to finish the honeymoon in Paris.

Franklin's fame as a contributor to geographical science had preceded him, and he found himself the recipient of marked attentions from Parisian society, both learned and fashionable. He had taken with him a letter of introduction to the Duke of Orleans, two years later to become the King of the French, who responded to his presentation of it by inviting him to dinner on the following day. 'The scientific men,' he writes to his sister, 'of whom Baron Cuvier is the head, have been no less kind to me, and I have enjoyed a very high treat in becoming known to the *savants* of France with whose names I have long been familiar. I have dined with Baron Cuvier and been at some of the public scientific meetings ; I have also dined with our Ambassador (Lord Stuart), M. Delessert, and Baron Rothschild, the great Parisian banker, whose dinners, in point of style and luxury, almost equal Oriental splendour.' In these honours and festivities, however, Mrs. Franklin, he observes, was not able to participate, ' it not being the custom for ladies to be invited to dinner.' *Soirées* were the special form of entertainment provided for them by the fashion of the time. 'She has been invited to one at Madame Rothschild's on Saturday, and also to one at Madame Cuvier's, and I hope more invitations will follow for her, for, though there may not be anything particularly agreeable in these *soirées*, yet they are among the sights of Paris.' Three visits, he says, have been paid to the theatres, of which there were then fifteen in the French capital, and the irrepressible explorer declares his intention of ' making the round of them ' before his return home. One of these visits was almost of a State character, as the following letter, interesting on other grounds, will show :—

Neuilly : Friday morning, December 5, 1828.

Dear Sir,—Accept my best thanks for the highly valued present you are so good as to make to me of the narrative of your second journey to the shores of the Polar Sea. Its value is still much increased by being indebted for it to its celebrated author.

My sister offers her best thanks for the note, also for the lines so well adapted to the circumstance, and both will be placed in the collection of *Autographes* of her friend le Marquis de Dolomieu.

Permit me to enclose an order for the Duchess of Orleans's box this evening at the Opera, which we have thought might be agreeable to Mrs. Franklin and to yourself. The box is roomy, and may hold twelve persons.

I remain, with great regard, dear Sir,
Your affectionate
LOUIS-PHILIPPE D'ORLÉANS.

The note and autograph above referred to were sent in response to a request made to Franklin on the previous evening when he dined with the Duke at Neuilly. The conversation, as recorded in his diary, turned principally, like that of the Imperial dinner party at St. Petersburg, on the exploits and sufferings of the distinguished guest. One subject, however, of a less personal character appears to have come up in the course of the evening on which the interchange of views between guest and host is worth noting :—

'The Duke,' writes Franklin, 'likewise conversed with me respecting the Canadas, Nova Scotia, and the Columbia River, on all which subjects he had a perfect knowledge, gained, as he said, by reading. He thought, as I do, that it was probable the Canadas must eventually be independent, and if this concession were granted with grace, the change would be beneficial in point of trade to England. He thought, however, and justly, that it would be necessary for us to retain Nova Scotia, for the sake of Halifax as a naval position.'

There is almost as much virtue in an 'eventually' as in an 'if,' since no prediction which it qualifies can of course be pronounced erroneous at any earlier date than the morning of Doomsday. All one can say is that, though nearly seventy years have passed since this conversation, the 'event' referred to seems both to Englishmen and Canadians further off to-day than it did then.

Of the banquet at the great financier's Franklin writes with more mixed feelings :—

There I saw magnificence and luxury in its utmost extent. To describe the dinner or even to name the wines is quite beyond my power. The party, however, was but so-so ; and the only person I felt a delight in meeting was M. Hauseman, the Professor of Geology at Gottingen, who is on his way to England. Baron ——— was of the party, the editor of the ———, who is considered a charlatan by the *savans* of Paris, in which opinion I should coincide from his conversation with me, which certainly did not show a person of any great research or genius. There was a Count Molé (whom I had met before at Baron Delessert's) and two other barons, but they all appeared to be like their host, money-making men. The conversation at dinner, as usual at the French table, was carried on with the next person to you. I was seated on the left of Rothschild by invitation, but I considered myself more fortunate in having Professor Hauseman on my left, with whom I principally conversed. For a time, however, the Baron addressed himself to me, and having heard a little of the nature of our voyages, of which he was till then ignorant, he became much interested, and asked many questions. The cloven foot, however, was shown by his inquiry, ' What did the British Government give you for all that ? '

After dinner we had coffee as usual, and, several gentlemen having gathered round me, Madame la Baronne begged I might be invited to come near her. She then talked to me, but not with much knowledge of the nature of my voyage, though she had evidently read a part of the narrative. She was, however, desirous of gaining information, and this from a woman, though her lips owed their pretty tint to a coating of rouge, sufficiently encouraged me to say what I could for her amusement. Her remark that the Indians, from my description of their moral character, were well fitted for becoming Christians surprised me not a little when I looked on her decidedly Jewish visage.

A few days later Franklin was presented to Madame la Dauphine, the Duchesse d'Angoulême of 1815, who learned with interest that he had been second in command of the British ship of war which had been placed at her service to convey her back to France at the close of her long exile.

The beginning of the year 1829 saw the Franklins back again in London and established for the time at a house in Devonshire Street, Portland Place. In April of that year, as has been already above recorded, he made that transforming obeisance to the Sovereign from which he ' rose up Sir John,' and in the following July he stood side by side with his gallant colleague and competitor in Arctic enterprise, Captain Parry, in the Sheldonian Theatre at Oxford, to receive the not too lavishly bestowed distinction of Honorary D.C.L. The deeds of the two explorers formed the subject for the Newdigate Poem of that year, and were celebrated by the prizeman, Mr. T. L. Claughton, afterwards Bishop of Truro, in verse which, though not inferior in smoothness to the average prize poem, undoubtedly partakes more of the frigidity than of the grandeur of its Arctic theme.

The new knight and D.C.L. was the last man to rest content with his honours or to look forward to a life of repose

after his toils and sufferings. He was already longing again
for active employment, if not in the work of exploration
—and the curt letter from the Admiralty in the previous year
had extinguished that hope altogether—then in any public
service which would afford room for the exercise of his
organising abilities and his conscious faculty of command.
Nay, it is evident enough that mere prolonged physical
inaction was irksome to him, and that his body no less than
his mind craved imperatively for exertion. His indeed was
one of those not uncommon cases in which the outer belies the
inner man.   One of the royal ladies to whom he was
presented in Paris had with some *naïveté* expressed her
surprise at the plump and comfortable appearance of the
traveller who had undergone such incredible privations in the
course of his adventures. The paradox, it need hardly be
said, was only apparent ; but we can understand the Duchess's
difficulty in associating the portly naval officer before her
with the idea of a prolonged diet of deer-hide and *tripe de
roche*.   Incidentally it appears from the correspondence
between Sir John and Lady Franklin that his weight at this
period of his career was fifteen stone, which for a man of no
more than middle height and but forty-three years of age is
very considerably above the average. Nothing, however, is
more delusive than the common tendency to connect mere
bodily bulk with indolence and love of physical repose. The
obese Napoleon, gorged with empire, who struck down
Prussia at Jena and Austria at Austerlitz, was a man of the
same untiring energy of body as the lean and hungry soldier
of the first Italian campaign. And there is no reason to
doubt that not only at this period of his life, but for a good
many years afterwards, Franklin's physical activity and his
power of sustaining fatigue and privation were, his bulk notwithstanding, unimpaired.

Nevertheless, he was not disposed to accept any form of
active employment which might be offered to him by any
body of employers, no matter whom. On the contrary, he
felt, and rightly felt, that as a naval officer some fitting
occupation should be found for him in the service not

merely of the country but of the Crown. Thus he records in the early summer of 1829 that he had just declined a 'very tempting and flattering offer from the Australian Company to manage their concerns in New South Wales.' The re-muneration proposed, 2,000*l.* a year, was for those days ample, and the work attached to the office must have had many attractions for him. But his resolve not to separate himself from the service to which he had devoted himself for now nearly thirty years was unalterably fixed. He looked to the Admiralty or to some other department of the State to find him employment, and after another year and a half of patient, or more probably perhaps of impatient, waiting he obtained it.

In the meantime, however, he never doubted the wisdom of refusing all solicitations to engage himself to any private body of employers. ' I felt,' he writes to his wife concerning this Australian offer, ' that such an occupation would with-draw me from my profession for some years to come, and might materially injure my future prospects in the service. Besides, having now been so many years employed in land service, I am particularly anxious to avail myself of the first opportunity of getting into active naval employment.' The appointment declined by Franklin was afterwards offered to and, at the urgent instance of many of his friends, accepted by Sir Edward Parry.

Franklin was not now to be exposed to any more temptations of this kind to quit the regular line of the service. Events in Europe during the closing years of this decade had already given some unexpected and indeed, so far as the British Government were concerned, undesired employment to the British Navy ; and though it was not Franklin's fortune to be among the officers engaged in the singular battle of Navarino—that affair of which a noble admiral of the period humorously remarked that ' it was a capital fight, only we knocked down the wrong man '—the international crisis out of which it had arisen created not long afterwards a neces-sity for increased activity among His Majesty's ships in the Mediterranean. The nascent kingdom of Greece, it was generally admitted in European Courts and Cabinets, required watching by the Powers. It was also thought in certain quarters (though this was not so generally admitted) that some, or at any rate one, of the Powers required watching by the others. By the middle of the year 1830, one, if not both, of these causes for increased activity in the Mediterranean was thought to have become urgent; and in 'prospecting' round for experienced and highly capable officers to employ in a service which was certain to be important, and might in conceivable circumstances become extremely difficult, the eye of the Admiralty fell upon Sir John Franklin. His application for employment lay before them with the high claims attached to it, and, since there is no evidence in his correspondence to show that he recalled their attention to it, they may actually have remembered him of themselves.

Be that as it may, he was selected for a command. On August 23 he received the long-looked-for and eagerly welcomed official notice to the effect that 'My Lords Commissioners of the Admiralty having appointed you Captain of His Majesty's ship the Rainbow, at Portsmouth, it is their Lordships' direction that you or your agent repair immediately to this office, and that you report to me the day on which you shall have joined the ship.'

The prospect of new employment was hardly more welcome to Franklin himself than to his ambitious and energetic wife. Her correspondence of this period shows signs that she was almost as much bitten with the longing for Arctic exploration as he. Parry, too, she reminds him, was meditating new voyages of discovery, with Lady Parry's concurrence and even encouragement. The idea was never to be realised, and the magnificent exploit of 1827 was Parry's last attack upon the Pole. There, in lat. 82° 45', was, in Othello's words, 'his butt, and very sea-mark of his utmost sail.' And not a bad one either, considering that it remained the seamark of the whole human race for nearly fifty years. But if there were to be no more Arctic expeditions for the present, it was at least something that Franklin should have got afloat once more. 'I look back,' wrote Lady Franklin to him, 'with almost remorse on our career of vanity, trifling, and idleness'—that is to say, from November of 1828 to August of 1830, a year and nine months, and part of it a honeymoon. To less restless spirits it does not seem so very shocking.

CHAPTER IX

A MEDITERRANEAN COMMAND

1830-1833

THE mission on which Franklin was now despatched presents so striking a contrast to any of his previous employments as a naval officer that it is desirable to suspend the progress of this narrative for a while in order to take a brief survey of the task before him and to point out its singularly difficult conditions. And, as a preliminary step to this process, it will be necessary to recall as concisely as may be the incidents of a now forgotten chapter of European history.

Greece, in the year 1830, had just succeeded, by the aid of the two Western Powers acting in formal concert but not in wholly confidential alliance with Russia, in throwing off the yoke of the Sultan and establishing its independence. Navarino, that 'untoward event,' as the victory was so frankly described by one of the victors, had been fought and won— or rather blundered into and out of—two years before. The Porte had formally consented a few months before to the erection of Greece into an independent kingdom ; and nothing remained but for the Powers to choose an eligible European prince for the new throne, to secure his acceptance of the honour, and to induct him into his sovereignty. But the second of these three steps was found to present unexpected difficulties. The first choice, or meditated choice, of the kingmakers was Prince John of Saxony, but the crown was declined by him with thanks. Leopold of Coburg, the next to be selected, showed a disposition to accept the offer, and the negotiations for the formal completion of the arrangement had, indeed, made some progress when the Prince, partly through disapproval of some of the conditions which were to be imposed upon him, and partly influenced, it is supposed, by the change in his prospects consequent on the death of George IV.—an event which brought his sister, the Duchess of Kent, within one remove of the Regency which would fall to her as the mother of her present Majesty, then a child of eleven—revoked his provisional assent, and the Greek crown once more went a-begging. Meanwhile the somewhat rotten reins of such government as Greece possessed remained in the hands of Capo d'Istria, an active and astute intriguer, of Greek origin indeed, but who had spent fifty years of his previous life as a minister of the Czar of Russia, a period during which he devoted himself incessantly, and in the end successfully, to the work of diplomatically undermining the authority of the Porte over its Hellenic subjects. Upon the definitive overthrow of Turkish rule he had contrived to get possession of the machinery of executive control in the newly liberated country, and to obtain an informal recognition of his *de facto* presidency.

Capo d'Istria possessed considerable ability, which, no doubt, seemed greater by comparison with the noisy and frequently ferocious mediocrities whom the Revolution had raised up around him. He appears to have been a man of sincere patriotism, and of disinterested if somewhat narrow ideals. But he overrated, says a well-known historian of these events, alike ' the influence of orthodoxy in the Ottoman Empire and the power of Russia in the international system of Europe,' an error natural in a politician whose experience of mankind had been acquired either in the confined and corrupt society of Corfu, or in the artificial atmosphere of Russian diplomacy. Other drawbacks he had which could not but detract in some measure from his efficiency as an administrator. Italian was his mother tongue, and, though he could speak Greek fluently enough, he was unable to write it, and both in conversation and in despatches he was in the habit of using French. 'For a statesman, he was far too loquacious. He allowed everybody who approached him to perceive that on many great political questions of importance to Greece his ideas were vague and unsettled. At times he spoke as a warm panegyrist of Russian absolutism, and at others as an enthusiastic admirer of American democracy.'

The Western Powers, it may be imagined, were more impressed by the panegyrics than by the admiration. The circumstances of his election were such as naturally induced the English Government to regard him as the nominee of Russia, and his own policy and declared opinions encouraged the belief that he was no friend to this country. Fifteen years earlier, at the European settlement which followed upon the victory of Waterloo, he had exerted himself, and had been allowed to employ all the influence of Russia, to re-establish that Ionian Republic which had been created in 1803, and at the downfall of which in 1807, by the annexation of the islands to the French Empire, he had transferred his services to the Czar. He never forgave the Government of Great Britain for having insisted on retaining possession of the Ionian group, and on holding complete control over their government as a check on Russian intrigues among the Orthodox population of the Ottoman Empire. And the view taken by the English Ministers of his sympathies and tendencies was confirmed by the part which he was believed to have played in the negotiations which led to Prince Leopold's withdrawal. It was in May 1830 that this event took place, and when Franklin received his appointment to the Mediterranean service four months later the relations between the British Cabinet and the Greek President were those of mutual distrust.

The situation in Greece, however, was destined to be yet more gravely complicated by a tragic incident which took place towards the close of the following year. On October 9, 1831, Capo d'Istria was assassinated by the brothers Mavro-michales, two political opponents with whom, it was alleged, he had treacherously and oppressively dealt; and with his death Greece entered on a period of almost absolute anarchy. A few hours after his murder a governing commission, consisting of three members—Agostino Capo d'Istria, brother of the murdered President, and two other prominent politicians, Kolokotrone and Koletti—was appointed to exercise the executive power until the meeting of the National Assembly. But the so-called Constitutional party, who had opposed the autocratic rule of the late President, were little inclined to submit to the improvised junta who proposed to carry on his policy. They prepared to resist it not only in the Assembly, but, in case they should be defeated there, in the field. The Capodistrians were strong in the Morea, in which—at Argos—the Assembly met, and their party succeeded in obtaining a considerable majority at the elections. But they were supposed to have derived much additional strength from the open support given them by the Russian Admiral Ricord ; and that they themselves were not deficient in the faculty of self-help is evident from the fact that in certain places where they were in a minority they succeeded in securing the return of their candidates by military force. The irregularity of these elections did not, of course, invalidate them, for the simple reason that the Capodistrians possessed a majority in the Assembly, and had no superstitious scruples about using it. Both parties circulated the most odious calumnies against their opponents, the Capodistrians accusing the French and English of being privy to the murder of the President, and the Constitutionalists alleging that the murdered man had himself bribed ' six traitors ' to murder the leader of the Opposition.

The art of ' working ' a popular assembly in such a way as to give a constitutional and even democratic air to the manœuvres of the men who have ' got hold of the machine ' was less thoroughly comprehended in those days than it is in these. If the Capodistrians understood packing a House, they evidently did not understand ' running ' it after it was packed. Probably there was not enough ready money for the work, and the eligible places were all filled. Anyhow, they found it impossible to manage the minority. Loud complaints were made that the elections had been illegally controlled by military force, and that a force exerted in favour of Russian domination. A large body of members accordingly protested against the competency of the Assembly to proceed to business, and were for their pains driven from Argos by a body of troops which the Provisional Government, fearlessly braving the calumnies of their opponents, had placed under the command of a Russian officer. The seceders repaired to Megara, formed themselves into a National Assembly, and declared themselves to be the only legal representatives of the Greek nation.

This, of course, made two bodies of 'only legal representatives,' each of them naturally animated with deadly hostility to the other. Geographically speaking, they were very unequally matched, the Morea alone adhering in general to the Provisional Government, while the population of all the rest of the mainland and of the Archipelago supported the Assembly of Megara. Nor were the insurgents long in demonstrating their superiority in physical force. Marching into the Morea, they easily overthrew the feeble rule of the younger Capo d'Istria and his two colleagues, and proceeded to establish a commission of seven members, to discharge the nominal functions of an executive till the Great Powers should have settled the destinies of the independent State which they had created.

And nominal indeed those functions were. They seem, in fact, to have consisted for some time to come in issuing admirably rhetorical manifestoes and proclamations from Napoli di Romania (the ancient Nauplia, at the head of the Argolic Gulf), which were read, doubtless with much interest, on the walls of that city, but received not the slightest attention outside them. The party of revolution, like other revolutionary parties before and since their time, possessed precisely sufficient strength to overthrow the government against which they rose, but were unfortunately left without a margin of power wherewith to establish any really authoritative government of their own. Conscious of this deficiency, they devoted the remainder of their energies to the work of farming out the revenues among their friends and favourites at half their value; the result of which financial operation was to leave an army of 8,000 men without any pay or other 'visible means of subsistence' than that of preying upon their fellow-countrymen—an industry to which they immediately adapted themselves with all the versatility of their race.

The situation, as it appeared to Mr. Finlay, an historian in thorough sympathy with the cause of Greek independence is thus described :—

The Roumeliots, after overthrowing Agostino's government, daily lost ground. The Commission of Seven was either unable or unwilling to reward their services. The soldiers soon determined to reward themselves. They treated the election of the Commission as a temporary compromise, not as a definitive treaty of peace, and they marched into different districts in the Morea to take possession of the national revenues as a security for their pay and rations. Wherever they established themselves, they lived at free quarters in the houses of the inhabitants, or were authorised to collect arrears due from preceding farmers. These proceedings gave rise to intolerable exactions. The chieftains often paid their followers by allowing them to extort a number of rations from the peasantry, and defrauded them of their pay. Some drew pay and rations for a hundred men without having twenty under arms. Numbers of soldiers were disbanded, and roved backwards and forwards, plundering the villages and devouring the sheep and oxen of the peasants. . . . Eight thousand Roumeliots were at this time living at free quarters in the Morea, and it was said that they levied daily from the population to the extent of upwards of 20,000 rations.

The financial administration [of the Commission] was not calculated to moderate the rapacity of the troops. They raised money by private bargains for the sale of the tenths, and the proceeds of these anticipated and frequently illegal rates were employed to reward personal partisans, and not to discharge the just debts due to the soldiers for arrears of pay. A small sum judiciously expended would have sent many of the Roumeliot troops to their native mountains, whither, as peace was now restored, they would have willingly returned had they been able to procure the means of cultivating their property. The troops were neglected, while favoured chieftains were allowed to become farmers of taxes.

These proceedings were naturally found very oppressive by the inhabitants of the country: multitudes fled for security to the Ionian Islands, while the peasantry sought protection against the military marauders by abandoning the village for the fortress, and sometimes even the field for the cave.

M

The representatives of Great Britain, France, and Russia, the three Powers to whom Greece owed its existence, found it much harder to protect than it had been to create their offspring. They stood helpless before this scene of anarchy, hesitating to act, and, when at last forced into action, taking it without effect. France had already landed troops in the Morea, and the Allies therefore possessed, nominally at any rate, the power to intervene by force of arms for the pacification of the distracted country, but their intervention, when it did take place, only made confusion worse confounded. Before the Commission had held power for a month they felt their position so insecure that they found it necessary to invite the French troops to occupy Nauplia and Patras as the only means of assuring their personal safety and the prolongation of their power. The former measure was successfully accomplished; but before the French arrived at Patras the place had been seized by the Capodistrians.

Nothing could have been simpler than the mode of its capture. The Greek troops by which it was garrisoned were well affected to the Commission, as they had previously been to the Capodistrians, and as, to do them justice, they would have been to any political party or person who would guarantee them their pay. But this the Commission had most unwisely allowed to fall into arrear; it was even rumoured that they were to be disbanded; and 'while they were brooding over this report' they heard that French troops had been invited to garrison Patras, a piece of intelligence which seemed to render their prospect of payment more uncertain than ever. In the mood produced by it, it was not difficult to convince them that patriotism forbade the surrender of an important place of arms to the foreigner. The Commission had accused the Capodistrians of selling Greece to the Russians; the Capodistrians now retorted by accusing the Commission of selling Nauplia and Patras to the French. Upon this hint the Greek garrison mutinied, and deposed their commander, who refused to sign a manifesto justifying the revolt; and a patriot of the name of Zavellas, who had fought with bravery against the Turks in the war of liberation, but whose political position at this moment is more than usually hard to define, was invited by them to assume the chief command at Patras. Zavellas, who was at the head of 500 irregulars, and who would not have been a Greek if he had declined an opportunity of making himself master of the persons and property of the inhabitants of a flourishing seaport, accepted the offer with alacrity, and, hastening to Patras, entered it before the arrival of the French. When they made their appearance he transmitted to their commanding officer a formal protest against the authority of the governing Commission, and refused to obey the order to admit the French into the fortress. The French commander, considering that, as the Allies had despatched him to Patras for the purpose of maintaining order, it would hardly be consistent with his mission to come to blows with any party who should have succeeded in obtaining the undisputed mastery of the place, withdrew his troops, leaving Zavellas in peaceable possession.

Having thus brought down to the summer of 1832 the turbulent history of this distracted little kingdom, we may once more return to Franklin. It has been necessary to enter with some minuteness into the course of local politics at Patras in order that the extremely delicate part which he had to play in connection with that port, its trade, and its inhabitants, may be rendered intelligible. His duties in the Mediterranean, however, had commenced more than eighteen months before the latest of the events just recorded. It was on August 30, 1830, that he was appointed to the command of the 26-gun frigate Rainbow, and on November 11 of the same year that she put to sea.

A backward glance at the chronology of the events concisely summarised in the foregoing pages may be necessary in order to recall the situation when Franklin's mission commenced. Prince Leopold's resignation of the sovereignty was now an incident some three months old ; and the political disquietude of the new kingdom had approached just so much the nearer to actual anarchy, while the relations of the two Western Powers with their Eastern ally were just so much the further from those of mutual confidence. President Capo d'Istria, it seemed, was more and more openly showing a hand, which was the hand of Russia ; and indeed, before Franklin had been many months in the Mediterranean, Russia herself had, by the conduct of her naval officers, given the strongest colour to the suspicion that she was playing a game of her own. In the summer of 1831, the municipality of the island of Hydra, which had revolted against the President, and which he was meditating how to reduce to submission by naval operations, suddenly turned the tables on him by seizing the greater part of the Greek fleet, then lying disarmed in the port of Poros.

Upon this, Capo d'Istria appealed to the Russian Admiral Ricord, then at Nauplia with his squadron, the French and English commanders being absent, to come to his assistance, an appeal to which the Admiral responded by sailing straightway to Poros and summoning the insurgents to surrender the ships and the arsenal to the Greek Government. The demand was refused, but before any action was taken on either side the French and English naval commanders chanced to put into the port on their way back to Nauplia, and on learning the condition of affairs agreed with Ricord and Miaulis, the insurgent leader, that the *status quo* should be maintained until they had had time to go to Nauplia and procure instructions from the diplomatic representatives of the Allies. This, however, was much as though two cats should go off to consult the wishes of the dairyman, leaving a third cat bound by an honourable undertaking to maintain a *status quo* with the cream bowl. The arrangement had its natural result. Before the French and English commanders could execute their mission Admiral Ricord prepared to attack the port, a movement to which the insurgents responded by blowing up the finest of the ships in their possession to prevent their capture. Meanwhile, the troops of Capo d'Istria, who were besieging the fort from the land side, rushed into the town and sacked it for twenty-four hours under the eyes and guns of Admiral Ricord and his squadron.

Franklin himself was at a considerable distance from the scene of these operations ; for the Rainbow during the year 1831 was stationed mainly at Corfu. But the English naval commander with whom the Russian Admiral had kept such peculiarly Punic faith was Captain (afterwards Sir Edmund) Lyons, an intimate friend and frequent correspondent of Franklin's ; and this circumstance may have deepened the resentment and distrust of Russia with which the affair of Poros generally inspired English naval officers in the Mediterranean. Later on it will be seen that the captain of the Rainbow was himself to have a taste of his friend's experience, and to find himself called upon to exert all his tact and vigilance for the defeat of Russian intrigue.

For the present, however, and for some time to come, the duties imposed upon him were light enough. His first destination in the Mediterranean was Malta, from which station he was at the end of January ordered to Nauplia, and while here he had an opportunity of paying a visit to Athens. This visit produced upon him, as it has upon so many other men before and since, a disenchanting effect. He had been despatched with his vessel to the Greek capital as the bearer of letters to Ismail Bey, the Turkish Commissioner for the affairs of Greece, and after executing his mission he seems to have 'done' the city and its antiquities with as much thoroughness as an unofficial tourist. Athens he found 'a mass of ruins, not having more than three houses habitable' —a result of the different bombardments which it had undergone at the hands of both Turks and Greeks. Nor did he omit to record the injuries which it had suffered at the hands of that third nationality whose name Macaulay united in a famous passage with those of the other two. 'It must be confessed,' he writes to Lady Franklin, 'that the pleasure we feel on looking at this famous edifice (the Parthenon) is mingled with a kind of indignation at the wanton rapacity of the Elgins and other mutilators of the sacred Temple.'

But the disillusionising experience of his visit to the Greek capital had begun earlier still, as regards the Greek people and their political leaders. The prepossession in their favour which nearly all Englishmen of that date entertained had been seriously shaken before he left Nauplia for Athens :—

I was formerly a Philhellene, a warm admirer of their cause, but I must confess the short residence I have had at the seat of government has somewhat cooled my ardour, since I have found that the leading Greeks, instead of uniting and doing their utmost to restore the agricultural and other useful occupations of the country, seem to be squabbling for power and places of trust, and all of them, either statesmen or would-be statesmen, soldiers or would-be soldiers, strolling about the streets of Naples, apparently idle, or occupied only by dress and parade.

His impression, too, of the very foremost of these statesmen, the President himself, was no less unfavourable, though on different grounds. After mentioning the civilities he had received from the foreign Ministers and the 'leading persons here' in general, he adds :—

Capo d'Istria, however, is to be excepted, for he neither deigned to return my call nor to take any notice of me ; but I do not feel this, as he is apt to treat others in the same way, and is an excessively unpopular man, and, it is said, most thoroughly dislikes the English, whom he considers as the main bar to the accomplishment of his arbitrary and selfish wishes. I have been told that his measures have been generally disapproved of by the Greeks, as it is likely they would be, on account of his having removed the most influential of the Greeks (and especially those who were the first promoters of the Revolution) from all places of trust and power, and put in minions and creatures of his own. The country of Maina is in insurrection against him.

It was, indeed, by the hand of a Mainote that, a few months after these words were written, Capo d'Istria was to fall. Franklin, however, had left Nauplia some time before the assassination took place. He was ordered back to Malta about the middle of March 1831, whence, after a stay of some six weeks, he was despatched to Corfu, where he remained for nearly a year. It was not till the Governing Commission which had succeeded in wresting the reins of government from the feeble hands of the younger Capo d'Istria and his colleagues had proved themselves incapable of maintaining order, and the whole of liberated Greece was being desolated by anarchy, that the services of the Rainbow were called into active requisition. But in the spring of 1832, as has been related in the summarised narrative of events with which this chapter opens, matters were at their worst. ' Liberated Greece was at that moment anything but free. The Turks had been expelled from the country, but the people were groaning under worse oppressors and a heavier yoke. The whole substance of the land was devoured by hosts of soldiers, sailors, captains, generals, policemen, Government officials, secretaries, and political adventurers, all living idly at the public expense, while the agricultural population was dying of famine.' It was at the crisis of this miserable state of things that the Rainbow was ordered, for the protection of life and property, to the port of Patras, shortly afterwards to become the scene of the events above recorded, and that Franklin was to have the opportunity of showing those high diplomatic qualities of firmness and tact which won for him the warm commendation of his official superiors. Meanwhile, however, he remained at his station off Corfu exchanging letters with Lady Franklin, not yet started on those Mediterranean travels of which she reported her experiences and impressions to her husband and sometimes to her sister in that picturesque and animated style which lends such unfailing charm to her correspondence. The state of her health at that time was causing some concern, and she was staying at Brighton for its benefit. But she was full of eagerness to be with her husband at the earliest moment, and their letters to each other often reveal an amusing game of cross purposes ; Lady Franklin suggesting every expedient possible or imaginable for rejoining him, and the less impulsive Franklin gravely pointing out the impediments, professional and other, to her various plans. During the early months of 1831 she had other subjects to occupy her mind.

The new King had just been paying a visit to Brighton, attended by the usual gaieties at the Pavilion :—

People here are living with their eyes staring, and their mouths gaping towards Royalty. There has been a party at the Palace of eight or nine hundred people, and Miss Langton was at it. The

King talked to her a good deal, and she mentioned your name. ' I know him,' said the King ; ' he is a very amiable man, but he is more than that, a man of great ability and an excellent sailor.', Miss Langton said, ' Lady Franklin is here.' ' Show her to me. Let me speak to her. Bring her up to me.' On Miss Langton's explaining, he said he was sorry I was not there, and must come next time. ' Give her my commands that she come to the children's ball, and bring her little girl with her.' So Ella and I are going, thus flatteringly· invited, and my only discomfort is that I have no one to go with.

On February 18, in reply to a letter from Franklin, who had been giving her some account of Maltese society, she writes :—

You describe everybody alike, as being so amiable and agreeable, that I cannot tell one from the other, and by that means do not care for any of them. Suppose you try your hand next time on some spirited sketches of character and portrait-painting. I know you *can*, if you will. As it is, they all go in a bag together, and tumble out all alike. I am much pleased, however, with all you say about Dr. C., and am willing to give him credit for every merit you endow him with. Pray give him, therefore, my special remembrance. I never disliked him, nor did I ever think so meanly of him as you imagine, and in the midst even of his lackadaisical manner there was a degree of brightness and drollery in his eyes which belied it. . . . I read your long letter to my aunt, and I think it amused her to think what a good husband I had got. How could she be so foolish? I had half a mind to tell her that you dearly loved writing long letters, and that you wrote long letters and the same things to every· body ; but I stopped myself, for fear that she should more than half believe me. Indeed, though, my dear, you are a very wonderful man, for you *can* write about the same things to everybody, with a patience which surprises me. What an irritable, impatient creature am I in comparison ! For I could not write about the same thing twice over, even to you, and consequently nothing is so terrible to me as to have the news of a marriage or anything else which requires detail to spread about among expectant relations and friends. I should like to have a copying machine, and dash off the sheets by the dozen. . . . Captain Rideout told me he had not been near the Admiralty lately. He considered it perfectly useless. They were doing and undoing, and there was nothing but fluctuation and con· fusion. I think you are a happy man to be where you are. I hope you will have an opportunity of confirming Sir Pulteney Malcolm's good opinion of you, and that you will be in the good graces of the new Admiral, Hotham. How is he related to the nice deaf old man who was as much pleased or obliged by your gentlemanly and kind refusal, as he would have been by some ruder captain's consent? Oh, what a coaxing, smooth-tongued rogue you are! I have got his letter by me, and was looking at it the other day. Who would think, my dear, that you had lived among the Polar bears?

But now at last the period of 'active' service in something more than the nominal and technical sense arrived for Franklin. The critical spring of 1832 had come; the Allied Powers, their diplomacy quickened by the spectacle of the ever-deepening demoralisation of the Greek people, had agreed on the nomination of Prince Otho of Bavaria to the newly created throne, and, in response to the representations addressed to them from Greece itself, were preparing to exert themselves in real earnest for the pacification of the country. In the last days of March or the first of April Franklin was ordered from Corfu to Patras, and his first despatch from that port to the naval Commander-in-Chief in the Mediterranean shows the official instructions he had received and the steps which he had already taken in execution of them. The Roumeliot insurgents were meditating, or believed to be meditating, an attempt to cross the Gulf from Lepanto, with a view to the seizure of either Drepano or Vostitza, and the Governor of Patras had appealed to the Allied Powers to use their naval forces for the protection of the Morean coast. No doubt there was all the vagueness which usually prevails in such cases as to the precise scope either of the request or of the assent to it, or possibly of both. There was, at any rate, all the opening which in such cases frequently presents itself for the suggestion by one of the Allies of a more 'active' policy than was agreeable to the others.

Franklin's first step on his arrival off Patras was to compare notes of instructions with his French and Russian colleagues, and he of course found, on conferring with them, that, so far as words went, 'their unanimity was wonderful.' They were all three agreed, that is to say, that they were to confine themselves to the exertion of 'moral influence;' and Franklin was 'happy to find' that, on the question of the particular mode in which this influence was to be exerted, the sentiments of the French commander, Captain Fournier, were in entire accord with his own. Captain Leroff, however, of the Russian brig, 'appeared from his questions and observations' to place a somewhat different construction on these two important words. This officer 'intimated the wish if not the intention to detain every boat that might be found carrying provisions or other supplies without having papers signed by the proper Greek authorities;' and he further thought that if the Roumeliots should attempt to cross the gulf, the 'moral influence' to be brought to bear upon them should take the form of 'opposing their passage by force.' Captains Franklin and Fournier, however, did not feel themselves called upon in their view of their duties to take even the former and milder step, while, as to the latter, 'we at once declared that it would be contrary to our instructions.'

No urgent necessity for taking 'concerted' action on this variously construed mandate was, for the present, to arise. A question of more immediate concern to Franklin as a British naval officer presented itself instead. On April 12 a complaint was addressed to Mr. Crowe, our Consul at Patras, and by him transmitted to Franklin, to the effect that a demand for 'an arbitrary and illegal contribution had been made on several Ionian merchants,' subjects, of course, at that time of the British Crown, by the Governor of Patras, and that, on their refusal to pay, a party of soldiers had been quartered on their houses, with orders to seize upon their property for the maintenance of the troops until the money was paid. One of them having goods to land from a vessel, the duty on which nearly amounted to the sum demanded, made the payment required. Another persisted in his refusal, with the result that the fifteen soldiers quartered upon him turned his wife and family out of their rooms, seized upon some butter belonging to him and sold it, demanded wine, and 'abused the family with the most insulting language.' A third recalcitrant had ten soldiers in his house, who 'took his cloak and two guns and put them in pledge for wine and victuals,' and two others were similarly treated.

On being informed of these high-handed proceedings,

Franklin immediately waited upon the British Consul and found him in the act of writing to protest against them. Having waited the return of the bearer of this letter, and finding that no immediate answer was to be given to it, Franklin called upon the Governor, ' to demand an explanation of these extraordinary proceedings, and to insist that either the soldiers should be withdrawn or the parties complaining should be permitted to embark their goods and families and place themselves under my protection if they chose to do so.' The account of the interview which followed is given in Franklin's despatch book, with remonstrance and reply in parallel columns, and the dramatic contrast which it presents between dogged British pertinacity and inexhaustible Levantine shiftiness is decidedly amusing :—

Sir John Franklin states that he called officially on the Governor to say that he had received an official communication from H.M. Consul, informing him that an arbitrary and illegal contribution had been levied on some Ionian merchants, and that, upon their refusing to comply with it, military force had been used to compel them ;

That he felt it his duty to demand that the soldiers be immediately removed from the Ionians' houses, and that, if the merchants chose, they should be permitted to embark their families and effects, and place them under his protection, and that time should be allowed to communicate with H.M. Resident and Admiral at Nauplia on the subject.

The Governor explained that he had received a communication from H.M. Consul on the subject, to which he would reply ;

That he could not allow the embarkation of the effects or remove the soldiers until the Ionians paid the sums which had been assigned to them in the contribution.

Sir John Franklin hoped that the Governor was prepared for the responsibility he would incur from the measures of force which it might be necessary to resort to in consequence of force having been used ;

That the Residents and Admirals of the Allied Powers had recommended a system of conciliation, and every effort to maintain tranquillity, that he regretted extremely such measures on the part of the Government here, which had quite a contrary tendency, and that it pained him to reflect on what might be the result of the measures he might be compelled to adopt in consequence of the refusal of the Governor.

He again requested that the soldiers might be removed until communication could be had with the Resident and Admiral on the subject.

The Governor stated that this contribution was not levied on the Ionians alone, that it was on the merchants generally, and that they were in all forty individuals, among whom were only seven Ionians, and that he would not remove the soldiers until the money was paid.

This, of course, amounted in substance to an admission that the levy was compulsory, and to a contention that the Ionians were liable to it in common with the Greeks of the new kingdom.

Sir John Franklin said that this town was not in presence of an enemy, or menaced by an enemy, to warrant any such contribution, and that it was extremely ungracious to act in such a manner towards the subjects of one of the Allied Powers who had sent vessels to this place for its special protection and the maintenance of tranquillity, and who had also abstained from taking any part in the disputes between Greek and Greek.

He again begged the Governor to reflect on the responsibility he would incur by persisting in the refusal to remove the soldiers or to permit the embarkation of the Ionians, with their families and effects

The Governor said that this was not a contribution, but a voluntary loan agreed upon at a public meeting, that eight Ionians had paid and only two had refused, and that he would not remove the soldiers until the money was paid.

Here it will be observed that the tax has now become a 'benevolence,' and that, though 'only seven Ionians' were subject to it, eight have paid it, leaving over a mere insignificant fraction of 'two' who refused to pay. The English of this very 'Greek' statement was, as appeared from the result of later official inquiries, that the demand had been in fact made upon five Ionians, of whom two had paid and three had refused.

Sir John Franklin said that if such a measure had been intended to be a general one it should have been announced by proclamation, and communication made to H.M. Consul of the same.

The Governor replied that he did not think it his duty to have made such communication, as the measure had been agreed upon at a meeting of the Greek and Ionian merchants, who voluntarily offered to lend the Government the money, and that only two had now refused what they had previously consented to.

Here, again, the Governor's Greek is thus 'Englished' in the Vice-Consul's subsequent report: 'A meeting at the Municipality was held of the merchants of this town yesterday, April 11, and one or two Ionian merchants were summoned to attend, but none complied.'

Sir John Franklin said that if the Governor did not feel it his duty to make the communication generally known, common courtesy required that he should do so to the representatives of the Powers who had taken so great an interest in the tranquillity and welfare of Greece.

He again required the removal of the soldiers, or permission for the embarkation of the families and effects of the Ionians. Sir John Franklin hoped it was not true that the soldiers had taken possession of their effects.

The Governor repeated that he did not think it necessary to make any communication when the arrangement had been voluntary, and when eight out of ten had paid the sums subscribed ['subscribed' is a happy word], and two only were refractory.

And that it was not true that soldiers had taken possession of the effects of the Ionians.

Sir John Franklin stated that he had not been informed that eight out of the Ionians had paid the sums, or consented to pay, that he would consult with the Consul on the subject, but that he felt it his duty to protect the two who objected to pay, and to demand permission to embark their families and effects if they chose, and for them to come under his protection.

The Governor said that he would have consented to the demands of the Consul and Sir John if the measure had been taken for the Ionians alone; but in this case the Ionians had agreed with the Greeks to advance to the Government the money, and two only were refractory.

That he would allow the embarkation of their effects, except as to such value as would cover the amount they had to pay.

It would seem here from the use of the word 'advance' that this singular impost had undergone a further modification. Having developed from a tax into a 'benevolence,' it had now blossomed out into a 'loan.' Had the Governor been pressed a little harder, he might perhaps have represented it as a 'bounty' from the Government to the Ionian merchants. Meanwhile it was at least satisfactory to find that the Governor's second enumeration of these persons, though it corresponded to nothing in the facts, had undergone no further change.

Sir John Franklin stated that he felt the same duty to protect one British or Ionian subject as he would have done to protect 500 ; that he regretted extremely that the harmony and good understanding which H.M. Resident at Nauplia held with the Provisional Government of Greece, and therefore expected to be observed by all other authorities, was so opposite to the conduct of the authorities here as to produce on his part the remonstrance he was compelled to make ; and again begged the Governor to reflect on the responsibility he incurred, and the consequence which might result from the continued refusal to allow the embarkation of the property and families of the Ionians, or the removal of the soldiers from their houses.

He again desired that the Governor would remove the soldiers until communication could be made through the Residents to the Provisional Government on the subject.

The Governor replied that he wished the harmony and good understanding might be preserved, and gave his thanks to the Allies that they had sent vessels here for the protection of the town.

He agreed to permit the embarkation of the effects of the Ionians, as they had other property to secure the payment of the money they had to pay ;

But that he would not remove the soldiers until they paid the money, or until he had an order from the Provisional Government on the subject.

Sir John Franklin stated again that the views of the Allies were to preserve tranquillity in Greece, but that the measures resorted to by the Governor had a directly contrary tendency.

At this point the Governor seems to have made the only 'hit,' such as it was—and it consisted, as will be seen, in what lawyers call 'taking advantage of his own wrong'—which he succeeded in scoring during the whole interview. He coolly replied

that he had taken this step for the purpose of preserving tranquillity by supplying the wants of the troops, who might otherwise pillage the town, and from this the Ionians as well as the Greeks might be the sufferers.

His measures, in fact, preserved tranquillity in the sense that levying 'blackmail' prevents breaches of the law by acts of brigandage. He concluded with the declaration— wholly unwarrantable, of course, in international law—that he 'considered the Ionians on the same footing as Greek subjects, and liable to the same fiscal regulations.'

Sir John Franklin demanded whether the embarkation of the families and effects of the two who refused might be considered as permitted.

The Governor answered in the affirmative.

Sir John Franklin then demanded a passport for a courier to Nauplia.

The Governor was ready to grant it.

Sir John Franklin again expressed his regret at being obliged to make such a remonstrance against a violation of the rights of the Ionian subjects ; and could not express the pain which the reflection on the consequences which might result gave him. He would consult with the Consul on the subject of the conference, and hoped that the Governor would give an answer to the Consul's letter.

The Governor was equally sorry at the circumstance, but could not withdraw the demand [for the contribution]. He would forthwith send a reply to Mr. Crowe.

Thus ended this singular interview, technically, no doubt in a drawn battle ; but as the Ionian merchants, with their goods and families, were removed under the protection of the British flag, the substantial gains of victory may fairly be said to have rested with Franklin. In the covering despatch forwarded to the Admiralty with the above-quoted report of this conference, Franklin adds that the Governor, in at last assenting to the removal of the merchants, 'intimated,' dryly enough, 'that their houses would remain.' What happened to this portion of their property, or what indeed was the sequel of the incident generally, does not appear ; but some time, probably, before the courier despatched to Nauplia could have returned with instructions from the Residents, stirring events had occurred at Patras, and the authority of the Governor had, no doubt, come to an end. It is, at any rate, certain that after a few days' delay—during which period, however, he seems to have actually removed the two merchants from their houses to the citadel—he fulfilled his undertaking to Franklin. From a despatch of the 18th it appears that, on the receipt of intelligence to the effect that there had been some change in the members of the Government at Nauplia, the Governor of Patras had released the Ionian merchants from their confinement in the citadel without enforcing the payment of the contribution which had been demanded of them.

CHAPTER X

BEFORE PATRAS

1832–1834

AFFAIRS at Patras were now rapidly approaching a crisis. April 19, the date of the seizure of the town by Zavellas and his irregulars, as above narrated, was now near at hand ; and the shadow of the coming event is plainly visible in Franklin's communications with his official chiefs. On the 17th the uneasy authorities, civil and military, of the town made a formal application to the French and British naval commanders to land troops for the preservation of order, meaning thereby, of course, the maintenance of their own tottering rule. They wished these troops, as they put it, to act in concert with the regular garrison to repress any predatory action against the town which, it was feared, might be made by the irregular troops. Franklin and Fournier immediately sought an interview with the Civil Governor, and satisfied themselves that, having regard to the suspicious movements of the irregulars, there was good ground for the Governor's apprehension that they would take advantage of the approaching Easter festivities to enter the town under pretence of joining in the celebration, but in reality to plunder the inhabitants. The military commandant, who entered during the interview, added, it is true, that, now that he had procured the means of paying the troops of the garrison 'up to a certain time,' he could rely upon them for the defence of the citadel and, 'perhaps,' of the town, though he must admit that the landing of a force from the allied ships would give greater encouragement to the troops, and entire confidence to the inhabitants of the town. It appeared to the two naval officers that, notwithstanding the confidence of the military commandant, the troops of the garrison, even though assured of their pay 'up to a certain time,' might not be proof against the temptation to provide for a more remote future, and that 'if the pillage once commenced on the part of the irregular soldiery, those of the garrison would join them.' They therefore determined on acceding to the petition of the inhabitants to land some men from each ship of the allied squadron. Before doing so, however, Franklin took the two following very judicious precautions. In the first place, he framed and furnished the officers and men of the landing party with a very carefully drawn and minute code of instructions as to the proceedings to be taken and the rules to be observed by them during the period of the occupation ; and, in the next place, he prepared the following proclamation for issue by the civil authorities of Patras to the inhabitants of the town :—

The captains of the ships of the Alliance, in compliance with the wishes of the inhabitants, and at the request of the authorities of Patras, are about to land some troops. This debarkation has no political object whatever, and is only done to prevent all kinds of disorder. The captains, therefore, trust that the inhabitants and the military will conduct themselves in such a manner as not to render necessary the employment of force on their part for the maintenance of tranquillity.

Given under my hand, on board the Rainbow, at Patras, this 17th of April, 1832.   (Signed)   JOHN FRANKLIN, Captain.

On the same day the English and French troops were landed. They consisted of 47 seamen and 23 Marines from the Rainbow, and 15 seamen and 16 Marines from the Pelican. The French landed 40 seamen, thus bringing up the total force to 141 men, exclusive of officers.

The next step was to seek an interview with the disquieting Zavellas, and to prevail upon him, if possible, to restrain the exuberant cupidity of his irregulars. The patriot was gracious to the point of condescension, but showed no great eagerness to impart information nor any conspicuous readiness to pledge himself to a strictly pacific action. Probably he was already meditating the *coup* which he struck a few days later.

N

He was, however, quite willing to give all due and becoming assurances that the preservation of peace and tranquillity, not only in Patras, but throughout Greece, was the object nearest to his patriotic heart. None of his men, he said, should come into the town, unless it might be some few who had families there and who might come in to purchase provisions. On the French Consul, who acted as interpreter, repeating the request that he would keep his men away, the General dramatically—or melodramatically—answered : 'The word of a Zavellas is to be depended upon. I am a soldier, and have never been known to break my trust. I am well known. I am that Zavellas who headed the Suliote rising. I am known in history.' The French Consul asked him how many men he had, to which the historic soldier made the not very direct answer that they were divided about Vostitza and the vicinity :—

French Consul : But let us know the exact number.

General Zavellas : About 700 men.

French Consul : How many men have you here, as it is necessary we should know, that we may be able to perceive if any more arrive?

General Zavellas : They are all officers who live in this place and have their families here.

French Consul : But what may be their number?

General Zavellas : About fifty (with *some hesitation*) ; with their retinue, 200.

The General went on to say that all the Allies could do was only to secure a temporary tranquillity, and that until the Prince arrived to occupy the throne of Greece they might take his word for it that Greece would never be quiet. The Consul then, by way of encouraging the hope of an early pacification, informed him that a commission was being formed to manage the government of the country until the arrival of the sovereign, which commission, the General might rely upon it, would do all in its power to secure the orderly administration of affairs. General Zavellas, however, was so rude as to reply that 'Greece had had enough of commissions. He knew what they were ; they had no means of enforcing their power. Give them money, give them money, and then something might be done.' The Consul said that every one should be perfectly disinterested and merely look to the general welfare of Greece. The General said that 'when he fought the Turks, then it was that he looked to the general welfare of Greece.' The Consul then told the General that the Residents of the Allies would be provided with a loan of money to issue, but 'they did not yet know to whom it should be given, as it was their desire only to apply the loan to the interests of Greece.' The General answered that 'it was of little import to whom the money was given provided it made its appearance in the country.' He did not add 'to be scrambled for,' but his meaning is sufficiently clear without that addition.

Franklin had another interview with this notable on the following day, to suggest that, in the peculiar circumstances of the situation, he should direct his irregulars to refrain from celebrating Easter, as they were accustomed to do, by firing volleys of musketry, which he promised to do.

The action taken by the allied squadron achieved its object. Order reigned in Patras throughout the Eastertide festival. The irregulars did not celebrate the festival by pillaging the town, and the townspeople gradually recovered their confidence. But after the lapse of some ten or twelve days a change took place in the aspect of affairs which compelled the two commanders to reconsider their policy. The attitude of Zavellas had become more and more threatening, and in the last days of April his designs were unmistakably disclosed. A communication was addressed by the civil authorities of Patras to Franklin and his colleague, Captain Dupont, who had succeeded Fournier in the command, to the effect that Zavellas had definitely refused obedience to the orders of the Governing Commission, that he had disobeyed the directions transmitted to him through the Governor of Patras to retire his troops to a distance from the town, and that it was his intention, as they were positively informed, to seize the citadel, provision it by levying contributions on the villages, and hold it and the town which it dominated until the arrival of the King-designate of Greece in his new dominions.

Upon consideration of this grave intelligence, Franklin

and Dupont came to the conclusion that no course was open
to them but to re-embark their troops. It was out of their
power to land any force sufficiently strong to prevent the entrance of Zavellas and his irregulars into the town if he chose
to make the attempt with the whole strength of his following.
It was known, too, that he was conspiring with the garrison,
and it was probable, as indeed the event proved, that its
troops would throw in their lot with him on his making his
appearance. And lastly, most important consideration of
all, the orders given to the allied captains expressly forbade
their making any promise of material support to one party
or threat of coercion to the other, and that no circumstance
whatever, except insult to their respective flags, was to
authorise or induce them to use force. Consequently,
though it may well be believed with some reluctance, the
two officers resolved to issue a proclamation to the people
of Patras, stating that, in view of the present tranquillity of
the town, and of the fact of the men being required for
their duties on board, it had been decided to re-embark
them. This proclamation was issued on April 30, and, the
step announced, it was at once executed.

There could be no question of its wisdom, or indeed, having
regard to the numerical inferiority of the troops of the allied
squadron—150 men against some seven or eight hundred—of
its necessity either. But that Franklin regretted the restraint
imposed upon him by circumstances it is easy to see ; and it
is pretty certain that, with a clearer mandate of intervention
and a more adequate force, he would not have hesitated to
make himself master of the town, and thus secure the ' preservation of tranquillity ' in the most effectual of all ways
This appears clearly enough in the disappointment afterwards
evinced by him at the retreat of the French contingent sent
to take possession of the town on May 19. In an extremely
interesting despatch some months later to the Commander of
the Mediterranean fleet he shows, in answering a series of
inquiries which Sir Henry Hotham had addressed to him, how
actively he and his colleague had exerted themselves to facilitate
the French occupation of Patras. Captain Dupont had sent

two couriers by different routes to meet the Commander of the French troops, to apprise him of the exact state of Patras, and to communicate to him their joint opinion as to the quarter from which they could most advantageously for themselves, and most effectively supported by the guns of the squadron, advance upon the town. 'You will imagine my disappointment,' he writes, 'at hearing the French General's determination, which was first communicated to me on my going on board his ship, taking M. Ruffa with me, who had informed me only a little before that he could at once place 300 men at the General's disposal and 500 in five days, which I thought of importance he should know.' But the French General had committed the signal and singular blunder of preceding the force under his command, and, writes Franklin : 'I repeat my conviction that if the French General had not thus come, Patras would have been at once given up to the French troops. His having made the demand for the surrender of the fortress before the troops were on the spot appears to me extraordinary, and I was not surprised at the answer Zavellas returned to his letters. His ordering the troops to retire when within six hours' march of Patras was still more inexplicable to me, and I am sure it had the effect of emboldening Zavellas and his followers to persevere in their opposition.'

Regrets, however, were vain. Diplomatic timidity and military irresolution had allowed this Greek condottiere to make himself master of a leading commercial seaport of Greece, of the lives and goods of its inhabitants, and of a considerable amount of property or proprietary interests belonging to the subjects of other States. Thenceforth, therefore, until the final or what was supposed to be the final settlement of the Greek question by the arrival of Prince Otho of Bavaria and his Council of Regency in the early months of the following year, the position of Sir John Franklin was one demanding the exercise of sleepless vigilance, inexhaustible patience, infinite tact, imperturbable temper, and unfailing promptitude. The situation, in fact, was really almost comic in its perplexity and involution ; and even in its worst and

most irritating entanglements there are many signs that
Franklin was not insensible to its humorous aspects. His
despatches, which are models of the clear and businesslike
style befitting such documents, and his private letters,
abounding in shrewd observation and reflection, to Sir Henry
Hotham are, for the next six months, so interesting as to make
selection difficult. But the difficult is here the unavoidable
also ; for they fill several manuscript books of correspondence
and would, in type, go far to. fill a considerable volume, which
indeed they deserve.

Let us briefly survey the situation in which the captain
of the Rainbow now found himself. In front of him lay a
considerable commercial seaport in the hands of a captain
of Greek irregulars and his men, whose proceedings, so far as
they menaced the lives or properties of British subjects or
the honour of the British flag, it would be his duty to restrain
if possible by 'moral influence,' but if not, then, in circumstances incapable alike of prediction or of definition, by the
use of material force. Behind the town, so to speak—that is
at the seat of the Central Greek Executive so called—stood a
Provisional Government, which Franklin was instructed to
co-operate with and assist in the exercise of an authority
recognised and obeyed precisely by that portion of the Greek
people whose self-interest or indifference induced them to do
so, and by nobody else. In his own rear—that is to say, at the
source of that international authority which was then nominally directing the affairs of Greece—were three Great Powers,
agreed indeed as to the future of the new kingdom, but quite
unable to grapple with its present disorders, and two of them
filled with a profound and not unreasonable distrust of the
third. By his side were two naval colleagues, of whom one,
the French commander, was to be relied on for loyal co-operation, but the other was vehemently, and indeed on the
strongest grounds, suspected of intriguing with the Greek
political faction whose adherents were then in possession of
the town.

Were it necessary to add a finishing touch to this picture
of confusion, the following passage from one of Franklin's

private letters to Sir Henry Hotham's secretary would supply it :—

I heartily wish the authorities on whom the termination of the Greek affair rests would speedily decide on what is to be done. Nothing can be more wearying for the mind and temper than to witness the vacillating measures which have been recently followed in these matters. There are three places, for instance, within sight of this anchorage occupied by persons acknowledging three different authorities : Patras by Zavellas, in avowed opposition to the Government; Missolonghi by Grivas, professing to be acting for the Government, but really, I believe, for himself ; and Lepanto, divided between the troops of Lambro Vecchio, who have faithfully adhered to the Government, and a party professing to be rather inclined to the Government but opposed personally to the views of the commandant, Lambro Vecchio.

The case, it will be here seen, was even worse than Franklin put it ; since the anti-Lambro faction may fairly be regarded as a fourth party. And, considering that they occupied 'the lower town' with their opponents 'holding the citadel,' this duality might at any moment become important—especially to the non-combatant population of Lepanto.

It was not long after the seizure of Patras by Zavellas that Franklin's minor difficulties began. The critical position of its civil population, especially the women and children, and the rough measures taken by the commander of the irregulars for their embarkation and expulsion, caused him much anxiety. But a more serious complication arose some weeks later, when, in response to a communication received from the Governor of Missolonghi, Franklin intercepted and seized a Greek pirate vessel which had recently committed depredations at that port, and detained its captain, a man named Chrysanthos Morartachis, on board the Rainbow. The pirate, it seems, was an adherent of Zavellas, who had the impudence to demand his release. To this application but one answer of course could be returned. After refusing in duly decided terms to listen to it, Franklin and Dupont, in a joint letter to Zavellas, went on to remark that since the principal object of their being sent to this place was to prevent all kinds of disorder and robbery by sea, he could not be surprised at their employing all means in their power to arrive at that object:—

But (they significantly continue) we also assure you that we will seize upon all boats under your orders, which under pretext of serving you employ their forces in robbing and pillaging merchant vessels of any nation whatever. If, on account of our not being able to release to you the pirates we have taken, you do not think yourself able to answer for the accidents and insults which may occur under the head of reprisals, we also, sir, cannot answer for the calamities which may befall this town, the whole responsibility of which will be placed upon you; for be assured that the least insult offered to the flags or subjects of our respective Powers will be at once resented with all our force, and with so much more reason as we have right on our side.

This resolute language had apparently its desired effect. Zavellas made no further attempt to obtain the release of the pirates, who were in due course handed over to the Government at Missolonghi.

A little later, however, Franklin was even more nearly 'coming to blows,' as he put it in a subsequent despatch, with the master of Patras. A Greek Government schooner was passing or approaching the port when Zavellas, without notice to the allied vessels or to any merchant ships in the neighbourhood, opened fire upon her from the guns of the citadel. None of the shots took effect, but instant preparations had of course to be made against the contingency of one of the ships of the Allies being struck. The crew of the Rainbow were signalled to their quarters in readiness, in that event, to return the fire; and 'though I should have deeply regretted the consequences to others,' wrote Franklin privately to Sir Henry Hotham, 'if we had been forced to the measure, I yet think a broadside or two would have been a just punishment to him and his soldiers for their insolence in firing upon a Greek Government schooner that was close to two of the ships without informing the captains of the Alliance of their intention. The only apparent reason of this dishonourable action was that the commander of the schooner preferred to consult with the Allies before he gave an answer whether or not he would go on shore to communicate with Zavellas.' Franklin, however, adds his suspicion that Zavellas was glad of some such opportunity to employ his captains and soldiers. Several of the former, it was reported, had expressed much disappointment at not receiving any pay for themselves or their men when they knew that the General had recently collected money from the villages. ' There is nothing like the excitement of a battle for putting aside such causes of irritation.'

But there was a more constant cause of anxiety to the English and French commanders than even the doings and designs of Zavellas ; and that was the attitude of their Russian colleague. From the very commencement of their patrol duty before Patras, Captain Zanetzky's behaviour had been unsatisfactory. His attitude towards Zavellas and the faction supporting him—foremost among whom was the Prince de Wrede, a Bavarian, who had held the post of military commandant under the Administrative Commission, but had subsequently struck up an open alliance with the insurgent general—was more than suspicious. His whole conduct, in fact, suggested that, instead of loyally co-operating with the other two officers of the Alliance, he was pursuing a purely Russian policy under the direction of his commander-in-chief at Nauplia, the too notorious Admiral Ricord. Hence his relations with his colleagues in the roadstead of Patras became daily more and more strained.

They must have reached a pitch of considerable tension when such a despatch as the following could be addressed by the English and French commanders to their Russian colleague :—

Sir,—Two nights in succession, and at different hours, the boats of the brig of H.I.M. of Russia under your command have been seen hovering round their Britannic and French Majesties' ships. We, the commanders of these ships, beg to be made acquainted with the meaning of this unusual proceeding, which we refrain from qualifying with a name till we have received your explanations. We also wish to be informed why your boats do not answer when hailed. If it has been your intention to row guard round this roadstead, we think that you ought to have informed us in an amicable manner of this desire, as we are in alliance with you, and are here, like yourself, to maintain good order. But if the rowing of your boats by night relates to your own particular protection, why, we ask, do they not confine themselves to the neighbourhood of your own brig, and not pull close round our ships, which need no protection of the kind? It is not our wish, Sir, to prevent your boats rowing about at night if you think it advisable, but we desire that they should not be sent into such situations as to present the appearance of watching our ships, and, above all, we require that their officers and men should be instructed to answer when hailed.

You must be well aware that every sentinel has the right to fire at any person approaching him by night without answering his challenge, and you must also know very well that no ship of war permits boats to pass by night within her buoy without being satisfied with their answer.

If our sentinels have not already fired upon your boats for refusing to answer them when hailed, it is because we have prevented them doing so from pure good feeling towards our allies, and until we could obtain an explanation from you as to the very unusual course of proceeding of which we hereby inform you.

We are, Sir, with consideration,

(Signed)   JOHN FRANKLIN, Captain of the Rainbow.
C. DUPONT, Captain of the Cornélie.

The 'concert of Europe' does not seem in a very harmonious condition when the sentinels of two of the Allied Powers have been brought so near to firing on the boats of the third. Captain Zanetzky, of course, explained that it was out of solicitude for the safety of the Rainbow and the Cornélie that his boats had been sent to row round these vessels.

Some three weeks afterwards we find Franklin compelled to complain to his superior officer of Zanetzky's refusal to act with his colleagues in the matter of an application made to them by the Governor of Missolonghi; and yet a few weeks later the French and English captains came to something so like a personal rupture with the Russian that Admirals Sir Henry Hotham and Baron Hugon [1] had to seek satisfaction for the wounded susceptibilities of their officers by means of

[1] Of this gallant sailor the Prince de Joinville, in his recently published Memoirs, relates the following anecdote: 'At Navarino, where he commanded the Armide, he came up and lay with true fraternal chivalry between the Turkish ships and a British frigate that had suffered very much from their fire, which same service the British corvette Rose rendered him in return and with equal gallantry towards the close of the engagement.'

a formal representation to Admiral Ricord. Zanetzky had asserted that signals had been seen from the Russian brig to have been made from the Rainbow, which were answered from the shore; and he had persisted in the assertion, after Franklin had given him an assurance that this was not the case. Upon which, says Franklin, 'I told him that after the imputation he had made on myself and my officers it was impossible any private communications could be kept up with him.'

Zanetzky was shortly after this relieved of his command, and Franklin, in a despatch to Sir Henry Hotham, records his satisfaction at the approaching departure of an officer 'who has countenanced the insurgents in every way, and has been the promoter of dissension in the Alliance from the day of his anchoring at Patras.' Yet the essential kindliness of his nature comes out in the little incident which he then records in a private letter to Sir Henry Hotham, written two days after the unpleasant interview of which he had given an account in his last official despatch :—

I told Captain Zanetzky that I could not avoid contrasting September 3, 1828, with that of 1832. On the former day I had the honour and pleasure of being present at all the ceremonies and rejoicings at Moscow on the anniversary of the coronation of the Emperor of Russia, and I dined with the Governor-General, Prince Galitzin, at the Palace, where were assembled all the dignitaries of the Church, as well as the nobles of Moscow and its immediate vicinity. But in 1832, on the same anniversary, I was not even reminded of the event, nor was either a British or a French flag displayed on board his brig. . . . I further told him that, as I had been honoured on my visit to Russia by the condescension and kind attention of the late Empress-Mother, and had been introduced by Her Majesty, in the absence of the Emperor, to her eldest son and to all the younger branches of Her Majesty's family, I should have had great pleasure in paying my congratulation on board his brig on the last anniversary if he had informed me of the day. Captain Zanetzky was evidently much affected by these observations, and immediately replied to me that he had acted on that occasion by his Admiral's orders. 'I wished to have asked you,' he said, 'but I could not. In fact, in everything I have done I have implicitly followed the instructions of my Admiral.' After this frank avowal I could not for any consideration have used another warm expression in speaking to him. I felt, indeed, that any officer who is obliged to act under such shameful orders is to be pitied, though I could not exonerate him from the duplicity he has practised on almost every occasion of our meeting. But his duplicity is light compared with that of Admiral Ricord, and I really shall rejoice if the means be afforded of exposing his conduct to the world, and shall feel not a little pleasure if any part of the clue to this exposition has been furnished from the accounts of his underhand working in this place. The proceedings of the Russian party in this quarter of Greece have been so manifestly in favour of the opponents of Government that a child might have discerned them.

But in no incident in Franklin's service in the Gulf of Patras is the comedy of the situation or his own remarkable adroitness in dealing with it so effectively illustrated as in a certain episode which may be shortly described as the 'affair of the currants of Vostitza.' Vostitza, situated some score of miles nearer to the head of the Gulf of Corinth, was, and perhaps is, extensively interested in currants. The storehouses of its local merchants, many if not most of them British Ionian subjects, were generally full to overflowing in the export season with vast quantities of the fruit awaiting embarkation, and in the autumn of 1832 there were at least two thousand tons of it ready to be shipped, and representing a sum of no less than ninety-six thousand pounds in export duty. Hitherto it would seem that matters had been amicably arranged between the producers, the merchants, and the military masters of the town by the simple process of paying the duties to the Commandant of the Garrison, General Fotomara, for application to the payment of his troops. Under this arrangement the soldiers had been entirely fed and a portion of their pay provided for them ever since the revolt of Zavellas. Where the Provisional Government 'came in' does not appear, but inasmuch as they were practically powerless to protect their nominal subjects or the foreign merchants trading in the town, they had perhaps no right to come in at all. Fotomara and his soldiers represented law and order in Vostitza, or so much of these blessings as its inhabitants enjoyed, and in return for the revenues appropriated to them they did at least prevent the citizens from being plundered by anybody else.

This happy state of affairs, however, was now threatened with disturbance from two causes—the appearance, namely, of two other claimants to the currant duties. One of these was a commander of irregulars of the name of Hadji Pietro; the other was the Provisional Government. The latter sent an emissary commissioned—or reputedly commissioned, for he could apparently produce no credentials—to receive the duties on behalf of the Minister of Finance; the former proposed to himself the simpler method of marching his troops into the town and crying 'halves' with the soldiers of the garrison. The situation, therefore, had become critical alike for the proprietors, for the merchants, and for Fotomara; the commandant foreseeing a distinct probability of being deprived of his soldier's pay, and the proprietors and merchants contemplating the even more unpleasant prospect of finding the duties demanded from them twice if not three times over. In these circumstances a pressing appeal was made to Franklin to come and 'protect the currant trade,' and in response to it the Rainbow promptly made its appearance off the port of Vostitza. The applicant most interested in his intervention was a Mr. Robinson, a British merchant with a large stock of currants ready for exportation, and the embarrassed recipient of 'an order purporting to come from the Minister of Finance,' directing that he was to 'retain' on that official's behalf 'the duties' payable in respect of them.

Before, however, Mr. Robinson's case could be dealt with, Franklin received a visit on board the Rainbow from the Abbot and two priests of the convent of Megaspelion, situated in the plain of Vostitza, outside the town, who begged him to prevent the soldiers of Hadji Pietro from seizing on some currants belonging to the convent which were ready for shipping in a fortnight. Ascertaining that the fruit was in a storehouse some miles away from the town, and at some distance from the seaside, ' I was under the necessity of informing these reverend gentlemen that the duties of the captains of the Alliance were confined to occurrences afloat, and that, however much we lamented the probability of the soldiers unjustly seizing upon their currants or those of any other proprietor, we could not prevent them without landing a force for that purpose, which we were not authorised to do. "But," replied the Abbot, "cannot you say they are yours and that you have bought them?" "Certainly not," I told him, "if that was not true. Besides," I said, "all officers in the Navy are forbidden to trade while on active service." I thought,' he gravely adds, 'that such a desire from the Abbot of a convent did not speak well for the morality of these priests.' Finding they could not gain Franklin's assistance, 'they begged to be shown round the ship before they left it.'

Meanwhile Fotomara had taken prompt and decisive action. Thrusting himself, with all the dashing strategy of Napoleon in the campaign of 1814, between the two other rival claimants to the currant duties, he resolved to stave off one of his competitors by force, and to forestall the other by negotiation. He despatched a body of troops to hold the passes against Hadji Pietro, a movement which was successfully executed, and at the same time called upon the proprietors to advance him the money required for his soldiers, on the 'security' of duties which had been already 'attached' by the Minister of Finance. Franklin was upon this invited by Mr. Robinson to come on shore and remonstrate, which he consented to do. To continue the narrative in his own language :—

I pointed out to Fotomara the illegality of such a proceeding, because the duties could not be paid to him or to any other person but the head of the Customs, who alone had the power of giving a clearance to the vessel that received the fruit, and that the proprietors must consequently lose all the money they now were called upon to advance. He contested this point for a long time, and did not, in fact, relinquish for some time the hope of persuading me that his order directing the Custom-house officer to discharge the loans from the proprietor, as he received the dues from the merchant, would be sufficient. I told him, however, that his order would be of no value, and that the taking of money from the proprietors under any such delusive idea as he cherished would be a robbery. I reminded him that his soldiers had hitherto borne a good character, and that their conduct in preserving this province in a state of quietness would certainly be strongly represented by the primates and proprietors to the Regency of their King, whose arrival might be looked for in a fortnight, and that their representations could not fail to procure for him the countenance and favour of the Regency. I told him also that the conduct of the soldiers formed a laudable exception to that of almost every other corps in the Morea, whose course had been marked with outrage and pillage, and had brought down on them the hatred of all the peaceable inhabitants and peasantry ; and then asked whether it was not most unwise to put his character at risk at this time by any act of oppression towards the proprietors and inhabitants. He seemed to assent to my observations, though he did not withhold the remark that those corps had, by the forcible means they had used, got more money than his. 'Perhaps that might be the case,' I replied ; 'but you may be assured a day of retribution for their bad conduct is near ; and besides, if it were not, can the possession of money be desirable that is wrung from the poor inhabitants in such a lawless manner?' Fotomara concluded by telling me he would inform the captain and soldiers of all that I had said, that for his own part he was persuaded my advice was the best to follow, and that he thought the soldiers would take the same view of it. And if they found the proprietors unwilling to advance the money to them they would not press the matter further, but would wait with patience to receive the dues. As to any imposition being laid on the British merchants respecting the duties, he said that was quite out of the question. I assured him that I would never allow that to be made, or their warehouses to be touched. I told Fotomara I should return immediately after the English packet arrived at Patras. Mr. Robinson thought the conversation would have a good effect.

Mr. Robinson was right. Six or seven weeks later he was able to report that some two thousand tons of currants had been shipped from Vostitza, representing dues to the amount of 96,000*l.* Franklin's ingeniously persuasive methods, as displayed in this curious negotiation, show clearly enough that Lady Franklin's playful compliment to her 'smooth-tongued' husband was not undeserved. The matter was hardly one of international importance, but it affords perhaps the most striking example of his diplomatic skill. There is a homely adage which affirms the impossibility of getting 'butter out of a dog's mouth,' but it was hardly a lesser feat to have rescued so large a sum of money from an impecunious commandant of Greek soldiery in the year 1832. The affair of the currants was the indirect means of bringing Franklin into contact with a young man destined afterwards to become a somewhat prominent figure, both in society and in the world of letters. His host's reference to him is worth quoting, however, for other reasons than that of the interest attaching to the person upon whom it bears :—

I cannot say Mr. Milnes particularly pleased me. He appeared to me to be one of those young travellers who, from a hasty passage through Greece, have drawn conclusions which the longer residents and better informed persons know not to be correct. These young gentlemen have for the most part come from the Universities full of the history of ancient Greece, and therefore strive to make the modern history bend to those descriptions, and to think we do not understand the Greek character. His exalted idea of the Greeks of the present day was much shaken by hearing and seeing what is passing in this neighbourhood, from whence sprung all the commotion that keeps the Morea in a state of agitation. I brought him from Vostitza to Patras in this ship, and then procured him a passage in an Austrian brig of war to Corfu, so that he tumbled upon his legs. He spoke of having seen you (Lady Franklin) daily at Athens, and of spending every evening in the society where you are, though I did not imagine he was a person after your taste.

Certainly the affair of the currants was calculated to shake the future Lord Houghton's 'exalted idea' of the Greeks. There was no flavour of the Homeric age about it, except perhaps in a certain faint suggestion of Ulysses. But how perennial a type is that of the academic politician here shown to be! And how well do we remember, as how much did we suffer, from the same class of 'young gentlemen,' in the years 1876–1878!

The rescue of Mr. Robinson's property was the last incident of any interest in Franklin's two years of patrolwork in the Gulf of Corinth. Early in the following year, or, to assign its precise date to so long-looked-for an event, on February 1, 1833, King Otho landed at Nauplia from the British frigate Madagascar, in which Franklin's friend, Captain Lyons, had conveyed him from Brindisi, and Greece was restored to temporary quietude. Zavellas, whose exactions, Franklin notes, had become heavier for the last few months, in pursuance perhaps of an 'old-age pension scheme' of strictly personal application, appears to have evacuated Patras without resistance; and, shortly after, the Rainbow was withdrawn from that port. It was not till December 1833 that she returned to England: but, as her period of active employment in the Mediterranean here ends, this chapter of Franklin's career may fitly conclude with the following testimonies to the value of his services, borne by the two persons best able to appreciate them, Admiral Sir Henry Hotham, the Commander-in-Chief, and Mr. Crowe, H.M. Consul at Patras. The Admiral writes :—

In the concluding operations of the service you have so long and so ably conducted in the Gulfs of Patras and Lepanto I have great satisfaction in repeating the approbation which I have already at different times expressed of your measures in the interests of Greece and in the maintenance of the honour and character of the English nation and of H.M.'s Navy on that station, wherein you have entirely fulfilled my instructions and anticipated my wishes. I also take this opportunity of commending the judgment and forbearance which you have exhibited under circumstances of repeated opposition and provocation. To your calm and steady conduct may be attributed the preservation of the town and inhabitants of Patras, the protection of commerce, and the advancement of the benevolent intentions of the Allied Sovereigns in favour of the Greek nation.

The Consul's letter, conceived in still warmer terms, was as follows :—

My dear Sir John,—While I beg leave to offer you my congratulations upon being at length released from the anxious and wearisome duty that has detained you before this town for the last twelve months, I cannot refrain at the same time from expressing the regret I feel upon my own account in losing your society and that of your officers, which has so agreeably relieved a period that would otherwise have been of unmitigated annoyance and vexation.

The humane object of your mission is now completely fulfilled. You have the satisfaction to witness the termination of the miseries of the inhabitants of this city, and of the misrule and violence that so long and heavily oppressed them—violence restrained from the worst and grossest excesses only by your presence, and awed into respect by the dignified calm which you ever preserved under circumstances of great irritation.

But for your forbearance the city just rising from its ruins had ceased to exist. You now see tranquillity and order restored to its homes, and a few days have been sufficient to reanimate the activity of commerce.

O

Patras owes you a deep debt of gratitude, and, I trust, feels the obligation. For myself, I hope I need not assure you that I can never forget your unvarying kindness, and I am sensible of the high value of the friendly and cordial regard which you have continued to bestow upon me. For weeks together your ship afforded a home— a kind home—to my family, and the Rainbow will ever be remembered by them with the feelings which home excites.

She was indeed regarded as something more than a home by others besides the family of the British Consul. The happiness and good feeling prevailing on board of her were proverbial on the Mediterranean station; and the story goes that 'she was called the Celestial Rainbow,' and that 'the sailors used to describe her as Franklin's Paradise.' It only remains to add that her commander, on his return to England, was made a Knight Commander of the Guelphic Order of Hanover in recognition of his services in the Gulf of Patras, and that King Otho of Greece shortly afterwards conferred upon him the Cross of the newly-founded Greek 'Order of the Redeemer.'

CHAPTER XI

LADY FRANKLIN'S TRAVELS

1831–1833

THE years of Sir John Franklin's active service in the
Mediterranean were years of almost equal activity for his
spirited and energetic wife in various other parts of the world.
They were not, indeed, separated throughout the whole of
this period, for they spent the winter of 1831–32 together
at Corfu. But the rest of the time was passed by Lady
Franklin mainly in the East, and the letters which constantly
passed between them during the two or three following years
reflect so valuable a light on their relations with each other,
besides abounding on the wife's side with bright impressions
of travel and lively sketches of character and manners, that
no apology is perhaps required for temporarily interrupting
the progress of this narrative for the purpose of giving
extracts from their correspondence with each other.

Lady Franklin's desire to visit Greece and the East was
as ardent as might be expected in a woman of her exceptional
abilities and strong intellectual curiosity, and it was evidently
somewhat of a disappointment to her that she was unable to
accompany her husband to his first destination in the Mediterranean. Her husband, however, naturally felt, and she
herself was too sensible not to perceive also, that it was un-
desirable, even if no official objection interposed, for the newly
appointed captain to take his wife out with him to the station
at which he was to commence his duties. The winter of 1830
and the first six months of the following year were accordingly
spent by Lady Franklin in London and Cheltenham. It
was an anxious time in England, as is well known, and her

o 2

letters, as has already been shown, reflect the then prevalent apprehensions of an imminent outbreak of European war over the eternal Eastern Question, as well as the widespread uneasiness with which the bulk of the educated classes in this country regarded the agitation for Parliamentary reform. Here and there it finds expression from Lady Franklin in language at which it is easier to smile in these days than it was in those. 'Funded property does not seem,' she writes, 'to be thought very secure. I think I told you that Fanny [her sister], by an express article in her marriage settlement, is enabled to invest part of her fortune in the purchase of land or stock in the British Colonies, thus contemplating a comfortable retreat in case of revolution.'

Lady Franklin, of course, has much to tell her husband about the health and·progress, bodily and mental, of her little step-daughter; and it may be worth while to extract the following brief passage from one of her letters, for the relief of an anxiety of which each successive generation of civilised mankind appears to become the inevitable victim. After referring to a somewhat serious illness from which the child had just recovered, Lady Franklin adds :—

> She is now quite well enough to walk for an hour every day, and I shall soon return to her books, though I care at all times but little for these compared with the strengthening of her health and the cultivation of her feelings. Her learning will come in due time, and much better *late* than *early*. At any rate, I shall have the comfort of thinking that I have not stultified her understanding nor cramped either her physical or mental energies, as seems to be the fashion in the present day, and which makes physicians (rightly, I fear) say that the next generation will present more weak and disordered intellects than ever afflicted mankind before.

Our anxieties in these days about the woman of the future are of a more varied, and indeed, to some extent, of a mutually incompatible character, though whether they aggravate or neutralise each other on this last account it were hard to say. As matters stand, however, we are divided between the two apprehensions—one, that the girl of the present is being ruined as the woman of the future by mental overpressure, and the other that she is being as fatally unfitted for it by excessive bodily exercise.

The severe and indeed dangerous illness of her step-daughter of course arrested for a time Lady Franklin's attempts to arrange for rejoining her husband, but after the child's recovery other anxieties of another kind arose. 'I am told,' she writes, 'that the Reform Bill is almost forgotten in London in consequence of overwhelming fears respecting the *cholera morbus.* It seems to be the prevailing opinion of the first physicians that it will visit this country, and you will see from the papers that the Government have taken some strong measures respecting quarantine and that a Board of Health is established. The prevailing complaint now in London is not however the cholera, but an influenza attacking the chest, accompanied by fever, and the sickness is sometimes fatal. We are better off here at present, and I linger to the last moment before venturing to take Eleanor back to the heated summer atmosphere of this now sickly city.'

It was to be Lady Franklin's last month in England for several years. After a few more weeks passed in anxious consultation and debate with her husband as to routes and methods of transport, Lady Franklin, accompanied by her father and her friends, the Kirklands, left Portsmouth on August 7, 1831, in a steam-packet bound for Cadiz and Gibraltar, whence, after a stay of some weeks in Spain and a visit to Tetuan, Mr. Griffin, who was of advanced age, and felt unequal to the fatigue of further travel, returned to England, the party pursuing their journey to Malta, where Lady Franklin had promised herself the pleasure of rejoining her husband. A signal disappointment, however, was in store for her. The Rainbow was under orders for Corfu, and Malta imposed a strict quarantine upon vessels coming from Gibraltar, so that the first meeting between husband and wife after nearly a year's separation took place under the unsatisfactory conditions thus described in a letter to her sister :—

We spent forty-eight hours at Malta, sleeping on board the steamer in order to save the trouble and expense of a stay at the lazaretto, and accepting the hospitality of our companions, who had established themselves in its desolate and spacious halls, for our meals. . . . My first communication with Sir John was by means of a letter brought me by Commissioner Briggs, which turned me sick and even continues to do so when I inhale its peculiarly offensive fumigation. Then he came alongside with his yellow flag and his yellow-cuffed guardians, and then I was put into a boat with *my* yellow flag and guardians (and to make the livery more complete I put on my yellow scarf also), and we were both landed on a narrow platform in front of the lazaretto, and narrowly watched on each side lest we should approach too near during half an hour's conversation.

The next day Lieutenant Aplin got permission to take Colonel Cochrane in his boat to look at Valetta Harbour, and I was landed on a rock with my guardians, and Sir John came off in a boat with his, and we had another conversation. They tell me it was two hours long. However this may be, the fatigue of standing a long while in the heat (though it was not so *very* hot), and of speaking at the top of my voice to make Sir John hear, united with the blinding effect of the bright water and the dazzling buildings, so overcame me that I was fit for nothing but my wretched berth on my return to the ship, and have been fit for nothing ever since we left Malta, the motion of the ship and the mosquitos which we brought away from the lazaretto aggravating my fever.

Corfu, however, was at last reached, and a house taken there, in which her husband, when not occupied with his duties on board the Rainbow, resided with her. Here is Lady Franklin's lively description of her quarters :—

We are now installed in our new dwelling at Mr. Crawford's, which is in a pleasant situation on the esplanade, facing the most romantic-looking rock that ever Nature or even fancy created, crowned by a citadel and lighthouse. We have a suite of four sitting-rooms in front, partly elegant, partly comfortable, but more than half shabby, having wretched stained and cracked walls, so thickly covered with spots of broken plaster that they look as if the young Crawfords had made it their business to discharge their arrows at them daily till a given portion was completed ; doors that seem falling off their hinges, chairs, tables, and sofas of various forms, most of which are groaning under the weight of all the newspapers, reviews, and other periodicals, maps and prints which bestrew them, and dirty open bookcases crammed with books which cannot always be drawn forth from their homes without bringing a variety of novel-looking and flourishing insects along with them. A dirty green baize covers the floor, and here and there a rich little Persian carpet forms a brilliant spot on the surface. The character of the whole is shabby elegance and somewhat dirty (certainly very dusty) comfort. The bedrooms at the back are more bare and less attractive. We have not yet proved their intrinsic merits.

The following extract from one of her letters to her sister, Mrs. Simpkinson, is in the satirical vein which it sometimes pleased her to adopt. The peculiar traits of character which she dwells upon in the personage whom she here sketches are already familiar enough to the world, but his personality still remains one of vital and enduring interest, and Lady Franklin's remarks have a right to be quoted as partaking, however slightly, of the historic quality of their subject :—

Young D'Israeli's follies on board the Hermes are of a piece with his and his companion's conduct here two years ago. They are quite a by-word at Corfu, the names of D'Israeli, Clay, and Meredith never being mentioned but to be laughed at. They apologised for being too late for dinner, because the scenery of the island did not enable them to think of such things ; accepted with hesitation an invitation to one of the regimental messes, saying it was a *trying* thing to dine at a mess ; avowed their utter inability to dine in anything but a large room, and with Sir Frederick Adam (who lives in what is called the Palace) behaved as if they thought their host was a very insignificant person indeed compared with themselves. Mr. Clay wore long ringlets down his cheeks, and was dressed in a complete suit of blue lined with velvet, with blue buttons and blue spurs ! Being asked by Sir Frederick what men deserved who drank port wine, he replied, ' They deserve to be sent to England.'

It is difficult to resist the suspicion suggested by the foregoing description of ' Mr. Clay's ' hair and costume that Lady Franklin has confused the identity of two of the young men. The third, Mr. Meredith, came, in the course of the very tour here spoken of, to a sudden and untimely end, to which reference is made hereafter.

Lady Franklin was as much charmed as are most of its visitors with the scenery of the island, especially with its magnificent olive groves—' trees as large and varied in their forms as the timber trees of a deciduous forest,' looking ' as old as the Creation, and as different from the dapper little olive trees planted in ranks in the South of France as are the wild Greek and noble-looking Albanian (whose picturesque and flowing costume is caught occasionally emerging from their shades) from the sprucely dressed gentry who display their Sunday coats on the promenades of that well-dressed nation on a *jour de fête.*'

But the unquiet England of 1831 was not to be forgotten even in this Levantine paradise. News of its disturbed condition reached them there from time to time, and produced its natural result :—

Sir John grows more anti-Radical and aristocratic in proportion as the people grow wild, and his are the most popular sentiments on board the Rainbow. The great mass of the society here being military, it is not to be expected that *they* either are very fond of the lawless rule of the mob, and the two regiments which are about leaving us, the 18th and 51st (to be replaced by others), feel, I believe, that they have no very pleasant prospects before them in returning to England at this moment.

Another of the letters of this date, a letter written by Lady Franklin to her father, from whom, it may be remembered, she had parted at Gibraltar, contains the following reference to a melancholy passage in the early life of the famous statesman whom the writer had previously criticised with her usual vivacious freedom in the letter above quoted :—

It was some satisfaction to me to see young D'Israeli on board, for though you may not be the companions best suited to each other, yet the sight of a familiar face and the identity of the scenes you had both recently visited relieve, I thought, the dulness of separation and departure. I thought young D'Israeli was looking very ill, and was told at Gibraltar that, though he assumed occasionally his usual vivacity, he was in fact in exceedingly depressed spirits, owing to the recent death of his friend and travelling companion, young Meredith, of whom report had spoken [as engaged to Miss D'Israeli], and whose marriage with her, since the difficulty occasioned by the late uncle's objection, might be supposed likely to take place.

In March 1832 Lady Franklin, having paid a visit to Malta, obtained a complimentary conveyance thence to Egypt in the Concord, an American corvette, to whose commander, Captain Perry, she took a strong liking, amusingly qualified at times by a certain patriotic jealousy to which the officers' remarks gave occasional provocation.

From Egypt she writes, giving an interesting account of an interview with a 'person of some importance in his day,' the famous Mehemet Ali :—

We had this day the good fortune to be introduced to the Pasha on board the Concord. He was accompanied by Mr. Boghoz (his first dragoman and Prime Minister), by Suleiman Aga (the last of the Mamelukes), and several other dignitaries. The yards were manned, salutes fired, and all the men called to quarters. The Pasha never receives ladies unless they disguise themselves in a man's dress, and the only European lady whom I have heard of as doing this is the wife of Colonel L., who seems a very extraordinary person. She is young and handsome, bold and romantic, and with these qualities has set off alone with only her janissary and two native servants for Thebes and the Cataracts. Captain Perry invited me and Mrs. K. to come on board, having previously informed the Pasha that we were the ladies whom he had brought out in the ship, so that we might be supposed to be living there. He seemed embarrassed, notwithstanding, at the first sight of us, and though advancing towards the cabin, drew back and turned round. Thinking better of it, however, he desired to be introduced to us, which being done, we took seats in his presence, as did also the Captain.

Here is Lady Franklin's word-sketch of this formidable personage :—

Mahomed Ali is a little and rather vulgar-faced man about 62 years of age, with an extremely quick little eye in perpetual motion, and a mouth expressive of humour and satire. Some people think they see in it the cunning and ferocity which mark the sagacious and bloody murderer of the Mamelukes ; and I am rather of their opinion, though in this it is not the English residing here who are my partisans, for with one accord they and, I believe, all the Franks residing here are disposed to palliate his crimes, and to regard him with admiration and respect, and something like affection. Interest may have something to do with this, but cannot account for it altogether. He is certainly a man beyond his country and his times. His dockyard has risen out of barren sands within three years, and his ready adoption of every improvement, as far as the means he has to work with admit, shows a character of no ordinary stamp. Ibrahim Pasha is thought to be a worthy successor of him.

Perhaps the part of this year's travel from which Lady Franklin derived the highest pleasure was her tour in the Holy Land. As everybody, however, who has made it knows, it is not an unmixed pleasure to the traveller, and so she found. 'I wished you yesterday at Jericho,' she writes to Mrs. Simpkinson, 'the first time perhaps that any one has ever wished you there, and certainly the first time you have ever been wished there with so friendly a meaning. But now that I know what it is to be at Jericho, I will not wish my cruelest enemy, if there be such a person in the world, ever there again.'

It was not, therefore, in order to herd with us under a filthy shed with our horses and Bedouins, obliged to cling close under the dwarf-walls of the most wretched of villages in order to be safe from robbers, devoured by mosquitos, so entirely lame in one inflamed leg in consequence that I was obliged to be carried whenever I moved or got up, and suffering much in head and stomach besides from having been eight hours on horseback under a hot and un-shaded sun, that I wished you at Jericho. I should have been con-tented had you seen us an hour before daybreak the next morning, mounting our horses to leave, my foot and leg much relieved by the poultice that had been applied to it in the night, and my head and stomach relieved by starvation and the freshness of the morning air.

The extraordinary elasticity, mental and physical, to which this rapid recovery testifies affords a singular commentary on Lady Franklin's repudiation, quoted a few pages further on, of her character for energy of spirit and vigour of body :—

I was mounted on my English saddle, with a white handkerchief on my head over sundry under-caps, the flaps of which are pinned in general over my face, partly in compliance with the custom of the country, which hides women's faces from view, and partly to save my face from the sun. I was attended by Owen [her maid] mounted astride, and by our faithful Egyptian servant, Achmet, by the guide of the Latin Convent at Jerusalem, by the Convent janissary, by our own janissary, granted us by Ibrahim Pasha the younger at the camp at Acre, by three others sent by the Governor of Jerusalem, and by twelve Bedouin Arabs, including their chief, three of whom were mounted on horseback with long spears or lances, and eight on foot—wild-looking creatures in striped blankets and coloured hand-kerchiefs on their heads, with muskets slung at their backs and swords or scimitars in their hands.

You should have seen our mounted guard as we crossed the desert plain of Jericho towards the Jordan, to which we were advancing, playing in their wild spirits at the game of war, exciting one another by wild screams, firing off their muskets and pistols, balancing and thrusting their lances at full gallop, wheeling, pursuing, receding, sweeping across our path, yet always with the nicest care avoiding being in our way. Then you should have seen the bright sun rise above the mountains of Moab beyond Jordan in front of us, and in another hour seen us arrive at the river's bank shaded with trees, and seen me with Owen, conducted by Achmet (all, as you may suppose, becomingly dressed, and with our guard keeping a respectful distance), walk into its rapid current and bathe in the sacred stream, dipping my wrought mother-of-pearl shells at the same time, and beads and crosses, and filling my bottles and phials with the water.

Then you should have followed us again through the desert plain for about an hour and a half to the Dead Sea, seen me carried out upon some stones that placed me fully in its transparent waters, and heard me choke and shudder at the intense nauseousness of the sip I took, and seen me fill a large can with the detestable water, for as rash and for much wiser folk than myself to sip and to analyse.

It was between ten and eleven o'clock before our jaded beasts arrived that night at the gate of Jerusalem, which had been left open for us. This excursion, which was one I had always set my heart upon, though I doubted my power of accomplishing it, was rendered much more fatiguing than it might have been by our exposure to the heat, though this was tempered by such beautiful mountain breezes that the suffering from it was at the time infinitely less than you might suppose.

Franklin's correspondence with his wife was, from the nature of the case and the pressure of his naval duties, of a less constant character; but his rare opportunities of communicating with her were always taken advantage of, and it is interesting to perceive from occasional passages in his letters how unwavering, amid all the absorbing preoccupations of his naval duties and the anxious work of diplomacy and maritime police, was his attachment to his old love of exploration. One may well suspect that for many an hour of his bodily imprisonment in Levantine waters his enlarged spirit was ranging the Polar Seas. It was just then a time well calculated to test the constancy of an Arctic explorer's passion. Sir John Ross and his nephew had been three years absent on that voyage in which all but the most sanguine believed that they had perished, and from which they did not return till after a fourth winter, like men risen from the dead. A search expedition was being organised in the autumn of 1832, and Back, it was said, was to be appointed to take command of it. 'But he has not written to me,' writes Franklin to his wife, 'and I have not the particulars of it. I am persuaded,' he adds, 'from the letters which passed between the Treasury and Richardson, who offered to go for half his former pay, that it will be settled on a most limited and economical scale.'

I shall be delighted to hear of his success, though I shall not be sanguine of it. He probably may learn where poor Ross met his fate, for I believe that to be sealed ; but I don't expect him to add much to the discovery of the northern regions.

I have written twice to Barrow, expressing my desire to command any ship or expedition to be despatched to the North Coast of America, and I am sure he has that friendship for me that he has borne my wishes in view. The present Government will not, I am convinced, allow of money being spent on any expedition that would permit me or any other captain to command. A ship being sent is quite out of the question in these economical days, and I much question whether I could bear the fatigue and anxiety of service by land without doing great injury to my constitution. I would try, however, if anything were to offer, and, if in England, should, I hope, be successful in my application. . . . I think my occupations at Patras may have brought me quite as much under the notice of the Admiralty and of the Government as the being employed on discovery. It has been a new field for me, and one in which I have had to act very much on my own responsibility in cases of difficulty not unconnected with the law of nations.

The Admiral's approbation of his conduct, though no immediate benefit resulted from it, might perhaps tell in his favour at some future day :—

The Admiralty, in their economical rage, are doing such remarkably odd things, and making so many clippings and alterations, that either promotion or employment seems to be hopeless even to persons of great influence. I cannot, therefore, hope any great exception should be made in my favour, though I believe (call it vanity, if you please) that Sir Thomas Hardy or Sir Pulteney Malcolm (who has much to say in the present naval alterations) would assist my views in case of anything turning up for which they thought me fitted, providing always, with them as with other public men, that it did not interfere with any of their plans for the increase of their own political interests or those of their immediate friends.

In the autumn of 1832 Lady Franklin was in Greece, and from Athens in November of that year she made one of the most interesting and most enterprising excursions of her Greek tour. It was made in company with a somewhat curious party of travellers, whose peculiarities, as well as the incidents of their companionship, she describes with her usual liveliness and spirit :—

We sailed on the 6th of November from the Piræus in a little Hydriote cutter belonging to a party of French military officers (one of whom had his wife with him), who had only on the preceding day, hearing of my wish to get away, come in a body, and in the most frank, cordial, and persuasive manner offered me a share of their accommodation, adding that they were going by Eleusis, Megara, and Corinth, and my only expense would be a dollar apiece for my party for this digressive excursion. I also of course added to the stock of provisions, which, after all, have only just lasted, such in particular was their enormous consumption ·of tea, sugar, and rum ! Of these three ingredients, they regularly at breakfast and tea made a great boiler full, which was handed round and round again in a metal pot.

This, however, was only one of their somewhat disconcerting habits ; for, continues Lady Franklin :

Kind as was their reception of me, it was impossible to be blind to their defects. Their noise and boisterousness, their incessant taking of God's name in vain [Lady Franklin perhaps attached a rather too serious English significance to the colloquial ' *Mon Dieu !* ' of the Frenchman], their gross and unblushing infidelity, glorying as they all did in the purest atheism, went far to counteract their amiable qualities. Of these, their extreme good-nature, the absence of selfishness in their dealings with one another, their desire to obtain and their willingness to communicate knowledge, their unconquerable vivacity and good-humour in all circumstances, were most remarkable. They all herded together in a small hold, where everything was cooked, besides giving up their cabin to us three females. It had a spacious locker all round, and in the middle of it we could stand upright and dress without being seen when a capote was thrown over the ladder-hole. As to all the rest, there are many reasons why it is pleasanter to travel with Frenchmen than with Englishmen with only insufficient accommodation, and such I experienced on this occasion.

Their 'desire to obtain and their willingness to impart knowledge' was thus amusingly illustrated :—

My French friends had all and each a journal, and if one of them had nothing to say he begged and borrowed from another or copied from books. This took up a good portion of their time, and was the only time when they were at all quiet. Their journals, which were generally of a quarto or folio size, were always in their hands whenever they landed, whether on foot or on horseback ; and the first bit of hewn stone they saw, down it went in the book. Perhaps part of it was buried in the earth, like a mutilated statue we saw at Eleusis ; no matter, they wrote down its length, breadth, and thickness. 'Voyons !' said they, 'that must be a torso.' They measured their pencils' length across it and said, 'Write down "The statue was fourteen feet high."'

At Eleusis I took on shore Gell's 'Attica,'[1] which, I saw, contained some account of it. They immediately fell rapaciously upon my book, and the first hut we came to they made me sit down in the middle of the room, surrounded by a number of wondering Palikari, and translate it into French, while they stood around with their books, copying and revising with much care from my dictation. Three pages I had to go through in this way; and thus an hour was spent before we began to look about us, though we were to return to the ship before we could get any breakfast.

The young lady of the French party, the officer's wife above referred to, 'also never moved without her paper in one hand and her pencil in the other ;' and here the shrewd Englishwoman lays a ready finger on a point of characteristic difference between the French and the English form of *mauvaise honte* :—

She did not care much about it, but she and her husband would have been ashamed for her to have neglected it. Her shame would have been misplaced, but surely the ridicule which attaches in England, or with some people in England, to be seen doing that before others which no one is ashamed of doing in private is scarcely less justifiable.

The eldest of our party, M. l'Intendant La Cour (a man of about fifty years of age), was possessed of a good deal of *esprit*, and was a poet. He excused himself from going to Eleusis, because during

[1] Of Dardan tours let dilettanti tell,
I leave topography to classic Gell.
—Byron, *English Bards and Scotch Reviewers*.

the night, he said, it being very hot so that he could not sleep, he had been making some verses on Salamis, which we had passed the evening before. 'C'est bien peu de chose, Madame,' said he ; 'mais, cependant, je crois y avoir mis quelque verve, et quelque chose de frappant.' 'Therefore,' added he, 'I will stay on board to put the last stroke to it and to look after your breakfast. At the Acrocorinthus we all knew that the classic Pierian spring is by some authors (as Pliny) supposed to have been here, while others fixed it at Parnassus.

Asked by M. La Cour for her own opinion on the point Lady Franklin was humorously equal to the occasion :—

I said that for *us* it must certainly be at the Acrocorinthus, unless he would agree to my proposal to go down the Gulf of Corinth and visit you at Patras, and in that case, *en passant*, 'Je le remettrai,' I said, 'au Parnasse.' 'Mais, que c'est charmant, cela !' replied the Intendant ; 'c'est une véritable muse, Madame, qui vous a inspiré cette idée.' As he understands a little English, I asked him if he knew the lines—

A little learning is a dangerous thing:
Drink deep, or taste not the Pierian spring.

On their being explained to him he was in raptures. 'Oserai-je vous demander, Madame, de me mettre cela en écrit?' He should, perhaps, be able to turn it to account in some happy moment of his own. We came to the Pierian spring, and the young and clever Dr. Ducis was holding the little wooden bowl to my mouth while I swallowed a thirsty draught, when he suddenly exclaimed, with great vehemence, 'Arrêtez, donc, Madame, arrêtez !' I looked up somewhat alarmed. 'Bien !' exclaimed he, looking slyly in my face ; 'car nous en avons plus besoin que vous.' Such are some of the truly French characteristics of my French friends.

'So you see,' she concludes triumphantly, 'I have been to Corinth in spite of the robbers and in spite of my disappointment at not going down the Gulf.'

To the tourist of these luxurious days, who may be apt to underrate the amount of 'roughing it' for which every traveller of either sex, robust or delicate, had to be prepared, the following graphic account of a melancholy experience of Lady Franklin's may well be commended. Touching at Myconi on her way to meet her husband at Syra, she found a young Englishman of her acquaintance whom she had left

but ten days before at Candia lying desperately ill in the
lazaretto. He had been reduced, he said, to this state by
'the villainous conduct of the Turks on board his vessel,'
where, although he had bargained for a place of better class,
he had been compelled to sleep on deck exposed for ten
successive nights to most tempestuous weather, with nothing
but his cloak to protect him. The vessel having put into
Myconi to take refuge from the gale, he had had himself put
ashore, but as, according to the despotic regulations of the
Greek Government, no quarantine could be performed and no
pratique obtained except at the islands of Syra and Hydra,
even his present confinement would avail him nothing, but
would have to be followed by another term of seclusion in
the former of those islands, to which he was bound :—

He had engaged (he said) a boat to take him to Syra, but was
not yet able to move. By degrees he seemed to recollect how strange
it was that I should be standing before him in conversation, and he
blessed the circumstances, whatever they were, that brought me there.
I told him I regretted that I could not stay with him, but if I did
so I should probably miss you at Syra, whither (as he knew) I had
returned in order to meet you, but probably I should do as much
good by returning to Syra and stating his case to our excellent Consul there, and procuring him as good quarters as could be had at the
wretched lazaretto here; but I advised him not to attempt moving
till he was a little better, which I trusted the medicine I should leave
with him would make him. He eagerly took my medicine, and
showed me his tongue, that I might see how very ill he was; but
could not ask me to feel his pulse, since I should then have put
myself in quarantine with him, for there were witnesses of our
actions. He asked me if I had ever seen so altered a man. I left
him a candle and a few utensils, and strongly recommended him to
the care of the Vice-Consul, as a gentleman well known and highly
respectable, and well able to pay for whatever he wanted, and I
begged the Vice-Consul to procure him a nurse instantly. It went
against my feelings and almost against my conscience to leave him
even thus; but if I stopped I missed you, and it was no use my
stopping unless I shut myself up with him in his single room, which
had only the earth for a floor, and where, if I contracted his quarantine, I should myself become a person whom no one could approach.
I had but lately come out of the Syra lazaretto—that is to say, out
of a shed of gaping planks a foot wide from each other in several

places, without a door to close the entrance, with the wet earth for a floor, swarming with water-rats, and with the rain coming down upon my bed through the roof of planks. I had been obliged to have the doctor immediately on leaving this shameful hole, and had scarce yet recovered from the effects of it.

At Syra, Lady Franklin immediately sought the assistance of the British Consul, and a boat was sent to fetch the sick man to the island. He arrived there some days later, worse than when she had left him—too ill, in fact, to be removed from the boat to a little chapel on the islet rock, which the Consul had kindly exerted himself to procure for him and thus save him from the unnameable horrors of the lazaretto.

I was too unwell on the first day after his arrival to go near him, but Mr. Hill, of Athens, who happened to be here and saw him, told me that Mr Lyons said I was 'an angel,' the best woman he had ever met in the world. There was he at Myconi, he said, sick and alone, when all at once I appeared before him and gave him medicines and comforted him.

'He was thought,' interjects Lady Franklin with a touch of her characteristic irony, ' to be a little light-headed.'

The next day I went alongside his little boat, but he was dozing in the confined hold, and I did not see him. Two or three days afterwards, having remarked to Mr. Jedder, the Church missionary here, that I could get no one to tell me exactly how Mr. Lyons was, and had been too unwell to go myself, he replied, 'I buried him yesterday !' They had concealed it from me because I was myself unwell and in low spirits ; and thus the poor man died in the hold of his tiny boat without a familiar face or friend near him, and only a hired Greek servant to watch his last moments. Mr. Wilkinson (the Consul) did everything that was possible, but he was speechless for some time before he died, and it was useless for him to shut himself up in quarantine in a hole a few feet in extent with a man dying of malignant fever. I would have given a great deal, however, to have been near him, so that he might have been conscious of it in his dying hour. I was the only human being here whom he could be said to know, and this reflection, together with the feeling that perhaps had I stayed with him at Myconi I might have saved his life, has made me feel the wish of paying the only atoning tribute to his memory, by having a stone erected at my own expense over the humble grave in the ground where he lies.   It will cost but a trifle, yet I did not venture to propose it to Mr. Wilkinson without diffi- dence, knowing that most common minds would sneer at the romance (to give it the prettiest name) of such an action.

With this pathetic story, so simply and touchingly related, these extracts from Lady Franklin's correspondence may fitly close.

CHAPTER XII

UNWELCOME LEISURE

1834–1836

AT the earliest moment after his arrival in England Franklin, as in duty bound, presented himself at the Admiralty, where, of course, he was warmly received. He had just been displaying an exceptional amount of that quality which the official, and especially the 'permanent' official, mind is wont to prize more highly in a British officer than any other human virtue—the quality of discretion. The First Lord was not on that occasion visible, but the staff of the department 'welcomed me,' says Franklin, 'most kindly, and each one spoke of the difficulties of my position at Patras.' An interview, however, of a far more interesting character, and with an infinitely more august personage, was awaiting him, and its circumstances must be related as he relates them in a letter to his wife :—

These preliminary duties performed, I went to Brighton and wrote to Sir Herbert Taylor that I had come down to pay my most dutiful respects to His Majesty by leaving my name in his book. About two hours afterwards I received a note from Sir Herbert to say that His Majesty would give me an audience at five the same evening, and that I was to dine at the Pavilion at seven   I was, of course, punctual to the time named, and was with the King three-quarters of an hour, and most closely questioned as to the present state of Greece, Turkey, and Syria.

His principal aim seemed to be to ascertain the state of feeling towards the Russian interest in each of these parts, and the means taken to thwart or encourage it. He inquired particularly about the position and strength of the forts of the Dardanelles, the public feeling at and about Constantinople and on the coast of Syria. He asked many questions about the harbours near the Dardanelles, of their fitness to receive and shelter fleets, of the distances from one part of the Archipelago to others, about the present state of Candia, about Ibrahim Pasha, and the opinion generally entertained in Syria as to being under the Egyptian Government. And, in fact, it was evident his mind was dwelling on the prospect of war, which then attracted general attention, but which was thought improbable. He asked what kind of person the King of Greece was, and said he sincerely hoped Greece would be established as an independent kingdom. He spoke of Sir Henry Hotham, of the intrigues of the Greek Capitani, which he said there was no doubt were fomented by the Russians; but he stopped me when I was proceeding to describe the manner of Ricord's conduct to Sir H. Hotham, and that of his captain to me, evidently showing that these were subjects he could not enter upon, though he gave me to understand he had been made acquainted with them. . . . On his rising and my retiring, the King thanked me for the information I had given him on several points upon which he required it, but had not met with any officer able to give it him so clearly; and he further added: 'This has been an interesting conversation to me. I shall see you (he further said) at dinner.'

I was there punctually at seven, and met a brother-officer (Lord Byron) as the lord-in-waiting. Sir Peregrine Maitland and Lady Sarah arrived soon afterwards (the former I had known in Canada), and in a short time the rest of the visitors appeared, and the members of the household, among whom there was interchange of conversation. The Queen entered the room with her attendants at a quarter after seven, followed by the Princess Augusta. She bowed to the gentlemen, who stood in line, in passing, and spoke to the two ladies who were visitors. The King appeared shortly afterwards. . . . Dinner being announced, the King desired the Duke of Dorset (the chamberlain, I believe) to lead out the Queen, and he offered his arm to the Princess Augusta. The Austrian Princess then followed, and the others according to their rank, each gentleman with a lady as long as any remained. I had none, and several others were so situated. I got agreeably placed next Lord Byron, though at the bottom of the table. Opposite me was Miss Wilson (maid of honour), whom my neighbour teased a good deal in directing her to look to every part of the table that she might find out Sir John Franklin, whom she much wished to see and had heard was at table.

The table was magnificently served—all the ornaments of gold. The King drank wine twice with me in company with my neighbours. The Queen withdrew at the time other ladies do at other tables, and the gentlemen in due time after. The Austrian Princess sat on the Queen's left, and the Duke of Dorset on her right; the Princess Augusta on the King's right, and Lady Saraa Maitland on his left.

The conversation was free, each with his neighbour, and the whole party very agreeable. On the King's rising to join the ladies, the gentlemen followed. He took his seat at a raised table, where also sat the Queen, the Princess Augusta, and the Duchess of Gloucester (who did not dine), the Countess of Mayo, Lady Sarah Maitland, and Lady Byron. The Queen and Princess were working, and conversation appeared to be lively among them, the King joining in it. At another table sat the maids of honour and three of the King's daughters, generally working; and at other tables gentlemen and ladies played cards. All were allowed to amuse themselves as they liked. None went to the royal table unless called, and the only person thus honoured was the Austrian Princess, who sat by the Queen. . . . The King did not speak to me in the drawing-room, nor to any other gentleman. Nor did the Queen speak to me. She looked closely at me, and I on two occasions caught her looking at me from her work-table with her spectacles. She is shy, and would perhaps have spoken if I had been near her. I only observed her speak to two of the visitors, except the Austrians. The King having at my audience yesterday asked whether I intended to make any stay in Brighton, I mentioned my wish to go to town the following day to see my child, if he had no further commands. He replied that it was quite proper I should go, and I accordingly left the next day.

Another interview of some interest, political and personal, took place a day or two later between Franklin and Sir James Graham, the First Lord of the Admiralty in Lord Grey's rapidly expiring Administration. Sir James, he says, 'kept me half an hour in close conversation, though there were many waiting to see him,' and the nature of the Minister's questions witnesses clearly enough to the keen anxiety of the official mind and to the threatening European situation which occasioned it. Franklin was most minutely interrogated as to Russian influence in Greece, the condition of Syria, the character of Ibrahim Pasha, and the opinion entertained of him by the Syrian population; whether, for instance, being a Mussulman and an acknowledged soldier, Franklin thought that 'in case of any overthrow of the Sultan by the Russians as a consequence of any insurrection' the Mahomedans of Syria would object to rally round Ibrahim if they were encouraged to do so; to which Franklin discreetly replied that, given that encouragement and an assurance of protection against the monopolies and exactions of Mehemet Ali, he thought they would not object.

He was then questioned, as he had been by William IV., with regard to the Dardanelles and its defences, the strong and weak points of the forts, the best means of taking them and of getting a fleet up the Straits. The Minister was especially searching in his inquiries as to the supposed state of feeling among the people generally at Constantinople, and what was likely to be the effect 'if the Russians were to march down among the mass of people not military or under the immediate influence of the Sultan. The Divan and higher classes, he thought, might be, and probably were, bought over by Russia.' Franklin replied, stating his impression that the people generally were not inclined to the Russian occupation, and that they would display this sentiment in action if warmly encouraged and assured of support.

It is worth remarking, as an illustration of the feeling in England towards the 'interesting people' in whose affairs Franklin had been for the last three years immersed, that hardly a question appears to have been asked him at this interview about the condition and prospects of the Greeks. What were the probable designs of the Czar, and what the state of feeling among the Mahommedan subjects of the Porte, were the sole questions of any interest to the ministerial mind at that moment. And not to the ministerial mind alone. On all hands it is the same story—a story which Franklin tells his wife not without a touch of mild disappointment in this same letter. We have seen already that he was no fanatical Philhellene, but it is evident that even he could have wished for a little more sympathy with the Hellenic cause than he found :—

You have been prepared to expect that Greece and its affairs occupy a very small portion of the public thought in England. The feeling is that of absolute indifference. The King, Sir James Graham, and Mr. Backhouse, the Under-Secretary of State, are the only persons who have spoken a word to me about them, and their conversation related to the political bearing of the subject with reference to Russia and to my transactions at Patras, which I may here mention seem to have attracted great attention. Though I thoroughly detest the modern Greeks, and would not for any consideration live among them, except from necessity, I take an interest in the welfare of Greece, and shall continue to do so, and therefore do not relish this indifference towards them.

An interest in the welfare of a country is, of course, not quite consistent with a thorough detestation of its inhabitants, but Franklin evidently meant no more than we all mean when we pronounce these sweeping judgments upon whole communities of men. They never amount to more than a hasty generalisation from certain conspicuous specimens of the nation condemned, and, on reflection, are usually felt, even by those who pronounce them, to be not wholly just. They are not perhaps wholly unjust, inasmuch as the offensiveness of the aforesaid 'prominent citizens' is usually due to characteristics common to the entire nation. The injustice consists in treating the exceptional exaggeration of these qualities as if it were no less common than the qualities themselves. Franklin, of course, knew well that behind the horde of greedy, lawless, and lying Greek adventurers with whom he had come principally in contact there was to be found, as there is in most countries, a community of honest, quiet, industrious, unsophisticated cultivators and traders, with all the virtues that the adventurer had 'shed' and with the vices which he had developed still dormant in the germ. These and not their unworthy leaders were the real people whom Franklin had been endeavouring to help, and it was their 'welfare' he was really thinking of.

Thus he concludes his account of his interview with Sir James Graham :—

Before I left him I said I hoped he would allow me to take this opportunity of representing to him that I was extremely anxious to be actively employed ; that during a professional life of thirty-four years I had scarcely been out of active employment, and therefore could not look upon the prospect of inactivity with any complacency. I was quite ready for any service. I knew (I continued) that there were many applicants with equally strong claims, yet I thought it due to my professional character to urge mine, on which alone I had to depend. Sir James answered that he feared he could not meet my wishes at present ; 'but if there was any stir,' he added, 'the case would be different. I should then, perhaps, be able to call for your services. I am well acquainted with your merits, and have received the strongest testimonials respecting your judgment and talents from Sir H. Hotham and Sir Pulteney Malcolm, and particularly in trans- acting the difficult affairs of Patras, and, believe me, I shall bear them in mind, and be happy to employ you when I can.'

To a First Lord overwhelmed with applications such urgency on the part of an officer who seemed to think that to have been scarcely out of active employment for thirty-four years was a reason for seeking, not repose, but renewed occu- pation, may well have seemed a little embarrassing if not unreasonable. But Franklin had no notion of allowing any such considerations to abate his insatiable thirst for work. His pertinacity, indeed, in hunting up the authorities seems almost to have astonished himself. For he continues, in his delightfully simple fashion :—

On reading all these details, you will fancy, my dearest, that your shy, timid husband must have gathered some brass on his way home, or you will be at a loss to account for his extraordinary courage. What will you say on learning that I have done all but the truly official part, principally because I knew you would have wished me to do so if you had been present, and therefore for your sake ?

Meanwhile Lady Franklin was still on her travels. About the time of his arrival in England she wrote to him from Alexandria, which she was about to quit in a few days' time for a trip up the Nile. There had been talk of her husband's joining her, but with her usual good sense and solicitude for his professional interests she declined to entertain a proposal which it is evident had been made mainly for her gratification. On January 8 she writes :—

It will be a good and sufficient reason why you should not come here (and that applies equally to your coming to Napoli or anywhere else), that by being at home you may be in the way of other employ- ment. There are some signs of a stir in the times—signs of war, and much talk, I am told, of various scientific expeditions. I should be sorry you were out of the way of profiting by any of these oppor- tunities, and if you stayed at home on this account I would instantly, on my return from the Nile, embark on a ship straight for England. . . . It would be equally unjust if you thought it was indifferent to me to part from you or otherwise than exceedingly painful ; but your credit and reputation are dearer to me than the selfish enjoyment of your society. Nor indeed can I properly enjoy your society if you are living in inactivity when you might be in active employ.

Then, reverting to a subject which was never long absent from Franklin's mind, and which his wife had trained herself to discuss with him in his own spirit, she continues :—

With respect to the expeditions, I regard them as affording a means of distinguishing yourself in your own peculiar line, which no command of a ship on any station in these times can by any probability present. The character and position you possess in society, and the interest—I may say celebrity—attached to your name, belong to the expeditions, and would never have been acquired by the career you have run, however fair and creditable, in the ordinary line of your profession. I am unable to judge, however, how far you feel equal to your former exertions, setting aside accidental sufferings, which, it is to be hoped, never need occur again. I would not have you go, to be like —— ; and God forbid you should go to the ruin of your health, if you should feel to be unequal to any of your former exertions. A *ship* expedition, however, does not seem liable to the objection, and a freezing climate seems to have a wonderful power in bracing your nerves and making you stronger. Mr. Thurburn tells me that an expedition is contemplated to the south, and that a north-west passage is still thought a feasible object. Now, young Ross cannot do both these at the same time, and if both are undertaken some one will step in to do the one while he undertakes the other. They tell me Parry is on his way home, and he will be working hard for the vacancy, or perhaps Richardson. I wish him well, and young Ross also. They are both fine fellows, and I grudge them nothing of their well-earned fame. But if yours is still dearer to me, even they could forgive me. . . I hope what I say will not displease you, and you must not think I undervalue your *military* career. I feel it is not that, but the other, which has made you what you are.

There are some of your friends who regret that you ever swerved from discovery to the beaten way of the majority of your profession. Is not Captain Beaufort of this opinion? I am not, however. You did not ask for a ship in the Mediterranean till you had again proposed yourself for another expedition, but it was not thought worth while. Now it is revived again. Have you thought of talking or consulting with Captain Beaufort on the subject?

The trip up the Nile was to be unavoidably delayed for some weeks, and in the meantime Lady Franklin continued her stay in Alexandria, sharpening her critical wits on the official and other native society in which she moved. She saw much of the *entourage* of the masterful Pasha, her description of whom has been quoted above. It was at the time of the troubles in Candia, when the defection of Osman, a trusted servant of Mehemet Ali's, was the theme of general conversation—' a crime,' writes Lady Franklin in her emphatic way, 'of the blackest dye, because he had been raised from nothing by the Pasha, and educated in Europe by him, loaded with riches and favours, and was in his confidence.' His sudden desertion, coupled with the wanton barbarities he had recently been committing in Greece (where he put to death some thirty people in the different towns and villages after they had at his summons dispersed quietly to their homes), excited the suspicion which the friends of Mehemet Ali would have been glad to see confirmed, that these acts of cruelty had been committed without the sanction of the Viceroy. ' I am sorry to say, however,' adds Lady Franklin, ' that Mehemet Ali does not disavow those executions, and thus deserves to draw down on himself the bitter consequences of such cold-blooded tyranny. I heartily wish that Candia may be wrenched from his grasp, for if it is not, and he deals with the poor Greeks in this manner, the island will soon be depopulated.'

Franklin's hopes of speedy employment, in so far at least as they were founded on the contingency of what Sir James Graham called a ' stir,' were but shortlived. Before the end of February we find him writing to Lady Franklin that the ' hostile appearances ' which were prevalent at the time of his audience of the King and interview with the First Lord of the Admiralty ' have been since removed,' though there is just a chance, he seems to think, that the thawing of the Baltic may again restore the warlike aspect of things by encouraging Russia to ' hold a higher tone than she has thought it prudent to do while her fleets were blocked in by ice.' On this account he does not think it advisable to ask the Admiralty for any prolonged leave of absence, which he would have to do if he were to accompany Lady Franklin on to Syria and

Greece, and to return by the Continent overland. Moreover, he evidently could not abandon the hope, which has beguiled so many another deserving officer, that his deserts had attracted the special notice of his official superiors. 'Sir James Graham at the Drawing Room the other day showed me a marked attention by leaving his wife's side to come forward and shake me by the hand, which I did not observe him to do to any other captain, though there were numbers around me.' And he goes on to relate how the Secretary had paid him a similar compliment, and introduced him to his daughters. 'These,' he adds, 'I admit, are in themselves trifles, though they show that I at least am not undeserving of being noticed in such a public place.' A more substantial recognition, and one which gave greater pleasure to his kindly heart, was the promotion by the Admiralty of two warrant officers at his request, and the provision of new berths for 'all the young mids of the Rainbow, mainly on account of the credit the ship had attained.' Their Lordships, moreover, 'had expressly appointed Kay (his first wife's nephew) to the Edinburgh in lieu of a candidate of stronger official interests, on my directing their attention to his merits and pointing out by letter the distinguished manner in which he had passed his examination.'

Having received all these proofs of the attention of the Admiralty to his professional claims, and having fully made known to them his earnest wish to be employed, it would surely be unwise of him, Franklin writes, to ask for a lengthened leave of absence, the very request for which might almost be taken to imply a change in his wishes with respect to active employment. At the same time, he did not himself regard the prospects of active service, at any rate of the kind which he preferred to any other, as hopefully as his wife. She had, he thought, been misinformed as to the probability of another expedition being sent to the North-west. 'The younger Ross,' he writes, 'has received an official reply from the Admiralty, saying that their Lordships had no intention of sending another expedition at present.' Nor had he ever heard the slightest hint of a South Polar expedition, of

which he felt sure he should have been informed through
Captain Beaufort if anything of the kind had been in contemplation. 'We may rest assured,' he adds, with, as the event
showed, an undue confidence in the possibility of forecasting
the operations of the official mind, 'that there will be no more
land journey after Back's return.'

You are quite right in thinking a cold climate would suit me. It
always has done, and I would rejoice in being sent on some service to
such a climate, but not to go for the mere desire of travelling, and
still less for the mere empty shadow of increasing my fame. I know
that my character has been appreciated by the officers of my profession, and others higher in station, whose good opinion I am proud to
have obtained, and you may rely upon it that they do not fancy me
to be so overcome with the love of repose as not to be ready and
most willing to obey any call for my services, to whatever part of the
world they may lead me.

Lady Franklin had in one of her former letters referred to
a Foreign Enlistment Bill then under consideration in Parliament, the result of which, if passed, would be, she seemed to
think, to enable Franklin, if all prospect of employment by
the Admiralty should fail him, to take service temporarily
under some foreign Government. It may be interesting to
cite his views, which were the general professional views of
his day, on a question not perhaps regarded as quite so free
from doubt in our own time. Observing on the fact that
Lady Franklin seemed desirous of directing his attention to
that field of activity, he continues :—

You will perhaps be surprised to learn that all officers of rank
who take such a step are considered by the heads of our profession
as mere adventurers. . . . I cannot agree with Mr. Thurburn that, if
a man distinguished himself in foreign service, it would aid him
when he returned to his own. I know, on the contrary, that there is
not a single instance of an officer who has been employed on foreign
service of late—since, in fact, such service has been solely a money-
getting adventure—who has returned to his own, or rather who has
been afterwards employed in his own profession ; and, therefore, if ever
I were to accept employment in a foreign service, I should consider
the act as putting a finish to all claims beyond the receipt of my half-
pay from my own, and in so doing I should only be guided by what
has happened to all the others. Except Lord Cochrane and Sartorius

and Napier, I know not any person of the rank of a captain who has been in foreign service.   And how many of junior rank have been compelled to quit foreign service by the neglect of their petty employers and disgust at the treatment they have received !   Your friend, Captain H., you see, had no idea of it after he was posted, nor, I will venture to say, will there be found above one or two in our whole 'Navy List' who would.   I cannot conceive a more humbling position than to place an officer of acknowledged merit in our service to be subjected to the whims and caprices of either Egyptian or Turkish rulers, or the equally unprincipled rule of Dom Pedro's or Miguel's advisers. The Dutch is the only foreign service that, in my opinion, a British officer of the rank of a captain could enter with credit to himself.

The year 1834 was saddened for Franklin by the death of his last surviving brother, James, who had returned from India in broken health and had now but a few months to live. He had led an active and distinguished life in India, and was a conscientious officer and a man of blameless reputation ; but during his closing days he seems to have become a prey to a religious melancholy almost as dark and despairing as that of Cowper.   John was unremitting in attendance at his brother's bedside, and in endeavours, at last, it would seem, successful, to console and cheer him.   He has left many notes of their conversations—notes not intended and not fitted for the public eye, but abounding in evidences of deep fraternal affection and full of a healthy and manly piety, which is all the more striking by its painful contrast with the morbid spiritual condition he was endeavouring to relieve.   James Franklin died on August 31, 1834, leaving one daughter, whom his brother virtually adopted and who accompanied him abroad on his next official employment, and remained a member of his household until her marriage.

In the autumn of 1834 Lady Franklin returned from her travels and took up her residence with her husband at a house in Gower Street, Bedford Square, where they appear to have stayed some months.   That weary wait for employment which has been the cause of so much heart-sickness to spirited officers in all piping times of peace, was still going on.   'You ask me,' he writes to Miss Franklin, whose affectionate sisterly anxieties as to his prospects had been accompanied by

inquiries after political news, ' how His Majesty and his people
get on together.' (It was four months after that historic *coup*
of William IV., the dismissal of the Melbourne Ministry by
an exercise of the prerogative.)

I think the people generally are much pleased with the King,
though there are several who are not satisfied with his Ministers [the
short-lived First Administration of Sir Robert Peel]. The Whigs
who held the government before have joined with the Radicals to give
every opposition they can to Sir Robert Peel's Ministry, and they are
expected to have a struggle for the majority on the subject of the
Tithes in Ireland. But though the Ministry may be defeated on that
question, it does not follow that they will go out, and I believe every
sincere wisher for the welfare of the country desires that they may
remain in office, since they are doing great good and have the confidence
of the country generally with them.

Alas for the desires of the sincere well-wishers! The sorely
pressed Ministry were thrice defeated in the course of the
next fortnight on the Tithe question, and at the third defeat
resigned.

You ask, secondly, what my prospects are. At present I have
no employment in view, though I have made application for it in
common with many others. Having been recently afloat, and there
being but few ships in commission, I cannot expect to be preferred
before many other officers of merit. I keep, however, on the watch
for anything that may offer.

Franklin did not, however, consider it necessary to maintain a watch of such extreme vigilance as would keep him
perpetually within half an hour's walk of the Admiralty. In
the course of the summer of 1835 he indulged himself and
his wife with the distraction of a tour in Ireland. They had
excellent introductions to many notable people both of the
social and the scientific world, and merely as an expedition
of pleasure their visit was a complete success. But Franklin's
untiring intellectual curiosity and thirst for information made
it impossible for him to regard any sojourn in a new country
from the point of view of mere amusement, and his well-filled
notebooks attest the diligence with which he endeavoured
to make himself thoroughly acquainted with the rural and

economical conditions of Irish life. The success with which he applied himself to this task was soon to receive public proof. Experience of his past services had, no doubt, satisfied the official mind that his shrewd observation and sound judgment would make his opinion worth having on a question of Irish maritime industry, even after but a brief visit to the country. He was invited to give evidence before the Royal Commission then engaged on the Irish Fishery Inquiry, and made several practical recommendations of considerable value. Like most other students of the peculiarities of the Irish people, as illustrated in their industrial habits, he had been equally impressed by the excellence of the Irishman's natural gifts and by his singularly ineffective employment of them. The West Coast population evidently struck him as a race of potentially admirable fishermen, who, as a matter of fact, did not know how to fish. He recommended accordingly, as 'politic means of improving the fisheries,' the stationing of 'substantial fishing vessels by Government on the Western Coast, to be manned with experienced fishermen and provided with a complete outfit of nets and other fishing gear, such vessels to be placed on several parts of the coast, two in company, to instruct the local fishermen in the best modes of fishing.' The commander and the mate of each of these ships would be the actual instructor, their crew of pupils being selected from the boatmen of the adjacent coasts ; and Franklin laid much stress on the point that these instructors should also be 'experienced seamen,' in order that the local fishermen might be taught to navigate square-rigged vessels into harbour, thus combining with the fishing industry the avocation of a scientific pilot. His idea, in fact, was that when the full benefits of the system of training were realised, every fishing vessel on the western coast might contain two fishermen capable of acting as pilots, whereby not a little saving of life and property might, he thought, be effected, inasmuch as many ships could then take shelter in western Irish harbours, to which vessels in distress had hitherto been unable for want of pilotage to resort.

Franklin, it is hardly necessary to say, was perfectly well

aware that nothing effectual could be done for Ireland, then as now, without a draft upon the British Treasury, and he did not suggest the establishment of these model vessels as a substitute for pecuniary assistance, but as a precaution against that futile squandering of aids and benevolences furnished at the cost of the British taxpayer which has been the sole outcome of so much of our legislative and administrative philanthropy where Irish industry is concerned. The witness 'does not believe,' run the minutes of evidence, 'that by the presence of the model vessels fishermen would be enabled to equip themselves properly for the sea-fishing, but he considers these vessels necessary for guides, by which any means placed within reach of the fishermen may be judiciously applied.'

Events had already shown, and were now to prove even more decisively, that there was some ground for the apprehension felt by Franklin as to the possibility of his falling out of the line of Arctic explorers if he sought other forms of naval employment. When, however, he accepted his Mediterranean mission, it certainly did not look as if there were much to be gained by waiting till it should please the Government to despatch another expedition to the Polar regions. Arctic exploration was distinctly at a discount at that moment in the official mind. With the return of Parry's third and most famous expedition in 1827, when he reached a latitude of 82° 45' and established a 'record' which was not to be beaten for nearly half a century—that is to say, not until Sir George Nares's party outdid it by half a degree in 1875—the British Government seemed to think that they had done enough for honour. Parry's gallant attempt had cost a sum of 9,900*l.*, which, though far from excessive, considered relatively to the splendid results achieved by it, was yet quite sufficient to chill the exploratory ardour of an average Chancellor of the Exchequer. No doubt, too, the British public, always liable to temporary qualms of conscience as to the value of adventurous enterprises in terms either of money or of human life, were not disposed to encourage any further undertakings of a dangerous and costly kind. After every great outburst of his maritime spirit John Bull is apt to fall into the mood of Sindbad and Gulliver, and to vow that he will never go to sea any more.

It was during one of these periods of reaction that Franklin had accepted his Mediterranean appointment, and the years which had elapsed had wrought no change in, at any rate, the attitude of the Government. On the contrary, it is natural to suppose that certain memorable incidents of Arctic adventure in 1829–33 may have done something to confirm them in it. But unfortunately for British Governments, their involuntary relation to this business of exploring the desolate parts of the earth is, after all, much the same as their equally involuntary relation to the no less characteristically British activity of penetrating its inhabited but unfriendly regions. They may discountenance exploring raids upon Nature as earnestly as they discountenance attempts to open up territory inhabited by savage tribes; but in both cases they are expected to help the adventurers out of a mess. Thus, when in 1829 Sir Felix Booth fitted out the Victory and sent out Captain John Ross, accompanied by his afterwards even more famous nephew James, to seek the North-West Passage, the Government had no means of foreseeing that, after a voyage most fruitful in scientific results and resulting in the discovery of the Magnetic Pole, the gallant vessel would be frozen up for no less than three solid years in its winter quarters, and that they would be called upon to send, and would send, an expedition to its relief.

Yet so it had been. In the year 1833, just at the close of Franklin's protracted struggle with Greek heroes at Patras, the British Government had to despatch a party under the command of Captain Back, with orders to proceed by the Great Fish River to the northern shore of Arctic America, whence he was to endeavour to reach Cape Parry, where it was anticipated that intelligence of the missing expedition might be obtained. For it was known that Captain Ross in some measure relied for support, in case of unduly prolonged absence, on the stores that had been landed from the Fury when that vessel was unfortunately wrecked in 1823. The Rosses, however, had already been picked up, and were being brought home by a whaler when the search party reached Arctic latitudes; and thereupon, in pursuance of his instructions—for, to do the Government justice, they seem to have thought that, whether he succeeded in rescuing the Rosses or not, he might as well do some exploring while he was on the spot—Back proceeded to trace the course of the Great Fish River, which has since borne his name as an alternative title, to its mouth. This work was completed on August 16, 1834, when his expedition reached its most northerly point on King William Island.

His success did much to rekindle scientific interest in the survey of the Arctic coast of America, and it is not impossible that the appetite of the Government itself for Polar discovery may have come to them, according to the French saying, *en mangeant*. It is, at any rate, certain that, at the instance of the Royal Geographical Society, they consented to attempt the completion of the survey of the North American coast between Cape Turnagain, Franklin's furthest eastward from the Coppermine River, and the point reached by Back from the Great Fish River, which debouches still further to the east. The connection of these two points would have completed the exploration of the American coast-line from Behring Strait to a meridian of longitude which had been already crossed by Parry travelling westward at a higher latitude. In other words, it would have caused the eastward line of exploration from Behring Strait and the westward line from Baffin's Bay to overlap, and have left nothing but a gap of some four degrees of latitude to be bridged over in order to complete the North-West Passage. Considering that more than half of the sixty odd degrees of longitude that divide Behring Strait from King William's Island had been explored by the two parties sent out under Franklin's command in 1819 and 1825, the leader of those expeditions would seem to have been naturally designated for the duty and the honour of completing the survey. The claims of Back, however, were at once too strong and too recent to be over-

looked; and Back accordingly was selected. A not un-
generous envy of his old comrade's good fortune is, I think,
discoverable in Franklin's correspondence of this period; and
his feeling in this matter was possibly strengthened by the
fact that, much as he admired Back's high courage and adventurous spirit, he does not seem to have formed an equally
favourable estimate of his abilities as an explorer. It was
wholly foreign, however, to his frank and friendly character to cherish either disappointment with respect to the
leadership of the expedition or misgivings as to its results.
When Back sailed from England in the Terror, that strenuous
and indefatigable challenger of Arctic and Antarctic dangers.
he was sped. upon his enterprise by no one with a more
cheery enthusiasm than by the former leader who had sustained and been sustained by him fifteen years before in their
deadly struggle with frost and famine in the Barren Lands.

It turned out an ill-fated and fruitless expedition. The
Terror left England on June 24, 1836, but was beset by ice
in Hudson's Strait in the following September, and for the
next ten months drifted helplessly in the pack. When at
last released she was found to have sustained such severe
injuries that all thought of further navigation northward had
to be abandoned, and her head was turned homeward.

Thus Back describes his experiences in a letter to Franklin
of the following year, the opening passages of which give
pleasant testimony to the strong attachment subsisting between
the two men. After warmly congratulating Franklin on his
success in the new sphere of duty upon which by that time
he had entered, the writer goes on :—

I know that John Barrow informed you of my arrival, after a most
trying time, among the ice, which was so close as to preclude the possibility of gaining ground. I overtook the Bay ship in the Strait, and,
had it been practicable, would have gone to the south of Southampton
Island ; but there was not the smallest chance, and, therefore, keeping
north, our advance was satisfactory enough until close to Frozen
Strait. There the northern and western ice came down in large floes
and packs, the detached pieces being old and heavy. Finally, we
were frozen in at sea, and for some time were drifted about with the
entire body without much injury ; at length we were nipped, and

subsequently the ice came in masses, throwing up pyramids and causing a devastation scarcely to be imagined, until long rolling waves from ten to thirty feet produced such confusion and havoc that the stern-post and twenty feet of the keel were forced over three and a half feet to port, the eighteen-inch square beams bent, bulkheads fell down, and lastly the ship was pressed upon the surface of the ice forward.   There she suffered for four months and eventually got clear from the ice in August, just completing the year from the day of entering in.   Two chain cables were passed across the ship to keep her together across the Atlantic, and often she was near sinking.   At length she got to Lough Swilly, and the following day she settled down by the head and was beached.   Being patched up, she was towed round to Chatham and paid off. . . . This business has shaken me much.

As well it might.   But there was good work left not only in the future Sir George Back, but in the stout ship which had struggled home with him, staggering under her wounds, across a thousand leagues of sea.   The Terror was refitted and, as all the world knows, made ready for further exploring service.   Two more journeys was the gallant ship to make to the two opposite poles of the world before the end of her days ; nor till she had seen the midnight sun shining in midwinter on the icebergs of a new continent in the furthest southern waters was she to take her last voyage northward and leave her tough old bones in the Arctic pack.

CHAPTER XIII

A NEW APPOINTMENT

1836

No doubt it was the feeling of having dropped out of the line of explorers that lent an additional stimulus to Franklin's desire for active service in some other form. A year or a year and a half ashore was always a sufficient spell of the landsman's life for him. Early in 1836 we find him stirred by the same longing after some outlet for his restless energies that had agitated him so often at former periods of his career. In these quiet times, however, and with his favourite avenue of adventure closed to him, he no doubt felt it vain to hope for any opportunity for service afloat, and it was in a spirit of complete readiness for official employment of any sort that he now proceeded to address the Government.

His claim to what he sought from them was undoubtedly strong. Even those who have followed his career thus far in these pages will perhaps hardly realise how strong it was until they see his many and varied services brought together in a concise statement, such as is embodied in the following formal application from him to the Board of Admiralty:—

I entered H.M. service in October 1800 on board the Polyphemus (64), Captain (now Admiral) Lawford, and was in that ship in the battle of Copenhagen, 1801. I soon afterwards joined the Investigator, Captain Flinders, and was employed for the greater part of the three following years in the survey of the coast of Australia. On that ship being condemned as unfit for the further prosecution of that service, I was sent with the officers and crew into the Porpoise, Lieutenant (now Captain) Fowler, late the first lieutenant of the Investigator. That ship and another being wrecked in company on a coral reef on the east coast of New Holland, their united crews, consisting of ninety-four persons, had to remain upwards of eight weeks on a desolate bank of coral, not of greater circuit than a quarter of a mile, subsisting on the provisions obtained by great exertions from the wreck of the Porpoise. Captain Flinders returned to Port Jackson, upwards of six hundred miles, in an open boat, and, having freighted a merchant vessel, brought her to our relief, and also a schooner, in which he proceeded to the Isle of France. I accompanied Mr. Fowler and the crew in the merchant vessel to Canton, where we were distributed among the different East India ships for a passage to England. I had the good fortune of having continued with my commander on board the Earl Camden, Captain Davies, and was appointed to the charge of the signals on the occasion of the East India Fleet beating off the squadron of Admiral Linois, which was lying in wait to intercept the fleet on its homeward passage.

On my arrival in England I joined the Bellerophon (74), under the command of Captain Loring, and was employed in the Channel Fleet, and, secondly, of Captain Cooke, who was killed in the battle of Trafalgar, in which action I was entrusted with the responsible charge of the signal department on board the Bellerophon. In the year 1807 I joined the Bedford (Captain the late Rear-Admiral Walker), and in a month afterwards was promoted to be acting lieutenant of the ship on the occasion of the royal family of Portugal embarking for the Brazils, whither the Bedford accompanied them. I was confirmed a lieutenant in February 1808, and remained in the same ship on the Brazil station upwards of two and a half years; then on the North Sea station; and had the honour of being in the Bedford when she formed one of the squadron under the command of His present Majesty when the Allied Sovereigns were escorted by H.R.H. the Duke of Clarence to this country.

On the conclusion of the war the Bedford was despatched with other ships of war to convey troops for the attack on New Orleans, and on the occasion of the capture of the American gunboats on Lac Borgne I commanded the boats of the Bedford, and was so fortunate as to be the first person on board one of their vessels. I received a wound on this service. I was subsequently employed for nine weeks in the boats and with the army on shore, and had the gratification of being mentioned in the official despatches of General Lambert.

The day the Bedford was put out of commission I was appointed first lieutenant of the Forth (48), then ready to convey H.R.H. the Duchesse d'Angoulême to France, and remained in that ship till she was put out of commission.

My next appointment was to the command of the Trent, as second to Captain Buchan, who was sent to attempt the Pole by steering directly north between Greenland and Spitzbergen, and I afterwards had the honour of commanding two expeditions by land to the Polar Sea, which gave me full occupation from 1819 to the close of 1827. At the close of this service I was honoured by having a knighthood conferred on me by His late Majesty.

In 1830 I had the gratification of being appointed to the command of the Rainbow, and was employed upwards of three years in the Mediterranean, under the command of Sir Pulteney Malcolm and the late Sir Henry Hotham, during the whole of which, except about two months, I had the honour of being entrusted by these distinguished officers with a detailed command. To one of these services I may be permitted perhaps more particularly to allude, on account of the importance attached by Sir H. Hotham to the careful execution of his orders, and because I know that the Admiral transmitted the whole of my correspondence connected with this service to the Admiralty, with repeated testimonies of his own approbation at my conduct, which documents are now either at the Admiralty or the Foreign Office. I mean the being stationed before Patras for eleven months as senior officer of the allied vessels while the garrison was held by an insurgent force, which at length I had the happiness of seeing delivered over to the troops of the King of Greece. This service procured for me the official approbation of the Admiralty, notified through my Commander-in-Chief, as well as letters of thanks from the British Consul and the Agent of Lloyd's, and the honour of the Golden Cross of the Order of the Redeemer, which was sent me after my return to England by His Majesty King Otho.

There seems an undesigned touch of the ironical in Franklin's observation that the official documents recording the commendations of his superior officers are now 'either at the Admiralty or the Foreign Office.' Much the same difficulty as attends the tracing of such testimonies to their departmental depositary has often before this been experienced in finding the recognition which it is hoped that these eulogies may insure. Governments are always officially grateful for services rendered to the State ; but the trouble with many deserving public servants is to discover the department—or it may be the pigeon-hole—in which that sentiment is kept.

Searches in the present instance seem to have been successfully instituted, and the ministerial gratitude was discovered. Indeed, in the spring of 1836 it had already begun to dawn upon the then Government that a naval officer of high distinction and proved ability had been for three years condemned to 'rust unburnished,' while the strongest desire of his heart was, now as ever, to 'shine in use.' The Colonial Office was, it seems, the first department to open its eyes, and its authorities then at once proceeded in thoroughly characteristic official fashion to ascertain what was the most unimportant post that the aforesaid distinguished officer could be prevailed upon to accept. Accordingly, the following correspondence passed between the Colonial Secretary, Lord Glenelg, and Sir John Franklin :—

Colonial Office : March 19, 1836.

Dear Sir,—I request to know if you retain the inclination which you once expressed to accept of some colonial office. The Government of Antigua is now vacant, and if it should suit your views, I should have great pleasure in placing your name before His Majesty.

I remain, dear Sir, yours faithfully,
GLENELG.

The reply of Franklin is notable for the homely simplicity with which he admits obligations to a counsellor whom a false pride might have prevented too many men in those days from acknowledging :—

My Lord,—I cannot sufficiently thank your Lordship for the very kind manner in which you have noticed the conversation I had the honour of having with you on the subject of some colonial appointment, and I feel much flattered and gratified by the offer your Lordship has been pleased to make me of the Governorship of Antigua ; but, as Lady Franklin is out of town, I will venture to defer giving my answer for a few days, till I have had the opportunity of consulting her.

I have the honour to be
Your Lordship's most obedient servant,
JOHN FRANKLIN.

Such a consultation was likely to have but one result. It is true that the great self-governing British colonies of our own time had not in those days risen into that importance which now dwarfs all our colonial possessions by comparison ; but even in the fourth decade of the present century Antigua must have held quite a third-rate position among the dominions of the Empire. Nowadays it does not even furnish a governorship to the Official List. Although the seat of government and residence of the Governor of the Leeward Islands, it is itself merely one of the ' Presidencies ' of that group, and its President holds the office *in commendam*, so to speak, with the colonial secretaryship of the Islands, at an addition of only 50*l.* a year to his official salary in the last-mentioned capacity. In 1836 it was assuredly no great catch for an officer of Franklin's distinction, as indeed he subsequently pointed out with his usual sailor-like bluntness to the Colonial Secretary himself.

Lady Franklin was against acceptance of the offer, and all the official acquaintances whom he consulted on the subject, among whom was his intimate and valued friend Captain Beaufort, the well-known Hydrographer to the Admiralty, concurred in her opinion. It was a lieutenant-governorship not in direct correspondence with the Colonial Office, and the salary, 1,200*l.* a year, was inadequate, Franklin was assured by those well acquainted with Antigua, to the social requirements of the position. Captain Beaufort, to whom Lady Franklin's letter of advice was shown by her husband, described it as 'the letter of a woman of most excellent sense, judgment, and feeling;' and added that, if he had ever entertained the least doubt as to the advisability of declining the appointment as soon as he knew that it was only a lieutenant-governorship, that letter would have decided him. He recommended his friend at once to call on the Colonial Secretary and lay before him the considerations which compelled a refusal of his offer. On this advice Franklin acted in the characteristic fashion described as follows in a letter to his wife :—

Accordingly, I went to Lord Glenelg (who received me with much cordiality), and began by saying that the gratitude I owed him, and the desire I had on every account to accept his kind offer, had made me take the time for consideration which I had done, and that it was with regret that the information I had gained had led me to the decision I should have to convey to him. I mentioned the inadequacy of the salary for keeping up the station as I should feel it my duty to do. He said he was aware of this inadequacy, and expressed his regret at being unable to improve it. I assured him, however, that this was by no means a primary consideration with me, and that I was even prepared to spend a part of my private income in this service (and that, too, with your consent) if other circumstances had been equally favourable in the appointment ; but that the point upon which my decision had rested was the not having to communicate with the Colonial Office directly, and that every official communication of mine must go through the Governor, which Lord

Glenelg admitted was the case. I had been accustomed, I told him, to holding positions of responsibility and command, and I mentioned the duties entrusted to me during my station in the Mediterranean; and I trusted that he would not consider me presuming in thinking, as did also many of my brother-officers, that I ought, in justice to my professional reputation and character, to look to some more responsible appointment than that of lieutenant-governor of an island where the chief could by any means, at any time, in six or eight hours, come in person to direct the affairs if he chose to do so. This seemed, I said, to be little more than being first lieutenant of a ship of the line.

The candour and straightforwardness of this behaviour had a good effect. 'Depend upon it,' said Captain Beaufort, when informed of what had passed, 'you have taken a step that will increase Lord Glenelg's respect and regard for you;' and the observation was speedily confirmed. Little more than a fortnight after this interview, Franklin received the offer of the governorship of Van Diemen's Land.

The terms in which it was conveyed were most flattering, and the dignity, independence, and amenities of the post gave it so marked a superiority over that which had been previously offered him, that Franklin felt he had no choice but to accept it. If anything could have made him hesitate, it would have been the doubt whether acceptance would definitely cut him off from naval employment in the future; and on this point Captain Beaufort reassured him in convincing if colloquial language. ' As for the idea,' he said, 'that the Admiralty might consider you as put on the shelf by accepting this appointment, depend upon it that is "all my eye." You may rely on their being glad to employ you later if you wished and they have a ship to give.'

The following letter from Dr. Arnold, whose acquaintance Franklin had made through the Stanleys, the family of the young officer who had served under him in the Rainbow, deserves quotation as showing how high an estimate of Franklin had been formed by men as appreciative of the moral aspects of character as the famous Head-master of Rugby :—

Rugby : May 1, 1836.

My dear Sir,—As Mrs. Stanley is going in a day or two to London, and is likely soon to see you, I avail myself of the opportunity to offer you my congratulations on your appointment to the governorship of Van Diemen's Land. I am not so sure, however, how far this appointment may be a subject of congratulation to yourself, as I am sure that it is to the settlement and to the public service ; and, feeling as I do the immense importance of infusing good elements into an infant society, it is to me a matter of most sincere rejoicing that a growing settlement like Van Diemen's Land will have the benefit of your management and character. But I am told that the climate and the country are agreeable, so that I hope that neither yourself nor Lady Franklin will dislike your new situation. Mrs. Arnold unites with me in the kindest remembrances to Lady Franklin, and in every good wish to you both for your health and happiness.

And a couple of months later an offer from Franklin to find some colonial employment for two of Dr. Arnold's sons drew from him the following letter, valuable not only for its characteristic expression of the writer's general views of life, but for the new light which it throws upon his inclinations with regard to his own future :—

The business part of your letter I attended to immediately by writing at once to say that I should have much pleasure in receiving your nephew after the Christmas holidays. . . . I delight to receive boys of good character and promise, and yet the pleasure is mingled with a proportion of anxiety ; for of all the painful things connected with my employment nothing is equal to the grief of seeing a boy come to school innocent and promising, and tracing the corruption of his character to the influence of the temptations around him in the very place which ought to have strengthened and improved it. And yet this does happen sometimes, though certainly in most cases those who come to school with a character of positive good are improved and benefited. It is the neutral and indecisive characters which are apt to be decided by the temptations of school—as they would be, in fact, by any other temptations.

And now let me thank you most heartily for your truly kind offer with regard to my boys. I shall be truly thankful to be allowed to bear it in mind as my younger boys grow up ; and if either of them were disposed to try his fortune in a new settlement, it would be an unspeakable comfort to me to be able to send him to Van Diemen's Land while you were Governor, and to recommend him to your kindness and to Lady Franklin.

But I sometimes think that if the Government would make me a bishop or the principal of a college or a school, or both together, in such a place as Van Diemen's Land, and during your government, I could be tempted to emigrate with all my family for good and all.

There can be, I think, no more useful, no more sacred task than assisting in forming the moral and intellectual character of a new society. It is the surest and best kind of missionary labour ; but our colonial society has been in general so Jacobinical in the truest sense of the word—that is, every man has lived so much to and for himself, and the bonds of law and religion have been so little acknowledged as the great sanctions and securities of society— that one shrinks from bringing up one's children where they must in all human probability become lowered, not in rank or fortune, but in what is infinitely more important—in the intellectual and moral and religious standard by which their lives would be guided. . . . Feeling this, and holding our West Indian Colonies to be one of the worst stains on the moral history of mankind, a convict colony seems to me to be even more shocking and more monstrous in its very conception. I do not know to what extent Van Diemen's Land is so ; but I am sure that no such evil can be done to mankind as by this sowing with rotten seed and raising up a nation morally tainted in its very origin. Compared with this, the bloodiest exterminations ever effected by conquest were useful and good actions. If they will colonise with convicts, I am satisfied that the stain should last not only for one whole life, but for more than one generation ; that no convict or convict's child should ever be a free citizen, and that even in the third generation the offspring should be excluded from all offices of honour or authority in the colony. This would be complained of as unjust and invidious ; but I am sure that distinctions of moral breed are as natural and as just as those of skin or of arbitrary caste are wrong and mischievous. It is a law of God's Providence which we cannot alter, that the sins of the father are really visited upon the child in the corruption of his breed and in the rendering impossible many of those feelings which are the greatest security to a child against evil.

Forgive me for all this, but it really is a happiness to me to think of you in Van Diemen's Land, where you will be, I know, not in name, nor in form, but in deed and in spirit, the best and chief missionary. My wife joins me in kindest, may I venture to say in most affectionate, good wishes to yourself and Lady Franklin.

Nothing, perhaps, could better illustrate the peculiar hardness of the philosophic Radicalism of that day than the views of this excellent and most kind-hearted man on the subject of the 'convict's stain.' The very same political creed which led some of those who held it into excesses of mawkish sentimentalism on questions of penal discipline was capable, in a mind like Arnold's, of begetting a theory of hereditary contamination which as regards its shock, both to the reason

and the sympathies, might compare fitly with the strictest
caste rules of the Hindoo. This tendency, however, of his
particular school of thought has perhaps been observed before.
To those who have noted it, it will be of more interest to
learn that even in 1836, only six years from his lamented
death, Dr. Arnold could look longingly from his work at
Rugby to a colonial bishopric.

Among the congratulations which poured in upon
Franklin on his appointment to the governorship of Van
Diemen's Land was one to which he attached a value that
the people of other countries would no doubt find some difficulty in understanding. The county is to the Englishman much what the clan is to the Scotchman, and the
sentiment of 'local patriotism,' so to speak, which the one
is capable of inspiring is no inadequate substitute for the
feeling of tribal unity which is the strength of the other.
Next to the approval of his Sovereign and his country, and
not so very far behind it, the typical Englishman of the
provinces will usually rate the applause of his county ; and
the strength of this feeling came out quaintly enough in
Franklin's acknowledgment of that traditional compliment,
the public dinner given in his honour by his Lincolnshire
brethren. The occasion was in one respect convenient, for
Franklin was at the time staying in the county for the
purpose of being present at the wedding of his niece, Miss
Louisa Selwood, to the Rev. Charles (Tennyson) Turner, who,
he writes, 'is described to me as being very good in temper
and disposition,' and whose 'two brothers, the eldest and
the third, Alfred (the poet), dine here to-day, and also the
eldest sister, as being very desirous to make my acquaintance.'

On June 11 the complimentary dinner came off at Horncastle. ' I felt very nervous in the forenoon,' says Franklin,
to whom no doubt the anticipation of returning thanks was
far more discomposing than the prospect of a battle with an
Arctic gale, 'but this passed off before I had to make my
speech, which I can assure you was very favourably received.
I had also,' he adds, ' to return thanks for you (Lady Franklin)

on your health being drunk, and for Dr. Richardson and Hepburn and Back. Great enthusiasm was shown. There was a large proportion of clergymen, with the Archdeacon at their head. The bells were ringing most of the day. Boys and girls had a holiday, and in the evening there was a grand display of fireworks. The latter, however,' he continues with amusing scrupulousness, 'was accidental, that evening having been previously fixed upon by the exhibitor.' Spilsby, his native town, had not associated itself with this tribute, its inhabitants preferring, instead of going to the dinner, to subscribe for a piece of plate, which was duly presented to their distinguished fellow-townsman, and by him duly acknowledged.

The sturdy local patriotism which animated him found characteristic expression in his reply to the toast of his health. No one evidently would have more warmly repudiated the description so repeatedly given of his native county by that well-known authority, Master Roger Wildrake, of Squattlesea Mere, as 'the moist county' of Lincoln. 'Some say,' exclaimed Franklin, that 'it is a county of fens; he would tell them to look at its fertile fields, to view its flocks, its crops of grain, and its general character; and, even with respect to the fens, what a mighty triumph had science and industry achieved in their drainage! Lincolnshire men,' he continued, 'were frequently called web-footed; he had no objection to be called web-footed; but let him ask them in what county would they find richer fields or richer crops, landlords more generally residing on their properties, the tenantry more respectable and intelligent, and the labourers more comfortable and contented?'

The same note was struck with even more decision by the speaker to whom it fell to propose the toast of 'Prosperity and Success to Van Diemen's Land.' There was another quality of the county besides its fertility, to wit its salubrity. It had to be shown that it could grow men and women as well as cereals. It had been said, remarked the Rev. J. B. Smith, that 'because of its damps and fens Lincolnshire was an unhealthy county—that it is a sickly clime wherein health withers and energies decay. In short, I verily believe in the opinion of some, and those, too, of rank and education, that to settle in Lincolnshire would be tantamount to coming to a premature grave.' A glance at the vital statistics of the county was sufficient, he held, to refute this groundless aspersion, and the reverend orator then went on to deal with the still graver charge that the minds as well as the bodies of Lincolnshire men were apt to undergo deterioration, that ' our mental energies are blunted and stunted in their growth here in the foggy Bœotia of England—that, in point of fact, we are half a century behind the rest of our country in intellectual advancement.' But how stood the case? With a good county history before him any one could almost complete the speech from this familiar outline for himself. ' To whom are we indebted for the invention of the chronometer? Gentlemen, it was Lincolnshire Harrison—Harrison of Barrow. Or again, in the department of natural history, where shall we look for a more splendid name than that of the late Sir Joseph Banks, whose persevering genius won its way to the proud distinction of President of the Royal Society? He, too, gentlemen, was a native of the Bœotian clime of Lincolnshire. Or if,' continued Mr. Smith, artfully preparing his climax, ' we look to the department of astronomy, that noble science, which affords ample scope for the most enlarged capacity, the most gigantic intellect—who, we ask, was the master genius before which all others bowed and acknowledged the prince of science? Who, gentlemen, but the immortal Newton—Newton, whose name will last as long as the sun and moon endure; and need I say, gentlemen, that Sir Isaac Newton was a Lincolnshire man? (Tremendous cheering, lasting some minutes).'

Dry, fertile, healthy above the average of English counties, and pre-eminent over all of them as the mother of illustrious sons, such was Lincolnshire by the time the dinner party at Horncastle broke up, and such, we are glad to think, is the character which could be as triumphantly vindicated for every county in England whose inhabitants meet together on any convivial occasion to sing the praises of their home. Smile as we may, and indeed must, at some of the more effusive manifestations of this sentiment, it is one on the prevalence and force of which we cannot but congratulate ourselves. After all, the debt of national to local patriotism is not inconsiderable.

A sheaf of friendly communications poured in on the new Governor of Van Diemen's Land during the months immediately preceding his departure. One might almost think that everybody of Franklin's acquaintance, besides a good many who were merely acquainted with his acquaintances, had a son or a brother or a nephew to place in the colony, for whom it was desirable to solicit the good offices of its future administrator. It was impossible, of course, that he could comply with all the requests made to him, though his good-nature made him desirous of serving as many people as he could ; and in some few instances, no doubt, the service was reciprocal.

Such reciprocity Franklin had reason to hope for in the case of the gentleman who had been recommended to him for the office of private secretary, and whom, as is shown in his correspondence with Lady Franklin immediately after his appointment, he took special pains to secure. But we shall hear more of Captain Mackonochie later on.

At length the day for their departure came, and in the late autumn of 1836 the Franklins took their last farewell of their friends, and set out in the Fairlie for their new home in the Southern Hemisphere.

Franklin's reputation had preceded him, and there was no doubt more than the average sincerity in the sentiments which found expression in the colonial addresses presented to him on his arrival. Certainly no administration could have commenced to all appearance under fairer auspices. It remains only to trace the history of the untoward events by which this hopeful prospect was so soon to be overcast.

CHAPTER XIV

TASMANIA

1836-1842

THE island of Tasmania, then and for some years afterwards known as Van Diemen's Land, was the first of our separate Australasian colonies to be 'shed' by the parent settlement of New South Wales. Tasman, its Dutch discoverer, first sighted it in December 1642, and he it was who encumbered it with its original name out of compliment to his patron, then Governor-General of the Dutch possessions in Batavia. Until 1798 it had been regarded as an integral portion of what was then called New Holland, but in that year Flinders discovered and sailed through the strait which divides it from the Australian continent, and named it after his fellow voyager, Dr. Bass. On September 12, 1803—during those very six weeks which the midshipman destined afterwards to be its Governor was spending with his shipwrecked messmates on the reef—the first settlement of the island was made by Lieutenant Bowen, acting under instructions from Governor King, of New South Wales. Like all the earlier of our Australasian settlements, it was planted in the first instance with an eye to the convict rather than to the colonist, and for two-and-twenty years its administration for penal and other purposes was conducted from Sydney. In 1825, however, it was definitely severed from New South Wales, and erected into a separate colony, Colonel (afterwards the distinguished Sir George) Arthur being appointed its first Lieutenant-Governor.

The period of eleven years which elapsed between this appointment and Franklin's succession was fruitful in the creation of difficulties for the second occupant of the post. It was comparatively easy to manage the island as a convict

R

settlement ; to govern it as a home of free settlers, and that, too, at such a time of national ferment as was the decade following on the Reform Act of 1832, was altogether another matter. Between 1825 and 1837 the stir of new ideas, philanthropic and others, had created a strong and growing feeling against the punishment of transportation, and the sharp conflict in which the mother country was destined to be involved with its Australian Colonies might already have been almost foreseen.

But the political troubles which were brewing for the new Lieutenant-Governor were insignificant in comparison with those of a private nature. Tasmania under the administration of Franklin's predecessor had become a seething cauldron of personal animosities and quarrels. It is, of course, an easy matter to assume in all cases of this kind that the Governor is to blame ; but such an assumption is not to be entertained in the present instance without special risk of injustice. The experience of his successor, a man differing widely from him in many important points of temperament and demeanour, goes far to show that the fault lay much more with colonial society than its rulers. Colonel Arthur's manners are said to have been too reserved ; Franklin's were certainly the reverse. The former, if we may trust a fairly impartial colonial critic, ' avowed hostility to liberal ideas.' The latter, though a Tory, as we have seen, in his politics, showed, at any rate at the commencement of his administration, a distinct leaning towards popular principles of government. On the whole, it seems eminently probable that even if the home Government of the day had been fortunate enough to find a Governor who combined the highest virtues of the Christian with the profoundest sagacity of the statesman and the most consummate tact of the man of the world, that paragon would, long before his official time had expired, have found himself by the ears with one or more of the cliques into which the hungry, jealous, self-seeking, and essentially parochial society of Tasmania, like that of most infant colonies, was divided.

If anything had been wanting to foment the petty passions of the community and to stir up strife among them, it would

have been found in the rapid rise and progress after the
separation of Tasmania from New South Wales of its local
press. When Arthur arrived to assume the governorship of
the colony, Hobart Town, its capital, boasted but two periodical prints ; before he quitted office their number had risen to
over half a dozen, and he had become embroiled with them
all. One knows what the journalistic style even of the
mother country was like in the late twenties and early
thirties ; or those who do not know may prepare startling
moments for themselves by consulting a file for that period
of any of the most staid and dignified 'dailies' of the present
time. Add a dash of the colonial vivacity to the editorial
style of the early century, and it may easily be imagined that
the resulting journalism becomes sufficiently remarkable.
The flowers of its rhetoric were harmless enough. 'We
esteem ourselves a beacon (capital letters) placed by Divine
graciousness on the awfully perilous coast of human frailty.
We contemplate ourselves as the winnowers (capital letters)
for the public. We desire to encourage the cloudless flames
of rectified communion, rejecting each effusion, however
splendid, of degenerate curiosity and perverted genius, of
misanthrophic (*sic*) ascerbity (*sic*) and calumnious retrospec-
tion.' When, on the other hand, the Tasmanian journalist
wished to pelt an enemy with something harder than flowers,
this was the style: 'I charge Mr. A., late overseer of the
Government farm, with stealing or embezzling a quantity of
hay, the property of the Crown ; and one J. B., the overseer of
Colonel Arthur's farm at the Marsh, with receiving the hay.
I also charge Mr. X., late superintendent of the Government
garden, with embezzling, and Captain Y. with receiving, four
Norfolk pines, value 20*l.*, the property of the Crown. I have
another distinct charge against Captain Y. and one against
Captain Z. for stealing or receiving certain building material,
the property of the Crown.'
  Thus did Tasmanian journalism treat human vessels
wrecked or alleged to have been wrecked on that 'awfully
perilous coast of human frailty,' from which its beacon had
failed to warn them. The specimens are taken from Mr.

R 2

John West's brightly written and well-informed 'History of
Tasmania,' and there is much quiet humour in the author's
explanation of these journalistic excesses. 'The violence of
periodical writings resulted partly,' he says, 'from the paucity
of topics, and was mainly a necessity of trade. The limited
field of discussion huddled all disputes into a squabble. The
writers could not forget the names of their antagonists ; they
espoused with vehement zeal the trivial quarrels of this or
that functionary. Officers who were dismissed supplied
anecdotes of those left behind which were worked up in every
form. The want of ideas and information would have withdrawn many writers from the combat had they not possessed
CAPITALS, exclamations (! ! !) and dashes (—), officered by
epithets of horror, as an army of reserve. These attempts to
impart energy to weakness and terror to insignificance gave
to the articles of many old newspapers the aspect of auction
bills rather than political disquisitions.'

Ignorance animated by self-interest and disguised by typo-
graphy : such was the prevailing note of Tasmanian journalism
at this period. And for the play of self-interest there was here,
as in all new societies, abundant room. There were few men
who had not still their fortunes to make, or were above competing for official help to the making of them. Every man might
claim or forfeit benefits that the Government could bestow,
and thus there were multitudes who suffered from those un-
satisfied expectations which so easily assume the shape of
personal grievances. A grant of land desired by one man is
given to another ; a valuable convict servant is denied to this
applicant and assigned to that. Here a trader complains
that his mercantile tenders are always rejected, while some
commercial rival mysteriously engrosses the custom of the
Crown. There some youthful stranger is invested with the
honour of a justice of the peace, while colonists of long
standing are passed over.

The accusation of favouritism was in those days a constantly reiterated charge against colonial Governors. Its
popularity is not surprising for the simple reason that it is a
charge which establishes itself. To convict a Governor of ap-

pointing none but friends or dependents to public offices is an easy task to those who know how to set about it. The accuser has only to point out that the very fact of any man's appointment by the Governor to a public office proves him to have been either a dependent or a friend. The reproach of nepotism is of more limited application ; for even though the dispenser of patronage may not be one of those ' kinless loons ' of Englishmen who provoked the contempt of the seventeenth-century Scot, yet the number of every man's relations is necessarily finite. If, however, he is of those who decline to disqualify an otherwise eligible candidate for office on the mere ground of consanguinity with himself, he must certainly be prepared for attack. On neither of these grounds had the late Governor escaped it. His enemies had accused him of filling vacant places with his friends ; and the undoubted ability of two officials whom he left behind him on his retirement in high appointments, was not permitted by his detractors to excuse the fact that they were his relatives. The attacks upon him increased in animosity until the news arrived that he was to be recalled, the Colonial Secretary informing him that the Crown, having allowed him to retain his office for the unusual period of twelve years, now intended to name his successor. Upon this the virulence of his enemies somewhat abated ; but the half-hearted recantations which follow when the object of men's abuse is about to lay aside all power to help or harm are not worth much. The retiring Governor was acclaimed by many on his departure, but signs of hostility mingled with the demonstration ; and no one who knew the state of society in the colony could have doubted that, had any unforeseen circumstance restored him to his post, the smouldering ashes of quarrel would have again burst forth into flame.

Such was the hotbed of dispute in which Sir John Franklin was about to fix his official abode. His nomination of course was highly acceptable to the colony ; his profession, career, and character being alike regarded as auspicious. His achievements and sufferings as an explorer were of course well known to the colonists ; and they could not but have felt

it as gratifying to their local patriotism, as well as carrying
with it a touch of romance, that a man whose name was
associated with Australian discovery, and who was actually
in those regions when the first party left Sydney to colonise
their island, should have been selected for its Governor.   His
reception accordingly was enthusiastic.   Crowds gathered
everywhere to greet him, and on his entry into Launceston,
the second town of the colony in point of importance, he was
escorted by 300 horsemen and seventy carriages.   Complimentary addresses poured in from every district ; and the
hearty frankness of the new Governor's replies was con-
trasted with the official coldness ascribed to his predecessor.

Misled by these delusive signs of peace and harmony,
Franklin took a step which, though eminently natural and
creditable to his generosity of character, was destined to sow
the seeds of future trouble.   Having sent home, as he felt it
his duty to do, a highly favourable report of the state of the
colony and the disposition of its inhabitants, he received
from the Colonial Secretary a reply expressing satisfaction at
such a confirmation of his estimate of Franklin's predecessor.
This despatch Franklin laid on the table at the next meeting
of his Legislative Council, and drew up a minute of his own
expressing his concurrence with Lord Glenelg's high opinion
of Colonel Arthur's services.

That was enough for the Opposition.   The late Governor
had, as has been already noted, left two nephews behind him
in official posts.   Captain Matthew Forster was chief Police
Magistrate, and Captain Montagu, a man of marked ability
and destined to play a chief part in the embittered conflicts
of the future, filled the still more important office of Colonial
Secretary.   Even if Franklin had distrusted them, which for
a man of his open and candid nature was impossible, he would
have had no choice but to accept them as coadjutors.   But that,
with the two nephews at his side, he should have pronounced
a eulogium on the uncle, was a circumstance from which no
thorough-going opponent of the late Governor was willing to
draw any conclusion but one.   It was clear to an enlightened

press that Franklin was about to become, if indeed he were not already, a mere tool in the hands of the ' Arthur faction.' If any confirmation of this suspicion were needed, it was surely to be found in the monstrous fact that the new Governor did not immediately reverse all the acts of his predecessor. Colonists aggrieved by the late Governor appealed to his successor for redress, and whenever Franklin discovered that they had no equitable claim, and that in fact Colonel Arthur's decision had been just and deserved to be upheld, he actually did not hesitate to uphold it. What could be clearer proof that the policy of the uncle survived in the nephews, and that it was to their insidious influence that the appellant owed the rejection of his appeal ?

But even before these unworthy suspicions had attained to anything like their subsequent growth, it had already dawned upon Franklin that Van Diemen's Land was not exactly the spiritual Agapemone which at a first glance it had appeared.

' In answer,' records Mr. West, ' to an address from Richmond which deplored the absence and invoked the restoration of social peace, he expressed his anxiety with touching ardour: " With my whole heart I agree with you. Let us be divided, then, if we cannot be united, in political sentiments, yet knit together as friends and neighbours in everything beside. Let us differ where honest men may differ ; and let us agree not in undervaluing the points of political dissent, but in respecting the motive which may produce it, in cherishing domestic virtues which will be found to characterise individuals of every party, and in making the generous sacrifice of private feelings for the general good, rather than aggravating the importance of grievances which must render such forbearance impossible." These sentiments, not less charming for their amiable spirit than happy in expression, are important as maxims of political life, and they depict the main difficulty of the Governor's position.'

They do more ; for it may here be added, though it would be anticipating the course of this narrative to dwell upon the point at any length, that the wisdom and geniality of these

sentiments on the part of the new Governor only deepen the
perplexity which the untoward course and issue of his six
years' administration can hardly fail to produce in the mind
of the impartial student, and which must always leave its
explanation to some extent a matter of conjecture. The difficulties of the situation have already been indicated ; but one
might have thought that, serious as they were, they could not
but be smoothed away or brushed aside by a hand at once so
firm and gentle as that which had now grasped the reins of
colonial administration.

Franklin himself was, at any rate, as full of hope in these
early days of his career as throughout he was full of zeal.
Writing to congratulate Captain Cumby on a naval appointment which had just been conferred upon him :—

I am glad (he says) to have my thoughts turned once more to-
ward ships and the course of my profession, in which my heart
delighteth. I begin, however, to find my present duties more congenial to my taste than I expected they would have so soon become ,
and if it were not that I have to deal with subjects of such a discor-
dant character, and with persons who have no common ground of
action, and, therefore, each pursuing his individual interests, there
would be much in my duty that would prove highly agreeable. You
will not, perhaps, be surprised that the management of the convict
discipline is not considered by me as the most unpleasant part of my
task, in consequence of it having been reduced to a system by my
predecessor, which, though not altogether unexceptionable, cannot
be easily amended, and works to the effect of giving security to property and an appearance of decorum even beyond what you find in
most large towns in our own country. The most irksome part of my
task is to adjust the various claims of settlers respecting the measure-
ment of their lands, the tracing out of roads through the districts to
the satisfaction of conflicting parties, and the assignment of prisoners
as servants. The revival of old and oft-refused claims for grants of
land is another source of continual application. The consideration
of the very numerous petitions presented by the wives and families of
prisoners for assistance, and of many who have come hither as emi-
grants, burdened with families, for employment and relief, forms part
of the daily routine of my business. When I add to this catalogue
that the society here has been torn by dissension and divided by
party spirit, and that the press is a most licentious one, living on and
delighting in personal scandal, you will be inclined to say with a friend
of mine : ' I don't envy you your berth.' Yet, let me tell you, I am

far from being either unhappy at or discouraged by the prospect before me. I indulge the hope that, through the blessing of God, I shall be able to go steadily forward in my duty, cheered by the prospect of finding the measures I may introduce beneficial to the colony, and that peace and happiness may follow in their train. I certainly have the assistance of some able men, who are the principal officers of the Government, and form the members of the Executive Council ; and I really have found them readily acquiesce in, and even suggest, measures and improvements differing entirely from some of those of my predecessor, to whom they are strongly attached. They are called by some here a 'faction,' but I have not had the slightest ground to consider them so. The Legislative Assembly is to meet in the course of a few days, and I have then to make my first appearance before that body, which consists only of fourteen members, all of them appointed by the Crown. I shall have to propose but few bills to them at present, as we are in expectation of receiving a new bill for the government of these colonies which might set aside all we now do.

Franklin's first 'thorn in the flesh' was his private secretary, Captain Mackonochie, a gentleman whom he had specially sought out for the appointment and for whom he entertained a high regard, but who, unfortunately, suffered from the malady—most inconvenient for a man in his peculiar position—of 'views' on penal discipline. Before Captain Mackonochie had held his post for many months, he felt moved to write a ' private and confidential letter ' of criticism on the existing system, in which, in the most unguarded terms, he spoke of the law dealt to the convicts in this country as one ' which in Scotland is called Jedburgh justice, or " hang first and try afterwards." ' The opinion thus expressed, and subsequently used to spice an article on the subject in one of the colonial newspapers, was not unnaturally regarded as reflecting on the whole character of the judicial administration from the Governor downwards, and particularly disrespectful, reckless, and unbecoming in the Governor's private secretary, who, *ex officio*, is considered to be the organ and echo of his own sentiments.

Captain Forster, the chief police magistrate, urged that the letter should be published, a step which would, of course, have compelled Captain Mackonochie's resignation ; but the

Governor objected, on the ground that it would excite the
convicts, irritate the magistrates, and convert the displaced
official into 'a hero and martyr of the Radical party.' The
situation was, moreover, domestically complicated by the fact
that the private secretary and his family were inmates of
the Franklin household ; and Sir John's reluctance 'to cast
them, as it were, on the wide world without office or home
was a feeling,' writes his wife, 'which, when at the height of
his utmost indignation, always calms and softens him.' In
the result, Captain Mackónochie's transgression was overlooked, an act of lenity of which Franklin had cause to repent,
while his escape was attributed to Lady Franklin's mediation,
an impression which she herself had equal reason to regret.

The incidents, however, which led to the final rupture
with Captain Mackonochie are so closely connected with the
question of penal discipline and of Franklin's policy with
respect to it, that it is desirable to defer the account of them
until the time arrives for treating of that subject as a whole.
Another public question, and one with respect to which
Franklin played a most active and beneficent part in his
capacity of Governor, has a prior claim to be considered. It
was a period of awakening interest in the cause of education,
and one of the earliest projects which engaged the mind of
the new Governor was that of founding a colonial college.
Four years earlier his predecessor had meditated the same
undertaking, but the scheme proposed by him had encountered serious obstacles, and was allowed to drop. The first
step taken by Franklin towards the realisation of his project
was to seek the advice of Dr. Arnold ; and the letter addressed
by him to that eminent head-master displays so much organising ability, as well as such close and acute study of the
social conditions of the colony, that a considerable portion of
it appears to deserve unabridged quotation :—

The charge (he wrote) which I wish to impose on you is to select
for me a well-qualified person to be head-master or principal of a
public school of the highest class, which we are preparing to establish
in Hobart Town, and which is to be primarily adapted to the present
limited wants of the colony, but capable of expanding into a more

liberal institution when the developed energies and increased population of the colony shall demand it. Under the character of a
university we contemplate its conferring at some distant period the
privileges of practising in law and medicine within the colony, if not
of qualifying for the pulpit, considering as the chief motive for this
that it would be a great inducement for parents to give their sons a
good and prolonged education if they could then be enabled to secure
for them its substantial rewards. In its infant state we trust to succeed in eliciting and cultivating native talent in whatever stations of
life it may be found, and in fitting our growing inheritors of wealth
to spend with credit the fortunes their parents have amassed, and to
become capable of acting an honourable and patriotic part as magistrates and legislators of their native or adopted land.

Then follows this comprehensive and informing survey of
Tasmanian society at this stage of its history :—

Perhaps I cannot give you a better preliminary guide to the
selection I wish you to be kind enough to make than by describing
briefly the condition of the population. It consists in all of about
44,000 souls, of whom about one-half are free immigrants and free
native-born youths. On the Queen's late birthday party, when its
(so-deemed) presentable persons were invited to Government House,
from nine hundred to one thousand cards to as many families or individuals were issued throughout the island ; but this has hitherto been
exclusive of the class of shopkeeper, not a few of whom are wealthy
and very respectable. Many of the settlers or landed proprietors
are worth 2,000*l.* and 3,000*l.* per annum, some 4,000*l.*, and a few from
four up to eight and ten thousand. In this free community (for I
leave entirely out of the question that class so influential in New
South Wales, called there by some 'emancipists' and by a late writer
'the felonry') there is a high degree of intelligence and activity of
mind ; in individuals much sterling probity, charity, and virtue ; and
in religious classes and self-incorporated societies much zeal for the
physical and spiritual welfare of their neighbours, according to the
particular understanding they may have of the means adapted to the
purpose.

But there is another and less pleasing side to the picture :—

On the other hand, there exists throughout the community generally a great lack of neighbourly feeling and a deplorable deficiency
in public spirit. Each man eagerly seeks his own individual advantage, with little or no reference to his neighbours, or is always
suspected of doing so. An extraordinary degree of irritability distinguishes the insular temperament, and all these anti-Christian peculiarities are fostered by a press which, though in the hands merely

of a few well-known individuals, some of whom are despicable in character and conduct, exerts a certain degree of vicious power over the public mind, which nothing but its interference with the privacies of domestic life, the origin, habits, and peculiarities of individuals, and the consequent dread of its vengeance or even its unprovoked malice, can possibly account for.

Thus a peculiar and elevated character of mind is called for in the man who, placed at the head of the Department of Education in this college, will become eminently exposed thereby to public or rather printed animadversion. He must be possessed of no common degree of prudence and firmness. With a single eye to the public good, he must give but little regard to calumny in pursuing it. Nowhere must a man set public opinion at first so completely at defiance as in Van Diemen's Land. He must resolve to live down imputations on his character and conduct, not expecting otherwise to overcome them. Such a person as this, however, would be supported and countenanced by the best part of the community, even though he were in some points open to censure. His office would be honoured, and his position would be honourable.

On the 'conscience' question, then as now and ever a burning one, Franklin writes with that combination of sincere piety and sound common-sense which one would have expected :—

I may add that such an institution as we are endeavouring to provide for has been in contemplation some years ; the hindrances have been the difficulty of finding a competent master in this quarter of the globe, and the still greater difficulty of obtaining any unanimity of opinion upon the principles on which it should act and the religious doctrines that should be taught in it. On the last point the utmost diversity of opinion prevails. The arguments on it are such as must be familiar to you on either side of the question, and need not be repeated. I believe, however, that it is the feeling of the vast majority of the community that the most important of all knowledge should not be the only knowledge which is set aside as uncertain or problematical. I, for one, and as the head of the community, cannot consent that religious instruction should be excluded, and religion itself thereby, as I conceive, dishonoured. . . . Though I have not stated that the person selected should be a clergyman, or even a member of the Church of England, yet I believe (putting my own predilection on that head entirely out of the question) that it would be more generally acceptable that he should be such than otherwise. Nearly three-fourths of the community are of that persuasion. He should also, I think, be a member of one of the English universities.

On the subject of the religious instruction to be adopted in the proposed school, I would only say that, while the instruction communicated must be founded on a strictly religious basis, and while it will
be the desire of the Government that the instruction should be as
little exclusive as possible, he will never be called upon to teach or
authorise the teaching of any doctrine which he may show to be repugnant to the tenets of the Church—in the present instance that of
England—of which he was a member.

Dr. Arnold's response to this appeal was most gratifying,
and the mission entrusted to him admirably executed. For
the principal of the contemplated college his choice fell upon
the Rev. J. P. Gell, sometime pupil of his own, who, after a
successful career of seven years both as organiser and teacher,
and, in truth, pioneer of the higher education in the colony,
returned to England to become the husband of Sir John
Franklin's daughter and only child, Eleanor, and, as the
venerable Rector of Buxted, in Sussex, still survives.

It is, however, one thing to choose the principal of a
college with sound professional judgment, and another thing
to frame its charter with administrative wisdom. Dr. Arnold
was an eminently able and justly celebrated preceptor ; but
as a politician he belonged to the peculiar school of doctrinaire
liberalism then dominant, and shared its essentially unpractical
and unworkable theories as to the adjustment of competing
denominational claims. It is anticipating matters a little to
quote in this place the letter which follows ; but to read it in
immediate succession to the preceding one will, perhaps, give
a fuller conception of Franklin's sturdy common-sense and
independence of judgment. High as was his respect for
Arnold's ability in the educational sphere, he was not in the
least overawed by his name and reputation in criticising
Arnold's proposals as an academic legislator. The Head-
master of Rugby had been requested by Lord John Russell,
who had succeeded to the Colonial Office, to draft the charter
of the new college ; and the result had been a scheme of the
most 'enlightened' and unpractical kind, and containing
a fantastic provision for appointing a Principal, 'turn and
turn about,' from the Anglican and the Scotch Presbyterian
communions. Besides this, it proposed an exquisite arrange-

ment for securing what was considered to be the just representation of each of these two religious bodies on the teaching staff. A more telling contrast between the methods of the academic legislator and those of the practical statesman could hardly be found than in Franklin's blunt, straightforward, not disrespectful, but wholly destructive criticisms of this notable scheme :—

I have need to crave your indulgence if, after having requested your aid in this matter by suggesting that a reference should be made to you, I now presume to question any one of the principles on which you have proceeded in complying with my request. I cannot but blame myself that, in a case in which I have such strong convictions, and in which, though I have no other advantage, I have that of some experience of the state of this colony, I did not foresee the conclusions to which you might possibly arrive, and against which I might at least have stated my objections. I did, however, in a letter to Lord John Russell—written, if I recollect rightly, a few months after requesting a charter—deprecate the introduction of any change from the terms on which the first principal was selected, in case any such liability to change should appear to be involved in the liberal principles advocated for the foundation. I was not unmindful of the argument of the Scotch, that in a British colony they are entitled to an equality of rights ; but this argument is virtually superseded by the fact that in this colony there are *three Established* Churches, the Church of Rome being one. In consistency with this unhappy Act of Sir Richard Bourke's [a former Governor of New South Wales, by whom this extraordinary arrangement had been recommended to the Colonial Office], we ought to have the headship of the college divided between the three Churches of England, Scotland, and Rome, a mode of reconciling matters which I need not say would be self-destruction. It has appeared to me that the only way to manage this difficulty is to give up the ground of ecclesiastical establishment altogether (a ground always offensive also to a large body of Dissenters who belong to no establishment), and to give the ascendency, if such an invidious word *must* be used, to the Church of the majority—such an ascendency interfering in nothing with the equal privileges of all the members of the college to refrain from joining in any religious ceremonies which they object to, or to observe any religious exercise which they had the means of attending.

'Denominationalism tempered by the conscience clause' is familar enough to us in these days as the governing principle of the State-aided voluntary school system, and indeed as the only practical principle on which the competing religious claims of majorities and minorities can be adjusted in educational matters; but in the second quarter of the nineteenth century the principle was by no means so well established as it is to-day, and it is interesting to note that it is not the schoolmaster-politician but the sailor-administrator who is the first to arrive at it. 'Would there be any difficulty,' Franklin continues, 'in stating in terms that the Principal should always be a member of the Church of England as long as that Church is the Church of the majority—I mean the majority of the students, not of the population? It appears to me that it is necessary for the uniform, steadfast, and independent conduct of the college that the Principals one after another should be of one Church, and if of one, it would be most fair that it should be the Church of the majority.'

Then, passing to the even more pedantic proposal with reference to the teaching staff, he proceeds :—

But if I feel a strong objection to the headship of the college being first of one Church, then of another, I have even a still stronger one to the special provision which it is proposed to make for the keeping up of two religious denominations within the walls of the college itself, and which, it appears to me, would be a provision for sectarianism and faction, the influence of which might embarrass and coerce those even for whose exclusive benefit it was intended. Might it not be better [continues Franklin, with undesigned but not the less searching irony] to make learning and character the sole qualifications for members of the college, rather than take any notice of denominational distinctions as qualifications for instructing the students in religious knowledge? The master and fellows, or by whatever name they are called, chosen on the latter principle would, I fear, scarcely fail to regard themselves as the representatives of their sect, and, like the members for boroughs in the Imperial Parliament, would feel that they were bound to advocate beyond all other interests the interests of their constituents, and to act as the organs of a party. The Principal would then be driven to act as the representative of his party, thus losing his dignified and proper position ; while among the students themselves would be engendered a spirit of clanship and party strife which would be found most tyrannical where the numerical power existed, and most bitter in the weaker party.

Franklin then goes on to reinforce his position by an

argument which for us in these days has an almost painful cogency :—

If at home our mixed nationality is still a source of jealousy and divided feeling, why should it be cherished at the uttermost extremity of the globe, in a country, too, where the present generations, strongly attached as they are to the soil, are more apt to regard themselves as Tasmanians than anything else?

Why, in other words, export Particularism from the mother-country to a colony which has shown no inclination thus far to manufacture that article for itself? There could be no sounder or more statesmanlike advice, and it availed. The later history of the college, however, was not a fortunate one. It became unhappily entangled in a complication of inter-local and denominational jealousies; the Imperial Government withdrew its support, and the scheme fell through. The colony had for the time to content itself with the establishment of a high school under the management of Mr. Gell, to the funds of which Franklin made a donation of 500l. before leaving the island, while Lady Franklin made the munificent gift of 400 acres of land on which she had founded a museum, in trust for the benefit of any collegiate institution that might afterwards be established. But the failure of the larger educational project was no fault of Franklin's. His management of the matter throughout was characterised by admirable good sense, fair-mindedness, and consideration for others. The responsibility for the defeat of his excellent intentions certainly does not rest in the smallest measure on Franklin's shoulders.

CHAPTER XV

THE COLONIAL GOVERNOR

1836–1842

It was not, however, in regard to educational matters alone, or even chiefly, that the period between 1832 and 1841 was so great a day for the proud possessor of the newest 'views.' We have seen from an above-quoted letter of Franklin's to his old friend and commander, Captain Cumby, that they were expecting from the Government a Bill for the future administration of the Australian Colonies as well as for the reorganisation of the convict system. In due time the project of the proposed legislation arrived, and all too faithfully indeed did it reflect the latest English Liberal ideas, exported 'in bulk,' after the fashion of the reformers of those days, for wholesale application to a community absolutely unfitted to adopt them. Thus, the reconstruction of the English municipal corporations being a triumph still fresh in the minds of Liberal politicians, nothing would content them short of the assumption that the materials of local self-government are necessarily and of the very nature of things to be found in all quarters of the English Empire, however remote, and among all societies, however rude. What, then, could be more hopeful, more rich in promise of future blessings, than to create municipal corporations by a stroke of the pen in—among other Australian settlements—the island of Tasmania?

Common-sense, however, and practical knowledge ultimately prevailed. The absurd project was dropped, and no more was heard of a representative system on the English model until a good many years later, when these Australasian communities were more fitted to receive them. But 'the ten-

S

pound householder,' who figured as the electoral unit in this abortive proposal, puts the finishing touch to it.   In England the ten-pound householder, after, so to speak, undergoing an education in the duties of citizenship extending over about six centuries, had only within the last six years been admitted to political power.   Tasmania, on the other hand, had only come into existence as a British settlement some thirty odd years before, and the political education of a large portion of its inhabitants had been acquired in that too elementary school of citizenship to which admission could be obtained by incurring a sentence of transportation for life or for a term of years.   But the Reformers of the ' Thirties ' seem to have been quite satisfied with the amount of resemblance between the two communities.   Popular suffrage was a good thing ; elective municipal corporations were good things ; representative assemblies, large or small, and as many of them as possible, were good things—for England.   Therefore they would be equally good things for a half-fledged colony, with a scattered population of settlers too busy to govern themselves, and a large sprinkling of reclaimed or half-reclaimed convicts, only too anxious for the opportunity of governing other people. As to the qualification, why, ten pounds was ten pounds all the world over.   One wonders how many similar projects of political theorists at home have in the course of our history been quietly killed by that practical good sense and administrative wisdom which have fortunately been seldom wanting to us in the more remote parts of our Empire.

The other proposal of the Colonial Office was of a less speculative and experimental kind, and had reference to a question on which there was room for legitimate difference of opinion among men of sound judgment and ripe experience in colonial affairs.   It has been observed already that the controversies connected with the subject of the transportation system—controversies bearing partly upon economical questions, and partly on the various branches of the difficult problem of penal discipline—had been maturing with some rapidity during the years immediately preceding Franklin's appointment.   In the year 1837 Sir William Molesworth obtained the appointment of a Select Committee of the House of Commons to investigate the whole question of transportation and penal discipline in general. Many witnesses were examined by this body and a large mass of evidence was accumulated, much of it of course, as was to be expected in such a case, of a violently partisan and exaggerated character. Franklin had from the first been a steady though moderate and fair-minded supporter of the existing system, and the criticisms of the evidence which were embodied by him in a letter to Sir Edward Parry, who, on the strength of his Australian experience, had been examined before the Committee, and which he afterwards substantially repeated in a despatch to the Secretary of State for the Colonies, form a document of high interest and value.

He protested, to begin with, against the unmeasured terms in which some of the witnesses had decried the discipline exercised in the colony under his administration. ' It is one,' he said, ' of coercion, certainly; but that coercion is tempered with compassion and with the most earnest desire for the amendment of the offenders.' To the assertion that ' the convict is beyond endurance miserable '—or, at any rate, to the inference sought to be drawn from that sweeping proposition —he opposed an indignant denial. ' When convicts are in that state of misery it is attributable, not to the laws and treatment to which they are exposed, but to their own determined perseverance in a course of hardened wickedness, and the same man would be in a similar unhappy condition anywhere.'

But to appreciate the significance of the more important observations of this document, it will be necessary to take a brief review of the history of a now almost forgotten incident of our then system of penal discipline in the Colonies.

Among all the questions incidentally connected with the main subject of transportation, none perhaps was more keenly debated than that of ' assignment '—the practice, that is to say, of allotting a convict after a certain term of penal discipline to the service of a master, under conditions varied from time to time by statutory enactment or administrative regulation.

It existed in our American settlements for a period of more than fifty years of the eighteenth century, and was introduced in Tasmania by Governor King in 1804. Under the system then established the master was bound by indenture to retain the servant for one year, a penalty of a shilling being imposed upon him for every day which fell short of that period. The quantity of work to be done was prescribed—contingently, however, on the nature of the soil, the state of the weather, and the strength of the workman. Wages were fixed at 10*l*. per annum for a man and 7*l*. for a woman. To restrict the habit of change, a rule was established by a subsequent Governor (Macquarrie) that no convict should be returnable to the authorities except for infirmity, sickness, or crime ; but when the supply exceeded the demand the condition was evaded, and the result, of course, was an accumulation of convicts on the hands of the Government. Theoretically, the advantages to the colonists of this virtually unlimited supply of labour appeared considerable ; but in practice this was not the case, for a large proportion of the convicts, coming from the manufacturing districts of Great Britain, were utterly ignorant of agriculture and required a tedious training before they paid the expenses of their support.

So far, however, as these cases were concerned, the principle of the system was sound enough. In theory at any rate all three parties—the employer, the convict, and the State—derived a benefit from the arrangement. The first obtained labour on moderate, perhaps on exceptionally easy terms the second regained his freedom and an opportunity, if he wished to reform, of earning an honest living; the third saved the present expense of the convict's maintenance and took the best means of preventing his return upon their hands in future. But in other directions the system was liable to gross abuse. Thus it was the custom to allot to the superior officers, magistrates, and constables, in proportion to their rank, a certain number of men who were subsisted from Government stores, the State thus continuing to defray the keep of men who by the hypothesis were fit for freedom. For instance, a skilled mechanic assigned on these terms was, of course, a highly valuable acquisition to his master, who allowed him to 'hire his own time' at from 5*s.* to 1*l.* according to its estimated weekly value, and while receiving this sum from his servant at the same time drew Government rations for his support. Other assigned servants rented farms and paid their masters in produce; and when these 'Government men,' as they were called, were unable to make good such an engagement with their masters, they were liable to be thrown back into their former position. Tickets of leave, on the other hand, were freely given to those incapable of much service to the Government or its officers; such as were useful, whatever might be their conduct, were detained, often for an indefinite period. Under a system so irregular, great practical injustice was inflicted, while advantages were enjoyed by artisans who could hire their time, and who, obtaining large profits from their trades, indulged in every form of vice and licentiousness. A writer in the 'Edinburgh Review,' whose style bears a strong resemblance to that of Sydney Smith, thus satirically illustrates the system: 'A little wicked tailor arrives, of no use to the architectural projects of the Governor; he is turned over to a settler who allows him his liberty for 5*s.* a week, and allows him to steal and snip what, when, and where he can. The nefarious needleman writes home that he is as comfortable as a finger in a thimble; that, though a fraction only of humanity, he has several wives and is filled every day with rum and kangaroo. This, of course, is not lost upon a shop-board, and for the saving of fifteen pence a day (to Government) the foundation of many criminal tailors is laid.'

Sometimes the inequalities of treatment which seemed inseparable from this system took a shape of almost comical flagrancy. Thus a convict named Clapperton, who had been assigned to a private master, and had risen to a position of trust in his service, was guilty of large embezzlements, for which he was tried by Captain Forster, the chief magistrate, and received a sentence of fourteen years' imprisonment. Clapperton, however, had the good fortune or the merit of being a skilful cook, and the Colonial Secretary, who was then in want of a *chef*, having first inquired whether the man's services would be required in the Governor's kitchen, and having been informed by Sir John's private secretary that he would 'waive the precedence,' forthwith engaged the convict in that capacity himself. On the way to his destination Clapperton thought it would be only neighbourly to call at his late master's and acquaint his former fellow-servants with the stroke of luck which had befallen him. This became known to the master, who thus found that the prosecution he had instituted had had no other result than that of adding to the domestic comfort of an official friend. He accordingly brought the case to the notice of Sir John Franklin, who at once interposed his veto on the projected arrangement, and sent the man to labour on the roads. It is hardly surprising that a case of this kind should have caused some public sensation, and provoked unfavourable criticism of a system which 'sent one man to toil in the chains and another to wear the livery of the second officer of the Government.'

That system, however, had a right to be judged not by its incidental abuses but by the modes of its ordinary operation. Anomalies of the precise description of the above could evidently be got rid of at a stroke by the simple expedient of abolishing assignments for domestic service. The question was whether, on the whole, and subject to the correction of these and other miscarriages, assignment was or was not a practice conducive to the material interests of the free settlers and the moral welfare of the convicts themselves. And Franklin, after a careful and dispassionate study of that question, had no doubt that it should be answered in the affirmative. Thus he writes upon the subject generally :—

I have entirely forbid the transfer of convicts, by which they could be removed from one service to another at the mere wish or convenience of the master. I have also forbid allowing convicts on assignment being hired out by the master to work for any other person, the master securing a certain portion of the wages, which I found to be a practice carried on to a considerable extent, though the act was punishable by fine. I have from the first discontinued the practice of assigning husbands to their wives, and servants to persons holding tickets of leave, though it is possible, notwithstanding all my care, this may have been done in some few instances since my order was issued.

But this increased strictness of discipline was not unaccompanied by reasonable efforts at reformation.

Whenever the abstracts of petitions for indulgence are presented to me for consideration, which is done weekly in special cases, and monthly in general cases, I devote myself to the examination of each case, and, whenever I find that the prayer of the petitioner cannot be immediately granted, I state in writing the reason, and point out his prevailing offence, and also fix a certain period of probation for him to conquer the habit ; and, if he does, the indulgence is then granted to him at once. My observations are directed to be forwarded to the petitioner through the master ; and I know that these warnings have had a beneficial effect on the conduct of the prisoners. The door of hope is thus proved to be open, and they perceive that the recovery of indulgence depends upon their own conduct. When the conduct of the applicant has been particularly good, I cause my notice of it to be conveyed to him. What is this but one of those 'moral appliances' of which the present system is said (by the Committee) to be wholly devoid?

Little recognition, however, of this or any other merit of the existing system was to be expected from that body. Their report reached Franklin after he had sat down to pen the above remarks, and his judgment upon it is that, though drawn up with much care and ability, he 'cannot look at it in any other way than as a one-sided view of the question.' Evidence relating to a wholly bygone state of things, and abounding in horrors which were matters of ancient history, appeared to have formed the main basis of the Committee's conclusions, later modifications and amendments of the system being entirely ignored. The system of assignment, denounced as 'slavery' by a class of politicians, themselves the slaves, in those days as in these, of words, was to be abolished on the strength of its nickname. Its evils were thrust into the foreground and perpetually insisted on ; the good effected by it was minimised or denied. Nor had there been any pretence of a desire to consider what improvements it might be susceptible of. 'I am not its bigoted advocate,' wrote Franklin, 'and would cheerfully assist in devising a plan by which the master and the man might mutually choose each other, and the latter receive moderate wages ; but I cannot reconcile myself to the idea that this or any other system is to be overturned by evidence which, if not altogether untrue, has been grossly exaggerated and misstated as regards this colony.'

And what was to be substituted for this maligned and misrepresented method of reformatory discipline ? Penitentiary systems, which, whether silent or social, did not appear to Franklin to be ' the best schools for inducing practical habits of labour and industry after the prisoners are released from them,' and in this respect were, in his judgment, much inferior to the employment of convicts in agricultural pursuits, in the felling of timber, and in mechanical labour apart from the towns. It must, indeed, have been difficult for a Governor of Tasmania in those days, and especially for one so eager for the material development of the country as was Franklin, to regard with patience such a wanton waste of human energy as the penitentiary system involved. Unreclaimed Nature, all around him, was crying aloud for the thews and sinews of reclaimable or irreclaimable man.

Franklin's pleadings for the system of assignment were vain. Peremptory instructions were sent to him and to the Governors of the other Australian colonies to discontinue it. His address to his Legislative Council at the opening of its session in 1840 records the official mandate, accompanied by such reassurances to the anxious employers of labour as Franklin felt able to offer. The assignment of ' domestic servants for purposes of luxury' had been put an end to the year before, and a month previously the practice of assignment for any purpose had, in the towns of Hobart and Launceston, ceased to exist. These changes would not, Franklin points out, reduce the number of prisoners who would become eventually available for purposes of field labour. On the contrary, it would ultimately increase that number by the addition to it of the convicts no longer assignable for purposes of luxury anywhere, or in the towns for any purposes whatever. But under the new system all convicts were on arrival placed in the public works, in what were called probationary gangs, for a minimum period of one year; and the consequence of this arrest of the supply of labourers, coming as it did at a time when there happened to be a specially urgent demand for them, had been so seriously felt that the Governor was compelled, without the sanction of the Secretary of State, to authorise the grant of a bounty for the encouragement of immigration.

To trace the vacillating policy of the Home Government, as Colonial Secretary succeeded Colonial Secretary and one theory of punishment ousted another, to be itself displaced by a third, is beyond the province of this work. The loyal but ineffectual endeavour of Franklin to work the new probationary system successfully belongs rather to the general history of penal discipline than to a biography of the man, and the subject, indeed, has only been pursued thus far because his treatment of it so strikingly illustrates the soundness of judgment and the shrewd common-sense which he brought to his administrative work. Unfortunately, however, it was also in connection with this subject of penal discipline that he became involved in the first of that series of personal differences with those about him which marred the whole subsequent course of his official career.

An early 'difficulty' which arose between him and his private secretary has already been noticed; a much more serious one was to follow. Captain Mackonochie in truth was, if not an 'impossible' private secretary, at any rate a private secretary in an impossible position. Officially attached to the service of the Governor, he was, or regarded himself as, in his unofficial capacity an emissary of an English society for the improvement of penal discipline to inquire into and to report upon the results of the system of transportation. He had, in fact, been furnished by this society with a list of no fewer than sixty-seven questions on which they desired to receive a statement of his views. The impossibility of thus dividing himself into two persons, and of loyally serving one master without breaking faith with the other, would have been apparent to any one not accustomed, like too many 'friends of humanity' at large, to neglect his obligations to individual members of the race. Captain Mackonochie presumably did not perceive it. He set to work to execute his unofficial commission, and with such industry did he pursue his inquiries that at the expiration of three months from his arrival in the colony he felt himself in a position to pronounce a sweeping condemnation of the system of penal discipline prevailing in the colony. Such, at least, was the substance of the report which he drafted and despatched to the society for whom he was acting. Of its manner we may judge by the following extract from the far from unfriendly criticism of Mr. West :—'Without circumlocution or reserve he spoke of the officers concerned in convict management as blinded by habit, as empirics who could patch and cauterise a wound, but were involved in the hopeless prejudices of a topical practice, and much too far gone to comprehend improvements founded on scientific principles. His deviations from the tone of philosophical discussion were not numerous, but they were marked. The chief police magistrate he compared to the lamplighter, by whom gas is detested. In praising that officer's administrative talent, he observed that he belonged to the martinet school, and that his estimate of human nature depressed it below its worth.'

A summary of this conciliatory document—which by condensing rendered more flagrant the charges against the colonists and more revolting the description of the prisoners— found its way, by a process to be hereafter explained, to the Colonial Office, and was handed by Lord John Russell to the committee then inquiring into the subject of transportation. Its next appearance was in an English newspaper, and it was in that form that it first came under the eye of Sir John Franklin. The report on which it was founded had indeed been laid before him, and his opinion of it was, as might have been expected, of a strongly adverse character. It contained, in his judgment, afterwards avowed in correspondence with its author, 'so many incorrect and even reckless assertions as to the condition and treatment of criminals, and so much offensive interpretation of the character of the free population, that I could not but feel apprehensive and even somewhat indignant at the probability of its being made public.' The appearance in the English press of a summary which unavoidably emphasised these objectionable qualities, and placed the Lieutenant-Governor's private secretary in a position of conspicuous if not contemptuous hostility to his chief and all the principal officials of the colony, left Franklin with but one course open to him—to dismiss Captain Mackonochie from his post. There was, however, no personal rupture between them ; the letters exchanged by them with reference to the incident which had rendered this painful step necessary are couched in terms of mutual respect and even regard ; and for some time after ceasing to be Franklin's private secretary Captain Mackonochie continued with his wife and family to reside at Government House. But for conclusive proof that the action taken by his chief was not only justifiable but inevitable, we need look no further than the admissions of the displaced official himself. Indeed, his very explanation of the particular proceeding by which the crisis was precipitated revealed a total incapacity to appreciate the true relations between the Governor of a colony and his private secretary.

Enough, however, of this unfortunate episode. It only now remains to trace the history of a sequel which demonstrated both the genuineness of Franklin's goodwill towards his former secretary and the practical value of the latter's disciplinary theories. Supported by an influential school of reformers at home, but also no doubt materially assisted by the good offices of a Governor whose recommendations would naturally derive additional value from the fact of the personal differences between them, Captain Mackonochie was shortly afterwards appointed Commandant of Norfolk Island, which had been selected, by way of halfway house to the abolition of transportation, as the sole future destination of transported convicts. He took up his new appointment apparently with full leave and licence to experimentalise on the lines of his own theories. Less than a year, however, sufficed to alarm the Home Government so thoroughly that they would at once have recalled Captain Mackonochie had they been provided with a successor. In little more than two years his methods resulted in catastrophe.

It was on May 24, 1840, the occasion of the young Queen's birthday, that the 'system' of the new Commandant received an illustration which scandalised colonial opinion and proved startling even to the boldest philanthropists of the mother country. A proclamation had been issued by Mackonochie describing the festivities by which he proposed to celebrate the anniversary. He had resolved, writes Mr. West, whose sympathy with his motives is not a whit less conspicuous than his consciousness of the absurdity of his methods, 'to forget the distinction between the good and bad, and to make no exception from the general indulgence; but he entreated the men to remember that on the success of this experiment his confidence would greatly depend; he warned them to suppress the first tokens of disorder, and by retiring to their quarters at the first sound of the bugle prove that they might be trusted with safety. On the morning of that day the signal colours floated from the staff, crowned with the union-jack; twenty-one guns collected from the vessels and from the Government House were mounted on the top of a hill and fired a royal salute. The gates were thrown open, and 1,800 prisoners were set free and joined in various amusements, of which Captain Mackonochie was a frequent spectator. Eighteen hundred prisoners sat down to dinner, and at its close, having received each a small quantity of spirits and water, they drank a health to the Queen and Mackonochie. Three times three for Victoria and the Captain rent the air. They then renewed their sports or attended a theatrical performance. New scenery, dresses, music, and songs contributed to the hilarity of the party. The performances were *The Castle of Andalusia*, in which the comic powers of the prisoners were exhibited to their companions; a variety of glees and songs; the tent scene in *Richard III.*; *The Purse, or the Benevolent Tar;* [this, perhaps, by way of compliment to the Captain], and finally the National Anthem. At the termination no accident had occurred, the gaol was entirely unoccupied, no theft or disorder had disgraced the day, and thus the notions of Mackonochie seemed to be illustrated by the experiment.'

The effect of this extraordinary performance was, the writer dryly continues, to give a violent shock to the 'long habit of connecting the notions of crime and punishment with those of guilt and misery,' and, in fact, of drawing that 'distinction between the good and the bad' which Captain Mackonochie had resolved to 'forget' in honour of the day. The novelty of the system 'gave to the policy of Norfolk Island the air of delirium ; the disciplinarians of the ancient *régime* raised their hands with astonishment. The place, once of all most hateful, painted by fancy, became an elysium ; employment enlivened by plays, rum, and tobacco, was described as a cheering vicissitude in a life of crime.' It was not, however, difficult to see, adds Mr. West—and certainly it is not difficult even at this distance of time for a reader to guess—' that a reaction would follow, and that any untoward accident would produce a recoil.' For a time, however, all went well. ' It is said that the prisoners at Norfolk Island deeply sympathised with their chief, and that they combined in a society for mutual reformation.' But the paper which contained the outlines of the plan was headed, we are told, with the surely somewhat ominous motto of the Irish Liberator :—

Hereditary bondsmen ! know ye not
Who would be free themselves must strike the blow ?

They struck the blow on June 21, 1842, when twelve convicts who had been told off to assist in unloading stores from the Governor Phillip, made an attempt to seize the vessel. A desperate struggle, in which several lives were lost, ensued ; but the mutineers were at length mastered and conveyed to Sydney in the vessel they had attempted to capture. Sentenced to death, they 'met their fate with fortitude, and their last words were in grateful remembrance of Mackonochie.'

By the following year the pendulum of policy had swung back again. Sir George Gipps, the Governor of New South Wales, announced in an address to the Council that after one year and a half's trial of the new discipline it was to be abandoned. The prisoners then in Norfolk Island were transferred to Van Diemen's Land ; and the former settlement, from being a school of reform, was converted into a limbo of the irreclaimable. The 'mark system,' which had been a capital feature of Captain Mackonochie's scheme, had signally failed. In theory it had seemed a felicitous idea to allow men to purchase discharge from a seven years' sentence by accumulating 6,000 marks for good behaviour, and from a life-sentence by 8,000. But in practice it proved fruitful in abuses. Convicts found means of accumulating marks without fulfilling the irksome condition of good conduct. Convict clerks falsified the accounts, and men transferred their marks to each other for a consideration. Moreover, they were awarded, as indeed it must have been difficult to avoid awarding them, for merits other than moral. Clever mechanics obtained them by their skill, the strong earned them by their strength, and both alike obtained an advantage over their less able or able-bodied fellows whose behaviour may have been in no respect inferior to theirs.

Captain Mackonochie's recall, which is said to have been in contemplation from the moment the news of the birthday festivities of 1840 reached the Home Government, was delayed for several years by the difficulties of finding a qualified successor ; but in 1844 he was at last recalled. He left the island, we are told, 'regretted by the prisoners,' but followed probably by feelings of a less tender character on the part of the colonists. He was unquestionably a benevolent and well-meaning man, but so was Mr. Walter Shandy; and if we could conceive that philosopher suddenly elevated to the government of a province, and empowered to apply his pet theory of 'Christian names' or any other of his eccentric crotchets to a portion of his subjects, he could hardly have set to work in a spirit of more opinionated self-confidence or of rasher contempt for the informations of common-sense and experience than did Captain Mackonochie in Norfolk Island. His administrative record in that settlement certainly afforded an ample *ex post facto* justification of Franklin's conduct in summarily closing his official career in Tasmania.

CHAPTER XVI

TASMANIAN INCIDENTS

1842

IT was characteristic of the insatiable adventurer that even within the comparatively narrow limits of his Australasian island he contrived to lose himself and an exploring party in the hitherto unthreaded bush, from which, indeed, they did not ultimately emerge into known or habitable regions until after his alarmed subjects had despatched at least one expedition for his discovery and relief.

Macquarrie Harbour, a port on the west coast of Tasmania, named after a former Governor of New South Wales, was the 'objective' of the arduous and perilous march, on which Sir John Franklin, with his wife, his niece, and their companions, set forth in the spring of 1842. The harbour, originally employed as a penal settlement, had been abandoned eleven years before in consequence of its difficult approach. Not easy of access even by sea, it was by land altogether inaccessible, being divided from the settled districts by a strip of country some eighty or ninety miles in width, and consisting of impervious forests, rugged mountains, tremendous gullies, impetuous rivers, and treacherous morasses. It is true that in the earlier portion of Colonel Arthur's governorship prisoners were still sent thither from other parts of the island as a punishment, but the difficulty of keeping up its supplies by sea was so great that its use as a convict station was at last discontinued. In the meantime, prisoner after prisoner had endeavoured to make his escape from it by way of the interior only to perish in the bush, or, as happened in two or three instances, to emerge from it so utterly worn out by fatigue and famine that the wretched fugitives were glad to surrender them-

selves on their arrival at the first human habitation. Sometimes the rash attempt had results even more terrible.   In the
year 1822 a party of eight men escaped from Macquarrie Harbour, of whom all but one perished, or were destroyed to satisfy
the hideous cravings of their famine-maddened companions.
The survivor, a man named Pearce, who had ultimately
fallen in with some bushrangers, with whom he was taken
and sent back to Macquarrie, actually made a second attempt
at escape with a fellow-prisoner of the name of Cox.   For
the first and second day they strayed through the forest, on
the third they made the beach, and travelled towards Port
Dalrymple until the fifth, when they arrived at King's River.
They remained three or four days in an adjoining wood, to
avoid soldiers who were in pursuit of them, and were all the
time from the period they started without a morsel of food.
Overcome by famine, each watched for an opportunity to
surprise and destroy the other, neither daring to snatch a
moment's slumber lest he should never wake.   Cox was the
first to give way to exhaustion ; he fell asleep, and Pearce
despatched him with an axe.   On the departure of the
soldiers, the miserable wretch slunk from his retreat, and,
living on the mutilated remains of his companion, spent a
day and a night in the place which they made their encampment.   Then, overcome with horror at his useless crime, he
returned to the settlement, and, declaring himself weary of life,
surrendered, confessed his guilt, and was tried and executed.

It was into the region so darkly associated with these
tragedies that Franklin and his little party fearlessly plunged.
Their purpose was to thread their way through scrub and
forest and mountain gorge, over river and torrent, and
round morass and swamp, to a point near the mouth of the
Gordon River, where a little schooner, the Breeze, was to
wait in readiness to convey them the rest of the way to Macquarrie Harbour.   They started in beautiful weather and in
a season, the best possible for their purpose, of unusually
prolonged drought ; but before they had got far on their
journey the atmospheric conditions underwent a complete and
most untoward change.   Heavy rains set in, flooding the

rivers and rendering the swampy ground impassable. For a week they were confined to their tents in a sheltered nook under a snowy mountain, and later on were compelled to make another considerable stay on the banks of a swollen river, waiting for provisions to reach them, and for a double canoe, now rendered absolutely necessary for their further conveyance, to be rudely fashioned out of the neighbouring pines. During the weeks of their enforced sojourn in the Tasmanian wilderness the travellers were entirely lost to the outer world. Neither sound nor sign of them seems to have reached Hobart Town, and the sinister reputation of the region in which they had disappeared tended of course to deepen public alarm.

In truth, the difficulties they encountered after the rains set in were sufficiently formidable. The swollen river, which formed the main obstacle to their progress—the 'Franklin' their surveyor had christened it—was some seventy or eighty yards wide, and quite impossible, therefore, to be bridged, like the others they had thus succeeded in crossing, by means of fallen trees. Their pioneering party was, in consequence, compelled to construct a rude kind of raft, which they had fastened by a rope across the river.

On our arrival (wrote Lady Franklin to her sister) the flood had carried away the warp, but the raft remained. On this, after the rise had subsided a little, two men (prisoners) volunteered to cross, a measure necessary to be effected as soon as possible, as the Breeze, which was waiting for us to take us back by sea, was to leave by order on the 18th, and if gone we should have had to make our retreat by land with increased difficulties through the country we had already traversed. The two men on the raft were whirled round in an eddy as soon as they pushed from the shore, and, unable to cross, were carried down the river over some rapids and disappeared from our eyes round a bend of the stream. Sir John declared, however, he had no doubt of their safety (they had been Thames and Bridgewater bargemen), and in half an hour afterwards their voices were heard on the opposite side ' coo-ee-ing' (the universal colonial cry learned from the natives), and, having given us that notice of their existence and safety, they darted deep into the forest on their mission, which was to arrest the Breeze in its departure.

The efforts of the two trusty convicts were successful.

T

They stopped the schooner when on the point of sailing, and the Franklin party eventually made their way to it in safety. But the pluck and loyalty of these criminal pioneers were virtues common to all their fellow-convicts engaged in this service. Few stranger or more paradoxical scenes have perhaps been ever witnessed even in a penal settlement than that which Lady Franklin here goes on so graphically to describe. After enumerating the members of their party, eight in all, she continues :—

The crew of the Breeze consists only of five persons, and a stranger to the country (particularly if he was a member of the former Transportation Committee) would take it for granted that twenty stout able-bodied convicts (chosen expressly for this service, because they are such) would find it an easy matter to overcome the resistance of thirteen persons, of whom two are women, and, taking possession of the Breeze, carry her off as masters and free. No such idea probably entered any of their heads. With the exception of trying whenever they could to get more than their share of our scanty provisions, which probably many free men of their rank in life would have done equally at home in similar circumstances, they have behaved admirably well, and we have all encamped together at night within a few yards of each other in open tents, without a guard and without a firearm among us, or a single instrument of defence against the axes and tomahawks which were continually in their keeping. You may think it was because the Governor was of the party, and that they all had much to *hope* from him, even though under the circumstances they could have little to fear ; and this is true, for they all look for indulgence for this service—that is to say, some alleviation of sentence according to law—and were promised it on good behaviour ; but, as far as safety be concerned, the sense of security would have been enjoyed just as much, I believe, by any other set of travellers as ourselves.

The safe return of the party was welcomed with the greatest relief by the colonists, who had, in fact, almost given them up for lost. New South Wales took an even more despairing view of the situation than Tasmania ; Sir George Gipps afterwards writing to Franklin to say that at Sydney the only difference of opinion as to their fate was as to whether they had been starved or drowned. They had indeed been at various times in very real danger of both these fates and, had the schooner sailed without them, it is but too probable that none of the party would ever have seen Hobart Town again.

Nor does this tale of perilous adventure end with their return. On their arrival at Hobart Town they found that a party of six prisoners had been sent out in search of them, and, as nothing had been heard of these men for some time, it became necessary to despatch a third expedition for the rescue of the rescuers, who, as it turned out, were themselves only narrowly saved from death by starvation. Arriving at Macquarrie Harbour after the Franklin party had left, they pursued their way along the coast in the expectation of finding traces of the explorers at some point on the shore. They consumed all their provisions, and, being at last stopped by a river which they had not strength to ford, they retraced their steps. After having been reduced to such straits for food that they had to devour their leather knapsacks, they at last regained a little canoe which they had constructed and left behind them, and got to a deserted island in Macquarrie Harbour, where they found potatoes growing wild from those originally planted there ten years before. After a few days' rest, four of the men with a small store of potatoes embarked again in their canoe for the Gordon River, where they left it. Plunging into the forest, they came to the Franklin, and crossed it in a canoe abandoned there by the Franklin party, which unfortunately filled and sank with their store of potatoes during the passage. Here providentially, at a moment when, according to their own account, they could not have held out another day, they fell in with the second relief party and were saved.

The two men left on the island were rescued by a boat sent from a ship which had been driven ashore. They, too, were reduced to the last extremity; their scanty stock of potatoes was almost exhausted, and they were on the point of building themselves another canoe with the view of attempting an escape from the island when the relief arrived. 'For myself,' writes Lady Franklin, 'I have suffered mentally very much indeed on the subject. It would have been a bitter pang for life if these poor fellows had perished in their attempt to rescue us. . . . Their image haunted me day and night, and you would be surprised to see how much this with other anxieties since our return from Macquarrie Harbour has worn and aged me.'

To a slightly earlier date in Franklin's administration than that of this too exciting journey belongs the following letter, interesting in right not indeed of its contents but of its author, the minutest scrap of whose correspondence is justly valued by the world :—

Park Lane : Feb. 13, 1841.

My dear Sir John,—Hearing at Lady Blessington's, a few nights back, that her brother, Mr. Power, was about to embark for the seat of your government in an official character, I could not resist availing myself of the occasion to communicate with a very old and very valued friend. I trust that Lady Franklin and yourself find health in the Tasmanian breezes, which, I hear, are very renovating, and I only hope the magic power of steam may some day, and perhaps soon, permit me to pay you a visit. In that case I shall have the pleasure of introducing you to Mrs. Disraeli, a lady who passed her Christmas last year at Bradenham in reading your adventures towards the Coppermine River, and who would be very much gratified in making the acquaintance of the hero of both Poles. You will be glad to learn that your old friends at Bradenham are well ; but my father, I deeply lament to say, though with apparently an unbroken constitution, has been stricken with blindness, for him a peculiarly dreadful visitation.

Last year, on our road between Augsburg and Munich, I met Mr. Griffin and Mrs. Simpkinson. He really seems younger than ever. I can only wish her the good fortune to seem as young as she always does.

We are apparently in this country on the eve of a change of government, which renders the world of politics turbid and excited. I hope, whoever may be in power, the colonial interests of this country will be maintained ; and I know no better mode than appointing governors as able and efficient as yourself.

You will find Mr. Power a very amiable man. I have always heard him highly spoken of, and can personally answer for his agreeable manners. Pray make my kindest remembrances acceptable to Lady Franklin, and believe me ever,

My dear Sir John, yours very faithfully,

B. DISRAELI.

Among other pleasant incidents of this chequered Tasmanian time is to be numbered the Governor's renewal of relations with the staunch comrade of his first Arctic expedition, John Hepburn. On his return to England in 1822 Franklin used his best exertions to procure from the naval authorities some fitting recognition of his late follower's services. A letter is extant addressed by him to Admiral Sir Byam Martin, then Comptroller of the Navy, in which he most warmly advocates Hepburn's claims—'the only English seaman,' as he says, 'who accompanied me to the shores of the Arctic sea, and who, during the whole time he was attached to the expedition, conducted himself with a degree of intelligence and zeal that called forth my repeated encomiums.' His conduct 'during a period of extreme difficulty and distress,' adds his late commander, 'was so humane and excellent as to merit the highest promotion that his situation in life entitles him to. When the officers were unable to advance any further he alone remained with them voluntarily, and at the imminent hazard of his own life. To his exertions at a period when his bodily weakness was extreme, Dr. Richardson and myself are indebted, under Providence, for our lives.'

Lord Bathurst, before whom a more detailed statement of Hepburn's services had been laid, had recommended him to the notice of the First Lord of the Admiralty for promotion ; and Lord Melville, also sensible of his merits, had expressed his intention of speaking to the Comptroller on the subject of procuring some situation for him. Franklin, indeed, had previously had an interview with Sir Byam Martin, the substance of which was by desire reduced to writing in the letter from which the above extracts are taken. We may take it that the application was successful, but that Hepburn's employment was either not permanent or not permanently satisfactory. It is, at any rate, certain that he reopened communications with Franklin some fifteen or sixteen years later, after the latter's appointment to his colonial post, and that, Franklin having responded with his usual kindness, Hepburn came out to Tasmania to be provided by the Governor with some more profitable situation than he could obtain in England. Some time afterwards the following correspondence, excellently illustrative of Franklin's untiring goodness of heart, took place between them. 'My dear Hepburn,' the Governor writes to him with all the *bonhomie* of a sailor addressing an old shipmate,

I heard yesterday that you are not satisfied with your situation, and that you have expressed disappointment with your prospects in this country and some regret at having left England. This information has given me much concern ; for though, as you remember, I did not urge you to come out with me, but at first discouraged your quitting England, I yet felt happy after you had decided, in the hope of being able to procure for you some comfortable situation. I appointed you, in consequence, to the very first that was vacant, the Superintendent of Government House, and when the present situation became vacant, which was more lucrative and of a higher class, I immediately offered it to you. I have had some reason to fear it is a situation the duties of which are not exactly suited to your taste ; but I have not had any other vacant which you are better qualified to fill, or that at all equals your present office in emolument and advantages. At one time, when I thought it not improbable there might be a vacancy in the situation of Harbour Master, you will recollect that I asked whether that appointment would suit you, and that you thought you were not now qualified to fill its duties with any degree of satisfaction to yourself or to the public. My first desire ever has been, and still is, to show my regard and esteem for you ; and I beg of you to let me know what situation you consider yourself better qualified to fill, or that would be more agreeable to your feelings, and I would endeavour to place you in such a position when a vacancy and opportunity occur. I cannot make situations, you must well know ; and I cannot know your wishes unless you communicate them to me. You must, therefore, write to me as soon as possible, and inform me as to your present feelings and wishes, and you may rely on the unaltered desire of my heart to prove myself your true and sincere friend, JOHN FRANKLIN.

Hepburn's answer, with due correction of the old sailor's somewhat breezy orthography, was in these terms :—

I have the honour to acknowledge the receipt of your Excellency's letter of the 15th inst., which I did not receive until last night, having been missent from Campbelltown to Launceston. I beg leave to state that your Excellency has been misinformed respecting the complaints said to have been made by me. In place of having expressed disappointment at my prospects in this country or regret at leaving England, I beg to *assure* your Excellency that it is quite

the reverse with me ; and, since I have been in the country, I have
added more to my stock of this world's riches than I did for the preceding twelve years. That I ever expressed dissatisfaction with my
present situation is also untrue. I am sensible that everything has
been done here to make me comfortable. I acknowledge for the
first six months that I often did feel at a loss for words to express
my disapprobation of the conduct of boys when brought before me.
From this circumstance alone I did feel uncomfortable and dissatisfied
with myself, and supposed that I was not a suitable person for such
a responsible situation. But in no other way have I ever had
occasion to complain. I well remember your Excellency's anxiety to
serve me before I left England, and I trust that I shall never be found
ungrateful for the kindness I have received, or so deceitful to a kind
benefactor as to make complaints in any quarter except to your Excellency. If it were not presuming too far, I would beg to be confronted
with the individual who has thus so basely misled your Excellency.
I am perfectly satisfied with my present situation, it suits me very
well ; my only fear is not suiting it. My wish is to remain until I
can save about two hundred pounds. Then, if my wife will come
out, we shall have enough to stock a small farm, should such be in
your Excellency's power to grant. I have received a letter from Her
Majesty's Paymaster-General containing four forms, one of which I
enclose herewith for your Excellency's inspection, being fearful that I
am doing wrong in receiving a pension while I hold such a lucrative
Government situation. Captain Booth has sent for me within the last
hour, and read a letter from the Colonial Secretary offering an appointment at George Town, which I believe would suit me very well ; and
I feel very thankful for your Excellency's kindness. Captain Booth
has in the kindest manner expressed his satisfaction with my services
here ; but, being very comfortable where I am, I beg to decline to
accept it. And I have the honour to be, &c.

Before taking final leave of these unofficial or semi-official
passages in Sir John Franklin's career in Tasmania it still
remains to record two of its most memorable incidents—one
of them touched with all the romance of past adventure and
of the memory of a cherished comradeship, the other fraught,
for us at any rate, if unconsciously to all the actors in it, with
the more tragic interest afterwards lent it by a fatal future.

No one could fail to be impressed by the singular chance
which had brought Franklin, at the age of fifty, to occupy
a post of authority in that very region of the world which,
as a lad of fourteen, he had assisted to explore. The
memory of those far-off days in the Investigator—days full of

young enthusiasm, and not free from youthful mischief—must have many a time recurred to his mind ; he may often have smiled at the recollection of the thoroughly middy-like trick by which he secured to himself the honour of annexing the Australian continent, symbolically at any rate, to the British Empire. The Investigator had lost one of its boats, which capsized and disappeared with its crew of seven men and a young officer, as it was returning to the ship. Franklin and several others were landed and sent out on the 'Heads' to watch for the appearance of any corpse that might be washed up on the rocks. Each carried a flag, which was to be un-furled as a signal in case any such object should come in view.

The temptation so obviously suggested to an ambitious middy by finding himself on the shore of a newly discovered continent with the union-jack in his hands was too much for the youthful Franklin. To have first descried or to have failed to descry the floating body of one of his drowned messmates was a mere detail : the really important thing was to be the first to unfurl the British flag on the coast of New Holland. It was accordingly not long before that beloved emblem was fluttering proudly in the breeze. In another moment a boat was lowered from the Investigator and was seen approaching the shore. It became necessary for Franklin either to discover one of the lost sailors, or to admit that the supposed signal had been in reality only in-tended to proclaim the annexation of the Australian con-tinent to the British Empire. He chose the former alterna-tive, and, pointing to a white object on the shore at some distance, he asked the officer in command of the boat whether he did not think that 'that white thing' was a dead body. The officer looked with interest at the crack in the rocks which was thus brought to his notice, and thought that it was a dead body. Indeed, he was for a short time pretty sure it was, while Franklin was 'sure of nothing but of the sweet consciousness that he had realised the longing of his boyish ambition.' No doubt, as his wife adds, ' it was a very young trick ;' but a daughter of sixteen is not, or in those days was not, apt to be critical of her father's youthful escapades, and it is therefore not surprising to hear that, 'though not of the first order of merit, it seemed very much to Eleanor's taste.' When, however, she told one or two people that 'her papa was the first who had unfolded the British flag in this part of the world when first discovered by Flinders, they looked almost incredulous.' That great navigator seemed to the South Australians almost as far removed from them as Tasman from the people of Tasmania. They looked upon him as a being not only of another generation, but of another century.

It was to Lady Franklin, while on a visit to South Australia, that the idea of erecting a memorial to Flinders on the scene of his greatest exploring triumph first suggested itself; and after a journey from Port Lincoln to Adelaide, the project, she says, 'had become an absolute mission in her eyes.' For in the near neighbourhood of this port, rising in an insulated and conical form to a height of some thousand or twelve hundred feet from the shore, stood the rock which the explorer had ascended to take the bearings of the gulf. This eminence, named by him after the town of Stamford in his native county, was obviously the very spot designated alike by nature and history for a monument to his memory. There was, however, a difficulty about the appropriation of a site. Land could not be purchased in anything smaller than eighty-acre lots; and to purchase such an extent of mountain, all stone and scrub, for the sake of securing an area of only a few feet, seemed a rather imperfect adjustment of means to ends. Colonel Gawler, however, the then Governor of South Australia, obligingly disposed of the difficulty by promising to make the site of the monument a Government reserve. Thus sanctioned and aided, Lady Franklin and her party started from Adelaide in a small schooner of about 100 tons, and, having landed at the foot of Stamford Hill, they ascended it, identified Flinders's bearings, and marked the spot.

The captain of their little vessel, himself a Lincoln-shire man, was much interested in the expedition, and 'bore on his back up the rugged ascent the heavy box containing the azimuth compass' required for the identification of the spot 'on which Flinders (from whose ponderous quarto we

were provided with the necessary extract) fixed his theodo-
lite.' The captain's wife played an involuntary, though to her
not an unpleasing part in the ceremony, as Lady Franklin
thus amusingly relates :—

Poor Mrs. Blackbourne's pocket-handkerchief was seized by me
by mistake, for when I found a white rag was wanted, I put back my
hand without turning my head to the person close to me, who I
thought was Eleanor, saying, 'Give me your handkerchief, my dear,'
and did not discover my mistake till the titterings and looks around me
made me turn round. Mrs. Blackbourne's blushes and pleased looks
convinced me I had committed a very venial mistake, and I therefore
made no difficulty in retaining my spoil. Since my return to Hobart
Town, I have sent the young person, who was then a bride of three
weeks old, a cambric handkerchief of surpassing fineness, trimmed
with deep lace, in room of the one she so obligingly allowed to be
raised upon Stamford Hill, and in remembrance of that pleasant visit.

The next step was to decide upon the character of the
memorial to be raised. 'Sir John,' Lady Franklin reports,
'is extremely well satisfied with my doings, and has not even
asked me what the memorial is to cost, which, indeed, I am
not able to tell till I get the opinion of Mr. Frome (the
Surveyor-General) on its dimensions; but I hope it will not
be extravagant, if the stone on the spot is made use of.'

Its cost appears to have been 250l.; its form that of an
obelisk, bearing the following inscription from the pen of Mr
Gell :—

THIS PLACE,
FROM WHICH THE GULF AND ITS SHORES
WERE FIRST SURVEYED
ON THE 26TH OF FEB. 1802 BY
MATTHEW FLINDERS, R.N.,
COMMANDER OF H.M.S. INVESTIGATOR,
AND THE DISCOVERER OF THE COUNTRY NOW CALLED
SOUTH AUSTRALIA, WAS
ON 12TH JAN. 1841,
WITH THE SANCTION OF LT.-COL. GAWLER, K.H.,
THEN GOVERNOR OF THE COLONY, SET APART FOR,
AND IN THE FIRST YEAR OF THE
GOVERNMENT OF CAPT. G. GREY
ADORNED WITH, THIS MONUMENT
TO THE PERPETUAL MEMORY OF THE ILLUSTRIOUS NAVIGATOR
HIS HONOURED COMMANDER
BY JOHN FRANKLIN, CAPTAIN R.N., K.C.H., K.R., LT.-GOVERNOR OF
VAN DIEMEN'S LAND.

The second of the two interesting events above referred to as marking the closing years of Franklin's administration was the despatch of the Antarctic expedition under Captain Ross. It may be imagined with what sympathetic enthusiasm this project was regarded by the famous explorer of the other Pole, and with what zeal and ardour he devoted himself to its furtherance. Hobart Town was for some time the head-quarters of the two officers commissioned to execute it; it was there that they made, or at any rate completed, the preparations for their journey; and it was thence they started upon their voyage. The officer in chief command was the Governor's intimate and attached friend, and received from him every assistance which it was in his power to render in the work of equipment for their arduous enterprise, a service which is amply acknowledged by Sir James Ross in his ' Voyage of Discovery and Research in the Southern and Antarctic Regions during the Years 1839–43.' In the report which the Council of the Royal Society had been requested by the Government to furnish, and which was appended to Captain Ross's instructions, much stress was laid upon the making of magnetic observations in Van Diemen's Land. When the expedition arrived at Hobart Town on August 16, 1840, the first thought of its commander was to procure the construction as soon as possible of the permanent observatory which he was instructed to erect there. His satisfaction may be imagined when he discovered the zeal with which the Governor had thrown himself into the project, and learned that the materials of which the building was to be constructed according to a plan sent out from England had been for months in readiness. Nothing remained but to select a site, which was done on the following morning; and by the afternoon a party of 200 convicts were at work digging the foundation, shaping the blocks of freestone which were to be its base and the solid pillars of the same materials which were to support the instruments, and bringing the prepared timbers from the Government store.

This was a pretty expeditious commencement of a public work, and its progress was marked by equal despatch. Under

Franklin's daily personal superintendence the building of the observatory proceeded so rapidly that the whole was completed and roofed in, the stone pillars fixed upon the solid sandstone rock, the instruments placed upon them, and all their delicate adjustments completed by August 27—a space of nine days, surely the quickest thing on record in observatory-building. Sir James Ross writes :—

I should be doing injustice to my own feelings were I to neglect to express my admiration of the cheerful enthusiasm which the convicts employed in the building displayed throughout the work. As an instance of this, I may mention that after they had been labouring from six o'clock on Saturday morning until ten at night, seeing that a few hours' more work would complete the roofing in, they entreated permission to finish it before they left off; but as it would have broken in upon the Sabbath morning their request was very properly refused. This is only one of several such instances of disinterested zeal in the cause, for from their unfortunate situation they could not derive any benefit from their additional labour, and must have on the occasion above mentioned suffered much fatigue from their unusually prolonged exertions.

There was less, one may suspect, of 'disinterested zeal in the cause' of science on the part of the convicts than of eager desire to please a Governor to whom they were devotedly attached. It was a case of 'personal magnetism,' not of the cosmical variety.

Nor were Franklin's services to the expedition confined to superintending the construction of their observatory. He took an active part, as of course he was well qualified to do, in assisting and furthering the observations. On September 23 it became necessary, too, for Ross to avail himself of 'the aid of volunteers under Sir John Franklin, who in his zeal for the advancement of science took his share of the duties of that day.'

That the voyage was not lacking in adventure will appear from the following passage of a letter dated Falklands, May 2, 1842, and addressed to Franklin by an officer of the expedition :—

You will be glad to hear of our safe arrival after our this time truly desperate cruise—forty-six days beset in the packed ice, not getting clear until February 2. Notwithstanding both ships losing their rudders, fitting new ones, we yet penetrated to 78° 11' S. and 160° W., tracing 150 miles of our last year's barrier further to the eastward, still preserving the same appearance. No land did we see; our soundings were from 190 to 200 fathoms along the walls of it. Heavy ice and rapidly forming young ice obliged us, on February 20, to bear away along the pack edge, tracing 1,100 miles of the most desperate work, and no ships ever had a more narrow escape from total destruction than we had in running our longitude down in the 60th degree. On March 13, in 147° W., blowing a gale of wind with a heavy sea, and pitch dark, a little past midnight, Captain Ross on deck, while close reefing the main-topsail, a very large iceberg was seen close to us on the starboard bow.

The ship running before the wind, her helm was put a-star-board to avoid the threatened danger, when at that moment an iceberg appeared on the larboard bow of her consort, and, on the latter immediately porting her helm, the two ships came into violent collision, the bowsprit of the former being carried away and their topmasts and foreyards remaining entangled for upwards of ten minutes.

No words of mine can convey an idea of the truly awful situation. Each crash you would have thought must be the last. However, after tearing the strengthening piece from the bows, the two ships parted company. We set the fragments of our main-topsail and fore-and-aft sails to try to weather the berg, which now towered fully 150 feet over, and drifted for more than half a mile along its perpendicular face. The heavy sea dashing against it fell off on board; it was only the violent drawback of the sea that kept us off. Had we once struck upon it the ship must have been dashed to pieces.

It may be imagined with what interest Franklin ac-companied his friends in imagination on their adventurous voyage, and how often he must have longed to exchange the storms of the Hobart Town Council Chamber for those of the Antarctic Sea. The results of the cruise are matters of geographical history, but Franklin's account of them in a letter to his wife, then in New South Wales, may here be given :—

I write to inform you of Ross's return after a successful voyage within the Antarctic Circle, being anxious that you should receive the intelligence as early as possible. He proceeded from hence to the

Auckland and Campbell Islands, where he procured the magnetic observations which he wished, and thence set forth to the southward. The ships entered the Antarctic Circle on January 1. The sea was there much encumbered with ice, and stormy weather caused other obstructions to their progress. However, Ross discovered land in the 70th degree south, which he traced to the 78th, and there, in the meridian of about 176° E., his further progress in that direction was stopped by a barrier of ice steep as a wall and about 150 feet in height. This he then skirted in the hope of finding some opening for his ships, but none was to be seen, and at last he was obliged by the formation of the new ice, which threatened to enclose the ships, to retreat to the northward. He was defeated in his attempts to effect a landing on the main shore ; but he succeeded on two small islands, one of them far to the south, which I believe he has named Franklin, from the name being attached to two specimens of rock brought from it which are on the table in the drawing-room. Ross, however, with his diffidence, has not even spoken to me about the island. The sea was so free from ice when he was sailing south beyond the 71st parallel that Ross was sanguine of passing over the pole of the earth when the unlucky barrier appeared. Near the extremity of their southern limit they discovered two volcanic mountains of great height, one of them emitting flame and smoke, which Ross has very appropriately called 'Erebus' and the other 'Terror.' They saw land over the ice as far as 79° S.

By the observations which Ross obtained to the south, to the north-west, and in the direction of the Magnetic Pole, he has been enabled to fix the position of it with as much accuracy as if he had been so fortunate as to reach the spot. He could not get within 160 miles of it. In sailing to the N.W. of his own discoveries in returning, the ships ran for eighty miles over mountains and other land which the American Exploring Expedition had laid down in their charts, and thus has stamped the proper value on their pretended discoveries in this quarter. . . . In fact, he has had complete success in his first undertaking, and I am happy to say without a single casualty or accident having occurred. The officers, crews, and ships are all in perfect condition. When the ships were first reported to be in sight, I felt most anxious and set off as soon as possible to meet Ross. My mind, however, was relieved before I got on board by the crew manning the yards and giving three hearty cheers. Ross was delighted to find that the officers at the observatory had been as energetic and persevering at their duties as his own companions, of which he received proof on landing by Kay laying before him the registers of their very numerous observations brought up to the preceding hour and ready to be at once forwarded to England. The only disappointment Ross has felt was at your absence at the time of his return, and in his expression of regret he was heartily joined by all his officers as well as by his own circle. However, we look forward to your early return, and I hope the ships will remain till you do.

The ships remained at Hobart Town for more than another month, and their stay there was signalised by an incident which, though slight in itself, cannot fail to strike any one at all curious of dramatic coincidence. It was singular enough that the Erebus and Terror, those two companion vessels which had done so much and were destined to do yet more battle with the Arctic ice, should have been selected for a service which brought them, at the other Pole of the world, into such close contact with the last commander that the Erebus was ever to have ; but this strange accident was to be yet more strikingly emphasised. During the sojourn of the explorers at the port of Hobart Town the hospitalities customary in such cases were exchanged between ships and shore, and among the Franklin papers of the year 1841 is still preserved one of those usually ' trivial, fond records ' of past festivities to which later events have lent a pathetic significance. It is the invitation card to a ball which was given on board the Erebus by the officers of that ship and of the Terror, and which the Government House party duly honoured with their presence. Virgil himself could have asked for no more grimly ironic commentary on his apostrophe of the

Nescia mens hominum fati sortisque futuræ !

than this light-hearted meeting of Crozier and Franklin, host and guest, on the deck of the doomed vessel which five years later was to bear the elder and accompany the younger to their Arctic grave, and to leave her own stout timbers, so gaily trodden throughout that warm southern night by the tripping feet of the dancers, to be slowly crushed in the cruel clutch of the ice-pack amid the iron fastnesses of the Pole.

CHAPTER XVII

FRANKLIN AND MONTAGU

1841-1844

IT was the warning counsel of Greek wisdom to 'call no man happy till he is dead ;' and what is true of the natural life has assuredly no less apt an application to an official career.

Safely to attribute happiness to the record of an Australasian governorship—especially in the uneasy times of our colonial history half a century ago—it was imperatively necessary to await its end. To any one who had watched Sir John Franklin's administration from a distance, who had noted the useful public works in which it abounded, the energy and success with which he promoted the material and moral development of the colony, the esteem and even affection which he won from the colonists as a community, it might have seemed incredible that a career in many ways so prosperous should be destined to so stormy a close. Nor even for one who most carefully follows the course of the events detailed in the course of this and the succeeding chapter is it easy, if indeed it is possible, to master the whole secret of their explanation. That the Governor was surrounded by factious and intriguing subordinates, that his policy was sustained with little loyalty, and often thwarted by petty spite on the part of those from whom he had a right to expect co-operation, that his chief adviser was a man of obstinate and masterful will, who may have cherished, as he was suspected of cherishing, ambitions inconsistent with faithful service to his chief—all this is patent enough as matter of actual fact, but is insufficient as explanatory material. These difficulties of his administration were known to Franklin from the first ; he had to reckon and to grapple with them from the very outset of his term; and it is not at first sight easy to understand how it was that after contending with them not unsuccessfully for a space of five years they should at last have overcome him.

Had he been other than the man which he had already proved himself to be, his failure would have been comprehensible enough. Many a man distinguished in the domain of action has before this proved himself utterly destitute of the qualities necessary to success in counsel. Energy and daring do not always go hand in hand with tact and discretion; the faculty of command is not invariably accompanied by the power of persuasion; a high and resolute spirit is often associated with an overbearing temper. But Franklin was no mere imperious martinet, no headlong and headstrong autocrat, deaf to criticism and impatient of opposition, and riding roughshod over the opinions and susceptibilities of those around him. On the contrary, he had already in his Greek mission proved his possession of all the moral and intellectual weapons of the diplomatist; he had shown his power of bringing an untiring patience, an imperturbable temper, and an inexhaustible ingenuity to the accomplishment of objects which he was forbidden to attempt, or could not hope to achieve, by force. How came it, then, we are constrained to ask ourselves, that he failed in a task for which the principal if not the sole and sufficient instrument might have been supposed to be simply skill in the management of men? How was it that he was unable to handle hostile and insubordinate colonial officials with the adroitness which he displayed in dealing with slippery Levantine adventurers and intriguing Muscovite colleagues?

No complete answer to these questions is now perhaps forthcoming, but a reply practically sufficient for its purpose and far from discreditable to Franklin may be deduced, it seems to me, from a comparison or rather a contrast between the circumstances of his Tasmanian administration and those of his Mediterranean command. It was not merely that in the Gulf of Patras he had the advantages which he lacked at Hobart Town—untrammelled authority and a free hand; that

in the former case his duty was to act with promptitude and
decision, and take the judgment of his official superiors afterwards, while in the latter case action could not always or
even generally be taken until the views if not the wills of
advisers had been consulted and objections of the captious and
sometimes perhaps even insincere or malicious order had been
laboriously refuted or in the last resort overruled.

To these new conditions of public service he could doubtless have accommodated himself. It was not the difference
between the circumstances of the two missions which led
to their unhappy divergence of result ; it was the difference
between the moral attitudes which he respectively assumed
towards them. The Greeks, official or insurgent, were approached by him in the neutral spirit and frigid temper of the
diplomatist. The objects which he sought to attain—the
protection, that is to say, of British interests, and, so far as
possible, the preservation of international order—were substantially identical with the ends which every commander of
a British war-ship has a standing commission to keep in view.
It was no more of a tax upon Franklin's patience to watch
the shifts and stratagems of Hellenic cunning, nor any
heavier demand upon his vigilance and dexterity to counteract
them, than he would have found it to have to await the
proper moment and select the best position for an attack
upon an enemy's ship.

But he was unable, and it was a generous inability, to
approach his colonial colleagues as he approached the Greeks.
He could not bring himself to regard them as so many human
instruments to be used for certain definite purposes, as so much
flesh-and-blood material to be moulded into, or as nearly as
possible into, certain desired shapes. That is the way in
which men are regarded by the ideal 'manager of men,' but
to observe such bloodless 'counsels of perfection' as these was
utterly beyond John Franklin's power. It needed a colder
heart and a less sympathetic temperament than his to be
able to treat his colleagues on the council board after any
such ungenial plan. No man was ever less fitted by nature
to act on the more cynical portion of the famous advice of

him who has counselled us always to 'treat a friend as if he might become an enemy, and an enemy as if he might become a friend.' To the latter recommendation, indeed, he would have promptly and cheerfully responded, but the former principle he would have regarded as morally hateful, and, for himself at any rate, practically impossible of application.

How, indeed, he would have asked himself, could he possibly apply it to any of the men around him? Were they not all English gentlemen like himself, all servants of the British Crown, under the same obligation as himself to promote the interests of the colony and the Empire by every means in their power, and, above all, to see that, in the memorable words of the Duke of Wellington, whatever else happened, the government of his sovereign 'should be carried on'? It was foreign to his nature to believe that any conscientious difference of opinion on questions of policy could ever array such men in personal hostility to himself, and it would be an insult to them to assume the necessity of treating them with the cautious reserve of a chief who saw a possible enemy in every one of them. So far from that, the kindly and open-hearted nature of the Governor but too strongly prompted him to extend not only his confidence but his friendship to any of those about him who seemed to invite it without too critically considering whether they were worthy of it. It was instinctive with him to seek to establish cordial and even affectionate relations with those under his control. Such a mode of government has its advantages, but it is also not without those dangers which proverbially attend the intrusion of 'sentiment' into 'business.' So long as the official machine runs smoothly, the chief who cultivates intimacy with his staff is no doubt served with a zeal and devotion which can never be commanded by one who, as the phrase is, 'keeps them at a distance.' But in the event of 'difficulties' arising between him and them the pre-existing intimacy is apt to react upon the situation with disastrous effect. Feelings of private injury add a sting to the irritation of public controversy; the warmth engendered by argumentative collision is inflamed by a sense of ill-requited friendliness and by resentment at real or fancied ingratitude; and the official dispute at last assumes the bitterness of a personal quarrel.

The influence of such a revulsion of feeling seems plainly traceable in the history of Franklin's difference with the most powerful and highly placed of his colleagues, and indeed, though in a less degree, in his conflicts with the other officials of whom he fell foul. In every instance one can plainly perceive that the irritation, never more than slight with sensible men, which a mere conflict of wills is apt to produce was indefinitely intensified by the smart of wounded susceptibilities, and that in each case the Governor's impulse was to regard his opponent not merely as a troublesome colleague, but to a certain extent as a faithless friend. It thus became impossible for him to take a tolerant view of those mere tactical devices of controversy which disputants whose personal feelings are not engaged find it easy to permit to their adversaries. To Franklin such strategy, purely defensive as it was, appeared only an additional cause of offence. Himself the soul of candour, a 'plain-dealer,' to use an old-fashioned term, of the most uncompromising kind, he was angrily impatient of any conduct in others which seemed to him to savour of obliquity or chicane, and it did not seem to occur to him that, as human nature is constituted, it is idle to expect absolute and unreserved self-disclosure from an opponent who is fighting for a victory on which his official position and prospects depend.

Thus, from resenting tactics which less sensitive men might have tolerated, Franklin went on to take that further step which is always so easy to a zealous and conscientious administrator in such circumstances. He began to feel a stronger and stronger indignation on behalf of the public service, struck at, as he conceived, in his own person. The men who were making this 'dead set' at him were also obstructing the government and imperilling the welfare of the colony committed by his Sovereign to his charge. Once convinced of this, his mere professional instincts and the training and traditions of his life impelled him to decided courses. It was almost inevitable that the civil Governor at loggerheads with his colleagues should have at last come to regard himself as a naval commander confronted with mutineers, and to deal with opposition in a manner so summary as to a certain extent to justify the criticism that he mistook his council chamber for the quarter-deck of a man-of-war.

No account, however, of these Tasmanian troubles would be adequate which did not include some estimate of Lady Franklin's innocent share in aggravating them. For innocent it was, in the strictest sense of the word, at least if a right to such a description can be earned by the absolute unselfishness of motives which began and ended in a benevolent desire to promote the moral and material interests of the colony, and a wifely ambition to contribute to the success and credit of her husband's rule. That her zeal was never in any instance untempered by discretion it would be too much to say. Prudence so unfailing and invariable amid circumstances often of extreme difficulty is not given to mortal man, still less to mortal woman. But this at least may be said in Lady Franklin's case, that her entanglement in the dispute between her husband and his colleagues was not the result of any unguarded word which may have fallen from her or incautious act into which she may have been betrayed. By this I mean that, though a connection might be plausibly traced between such word or act and the events that followed, it is assuredly not the fact that the avoidance of the indiscretion would have saved her from the entanglement. From that nothing would have saved her, except perhaps (for even thus much is not certain) an avowed and inflexible refusal to express, or even to admit having formed, an opinion of her own on public affairs. Even this, it must be repeated, would not have absolutely insured her against misrepresentation, for it is always possible for those whose interest it is to do so to insist that the wife of a Governor is 'a power behind the throne,' and even to find proof of the charge in the very fact that she, as they would put it, 'ostentatiously' disclaimed all concern with political affairs. Had Lady Franklin confined herself with the utmost strict-

ness to the ceremonial duties of her position, she could not
have concealed the fact of her bright intelligence, of her keen
interest in social questions, and of her eager desire for information on all colonial matters. Still less would her husband have
consented to disguise his high opinion of her judgment or
his readiness to consult it. It would always have been known,
or at any rate suspected, and by persons who would not hesitate
to treat suspicion as knowledge, that she shared the Governor's
counsels; and those who desired, as more than one of the
colonial officials did desire, to embarrass or to wound their
chief by representing her influence as supreme, would have
had little difficulty in finding or inventing evidence on which
to found the charge.

That charge is, in truth, one of the most embarrassing,
not to say the most offensive, which can be brought against
either of the two parties who are its object. To say of any
person in high authority that his policy is dictated by his
wife, is to level at him an imputation to which he cannot
submit without confession of weakness and incapacity, yet
which a man of generosity finds it impossible to repel with
the indignation which, had he only himself to consider, he
would probably display. Franklin was far too magnanimous
to throw his denial into such a form as might imply that he
excluded Lady Franklin from all participation in his public
cares, while she herself must have suffered acutely in feeling that this magnanimity necessarily weakened him for
defence. Nay, she was no doubt conscious that she had
in fact endeavoured, within the limits of legitimate persuasion,
to impress her own views of certain social questions upon her
husband's mind; while her concurrent consciousness that she
had never exceeded these limits, and, indeed, that beyond
them she would have been powerless to deflect the course of
Franklin's policy, made the misrepresentations of the malicious
peculiarly hard to bear. We have already seen how improper
a use had been made of her name, though in that case, doubtless, with no unworthy purpose, by Captain Mackonochie, and
how stern a rebuke he had provoked from the Governor in
consequence. Lady Franklin was guiltless of anything save

an abstract sympathy with the private secretary's ultra-humanitarian views as a reformer of prison discipline, an unfeigned esteem for his personal character, and a feeling of tenderness for a family who were in some sense her guests, and who had at any rate lived for months with her in the intimacy of a common household. It was in response to these sentiments, and to these alone, that she had laboured to prevent the final rupture between him and her husband, and had used her good offices at an earlier stage of their intercourse to soothe those natural feelings of resentment which Mackonochie's singular disregard of the obligations of his confidential post had created in Franklin's mind. Yet she had had reason to repent even this act of simple friendliness, and she was fated to learn that conduct of equally innocent motive could be even more unwarrantably perverted.

Franklin, it is true, was to have no more trouble from private secretaries. Captain Mackonochie was succeeded by Mr. (afterwards Sir) Henry Elliot, then only just commencing the distinguished career which he was afterwards to pursue through various diplomatic offices to that important post of Ambassador at Constantinople, which he served with such marked and memorable ability in the Eastern crisis of 1876–77. Between Elliot and the Franklins relations of the highest mutual esteem and confidence at once established themselves, and were not long in developing into those of close personal attachment. Nor did the intimacy cease with the private secretary's relinquishment of his office a couple of years later and his return to England to enter the diplomatic service. A correspondence was for some time maintained by him with his former chief, to whose character and capacity he took occasion many years later to bear a testimony which will be cited in a later page of this volume.

But trouble was brewing for the Governor elsewhere, and in more quarters than one. Reference has been already made to the singular and almost ludicrous acrimony of the quarrels which raged from time to time in the official circle of the colony. The gentleman who then filled the office of Attorney-General had come into violent collision with one of the judges

a short time after Franklin's arrival. He was said to have
'eaten sandwiches' in the judicial presence, to the derogation or
delay of the proceedings ; and the judge, among other words
of reproof, had thus addressed him : 'Sir, in your official
capacity I shall always treat you with the courtesy and respect due to you. Were you elsewhere I should treat you,
after your conduct, with less courtesy than a dog.' The difficulty was settled by the transfer of the Attorney-General to
another colony, but his successor failed to hit it off with his
colleagues, and later on the legal business of the Government
was somewhat embarrassed by the circumstance of its two
law officers not being on speaking terms with each other. In
the legislative session of 1839 the superior of these two func-
tionaries felt it his duty to oppose one of the measures
brought forward by the Governor, the principle of which had
been also denounced by the Solicitor-General as ' iniquitous
and unprecedented ;' but upon the resignation of the Attorney-General his colleague accepted his place and voted for
the Bill. His defence of this conduct was that he had expressed the former opinion in ignorance of its details ; but
so much public indignation was excited by his remarkable
change of front that Mr. Solicitor himself soon deemed it expedient to follow Mr. Attorney into retirement, and both
officials had to be replaced by successors.

A difficulty, however, of a still graver nature awaited
Franklin in connection with this measure, the principle of
which, it must be admitted, was legitimately open to dispute.
The Bill was supplemental to another which had just previously passed the Council for prohibiting private distillation,
and which had included a provision for the compensation of
the distillers at an amount to be settled by a committee.
To this mode of settlement the Chief Justice, as was perhaps
natural, took strong objection ; and the Government, being,
on the other hand, unwilling to accede to his proposal that
the claims of the distillers should be referred to a jury, yet
anxious that the enactment should not be delayed, had passed
it with a substituted section simply affirming the general
principle that compensation should be paid. To apply this

principle, however, to the actual circumstances of the case turned out to be no easy matter. The laxity of the distillation laws had enabled the manufacturers in many instances to realise illicit profits by paying duties on a lower denomination of cereals than those actually employed by them in their trade. Their past gains could not of course be questioned, but Franklin strenuously and reasonably objected to allow the rate of compensation to be based on a rate of profits which had been only maintainable by defrauding the revenue. So far, no doubt, he carried all his colleagues with him ; it was on his proposed method of giving legislative effect to his views that differences arose. A resolution was introduced to the effect ' that any applicant having been proved, to the satisfaction of this Council, to have been in the habit of distilling contrary to law, has by such practice destroyed any claim he might have otherwise had to compensation.' This resolution, perhaps because it was only a resolution, passed the Council. When, however, it was followed by what was called a Feigned Issues Bill—that is to say, a measure providing, by means of an action at law between two hypothetical litigants, for the judicial determination of the question whether any individual distiller applying for compensation had or had not increased his profits by the illicit practices above mentioned—Franklin failed to carry his colleagues with him. The lawyers on the Council, together with all the non-official members, opposed it, and the Bill was ultimately lost.

It was, however, opposed also by a member of the Council who was neither legal nor unofficial, but was in fact as closely concerned in the financial administration of the colony as the Governor himself. This was Mr. Gregory, the colonial treasurer, whose conflict with his chief on this question soon reached an acute stage. It could hardly, indeed, have been otherwise ; and the only matter for surprise in the whole business is the apparent assumption of the dissentient minister that his official position, after his difference with the Governor had proved to be an irreconcilable one, was for a moment tenable at all. The policy or even the equity of

Franklin's proposed measure was not the question.   There is undoubtedly a good deal to be said for the objectors, whose contention presumably was that, though a distiller's past violations of fiscal law might properly and indeed ought obviously to be taken into account against him in assessing his losses by the extinction of his trade, they did not and could not justify the Government in fining him to the extent of the whole profits, lawful as well as unlawful, which that trade had brought him in.   But the merits or demerits of the measure no more affected the question as between Franklin and Gregory than it would have affected similar questions arising in the mother country between a Prime Minister and a member of his Cabinet.   In each case the duty of such a member, either to support the policy of his chief or to resign his office, would be plain ; and probably nothing but the personal animus which seems to have been engendered by every official difference of opinion in Tasmania prevented Mr. Gregory from seeing this.   Franklin's rough manuscript memoranda of his various interviews with the Colonial Treasurer are still in existence, and they show conclusively enough that he spared no pains to dissuade that officer from taking up a position of active hostility to the policy of his chief.   It would even appear that the Governor, on the advice of his Executive Council, went the somewhat illogical length of acquiescing in Mr. Gregory's opposition to the Bill, provided that he would be content to confine that opposition to a silent vote, and would refrain from addressing the Council against the Bill.

All these efforts were, however, vain, and Franklin at last conceived it to be his imperative duty to suspend the Treasurer from his office, and to report the case and his action upon it to the authorities in Downing Street, by whom it was, apparently after some hesitation, approved.   They could hardly of course have done otherwise under the circumstances.   Franklin's case was too good in the merits for that.   Still it is, I think, evident that the authorities in Downing Street were a little taken aback by the vigour of his action, and that they would have preferred his proceeding by the more leisurely and ceremonious method of suspending the

legislation first, and the hostile official only after reference to
and permission from the department.

The Colonial Secretary, Mr. Montagu, was an antagonist
of a different and more formidable kind.   He was a man of
marked administrative ability, engaging manners, and a considerable gift of persuasive speech ; but his disposition was
masterful and ambitious, and he was quick to resent any
slight to his dignity or any check to his influence as the
officer next in colonial rank to the Governor.   That he would
eventually come into conflict with Franklin was certain ; the
wonder is that the collision was delayed so long.   What
seems to have precipitated, or to have helped to precipitate
it, was a visit paid by Mr. Montagu to England.   His leave
of absence was granted to him on private grounds, but his
chief, whose unqualified confidence he then possessed, was of
opinion that his presence in England 'might be of infinite
advantage to the colony if he had legitimate access to the
Colonial Office, and had means of making available his knowledge and experience in colonial affairs, and especially on
the subjects of emigration and convict discipline.'

The result, however, was disappointing.   It was said by
Mr. Montagu's friends in the colony, and the admissions of his
brother-in-law and *locum tenens*, Captain Forster, lent credit
to the statement, that he did not intend to return to Tasmania
at all unless he failed to obtain a certain appointment elsewhere, of which he was ambitious, and which he had gone
to England to seek.   All this time, however, Franklin was
receiving from him most positive announcements of his intention to return.   This, and the fact that Mr. Montagu
continued to keep his relative informed of his interviews with
and advice to the Secretary of State on the contemplated
changes in the convict system, while he withheld all information on these points from the Governor, tended to produce a
certain strain in the relations between them ; and though, on
his return to the colony in the summer of 1841, Franklin
attempted, ' after some necessary explanations,' to re-establish
the old footing of cordiality, it seems clear enough that the
attempt was but imperfectly successful.

About six months later the crisis came. Franklin had removed from the post of district surgeon (which included the medical charge of prisoners within certain limits) a young man who was represented to him as having carelessly and inhumanly neglected his duty in a particular case. The principal medical officer recommended that he should be severely reprimanded. The Colonial Secretary, through whom the report came to the Governor, added the recommendation that he should be dismissed. After examining the papers, Franklin concurred in the advice offered him, and annotated the documents with some severe animadversions on the surgeon's conduct. Facts, however, which were subsequently brought to his knowledge convinced him that he had acted with some precipitancy, and, 'not having yet learnt,' as he afterwards characteristically observed, 'that it is a greater blunder in a ruler to repair than commit an error,' it was a relief to his mind to receive a memorial from some of the most respectable inhabitants of the district in question— headed by the very foreman of the coroner's jury, who had previously passed some severe strictures on the surgeon's conduct—expressing the sense entertained by the neighbours and friends of Dr. Coverdale of his general humanity and skill, and their desire to retain his professional services. To the revision of the original sentence Mr. Montagu offered the most strenuous opposition. He pressed his chief to withhold his reply to the memorial until he had read and considered a memorandum which the Colonial Secretary desired to address to him on the subject. With this request Franklin, of course, complied, but when on receiving this paper he found Mr. Montagu's arguments insufficient, and, moreover, founded in part on mistaken data, he adhered to his decision, of which Montagu had, as usual, to be the official organ of conveyance. It was this reversal of a decision recommended by him which brought about the rupture.

After absenting himself for several days and sending his papers to the Governor without note or comment, contrary to his usual custom, Franklin found it necessary to send for him on business which was to be transacted in the Legislative Council. At the close of this interview Montagu in a very deliberate and formal manner declared that evil consequences would ensue from the step which had been taken with respect to Dr. Coverdale; that great excitement prevailed in the district of Richmond; that the petition was an entirely political movement; that he knew how it was 'got up;' that Dr. Coverdale's punishment was stated to be *his* (Montagu's) act, and that to restore him was to degrade his (the Colonial Secretary's) office; and, most important notification of all, as the event proved, that Franklin 'must not in future expect the same assistance he had hitherto rendered, though he should keep within the line of his official duty,' and that he 'feared that Franklin's official labours would thus be greatly augmented.' He concluded by expressing a hope that the evil consequences which he apprehended might not take place.

Franklin replied in effect that he shared the hope, and united to it the expectation, that they would not; that he knew nothing of any agitation whatever in the Richmond district, nor why there should be any; that he neither knew nor cared whether the petition was 'got up' as alleged or not; that he saw no reason why Mr. Montagu's office should be 'degraded,' or his usefulness diminished, or his chief's labours increased; but if that were to be the case, that he hoped he should be able to bear it. 'My reply,' continued Franklin in the subsequently published 'Narrative,' from which I have been quoting, 'might certainly have been couched in less forbearing terms, but, hoping that Mr. Montagu was labouring under some delusion and would soon see the folly and impropriety of these idle and disrespectful observations, I treated the subject as an ebullition of personal feeling of which he would soon himself be ashamed. Mr. Montagu's, however, were no idle threats. From that day, or more correctly speaking, perhaps, from the day when he reluctantly transmitted my answer to the petition, the current business of my office assumed a very different aspect. Mr. Montagu absented himself as much as he could from personal attendance ; the papers he forwarded to me were no longer accompanied by the necessary information which had to be elicited step by step from the Colonial Secretary's office ; needless questions were referred to me ; every effort was made to overwhelm me if possible with the investigation of minute details, and to make me feel that my dependence on Mr. Montagu's ordinary services was not to be broken with impunity.'

Matters, in fact, had by this time reached a stage at which any man of a colder and more calculating nature than Franklin's would have seen that a choice between two courses was open to him. Confronted as he found himself by a hostile and indeed secretly mutinous subordinate, with whom further official co-operation was impossible, such a Governor would either have reported the whole affair to Downing Street and requested the authorities to transfer his secretary to some other post ; or, if he found the situation created by Montagu so intolerable that his summary dismissal or suspension was imperatively called for without awaiting the sanction of the Colonial Office to the step, he would at least have taken care to provide himself with a good *casus belli* by putting his refractory minister in some definite official issue conspicuously in the wrong.

Franklin took neither of these courses, or at least adhered to neither. He tried forbearance without forbearing long enough ; and when he at last took action he injudiciously permitted a complaint of an unofficial, or, at any rate, of a not strictly official character against Montagu to be mixed up with the cause of dissatisfaction which already existed. And, gravest imprudence of all, this complaint was founded upon the always doubtful and generally quite unprovable charge of having countenanced anonymous attacks in a newspaper. The 'Van Diemen's Land Chronicle' began to publish articles reflecting, in the offensive tone characteristic of the colonial press of those days, on the conduct of the Governor, and generally supporting the Montagu side in the quarrel ; and the 'Van Diemen's Land Chronicle' was a recently founded newspaper, for which on its establishment the

Colonial Secretary had undoubtedly solicited Government patronage. Its editor and some of its principal writers were known to be his personal friends. On the appearance in its columns, therefore, of these attacks, it began to be said by the Franklin party that the Colonial Secretary was 'using the newspaper directly or indirectly to abuse and degrade the Lieutenant-Governor and his family.' It is a question, perhaps, whether it would have been wise even for Franklin himself to call Montagu's attention to these reports: it was certainly not advisable that such a step should be taken by any third person acting on his own initiative. Sir John's then private secretary, who seems to have been a gentleman of considerable officiousness and a somewhat plentiful lack of discretion, wrote on his own account, and premising that he had no authority from his chief, to invite from Montagu a denial of these imputations. The Colonial Secretary 'first evaded any direct reply,' and then (and it must be owned not unnaturally) 'expressed his resentment at the interference.'

This correspondence took place during a few days of Franklin's absence from the seat of government. On his return it was laid before him by Mr. Henslowe, when no doubt the most judicious mode of dealing with it would have been to lay it quietly on one side, and perhaps at the same time to administer a gentle rebuke to the private secretary for his excess of zeal. Franklin, however, as has been already stated, was somewhat over-sensitive, and his wife even more so, to newspaper abuse, and, 'the Colonial Secretary having taken no steps to repudiate the insinuations referred to in the correspondence,' he deemed it impossible any longer to overlook or delay notice of the very singular position in which Mr. Montagu appeared to have placed himself. He accordingly addressed a memorandum to Montagu reminding him of the conversation in which he had solicited, or had, at any rate, been understood by his chief to solicit, Government patronage for the 'Van Diemen's Land Chronicle,' calling attention to the scurrilous articles against the Governor and his family which had appeared in its columns during the last month, and inquiring whether the Colonial Secretary had 'taken any steps to uphold under such circumstances the dignity of my Government.'

To Franklin's great astonishment, Montagu informed him in reply ' that he had no recollection whatever of anything I had said respecting the newspaper,' except that he (Montagu) had conveyed a request from the editor that Lady Franklin would send him for editorial purposes the literary and other periodicals she was in the habit of receiving from England, and had further made a voluntary communication to the Governor of the editor's intention to support the Government in his newspaper. Consequently, Montagu went on to say, it was entirely out of his power to ' withdraw assistance he had never given,' or to ' assist the dignity of the Government ' by any step of the kind suggested. And, to trace the disagreeable affair to its close, as described in the words of Franklin's ' Narrative :'

The climax of Mr. Montagu's language in the correspondence which passed on this subject was contained in the following insulting remark in his letter of January 17 : 'But I trust your Excellency will also pardon me for submitting to you—and I beg to assure you that I do so under a deep conviction of the necessity of supporting my statement—that while your Excellency and all the members of your Government have had such frequent opportunities of testing my memory as to have acquired for it the reputation of a remarkably accurate one, your officers have not been without opportunity of learning that your Excellency could not always place implicit reliance upon your own.'

Unwilling to bandy more words with Mr. Montagu, I paused on the receipt of the letter, and, having again patiently reviewed the events of the last few months, and considered the little prospect there was of any real and healthy confidence being re-established between us, I felt that without detriment to the public service and dishonour to myself I could not retain Mr. Montagu as Colonial Secretary, and accordingly used the powers vested in me of suspending him from office until Her Majesty's pleasure should be known. This determination I conveyed to Mr. Montagu on January 25, 1842, exactly three months after his announcement of his intention to withhold the assistance he had previously rendered to me as Governor.

The 'insulting imputation,' as Franklin, not without reason, describes it, was the worst blunder Montagu had

made, and with his usual acuteness he saw the necessity of
hastening to repair it.

On the eve of the day named by himself for handing
over the business of his office to his successor, and six
days after his suspension had been made known to him, he
apologised for the expression above quoted, which he begged
to withdraw, and disavowed any intention of disrespect.
Franklin conveyed to him his appreciation and acceptance of
this apology, but, his decision having been formed on public
grounds and on the whole of Montagu's conduct, he felt that
he could not reverse it for an act of tardy reparation
addressed especially to his personal feelings. 'This act of
Mr. Montagu's enabled me, however,' he adds, 'to inform him
of my intention to recommend him to the Secretary of State
for employment as an able and experienced officer whose
services might be useful to the Crown in any country but in
Van Diemen's Land. The Secretary of State,' continues
Franklin, 'is well aware how amply I redeemed this pledge.'

So amply indeed, and with such effect, did he redeem it,
that Mr. Montagu, as will be seen, obtained immediate
transfer to an official post of equal if not of higher rank and
emolument; but the giving of such a pledge must nevertheless be regarded as a generous error. Mr. Montagu's ' ability '
and ' experience ' were unquestioned ; but it was another
matter to say of an officer who had for the past three months
been executing his threat of withholding from his chief ' the
assistance he had hitherto rendered him,' that ' his services
might be useful to the Crown in any country but in Van
Diemen's Land.' They might or they might not be, according as he got on or not with his official superior. Franklin's
own case against him was that under existing circumstances
Mr. Montagu was so much the reverse of ' useful ' that he felt
it impossible, without ' detriment to the service ' of the Crown
and ' dishonour to its representative,' to retain him as Colonial
Secretary. To admit his usefulness ' in any country but in
Van Diemen's Land ' was equivalent—or was sure to be
understood as equivalent—to an admission that the individuality and personal characteristics of the Governor had

X

something to do with the Secretary's contumacy.   It would, in fact, have been only too easy for an unfriendly criticism to attribute it to a conscience-stricken acknowledgment on the part of the chief that he had dealt too harshly with his subordinate, and to a desire to make him such amends as lay in his power by recommending him for official employment elsewhere.

CHAPTER XVIII

FRANKLIN AND DOWNING STREET

1842-1844

MR. MONTAGU was not the man to accept dismissal from any official post in a meekly submissive spirit. He had influential friends in England, and, as he believed, the ear of the Colonial Office, and he at once made his preparations for an energetic appeal against Franklin's decision. He lost no time in leaving for home, in order to plead his own cause on the spot, and, by the same ship which took him to England the Governor addressed his despatches to the Secretary of State for the Colonies announcing the suspension of his officer, and giving a detailed account of the incidents which had led to it.

Meanwhile, the quarrel, as often happens in such cases, had become complicated with and embittered by other and irrelevant topics of dispute. Lady Franklin's name had been drawn into it, Mr. Montagu asserting that it was she who had attempted to agitate or had, at any rate, favoured the agitation of the Richmond district, in favour of the medical officer whose reinstatement had led to the breach between the Governor and the Colonial Secretary. The charge was, of course, indignantly repudiated by Lady Franklin, and no doubt was destitute of any other basis than local gossip seizing upon private expressions, not always withheld perhaps from unsuitable audiences, of her sympathy with a young man who had been treated with undue severity Mr. Montagu, however, persisted in and doubtless believed the imputation ; it was taken up, *more suo*, by his partisans in the colonial press, and for both husband and wife it constituted, as may well be imagined, the most painful part of the affair.

X 2

Another and minor difference arose between the suspended Secretary and his chief on conflicting allegations of fact. The Director of Public Works had been censured by Franklin for having without his authority engaged in very costly improvements of a church for which the Governor had sanctioned only some necessary and simple alterations. Captain Cheyne, the officer thus rebuked, pleaded Mr. Montagu's sanction. Mr. Montagu denied that he had given it, and declared that he had 'never seen' the authority on which the Director had commenced the work. After his departure for England the plans were found and shown to have been approved and signed by the late Colonial Secretary. There is no reason to suspect him of anything worse than a lapse of memory; but when two men are at daggers drawn mutual suspicions are easily excited, and Franklin despatched these plans and the details of the incidents connected with them to the Colonial Office, as a separate head of complaint against his suspended subordinate.

The contest between them, however, was an unequal one. Montagu was on the spot, that is to say, in Downing Street, Franklin thousands of miles away. The latter was personally unknown to the higher official staff of the Colonial Department; the former had but recently been conferring with them on colonial matters, and had produced upon them that favourable impression as to his personal abilities which no man knew better how to create. And lastly, in the minister at the head of the Department Mr. Montagu had the good fortune to find a statesman whose brilliant political powers blinded and still to some extent blind the public to those grave defects of character with which his intimates had too good reason to be acquainted. He was not at all the sort of minister who, if he happened at a first impression to form a strong view of the merits of a particular case, would be at all likely to reconsider it on any grounds of conscientious scruple or from any sense of judicial duty. Nor was it in his haughty and imperious temper to consider the feelings of others as to his mode of signifying the conclusions at which he might have arrived.

Lord Stanley, as it happened, took a very strong view of the Franklin-Montagu dispute in Mr. Montagu's favour, and this view found ultimate embodiment in a despatch which was not only in itself so remarkable a document, but received so large an addition to its importance from the truly extraordinary circumstances of its promulgation, that it will be necessary to quote it entire. It is dated from Downing Street, September 13, 1842, nearly eight months after Mr. Montagu's suspension, and is in these words :—

Sir,—I have received the series of despatches enumerated in the margin, reporting the various occurrences which led to the suspension from office of Mr. Montagu, the Colonial Secretary of Van Diemen's Land, and to the arrival of that gentleman in this country.

This voluminous mass of papers has occupied much of my time, and has engaged my deliberate attention. In proceeding to announce to you the decision at which I have arrived I shall not attempt to enter with any minuteness into the various details and circumstances of the transactions to which they refer. Unfortunately, the merits of the question are so much darkened by the redundancy of the discussions in which it has been involved that any addition to their length and number would increase rather than dissipate the obscurity. I shall, therefore, confine myself to a brief recapitulation of the charge preferred against Mr. Montagu, and to a statement of the conclusions which I have adopted respecting each of them first. You have represented in substance (I purposely abstain from the quotation of the pages over which the complaint is spared) that Mr. Montagu had acquired an influence and authority in the affairs of your Government far exceeding that which properly belonged to his office ; that this influence was maintained by means which, if not culpable, were at least objectionable, and was used in such a manner as to render his continued employment incompatible with the freedom and independence of action which the Lieutenant-Governor ought to maintain.

I am not disposed to controvert, but rather to adopt, your opinion that various circumstances had concurred to place in the hands of Mr. Montagu a degree of authority which, if not balanced by great energy and decision in his immediate superiors, would probably tend to invert the relation which ought to subsist between them. But I find no reason to impute to Mr. Montagu the blame of having acquired the power by any unworthy means or dishonest acts ; or of having employed it for any sinister purpose or in an unbecoming spirit.

2nd. It is represented that when you overruled Mr. Montagu's advice in the case of Dr. Coverdale, Mr. Montagu manifested his discontent by words, and by a course of conduct unbefitting his position and yours, disrespectfully intimating that the zeal which he had till then exhibited in the performance of his duty would be relaxed ; and carrying that intimation into effect under such circumstances as to justify the belief that it was his design to embarrass you by suddenly exposing you to what he esteemed insuperable difficulties.

I am not able entirely to acquit Mr. Montagu of having, in reference to Dr. Coverdale's case, employed some language which you not unnaturally regarded as a menace or of having ceased to render you his efficient services in the same cordial and zealous spirit which till then he had been accustomed to evince towards you.   It may be difficult to condemn a public servant who faithfully and ably performs whatever lies within the strict range of his duty for not advancing further and yielding the aid which public spirit would prompt, or which a stronger personal regard for his employer would suggest. But the abrupt abandonment of a cordial co-operation for a service confined within the exact limits of positive duty may be the subject of a legitimate reproach, and from this reproach Mr. Montagu is not, I think, altogether to be exempted.

3rd. Mr. Montagu is charged with having made an improper use, in the course of these proceedings, of the name of a lady the most intimately allied to yourself.

I pass as rapidly as possible from such a topic, confining myself to the single remark that the imputation does not appear to me to be well founded.

4th. The next ground of accusation is Mr. Montagu's neglect to take proper notice of articles insulting to yourself and your family which appeared in a newspaper established under his auspices, and for which he had obtained your patronage, and his having, by his conduct, given countenance to the opinion that he had some personal connection with these injurious paragraphs.

After fully weighing every part of this case, I entirely acquit Mr. Montagu of all connection with the offensive articles in question, or with the authors of them, or of having omitted to do anything which from his position in reference to yourself and your Government might reasonably have been expected of him to prevent and discourage them.

5th. You complain of the language addressed by Mr. Montagu to your private secretary and to yourself on the subject of these newspaper paragraphs as having been wanting in the respect which it was his duty to observe towards you, and as having in one instance conveyed an insulting imputation on your credibility.

On this part of the case also I think that Mr. Montagu is entitled to be entirely acquitted of blame.   He did indeed make use of an inadvertent expression in one of his letters to you, but the frankness and earnestness with which the error was acknowledged, and with which your forgiveness was solicited, seem to me to have been an ample atonement for an unfortunate selection of words ; for such, and not any intentional insult, was the real character of the offence.

6th. It is imputed to Mr. Montagu that he made an improper appeal against your suspension of him to the public at large through the local newspapers at the very moment when he was contemplating a return to this country to prefer his appeal to myself.

I think that he has fully exculpated himself from this accusation.

Finally, you represent that Mr. Montagu authorised the expenditure of large sums of public money in erecting the tower and spire of a church, not merely without your authority, but with a studious intention of keeping you in the dark on the subject.

Here again I think that Mr. Montagu is entitled to be completely absolved of the fault imputed to him. He had no notice of the charge before leaving Van Diemen's Land, but he has since repelled it to my entire satisfaction.

The result of my consideration of the whole subject is, as you will see, to relieve Mr. Montagu from every censure which impugns the integrity or the propriety of his conduct, while I am compelled to admit that the circumstances of the case are such as to render his restoration to his office in Van Diemen's Land highly inexpedient. It was, therefore, gratifying to me to have it in my power to offer him an equivalent which, while it would mark my undiminished confidence in his disposition and ability to render effective public service, would direct his talents to a field of labour in which they could be exerted without the inconvenience which must attend his resumption of his duties as Colonial Secretary at Van Diemen's Land.

I offered for his acceptance the vacant office of Colonial Secretary at the Cape of Good Hope, and he has cheerfully accepted it. It cannot be too distinctly understood that Mr. Montagu retires from the situation he has so long filled with his public and personal character unimpaired, and with his hold on the respect and confidence of Her Majesty's Government undiminished.

Mr. Bicheno has been appointed to succeed Mr. Montagu at Van Diemen's Land, and his arrival may be expected shortly after your receipt of this despatch.

I am not aware it could answer any useful purpose to enter more fully into the merits of this protracted controversy. But, reluctant as I am to employ a single expression which is likely to be unwelcome to you, I am compelled to add that your proceedings in this case of Mr. Montagu do not appear to me to have been well judged, and that your suspension of him from office is not, in my opinion, sufficiently vindicated.

I have the honour to be, Sir,

Your most obedient humble servant,

STANLEY.

A despatch of such uncompromising not to say brutal severity can seldom have been addressed by a Cabinet Minister to a Colonial Governor; but the harshness of its terms is not more conspicuous than its signally unjudicial spirit. That Lord Stanley arrived at a conclusion adverse to the Governor and declined to approve his action, no reasonable supporter of Franklin could perhaps have complained. The point was distinctly an arguable one, and a Minister might in perfect good faith and with fullest deliberation have held that, the Governor having overlooked or condoned the Secretary's extraordinary intimation of his intention to reduce the amount of assistance his chief might expect from him, no adequate cause for his suspension had subsequently arisen. But Lord Stanley was not content with pointing out the insufficiency of the grounds on which the Secretary was actually suspended; he went out of his way to extenuate conduct on the Secretary's part which would have been amply sufficient to justify any Governor in suspending him.

His observations on this are almost absurdly lenient. Thus: ' I am not able entirely to acquit Mr. Montagu of having used language which you not unnaturally regarded as' (it would have been highly unnatural to regard it as anything else than) 'a menace.' And again: 'It may be difficult to condemn a public servant' for not going beyond the line of strict official duty; but 'the abrupt abandonment of a cordial co-operation for a service confined within the exact limits of positive duty may be' (not, as one might expect to read, the cause of a total disorganisation of the work of the Government, or a possible administrative collapse, but merely, and mildly) 'the subject of a legitimate reproach.' Surely the real question was not so much as to the propriety of 'cordial co-operation' or the inconvenience of its 'abrupt abandonment,' but as to the meaning and effect of a formal notice on the part of an officer who hitherto had cordially co-operated with his chief that he intended to do so no longer. It is impossible to draw any such hard-and-fast line between the course of conduct demanded by public duty and that which is suggested by private goodwill as Lord Stanley assumed; and a Colonial Secretary who deliberately warns a Colonial Governor that he no longer intends to pursue the latter course of conduct is likely sooner or later to deviate from the former. There can, at any rate, be little doubt as to the action which would have been taken by any man of less forbearing or of a more coldly calculating temper than Franklin on receiving a formal notice from a subordinate that his services would in future be unwillingly instead of ungrudgingly performed. Such a man would immediately have called upon his lieutenant for explanation or withdrawal, and, failing this, would have pointed out to him that if his sentiments towards his chief had really become such as to preclude him from co-operating with him as cordially as heretofore, it was his manifest duty to resign.

Lord Stanley's prepossession, however, in favour of the subordinate officer is conspicuous in every paragraph of the despatch. He may have been right in disregarding a complaint so indefinite as that Montagu had 'acquired an influence and authority' in excess of that 'which properly belonged to his office,' and he may have been justified in acquitting him of having acquired this power by 'any unworthy means or dishonest acts, or having employed it for any sinister purpose or in an unbecoming spirit.' But it was gratuitously offensive on Lord Stanley's part to suggest, as he quite distinctly does, that the Colonial Secretary encroached upon the authority of the Governor because he was the stronger man of the two. Nor, considering the person to whom the despatch was nominally addressed, do the elaborate testimonial to Mr. Montagu's high official qualities and the emphatic assurance of Her Majesty's Government's undiminished confidence in him with which the Secretary of State concludes appear particularly well placed. As addressed to his late chief it is hardly explicable, except on the assumption of a deliberate intent to humiliate the Governor by whom this warmly eulogised official had been suspended.

But it was in truth only nominally that the despatch was addressed to Franklin at all.   It might just as well have been sent as an enclosure in a covering letter to Mr. Montagu ; for, incredible as it may seem, its contents were not only made known to that gentleman, but had been freely circulated by him among his friends in the colony months before they came to the Governor's knowledge.   'The ink,' as Franklin puts it in the ' Narrative,' was ' scarcely dry on his Lordship's despatch before its import was mentioned by a relative of Mr. Montagu's in the hall of the Admiralty ; it was sent to Mr. Montagu, who, it will be recollected, was then on the spot, four days after its date, unaccompanied by any injunction of privacy, but, on the contrary, bearing on it the stamp of being Mr. Montagu's own authorised property, to be used as he thought proper.'   The natural result of handing a copy of it to him without any precautions, an act eminently characteristic of Lord Stanley's haughty want of consideration for the feelings and interests of others, was that the recipient felt, as he afterwards wrote in formal vindication of his conduct, that he had a right to show it to whom he pleased.   ' I imagined it was sent to me for that purpose, to enable me to satisfy those who were aware of my suspension from office that I had obtained a complete and honourable acquittal.   I did not hesitate to distribute many copies for that purpose in England. . . . For the same reason I sent two copies to Van Diemen's Land—one to Mr. Forster, and one to Captain Swanston.   I requested them to show it to my friends and to those who took an interest in my case ; but I stipulated that no newspaper was to have one word of the despatch communicated to it.'

Unfortunately, however, for official decency, the despatch obtained nearly as much publicity as though it had been circulated through the press.   By some untoward mischance, which was to repeat itself with even more serious consequences later on, the Colonial Office proved slower in its communication with Tasmania than did private correspondents.   Docu-

mentary evidence existed, Franklin declares, in his possession
that Lord Stanley's despatch was known to be in the colony
before he himself received it on January 18, 1843, and he had
besides the testimony of a resident at Port Phillip to its
having been publicly read at a dinner table in that colony, at
any rate at a date prior to his (Franklin's) own receipt of it.
Immediately on its reaching the Governor, the friends of Mr.
Montagu threw aside even the very slight reserve that they had
maintained; and Mr. Swanston, the late Colonial Secretary's
agent and manager of the principal bank in Hobart Town
placed a copy of the despatch for general inspection on his
office table.   Its contents became the leading theme of every
local newspaper, and were made the text for commentaries
abounding, as Franklin bitterly complained, in 'every species
of vulgar insult.'

But the cup of indignity was not even yet full, nor had
the Secretary of State as yet exhausted his ingenuity in the
selection of inconsiderate and oppressive methods of per-
forming what should have been a painful duty.   To a high-
spirited man like Franklin, the mere tenor of the despatch
would in any case, and apart from the needless affront
inflicted upon him in the manner of its communication, have
appeared to suggest but one possible course of action.   'On
receipt of it,' he writes, 'I hastened to request of Lord
Stanley that he would lose no time in appointing my
successor, unless he was enabled to give me the assurance of
possessing what the despatch seemed to render so equivocal,
the continued confidence of Her Majesty's Government.   But
long before this conditional resignation could reach England
my successor was on his voyage out,' and, as will be afterwards seen, he arrived in the colony four days *before* Franklin
received the official notice of his recall.

The vast absurdity of this last administrative blunder
almost dwarfs the monstrosity of the outrage.   Lord Stanley
did many remarkable things in his life besides taking his
famous political 'leap in the dark,' but one may well doubt
whether he ever rivalled the feat of appointing a Colonial
Governor to fill a chair which had not yet been vacated.   It

was a 'supersession' of the occupant in the strictest etymo-
logical sense—a supersession in the sense in which the Archbishop of York understood the word when in the famous
mediæval struggle between the northern and southern
archiepiscopates for precedence he asserted his claim to the
place of honour on the right of the Sovereign by the direct
method of seating himself in his brother of Canterbury's
lap.

Sir Eardley Wilmot, the new Governor, a worthy country
squire and excellent chairman of quarter sessions, was the
last man in the world to covet the aggressive *rôle* of the
Archbishop of York, and was probably much more distressed
by the consequences of this gross departmental blundering
than Franklin himself. He had come out in the Cressy,
convict ship, the captain of which, as though entering into the
spirit of these irregular proceedings, missed the entrance to
the port and landed him 'on an unfrequented part of the
coast.' This was on the evening of August 17. On the
following night he entered Hobart Town, but he brought with
him no communication from Lord Stanley as to his appointment, nor any official explanation of his arrival. On the
20th of the month, however, the Gilmore, convict ship, arrived,
with the duplicate of a despatch from the Secretary of State
announcing to Franklin the appointment of a successor in
the government of the colony ; and on the following day he
received by the Eamont, merchantman, the precious original
itself, bearing date February 10. It had been entrusted to
a vessel described by Franklin in a subsequent despatch
to the Colonial Office as 'a notoriously slow sailer,' an
expression the use of which, he afterwards admitted with his
usual good-humoured candour, was 'a weak point in his
remonstrance upon the unbecoming mode of his recall, as it
certainly savoured more of the captain than of the governor.'
The vessel in this case had been obliged by stress of weather
to put back, and had been detained for no less than six weeks
in Ireland. No care, however, was taken to send on the
duplicate of the despatch by any of the intermediate sailings
prior to the departure of the Gilmore, and in any case to

appoint a new Governor within a fortnight of the date of the despatch announcing his predecessor's recall, and to allow only a few weeks at the utmost to the former for winding up his public and private business in the colony, was a gratuitous experiment in the art of 'running things fine' which well deserved to meet with the discreditable *fiasco* in which it resulted.

The recall despatch was of the following strictly official tenor, its precise and methodical arrangement of dates presenting rather a ridiculous appearance in the light of subsequent events. 'Sir,' wrote the Secretary of State,

as your administration of the government of Van Diemen's Land will at the time of your receipt of the despatch have continued for more than six successive years, and as after the lapse of that period the general regulations of the public service will probably have induced you to anticipate the appointment of a successor, I trust that I shall not subject you to any serious inconvenience by the announcement that such a change may be shortly anticipated.

I am not at present able to state with precision at what time your successor in the government of Van Diemen's Land will sail from this country to assume that office, but I think it most probable that his departure will not be delayed for more than six weeks or two months beyond the present time. The interval will, I hope, be sufficiently long to enable you to make, with satisfaction to yourself, all the domestic and official arrangements incident to the transfer into other hands of the office you at present occupy.

The unseemly hurry in which the change of governors was at last effected reflects no little discredit on the Colonial Office, because Franklin's recall had, it seems, been resolved upon when Montagu's successor, Mr. Bicheno, was despatched to Tasmania in December 1842; it was indeed, in Franklin's belief, a matter of notoriety in England at that time. Yet Mr. Bicheno was the bearer to him of no communication, either official or confidential, of the impending change. On the contrary, the new Colonial Secretary brought out some important despatches respecting the changes which Lord Stanley was about to introduce into prison discipline. In these despatches Franklin was addressed as the person who was at once to commence initiatory steps for this purpose, and his zealous solicitude was bespoken, or rather (apparently) assumed, for the due execution of the duties confided to him. Lord Stanley subsequently explained his proceedings in the matter as dictated by a desire that Franklin's recall at the expiration of the usual term of colonial government should not have the appearance of being connected with the Secretary of State's disapproval of Mr. Montagu's removal. All, then, that can be said is that Lord Stanley's measures did grave injustice to his motives, and that they fully warranted Franklin in declaring, as he did, that, having regard to the embarrassments and humiliations which were inflicted upon him by the course actually adopted, he considered that his 'immediate recall would have been a much less injury.'

It was most unfortunate, too, that a Minister anxious to divest his action of a punitive appearance should have omitted the customary and indeed almost conventional expression of the satisfaction of the Sovereign with the Governor's services. This slight also was tardily and not too graciously apologised for, but undoubtedly it afforded only too just provocation for Franklin's bitter remark that the acknowledgments usually conveyed from the Crown in such cases were, under all the circumstances, scarcely perhaps to be expected. The Secretary of State, he said, had already stated in the case of Mr. Montagu that 'it could not be too distinctly understood' that that officer 'retired from the situation he had so long filled with his hold on the respect and confidence of Her Majesty's Government undiminished,' and, 'the inferior officer thus complimented, what terms remained for the Governor?'

On the day when the original of this despatch arrived— that is to say, four days after the disembarkation of the incomplete Governor on the 'unfrequented part of the coast'— he was in a position to take the oaths of office and was duly sworn in. Franklin, however, was not yet, on his part, in a position to turn out, but was obliged to remain still ten days longer in Government House, unable, in spite of the exertions of the utmost diligence, to remove his family and dispose of his effects in a less time. During this period Sir Eardley Wilmot resided with the Colonial Secretary, and paid a visit to Launceston, where there was an official residence. At its close Franklin shifted his quarters to the house of the Brigade-Major, where he remained for another two months busily occupied, until such time as the Rajah, in which he had engaged his passage, could complete the lading of her cargo at Port Phillip.

The intervening weeks were passed amid circumstances strangely unlike those which usually attend the departure of a superseded Governor. They were weeks of continuous leave-taking, and of preparations spontaneously made by the colonists of all classes for speeding Franklin in almost a triumphal fashion on his homeward journey. Letters of respectful and cordial sympathy poured in upon him from all sides. Addresses were presented to him from the bishop and clergy of the new diocese of Tasmania, from landholders and occupiers of land in various parts of the colony, from popular bodies like the Mechanics' Institute of Hobart Town, from scientific associations like the Royal Society of Tasmania. Even the colonial press relented towards him, and one enthusiastic editor expressed his wish 'that Sir John had remained twenty years longer.' A brother officer of Franklin, Captain Parker King, wrote to congratulate him in bluff sailorly fashion on having stuck to his post. 'I was delighted that you remained for your successor. All the blue-jackets have done so. 'Tis only the soldiers,' adds this par-ticular blue-jacket, 'who have walked off, afraid of being lampooned and insulted after the honour of government was taken off their shoulders. I was told you wouldn't stay. I said you would, and I was right; and so were you.' Even among those who took no side in the Franklin-Montagu quarrel, or whose leanings may actually be supposed from their position to be against the late Governor, many were shocked at the extreme harshness of Lord Stanley's despatch. Lady Franklin, in a letter to her sister, records a humorous utterance of Mr. Bicheno on being shown in the Colonial Office a copy of the despatch about to be sent to Sir John Franklin. Well might he exclaim, 'Hallo! Is this the way you snub the Governor? What, then, has a Colonial Secretary to expect?'

Franklin's final leave-taking of the colony was more like
the departure of a Governor summoned to receive some
special honour at the hands of the Crown than that of a
censured and virtually recalled official.   On the afternoon of
the day of the embarkation a dense crowd lined the streets
through which he had to pass to the vessel.   Every head
uncovered when he issued from the house in which he had
been staying, and his progress on foot to the water's edge was
a veritable triumphal march.   'As their beloved Governor
passed from among them,' writes an eye-witness, in language
of which the sincerity speaks for itself, 'many could recall to
memory his goodness, his charity, his honest, firm uprightness
of purpose ; and the recollection was now apparent when his
power had ceased, when their object was no longer the
Governor invested with the patronage and the panoply of
office, but the man.'   And the same observer goes on to give
a more minute description of the scene :—

Sir John was dressed in full uniform as a captain in the Royal
Navy, and wore the stars of the several orders which have been con·
ferred upon him for distinguished services rendered to his country
and the cause of scientific discovery.   He halted occasionally for
an instant to acknowledge the enthusiastic cheers which burst forth
from the assembled multitude.   The procession was swelled by new
arrivals at every step, the cheering being renewed at intervals as the
moving mass received fresh accessions.   Handkerchiefs were waved
from verandahs and open windows along the line of route, and there
were few who felt entirely unmoved at the scene before them, a loyal
and generous people paying a heartfelt tribute of affection to a truly
good man with whom their destinies had been bound up for years.

Near the point of embarkation a captain's guard of honour
(fifty men) had been stationed, soldiers of a famous British
regiment which had served through the Peninsular campaign
and bore the name of its glorious battle-fields on its colours.
They presented arms as Franklin approached, and a shout
from sea and land rent the air as the departing Governor
turned round to address the throng of assembled colonists
in a few words of kindly farewell.   They were very few, for
he was much overcome by the manifest tokens of public
affection which had been showered upon him, and, shaking

hands with those around him, prepared to enter the barge which was to convey him to the Flying Fish, circumstances having prevented him from availing himself of Sir Eardley Wilmot's offer of the Government vessel, the Rajah.

But as those near him retired numbers took their places, and anxiety was visible on every face once again to touch his hand. So many were the crowds succeeding crowds anxious for this last honour that there was a considerable delay. At length the signal was given, the oars fell into the water, the battery fired a salute of thirteen guns, a cheer burst from the assembled multitude and was echoed back from the shipping and the boats, which filled with spectators and crowded to accompany him to the vessel. Sir John Franklin bowed his acknowledgments, and the barge, surrounded by a perfect flotilla, pulled towards the Flying Fish, which lay in the stream.

And the character of the departing Governor is summed up by the same writer in these words :—

Thus departed from among us as true and upright a ruler as ever the interests of a British colony were entrusted to. It has been said, nay, insisted upon, that he was not popular, and every effort was made by a few vindictive enemies to make it appear that he was not so. Even a portion of the press, we shame to confess it, was either forced or lent itself to the delusion. But has it, or have they, been successful? Let the proceedings above described be their answer ; let them hear it in the voices of that crowded multitude, and learn how futile are the attempts of malice when opposed to honesty of purpose. It is difficult to corrupt or destroy the moral principle of a whole community, and until that is done appreciation of rectitude in another must ever hurl back denial upon those who say that the people he governed did not admire the honesty of Sir John Franklin.

Like all men, he had his failings and his errors ; he trusted too implicitly when he should not. He believed that the honour and honesty which influenced his own actions and his own conduct would influence others. He trusted and was deceived, but it was to his virtues, not his errors, that he owed his enemies. Had he forgotten what was due to the colony he governed, and to himself, had he consulted the advantage of a few, disregarding that of the many, Sir John Franklin would have perhaps found a few dubious supporters, but he would never have seen the sight which cheered him on his departure with the consciousness of duty performed and a popularity none can gainsay.

From the moderation and the evident effort after critical impartiality with which this judgment is expressed, it may

Y

safely be taken as representing the best opinion of the
colonial community themselves, far better judges of the
character, career, and services of their late Governor than it
is possible for any biographer to make himself, with his much
fewer opportunities and at this distance of time.   It is, therefore, with no little satisfaction that I record its substantial
confirmation of the view already expressed in these pages,
and arrived at altogether independently of the evidence which
it supplies.

CHAPTER XIX

A RETURN TO THE SEA

1844

'THE remaining part of my story must be quickly told.' So writes Franklin in the 'Narrative,' from which, with all due allowance for its being an *ex-parte* statement, I have gathered most of the facts of this unfortunate affair; and a biographer cannot do better than follow his example. It is impossible to dismiss the matter altogether at the close of its colonial stages, for that would be to leave the history of Franklin's struggle with Downing Street incomplete; but the final passages of the conflict shall be related with all possible brevity.

Immediately on his arrival in London, during the first days of June 1844, Franklin called on Lord Stanley in Downing Street, and left with him a note requesting the honour of an interview. A letter, which appeared to have been waiting his arrival, was then placed in his hands, and proved to be a stiff official reply to his last despatch of self-vindication, informing him that the Secretary of State 'did not think it consistent' with the relative position held by himself and the late Governor of Tasmania to 'take notice,' as Franklin puts it, 'of my charges and insinuations,' and stating that 'he would not make to his subordinate officer explanations which he used to Her Majesty the Queen and to Parliament alone.'

On June 18, however, Franklin succeeded in obtaining the personal interview which he sought. At this interview his Lordship 'said little and listened patiently;' but the result was unsatisfactory. The Secretary of State assured Franklin —as indeed he had already assured him by despatch—that his recall was unconnected with Mr. Montagu's suspension;

but this, of course, was not at all the form of solace for which his visitor's wounded feelings craved. 'I assured his Lordship,' said Franklin, 'that it was not of my recall at the usual period, and still less at a period beyond even the usual one, that I should have thought of complaining had it not been for the circumstances which preceded and attended it ; neither was it his Lordship's disapproval of a particular act of my government, of which he was the official judge, that I felt I had a right to arraign, but because no reasons whatever were given me for that disapproval, because Mr. Montagu's assertions had in every case been preferred to mine, and the grounds for such a judgment withheld from me ; moreover, because the terms in which that judgment was conveyed could not but be exceedingly painful and injurious to me ; yet, being such, they had been given to Mr. Montagu, who had no right to them, without any shadow of consideration for me, and had been by him, as might have been expected, made public.'

This last—at any rate for us of to-day—is the point. Upon all personal and upon most official disputes there is always room for difference of opinion, and it is quite possible that among the readers of the foregoing narrative there may be those who agree with Lord Stanley that Franklin's proceedings in the case of Mr. Montagu were 'not well judged,' and that his suspension of that officer was 'not sufficiently vindicated.' But, as to the character of the treatment which the censured Governor received from the Secretary of State, and as to the discredit which that treatment reflects upon Lord Stanley, there can be among men of good sense and good feeling but one opinion. No such man could withhold his sympathy from a public servant who has such a complaint to make as is embodied in the following words : 'I took the liberty of remarking to Lord Stanley that I believed the act of giving to an inferior officer a transcript of the exact terms in which his superior was censured was without a parallel in the annals of his office.'

Into the many aggravations of this original grievance it is unnecessary to enter—not, indeed, because they were unsubstantial, but because they do not strictly belong to that side of the affair to which alone I desire to confine myself—the treatment, that is to say, of Sir John Franklin by the Colonial Office. Some of them, such as that connected with the dispute between the Governor and the Secretary as to the authority for the expenditure on St. George's Church, arose from Lord Stanley's having erroneously, but perhaps pardonably, accepted Mr. Montagu's version of the facts as correct. Another, and that a very outrageous offence—the private circulation throughout the colony of a manuscript book containing defamatory statements about the Governor and his wife, and 'purporting to be minutes of conversation which Mr. Montagu had had with Lord Stanley *before the despatch was written*'—must, so far as it concerned the Colonial Office at all, be regarded as one among the natural consequences of the original indiscretion and inconsiderateness with which the Secretary of State acted in the delicate matter of receiving and adjudicating upon the complaint of a displaced official against his chief. One incidental affront, however, for which Lord Stanley was directly responsible, it would be wrong to omit. Shortly after the departure of Mr. Montagu for England, Sir John and Lady Franklin made the adventurous expedition related in a preceding chapter, and in May of 1842 a Tasmanian newspaper published a ridiculous story about the Governor's having granted a free pardon to the convicts who had acted as 'Lady Franklin's palanquin-bearers.'

Upon this being brought to Lord Stanley's notice he immediately addressed a despatch to Franklin, in which, after the usual conventional expression of disbelief in 'the unworthy motives attributed to you,' he requested the Governor to furnish him with 'an explanation of the unusual course which appears to have been taken with respect to these pardons,' and to inform him 'whether there is any truth in the assertion that some of the convicts had been thrice convicted in the colony.' There was no truth in the assertion, nor had there been anything unusual in the course pursued, which indeed was prescribed by and taken

in strict conformity with statute. Of the men to whom
the indulgences were granted, some would have 'obtained
them within only a few months' in the natural order of
events ; and all had, in the Governor's opinion, merited
them, not for their services as Lady Franklin's 'palanquin-
bearers,' but for the energy, patience, courage, and loyalty
which they had displayed on a most toilsome, difficult, and
even dangerous expedition undertaken in the interests of
the colony and the Empire. Of the sixteen who obtained
tickets of leave, eight had previously established a claim to
indulgence by uniform good behaviour. The two who
received free pardon, one of whom was within about ten
weeks of the expiration of his sentence, had risked their lives
in effecting a crossing over a rapid and swollen river, and
thereby rescuing the whole of the party from an exceedingly
perilous situation ; and one of the men who received a conditional pardon 'had suffered the loss of an eye in his
exertions to force a passage through the thick scrub.' At
any other moment, perhaps, it might have been less irritating
to be called upon to furnish these explanations, but to
receive the official demand for them—as, in fact, happened
—by the same mail as that which brought the despatch of
censure must have been felt as intensely provocative, even by
the most patient of men. 'No wonder'—Franklin naturally
said to himself—'no wonder the Secretary of State believes
my displaced officer's story in preference to my own, when he
can attach importance enough to the scandalous tittle-tattle
of a colonial newspaper to make it the subject of a formal
request for explanation.'

He gained nothing by his interview with Lord Stanley.
Seven weeks passed without bringing him any nearer the
redress which he sought, and on August 3 he addressed a
letter to the Secretary of State, with a respectful reminder that
he was still anxiously awaiting the result of his application.
And with a view to simplifying Lord Stanley's consideration
of his claims he submitted seven heads of request to the
Minister, bearing respectively on the various points upon
which he felt that he had a right to solicit some more

satisfactory declaration than he had yet received. Omitting those which relate to collateral and more or less irrelevant controversial issues, Franklin's requests reduce themselves to the following five :—

1. I submitted how indispensable it was for me to be assured by his Lordship of his belief that in my suspension of Mr. Montagu I was actuated solely by a desire of the public good, and not by personal or private motives.

2. I trusted that if the explanation I had been called upon to give of my conduct in granting certain rewards to meritorious convicts which had been called in question on the authority of a local newspaper appeared satisfactory to his Lordship, I might be favoured with a communication to that effect.

3. I solicited the written expression of Lord Stanley's assurance that my recall was unconnected with Mr. Montagu's suspension, and that the circumstances attending it were unintentional.

4. I reminded Lord Stanley of his personal assurance to me that the omission of any expression of approbation in the despatch announcing my recall was not intended for censure, and expressed my conviction that if the anxious efforts I had made worthily to keep the high trust which had been reposed in me during the usual period of a colonial government were appreciated by him, as they had expressly been by the great body of the colonists, this indispensable testimony would be supplied.

Lastly. I requested that a copy of any communication embodying those points with which his Lordship might be pleased to honour me should be transmitted to the Lieutenant-Governor of Van Diemen's Land, with directions that it should be laid before the Legislative Council at their next sitting.

Anxious that a reply which would have such important consequences for him should not be too hastily given, Franklin requested that Lord Stanley would either grant him another interview or would, if that course were preferred, allow him to instruct his friend Mr. Robert Brown to attend at the Colonial Office as his representative. Lord Stanley selected the latter alternative, and received Mr. Brown, who appears from his manuscript memorandum to have stated his friend's case with equal skill and propriety. On the following day Franklin received a letter from Lord Stanley which, at an earlier stage, might have had some mollifying effect. But matters had now gone too far, and one can hardly feel much surprise that to a man still smarting under the clumsy indignities which had been inflicted upon him in the method of his removal, the terms of this *amende* should have seemed cold and grudging. The following reply to it brings the official stage of this most disagreeable controversy to a welcome close :—

My Lord,—I should have had the honour to acknowledge earlier your Lordship's letter of the 13th inst. if I had not considered it right to wait for some time after your Lordship's receipt of mine of the same date.

It is with infinite pain that I am under the necessity of stating to your Lordship that the terms of your Lordship's letter are inadequate to afford me the satisfaction I expected from you ; and I regret that the more because your Lordship, having partially conceded to me a few of the points I had the honour to lay before you, though in language little conciliatory to my feelings, would appear to have anticipated a different result.

This may be a sufficient reply to the question your Lordship has been pleased to refer to me respecting the communication of your Lordship's letter to Sir Eardley Wilmot. As far as my own wishes are concerned, I can have no desire that a copy should be forwarded to Sir Eardley Wilmot.

It would have been satisfactory to me to have been permitted to point out to your Lordship the grounds of my inability to accept your Lordship's letter as a reasonable reparation for the injuries I have received, but your expressed desire that the correspondence should terminate forbids my doing so.

It may not be superfluous for me in the meantime to state that neither in Van Diemen's Land, where the injuries I have received in my government are best understood, nor in this country, where, as well as in the colony, the unprecedented act has been witnessed of the publication in the newspapers of a despatch condemnatory of a Governor who was still in the exercise of his functions, can your Lordship's letter, either in its substance or its terms, produce an impression which can at all counteract the evil that has been inflicted.

I have the honour to be, &c.,

JOHN FRANKLIN.

Many men would at this stage have, from sheer weariness, allowed the controversy to drop. But Franklin could no more resign himself to defeat in Downing Street than in Lancaster Sound. Whether the obstacle which barred his way was a literal or a figurative iceberg, it was not in his nature to rest until he had exhausted every means of making his way past it towards his goal. In the present case he was making for the 'open waters' of justice, which he saw, or believed he saw, distinctly ahead of him, and it would have taken a good deal to make him abandon the attempt to reach them. To appeal to the public, after the fashion of the present day, against the treatment which he had suffered would have been invincibly repugnant to one in whom the scruples of the time were strengthened by his naval training and traditions. But at least, he thought, he could set himself right with the members of his own profession, and with the official world in general. He accordingly set to work in the autumn of 1844, and no doubt immediately after the last interchange of letters with the Secretary of State, to compose for private circulation the 'Narrative' from which so many extracts have been made. From the first, no doubt, he availed himself of Lady Franklin's assistance in the purely literary part of his labours, and it seems probable that when, later on in the year, the preoccupations connected with the projected Arctic expedition withdrew him from his 'apologia,' it passed entirely into Lady Franklin's hands. There are evidences to this effect in the correspondence between them ; and in any case the 'Narrative' was not out of the printer's hands and ready for the private circulation for which alone it was intended until a few weeks before Franklin started on his last journey.

It is a distinctly able piece of work, lucid and well arranged, temperate in tone, strictly fair in its dealings with facts, and on the whole as reasonable in spirit as could be expected in the *ex parte* statement of one of the combatants in a long and embittered dispute. But whether it was worth while to prepare it, or whether it won over any judgments among those before whom it was laid, is exceedingly doubtful. Franklin sought the opinions of several of his oldest and most trusted friends as to the expediency of circulating it, and, as invariably happens with all such applications, each of them replied in accordance not so much with his view of the facts (on which indeed there was no difference of opinion) as with his own individual temperament.

Sir John Richardson took up his cause with enthusiasm, assisted him in his correspondence with Lord Glenelg and others on the subject of dispute, and abounded in suggestions as to the most effective mode of prosecuting his claims. Sir James Clarke Ross, on the other hand, though equally convinced of the justice of his friend's position, recommended him to waste no more time on the affair, and to dismiss it and its vexations from his mind. His letters on the subject are models of cool-headed good sense; but there are times when the very plenitude of this quality has an irritating rather than a soothing effect upon the recipient of the counsels which it inspires, and this, no doubt, was just such a time with Franklin.

Alien to the general character of Franklin's career as was this unpleasant passage, one cannot, unfortunately, dismiss it as a pure irrelevance. On the contrary, there is reason to believe that it was not without its share in determining the events of his future life for the brief span which still remained to it, and indirectly, therefore, in devoting him to his heroic death. This appears strikingly enough in a letter from his wife to Sir James Clarke Ross, written after the project of a new Arctic expedition had been mooted, but before its commander had been decided upon.

It is a subject (she writes) on which I have the most conflicting feelings, but if you who are the right person do not go [Sir James had already written to Franklin that he should 'certainly decline the command' if offered to him], I should wish Sir John to have it in his power to go and not to be put aside for his age. . . .

I do not think he would wish to go unless he felt himself equal to it; but what most weighs on my mind is this, that at the present crisis of our affairs, and after being so unworthily treated by the Colonial Office, I think he will be deeply sensitive if his own department should neglect him, and that such an appointment would do more perhaps than anything else out of the Colonial Office to counteract the effect which Lord S.'s injustice and tyranny have produced. I dread exceedingly the effect on his mind of being without honourable and immediate employment, and it is this which enables me to support the idea of parting with him on a service of difficulty and danger better than I otherwise should.'

Of Franklin's almost passionate eagerness to obtain command of the projected expedition there is abundant evidence in his correspondence. Apart, indeed, from his desire to get back to his old and proper work of adventure, and to exchange vexatious bickerings with his fellow-men for that nobler strife with Nature for which he was so much better fitted, the prospects of the new enterprise were specially tempting to his ambition. During his absence from the field of Arctic exploration, important additions had been made to his own discoveries. The gap of 160 miles of North American coast line, which was left after the expedition of 1825-28 between Beechey's furthest eastward and his own furthest westward, had been bridged over by Dease and Simpson, two officers of the Hudson's Bay Company in 1837; and the same resolute explorers had carried Franklin's furthest eastward of 1821 still further to the east by surveying the coast-line from Cape Turnagain to the Great Fish River. Nothing, in short, was lacking to the completion of the North-West Passage but the discovery of a channel less than 300 miles in length to connect the already overlapping lines of exploration traced respectively by Parry westward along the 74th parallel of N. latitude and by Dease and Simpson eastward along the 70th. It was, indeed, the fascinating effect of this situation which impelled Franklin's old friend, Sir John Barrow, then Secretary of the Admiralty, in concert with Captain Beaufort, the Hydrographer of the department, and other men well known either as Arctic voyagers or generally as leaders in geographical or other forms of science, to propose another Government expedition, and to exert himself as energetically as he did to procure its despatch.

In the course of the month of January, Franklin was formally requested to consider and report to the Admiralty on the practicability and prospects of the proposed expedition, and sent the following reply :—

My Lord,—In obedience to your Lordship's command, I lose not a moment in giving my written opinion on the question your Lordship did me the honour of putting to me this morning.

1. As to whether I considered the question of a N.W. Passage as

one which ought again to be entertained ; to which I have no hesitation of answering in the affirmative, for the following reasons :

The discoveries of Parry and Ross have narrowed the parts in which the passage should be sought, namely, that space between Cape Walker and Banks's Land of Parry, where I should recommend the trial first to be made, and in case of the passage not being forced in that direction, then to the northward by the Wellington Channel. The ships commanded by these officers had not the advantage of steam, and I need hardly say that the benefits to be derived from the aid of such a power are incalculable.

Having pointed out to your Lordship to-day, I will not dwell further on this matter than to say that the addition of steam to the ships is, in my opinion, indispensable.

It is gratifying also to know that it may be efficiently applied to the ships without destroying their capacity for stowing the requisite stores and provisions.

If the proposed expedition should unfortunately not be entirely successful in effecting a passage, it must contribute to our geographical knowledge, and it cannot fail to make important additions to the series of magnetical observations which are now carrying on in every part of the world.

I conceive that the greatest impediment from ice will probably be met between longitude 95° and 125°. The latter meridian being passed, I should expect to find the ice less heavy and such as may be penetrated with comparative facility. We know of no islands to the north-west of 120°.

Should there be any who say of these Arctic expeditions, To what purpose have they been ? I would desire them to compare our present map of that region and of the northern coast of America with that of 1818, when these expeditions commenced. They will find in the latter only three points marked on the northern coast of America, and nothing to the northward of it. Surely it cannot be denied that so large an addition to the geography of the northern parts of America and the Arctic regions is, in itself, an object worthy of all the efforts that have been made in the course of former expeditions.

I have the honour to be, my Lord,
Your Lordship's most obedient servant,
JOHN FRANKLIN.

Franklin from the first was keen in obtaining the commission to command it, and, on ascertaining that Sir James Ross was not competing with him for the honour, he sought the good offices of that distinguished navigator in support of his own application, and was most loyally seconded by him. Jealousy, however, is a weakness to which Arctic explorers are certainly not less liable than other people, and Franklin had, or thought he had, cause to suspect that a former comrade of his was opposing his claim. In a conversation with Ross on the question of the fittest appointments, 'he (Lord Haddington) spoke of my age,' writes Franklin indignantly to his wife, 'and of my suffering greatly from cold. Ross expressed his astonishment at the latter reason, for he had never heard it even hinted at before, which, if it had been the case, must have been spoken of by some one or other of the officers and men who served under him ; while, as for his age, he knew from actual observation that he was as active and vigorous as he had ever been, both in body and mind.' Franklin hastened to confirm this at an interview with Captain Beaufort. If his age was objected to him, all he could say was that, as to bodily health and energy, he was as fully competent to undertake the duty as he ever was. 'Then, hinting at my suffering from cold, but most carefully avoiding the mention of my having heard that it was supposed I did, I told him that I believed no one in the expeditions I had commanded suffered less than me. Besides, I had mentioned to Richardson my wish to go, who approved of it, and would certainly have advised me not if I was so very susceptible to cold.'

What this 'susceptibility' amounted to will be seen in a later chapter. The charge, due to a misconception, needed medical testimony to refute it. Franklin accordingly asked for and obtained the following certificate to his powers from his old friend and companion in hardship, Dr. Richardson. 'My dear Franklin,' wrote that staunch ally, then filling an appointment at the Haslar Hospital, Chatham,

I was rather surprised at your desiring my opinion with respect to your age, strength, and power of withstanding cold, in reference to the prospect of your obtaining command of a Polar expedition. It surely cannot be for your own satisfaction, for I firmly believe that you would not undertake such a command unless you considered yourself fully capable in physical as well as in mental power to perform all the duties it involves. To satisfy others, however, I shall have no hesitation in signing a certificate stating that I believe your constitution to be perfectly sound, and your bodily strength sufficient for all the calls that can be made upon it in conducting a squadron even through an icy sea. When you were a younger man I had ample opportunities of witnessing the way in which you stood the fatigues of a land journey, such as few who had spent their previous lives at sea as you had done would have sustained ; for it is a fact that seamen in general march badly. Your recovery from the effects of the privation and hardship was more rapid than my own.

As to your power of enduring cold, Back and Kendall can testify as well as myself. I think I am correct in saying that you were not once frost-bitten in the course of both land expeditions, including six winters spent in the country and a journey of some thousands of miles through snow and ice in the most intense cold.

From Captain Beaufort, Franklin went on to see Sir John Barrow, to whom he had repeated what he had said to the Hydrographer, and then back again to Beaufort to repeat the conversation with the Secretary. The Council of the Royal Society were approached on the subject, and sent a strong recommendation of Franklin to the First Lord of the Admiralty, who forwarded it to the Prime Minister. These energetic efforts, which occupied the closing days of December 1844, were crowned at last with success. On February 5 he received the much-desired summons from Lord Haddington, and waited upon that Minister at the Admiralty.

The following account, so graphic and animated that it would be a pity to spoil it by paraphrase, is given of this important interview in Lady Franklin's diary notes :—

Wednesday, Feb. 5, 1845.—Sir John went to Lord Haddington at the hour appointed. Lord H. said he had sent for him for the purpose of telling him that Sir R. P. (Robert Peel) had approved of expedition—that he naturally looked to Sir John, whose experience and judgment entitled him to command it, but said, ' Have you really thought seriously of the nature of the undertaking at your age, for, you know, I know your age : you are 59.' ' Not quite,' said Sir John.[1] Lord Haddington asked if his constitution was able to bear it. ' You'll

---

[1] The popular story to the effect that Lord Haddington said, ' You are 60,' and that Franklin replied briskly, ' No, no, my lord, only 59,' is the better of the two, and I am sorry to have to reject it ; but Lady Franklin's record of the interview is of course conclusive ; and, moreover, her husband would never have owned even to 59 in that conversation, when he was still two months from attaining that age.

examine me,' said Sir J. ; he repeatedly said this. Lord H. said he felt great responsibility in the matter (meaning, Sir J. says, that if Sir J. broke down he would be reproached for having appointed so old a fellow). He said that Sir J.'s services had been very arduous ones from an early age. 'I know all your services ; they have been very various, and latterly you have been on a civil service which must have caused you great care and anxiety.' Sir J. replied that no anxieties of his present service could equal that. However, it was bodily wear and tear that Lord H. thought of. 'I cannot,' he said, 'conceive anything more trying ; I know time has made great inroads on my constitution. Everybody knows how arduous were your land expeditions, and how you got through them, but you are not so young as you were.' Sir J. replied that if he did not think himself equal to it he should not wish to go. When he heard of the expedition from Barrow and others he wrote to Richardson (Lord H. said he knew him), and Richardson declared his fitness. Lord H. said he did not want any other person's testimony to his fitness, 'only your own.' Sir J. said, had it been a walking expedition he should not have undertaken it, being a much stouter man than he was. He might have delayed it. In a ship it was different. Lord H. said in one of the propositions there was a scheme of going to the Pole. Sir J. said in that case he should select the best officer of his party for the purpose. Lord H. said he was glad to hear that, and would take care that he had the best officers.

Sir J. said at one time, 'I've nothing to gain by it.' To this Lord H. did not reply. Sir J. said his manner was exceedingly kind ; it seemed to be done out of tenderness to Sir J. and a sense of responsibility in himself.

At close Lord H. said : 'We'll consider the conversation as not having passed' (or something to that effect) ; 'it requires a little consideration. In a day or two you will hear from me.'

Two days later he received a letter from the Admiralty informing him definitely of his appointment to the coveted command.

CHAPTER XX

THE LAST VOYAGE

1845

THE ships commissioned for the service were Franklin's old friends of the southern latitudes, the Erebus and Terror. The former was to be under his own command. To the latter he had succeeded, with the support of Sir James Ross, in procuring the appointment of Captain Crozier, the officer who had commanded the same ship in the Antarctic expedition a few years before. Commander James Fitzjames, an accomplished officer, to whose admirable letters we owe the best account we possess of the earlier incidents of the expedition, was appointed Franklin's second in command, while with him were associated Lieutenant Graham Gore and Mr. Charles F. Des Vœux, who were both of them destined to play an important part in the actual work of discovery. The complement of each ship was sixty-seven officers and men, and they carried stores and provisions as for an anticipated absence of three years. In accordance with Franklin's · suggestion, they had been furnished with auxiliary steam power, and were the first vessels to carry the screw-propeller into the Arctic seas. As compared with those of the present day, their fifty horse-power engines were pathetically weak. But many another vessel before them had faced the direst dangers of Arctic exploration, and yet returned unscathed. The memorable voyage of the Rosses in 1830–33 was example enough of this. The Erebus and Terror were exceptionally well found according to the appliances of the time. They were excellently officered and manned. They started on their enterprise with every advantage that human skill, bravery, and experience could superadd to material equipment. No adventure could have seemed less likely than theirs to be fated to so tragic an issue.

Nor did any Arctic explorers ever start in a spirit of more buoyant confidence than did these doomed men. 'Should you hear nothing till next June,' wrote Fitzjames from the last point from which communication was possible, 'send a letter *viâ* Petersburg to Petropaulovski, in Kamschatka.' So sanguine were this officer's expectations that the North-West Passage would be discovered and navigated after the first winter, and that by the summer of 1846 they would have made their way into Pacific waters. Alas! at that date they were either still confined to their first winter quarters or were already advancing towards that deadly embrace of the ice-pack from which they were never to escape.

Franklin himself appears to have been at first as hopeful as Fitzjames, and, indeed, to have contemplated at least the possibility of accomplishing his work in an even shorter time than the calculation of that officer. 'If we could but penetrate to the westward of 125° W.,' he wrote to Mr. (now Sir Henry) Elliot, at the time of his departure, 'I should not fear of getting through the remainder to Behring Strait this season.' But he adds : 'We are quite prepared to winter, and are taking with us provisions for three years.' Incidentally, this letter shows that the route which he originally suggested to the Admiralty, but which he did not ultimately take, was still in contemplation. He intended, he writes, 'to follow the track of Parry through Lancaster Sound and Barrow Strait, but instead of continuing on to Melville Island we purpose turning off to the south-westward after passing Cape Walker (the extremity of Parry's North Somerset Island), and endeavouring to effect a passage by that course of proceeding as direct as we can to Behring Strait. The space to the south of Banks Land and the islands which are close to the main coast of America is entirely unknown. We are as yet ignorant whether it be occupied by detached islands or by a large extent of land stretching north from the coast of America. This, in itself, is a geographical question desirable

z

to be settled.   We hope, however, to find it in that state
which will admit of a passage to the westward.'   He goes on
to say that, should they be checked in the course they first
intended to pursue, they would 'try to get to the north of
Melville Island through the Wellington Channel or some
other channel on the north side of Barrow Strait.'   As we
now know, this plan of procedure was entirely changed.   The
first summer was spent in an unsuccessful attempt to penetrate Wellington Channel, and in the following year the
Erebus and Terror took not a south-westerly, but an
almost due southerly course, through Peel Strait, between
Prince of Wales's Island and North Somerset Land, steering
straight towards the north coast of America and the line
of exploration of Simpson and Dease.

The former of these variations is less easy to understand—
unless, as has been conjectured, they were stopped by ice
at the mouth of Barrow Strait—than the latter.   For the
latter would only have been a reversion to a former preference of his own.   This southern course, declares Captain
Sherard Osborn, writing in 1860, 'was that of Franklin's predilection, founded on his judgment and experience.   There
are many in England who can recollect him pointing on his
chart to the western entrance of Simpson Strait and the
adjoining coast of North America and saying, "If I can but
get down there, my work is done ; thence it's plain sailing to
the westward."'   It is clear, however, that at the moment of
his departure he favoured the idea of the south-westerly
course in the direction of Banks Land, to the south of which,
sure enough, there is a channel, as Sir Robert McClure afterwards proved.   But Franklin was evidently quite confident
that whether by this route or another the expedition would
reach its goal.   It was one of those occasions on which his spirits
always rose.   Canon Wright, then a schoolboy full of the
healthy schoolboy's hero-worship, retains a vivid recollection of
Franklin's farewell visit to Mrs. Wright on the eve of this fatal
voyage, and recalls the cheery raillery with which he put aside
his ambitious young nephew's entreaty to be allowed to accompany him.   'No, my boy,' said he, 'we are not allowed to

take any cats with us that can't catch mice.' One can almost see the discomfiture of the youthful volunteer and the kindly twinkle in the stout old sailor's eye.

As the time, however, drew near for his departure, that strong but sober piety which was so marked an element in his character was deeply stirred, and its spirit breathes impressively through his various letters of adieu to those near and dear to him. On the night before the vessels sailed from Greenhithe he took solemn and prayerful leave of his father-in-law, then a very aged man, though not without the expression of a hope, so complete had been Mr. Griffin's recovery from a recent illness, that they might meet again after his return. 'I wish,' he adds, 'that you could see the ship now. She is about as clear as she will be at sea, and quite ready for sailing ; the officers and the crew all fine young men and in excellent spirits. This day we had the happiness of joining together on board in Divine worship, to praise God for His past mercies and to implore His guiding and protecting providence. In this spirit we all hope to begin, continue, and end our voyage.'

A melancholy interest attaches, indeed, to all the letters written by him on the eve of his departure for this fatal voyage. All, or almost all, of them have been preserved, not only of course those received from him by his wife and daughter, his father-in-law, and his sisters, but also his friendly and hearty leave-takings of old friends like Mr. Robert Brown and Sir James Ross. Their number, indeed, when considered as an addition to the voluminous correspondence on matters connected with the expedition and his preparations for it, which he had to keep up incessantly for the last two or three months of his stay in England, affords striking testimony to his extraordinary energy. In the midst of it all he seems to have been for some time prostrated by an attack of a malady of which the terribly debilitating effects are better known in these days than they were in those ; but his elasticity of spirits and mental if not physical recuperative powers triumphed even over the depression of influenza. His letters of farewell begin at Greenhithe ; one or

two are sent from Aldborough, on the Suffolk coast, a port
into which the two ships put for a day or two under stress of
weather ; from Stromness he wrote several, and the last under
his hand—the final message received from him ere he passed
into that dark shadow which was so long in being dispersed—
is dated from Whalefish Island, off Disco, on the Greenland
coast.

Thus he writes to Lady Franklin, under date of June 7,
1845, from Stromness :—

I was delighted last evening, on my arrival at this anchorage, to
receive your very interesting letter, with those from Eleanor and
Sophy, and the papers accompanying them. It was especially gratifying to me to find that you were not alarmed by the reports which
the newspapers had given of our position at Aldborough, though they
appear to have caused the Admiralty to send me an order, if the NE.
winds continued, that I should immediately proceed down Channel.
This was dated May 23, and sent to Harwich for Captain Stanley to
bring to me. He, however, did not overtake the ships before the
afternoon of the 29th, then to the north of Aberdeen. The return
to the Channel course was, in that position, out of the question ;
indeed, the taking the course we have done has never been a
question after leaving Aldborough. We have had only one other
strong breeze, and that off the Faroe Islands, in which during thick
weather we separated from the Rattler and the transport. The old
Erebus and Terror, however, managed very well together, and were
making tolerable progress when we were joined by the Blazer, and
afterwards rejoined by the Rattler (the two steam-tugs). It is satisfactory to perceive that the Erebus and Terror sail so nearly together
that they will be good company-keepers. The transport sails better
than either, but we must keep her close in hand going across the
Atlantic. Our squadron is now anchored around us, and by to-
morrow afternoon will, I hope, have finished the little fittings we
require, and be ready to sail. I purpose retaining the two steamers
to tow us about thirty or forty miles off the land, when we must part
with them, but we shall be thankful for the assistance they have
given us.

You will be glad to learn that the most experienced Davis Straits
seamen here and at Peterhead declare that we are quite in time. This
intelligence ought to please Beaufort and Sir James Ross. What a
kind note the latter has sent me ! . . . His conduct towards me has
been kind throughout as regards this expedition, and he has acted as a
man ought to do who is convinced that I should have spurned taking
the least advantage of him by proposing my services had he the greater

desire to have gone. I was aware, for he told me, that the suggestion was made to him that if he would go the next year the expedition might be postponed for that time, and also that a baronetcy and a good service pension were spoken of as an inducement for him ; but I suspected then, and believe now, that each of these propositions was suggested to him by —— and —— as considerations and rewards which would follow his acceptance of the command, and that they had received no express authority to make them as promises to be immediately fulfilled. However, he richly deserves these honours for his past services. I agree with him in the opinion that the navigation of the Arctic Sea is not near so full of danger as that of the Antarctic, nor, as far as I can learn, of the Spitzbergen Sea. It is very consolatory to me that you and my dear girl and Sophy have such correct views of the nature of our service. It is one unquestionably attended with difficulties and dangers, but not greater than those of former voyages ; and we may trust in God's merciful support and protection if we seek it, putting forth at the same time our earnest endeavours to overcome them. I am flattered by S.'s reasons for his supposing me so well fitted for the command of the expedition ; even in some respects, you tell me, he thinks, better than Ross. I think perhaps that I have the tact of keeping the officers and men happily together in a greater degree than Ross, and for this reason : he is evidently ambitious and wishes to do everything himself. I possess not that feeling, but consider that the commander of any service, having established his character before, maintains it most by directing the exertions of his officers and studiously encouraging them to work under the assurance that their merits will be duly brought forward and appreciated. S.'s remark is a just one, that my officers are from a different class of society and better informed men than on any former expedition. So says Parry ; and certainly, if we call to mind those others who were with Ross, there was scarcely one with the exception of Hooker above the ordinary run of the service. However, I feel my responsibility the greater from having these men to govern, and pray God to aid me in this work. I have the satisfaction of perceiving that they all defer to my opinion, even on points not immediately connected with our present pursuits. Fitzjames even looks surprised when it comes out that I have been in this or that kind of service, of which he had not previously been informed.

Then follows this interesting and, as it must have been afterwards felt to be, consoling testimony to the efficiency and high qualities of his officers :—

The more I see of Gore, the more convinced am I that in him I have a treasure and a faithful friend. I am particularly pleased with the manner in which he commenced and continues making the sketches for you. I expect to derive very great assistance from him if we have to winter, from his previous knowledge of the Terror when encumbered with ice. Stanley, who is often with us, tells me he is a very valuable fellow to have near you. I like the ice-master, Reid, and so do the other officers. As he begins to feel himself approaching the scene of his labours, he opens out and becomes communicative on the subject of ice and its motions.

Crozier has not had the opportunities of being much on board, on account of the weather ; but when he does come he is cheerful and happy, and seems to think we are making good progress. He could not bear the thought of going down Channel. Captain Smith, of the Rattler, has been uniformly attentive. Both he and his friend Mr. Smith, the great improver if not the inventor of the screw, a passenger on board, are quite delighted with the manner and speed in which, against wind and swell, the Rattler has towed the Erebus and Terror together. Yesterday she towed the Erebus alone in calm weather near six and a half miles an hour. This was proved on repeated trials. . . .

Let me now assure you, my dearest Jane, that I am now amply provided with every requisite for my passage, and that I am entering on my voyage comforted with every hope of God's merciful guidance and protection, and that He will bless and comfort and protect you, my dearest, my very dear Eleanor, dear Sophy, and all my other relatives. Oh, how much I wish I could write to each of them to assure them of the happiness I feel in my officers, my crew, and my ship !

Most heartily were these feelings reciprocated. Crozier, as we know, was an old friend of Franklin's, had enjoyed his hospitality in Tasmania, and had profited by the enthusiastic and untiring help rendered by him to the Antarctic expedition. But the other officers, who had but just made their commander's acquaintance, had already become equally attached to him, and their letters of this period bear abundant testimony to the respect and affection which their commander inspired. Thus Fitzjames writes of him :—

I like a man who is in earnest. Sir John Franklin read the Church service to-day and a sermon so very beautifully that I defy any man not to feel the force of what he would convey. The first Sunday he read was a day or two before we sailed, when Lady Franklin and his daughter and niece attended. Every one was struck with his extreme earnestness of manner, evidently proceeding from real conviction

Again :—

Sir John is delightful, active, and energetic, and even now per-severing. What he *has been* we all know. I think it will turn out that he is in no ways altered. He is full of conversation and inte-resting anecdotes of his former voyages. I would not lose him for the command of the expedition, for I have a real regard, 1 might say affection for him, and believe this is felt by all of us.

In a later letter he writes :—

Sir John is full of life and energy, with good judgment and a capital memory—one of the best I know. His conversation is delightful and most instructive, and of all men he is the most fitted for the command of an enterprise requiring sound sense and great perseverance. I have learnt much from him, and consider myself most fortunate in being with such a man, and he is full of benevolence and kindness withal.

Here again is valuable testimony to his powers as well as to his attractions :—

We are very happy and very fond of Sir John Franklin, who im-proves very much as we come to know more of him. He is anything but nervous or fidgety—in fact, I should say remarkable for decision in sudden emergencies ; but I should think he might be easily persuaded when he has not already formed a strong opinion.

Another and a younger officer with whom Franklin was no less popular sings his praises equally warmly if with some-what too much of the irreverence of youth ; and we ought also perhaps to take his years into account as qualifying what seems a rather exaggerated estimate of his commander's advanced age. In one of Mr. Couch's letters, beginning appropriately enough in the familiar schoolboy tone, we find the following :—

Old Franklin is an exceedingly good old chap—all are quite delighted with him—and very clever. He is quite a *Bishop*. We have Church morning and evening on Sundays, the evening service in the cabin to allow the watch that could not attend in the forenoon. We all go both times. Gives sermons out of his sermon books, and I can assure you adds a great deal himself. They say they would sooner hear him than half the parsons in England. He has three [officers, of course, not parsons] every day to dinner with him, and when the weather permits the captain and officers of the Terror. He ordered stock and wine to be laid in enough for four every day, and for a cabin-full twice a week for three years. So you see what a liberal old man he is.

The coast of Greenland was reached by the beginning of July, and the work of provisioning the ships with the stores which had been conveyed in the transports now commenced. The voyage had, as usual, a rapidly restorative effect upon Franklin's health. In his last letter from this station to his sister, Mrs. Wright, after describing the *morale* and spirit of his officers in enthusiastic terms, he continues :—

I rejoice likewise to say that the coming to sea has entirely removed my cough, and that my health is so good that the officers often exclaim that I am quite a different-looking person since I sailed. When they first became known to me I was suffering from the severe influenza which first sent me to Brighton.

To his friend Mr. Robert Brown, under a date a few days earlier than the above-quoted letter, he had written in the same buoyant strain :—

Here we are, having been one month from Stromness. Busy as bees, and, like those useful animals, laying in plenty of stores. We hope to get our portion from the transport this evening, and then we shall have on board three complete years of provisions and fuel. The ships, however, are very deep, which is of little consequence, as the sea is for the most part smooth when there is much ice, and by the time we get to Behring Strait or through the winter we shall be in good sailing trim and have room to stretch out our limbs, which we have hardly room now to do, so perfectly full is every hole and corner.

The Danish authorities are all absent from Disco making their tours of inspection, so that I have not been able to make inquiries as to the ice at the fountain head ; but I have conversed with an intelligent man, a carpenter, who is in charge at a station near the anchorage, and learnt from him that, though the last winter was unusually severe, the spring was not later than usual, and that the ice broke away from the land here about the close of April. He had also understood that the ice had separated from the land as far north as 73° lat. early in June, from which circumstance he considers that we shall have a favourable passage to Lancaster Sound—which is the limit of his knowledge. . . .

What I most fear respecting my wife is that, if we do not return at the time she has fixed in her mind, she may become very anxious,

and I shall in such a case be greatly obliged to my friends to remind
her that we may be so circumstanced at the end of the first winter
and even of the second as to wish to try some other part in case we have
not previously succeeded, and, having abundance of provisions and
fuel, we may do that with safety.   In order to prevent too great
anxiety either on her part or that of my daughter, they should be
encouraged not to look for our arrival earnestly till our provisions
get short. . . . Our next chance of writing may be by a whaler, if we
chance to meet any ; if not, this note must convey to you the sentiments of affection and esteem which I feel for you.   May God bless
you !

From Whalefish Island, in Disco Bay, came the last letter
which his wife was ever to receive from him.   It covers
sixteen closely written sides of quarto paper, and is indeed
a methodically kept journal of his stay at this last station of
equipment and preparation for his voyage—a stay extending
over some ten or twelve days.   He was still at sea, about
thirty miles from the coast of Greenland, when, on July 1,
the entries on these faded, long-treasured sheets commence :—

I begin the month in your service.   Our voyage hitherto has
been favourable.   The passage across the Atlantic was, as usual,
attended with strong breezes, and these generally from the west and
south-west, so that making our way across we were led to the north
and even carried within sixty miles of Iceland before we could get past
Cape Farewell, but we did not see Iceland.   It would have been
contrary to the long experience of Greenland seamen if we had gone
round Cape Farewell unattended by a gale.   We had a very strong one
from the south, with much sea, which drove us rapidly past the Cape
on the 22nd of June, and continued to favour us till the 25th of June,
when the gale gave place to calm.   The weather, which had been thick,
now became clear, and we obtained our first view of the shores of Greenland, distant about forty miles ; the astronomical observation told us it
was land in the neighbourhood of Lichtenfels.   Here, to our surprise,
we found a bank of forty fathoms water, on which we caught many
codfish.   Here also we communicated with an English brig which
had sailed from Shetland the same day we left the Orkneys, and had
come out to procure salmon in some of the fiords. . . . From the
last date to this time we have been generally in sight of the coast,
advancing gradually to the north, aided by light winds, as also we
are now doing.

The calm weather and smooth water had been specially
favourable to the dredgings of Mr. Goodsir, who was attached,

it should have been mentioned, to the Erebus in the capacity of naturalist.

The magnetic observations are likewise carried on with zeal and energy by Fitzjames, who never omits an opportunity of obtaining them. Each officer, in fact, directs his attention to some point or other of inquiry or observation, and it is this mode of fixing their energies specifically that I have encouraged in them, and shall continue to do so, as it is the best means of the expedition obtaining results on [scientific] points. I impress at the same time upon them the assurance that these individual exertions will prove their best claim to the favourable notice of the Admiralty. Of this they are all aware, so likewise are they that I shall have pleasure in bringing their services duly before the proper authorities. I shall be excused by *you* if I add that it is gratifying to me to know that they have the confidence in me that I shall do them justice. . . . We have, however, as yet seen but very few icebergs, and none of large size. The land we have seen is generally bold and picturesque, with openings that indicate the entrances into the different fiords which indent the whole coast. There appears less snow on the lower parts of the hills than I had expected to see there. We hope to hear from the Danish commandant at Disco what had been the prevailing winds during the winter and spring, and in what state he supposes the ice to be now to the north and north-west, and where the whalers are.

After I had issued such written orders as I thought necessary for the internal discipline and arrangements of the ship, as well as the instructions to the officers respecting the various observations which they would be required to make, and for their general guidance, I devoted myself to the preparation of a code of signals to be used between the Erebus and Terror when amongst the ice after parting from the transport, and in this duty I was mainly assisted by Parry's signals in a similar situation, which he had most kindly lent me. Indeed, I had little more to do than to introduce into his code some signals that are related to the steam machinery with which we are furnished. These first duties over, I have employed my time in carefully reading again the voyages of the earlier navigators as given in Barrow's collection of them, and still better in the numbers of the 'Cabinet Library,' article 'Polar Seas and Regions.' You will conclude, of course, that Parry's voyages have not been overlooked, nor Ross's (Sir John, I mean), in this examination, and yesterday I spent the morning most agreeably in reading the letters which you had kindly collected and put into my writing-desk, some of which I find to contain opinions and discussions of Richardson and myself on the very objects of my present expedition which will be useful to me. The despatches of Dease and Simpson to the Hudson Bay Company, and the letters of Richardson and myself to the Geographical Society and Beaufort, on which Back's last expedition was based, are also among them ; these likewise will be serviceable to me. These readings I consider matters of duty, but I occasionally take up some of the interesting little volumes with which you furnished my library. I have begun, since leaving England, reading a chapter of the Old Testament with the commentaries of Henry upon it, which I hope to continue. The Sunday is by all observed properly. We have Divine service on the main deck every forenoon, and in the evening of that day all those who choose, and are not on watch, may attend the service in my cabin, which in fact all do, and a most interesting assembling of ourselves together it has proved and will, I trust, prove in future to be. It is a source of sincere gratification to me when I think upon your prayers ascending with Eleanor's and mine for our mutual protection, and for God's blessing on each other. The heart is refreshed and comforted by such thoughts, and strengthened for the faithful discharge of our relative duties. . . .

July 4.—We arrived at the anchorage in Whalefish Island at four this morning, which, but for thick and blowing weather, we should have reached on the evening of the 2nd, thus making one month's passage from Stromness. We made our appearance off Lievely, the residence of the Governor of Disco, on the evening of the 2nd, though we could not communicate with him. The next day proved beautifully fine, which afforded us an opportunity of examining the state of the ice in the Waysgat Passage before we came in here. It was satisfactory to find from this news that the ice thereabout had broken up, though enormous masses were floating about.

As Parry has described our anchorage, so have we found it to be, a most snug place for clearing the transport (which is now alongside for that purpose) as well as for the magnetical and astronomical observations which have very soon commenced, under Crozier and Fitzjames, on the same spot which Parry occupied in 1824. I accompanied Mr. Le Vesconte to the top of the highest land, that we might procure a view of the groups of islands and rocks in this neighbourhood, and take bearings for placing them on the chart. Nothing can be more sterile than these islands are, a mere collection of rocks with a few mosses and swamp-loving plants in the water-courses. Mosquitoes, however, are most abundant and of large size. I have not yet heard many complaints made as to their biting.

July 5.—This is a Danish station, at which live several Esquimaux. The officer in charge of them is now absent at Lievely, where the Governor-in-Chief resides, so that I can give no account of the establishment at present. The Esquimaux came off before we entered the harbour, and two of them piloted the Erebus to the anchorage by keeping their canoes just ahead of the ship. This morning we had a visit from their wives and children. All of them had clean-washed faces, and hair neatly combed and put up. Their dresses were likewise clean and good, some of them of sealskin and the others of cotton. All the grown women had handkerchiefs on their heads, procured, I presume, from the Danes. The Danish Government, or perhaps merchants of that country, have several colonies on this side of Greenland, at which they procure furs, seal-skins, and oil from the natives. At each of these establishments, I believe, are missionaries for the religious instruction of the Esquimaux, several of whom are Moravians. Mr. La Trobe could perhaps give you more information than I can as to the latter esta-blishments. The Esquimaux who have been on board appear to me cleaner in their dress and persons than those I have before met, which shows, I think, that attention is paid to them in this respect. I have to-day employed two of them to convey a letter which I have written to the Governor at Disco. One man would not undertake to go across the bay (twenty miles) alone. Each went in his own canoe ; it, in fact, holds but one.

Sunday, July 6.—The messengers returned this afternoon with a letter from the officer in charge at Lievely, who communicated to me that, not understanding English, he had been unable to read my letter. He, however, referred me to the coxswain of a boat which had crossed over from Disco, whom he begged me to acquaint whether he could render me any assistance from Disco. This man I saw, as well as a still more intelligent person, a carpenter, and from the latter received the information that, from the last winter having been severe and the winds high, and from the ice having broken up hereabouts early in May, our prospects, he thought, were favourable as to getting to Lancaster Sound. He had heard that our whalers were off the Woman's Islands in 74° N. We, of course, shall rejoice to find his opinion correct, as the getting into Lancaster Sound early and across the barrier of ice in Baffin's Bay will be great points attained. It seems the Governor of Lievely is absent on leave. The inspector is also away, at some other station, and there is a supercargo only in charge ; so that in all probability I shall gain no further information than we have gained already from these parties.

I went after church to-day on shore to visit the Esquimaux' huts and tents, which with one dwelling-house have received the designa-tion of a station. It belongs to the Danish Government, and there are belonging to it 130 Esquimaux, all of whom except thirty are away catching seals. I have already mentioned their being comfort-ably dressed and apparently well taken care of by the Danes, and I was delighted that many of them read their Bibles, and that the children are taught at school to read and perhaps to write. One of the turf-built huts, which I observed to be fitted up with seats and forms, was pointed out to me as the schoolroom. There was nothing to invite your staying long in a seal-catching station, and, therefore, I stayed but little longer in many of these huts than to ask the questions I wished to have answered. The parties I prefer seeing alongside of the ships apart from the odours that surround their residences.

Monday, July 7.—Still busily employed clearing the transport, which we shall not be able to empty to-day. We are cramming the ships as full as possible ; both care and time are requisite to make the best stowage. This necessary delay is favourable for the magnetic and other observations which are carrying forward on shore, and it will be satisfactory to Colonel Sabine to know that the results by the observers from both ships accord very well. I have no doubt Crozier and Fitzjames will write to him on magnetic matters. I shall also write to him. I shall also write to Richardson, and send him tracings of two rare fish which Mr. Goodsir thinks he will be glad to have . . .

I yesterday saw Fitzjames making a sketch of the harbour, of which he intends sending you a copy. Mr. Gore has made a very faithful drawing for you of our parting with the Blazer and Rattler, and of them cheering the Erebus, which he has kindly framed also, . . . My own contribution to your Arctic stores is a pair of sealskin boots, made by one of the Esquimaux, and I send Eleanor and Sophy pockets for holding a watch, also made of sealskin, as specimens of the female work. Lieutenant Griffiths, the agent of the transport, will kindly take charge of them for you. I shall ask him to call at Bedford Place, for the purpose of seeing you or some member of the family. He is an intelligent person, and will give you full particulars of our progress hitherto. . . .

I had written thus far when Mr. Gore brought me in the sketch of our present anchorage for you, taken from the opposite side to that by Captain Fitzjames. The two ships together are the Erebus and transport, and the single one the Terror. It is a correct representation of the land and of our position. Almost immediately afterwards Captain Fitzjames brought me his sketch to look at, which he will himself send you. This is taken from Boat Island, in which Parry took his observations, as our officers are now doing. It will, therefore, be an interesting momento of the scene to show him.

I feel much gratified by the kind feelings of the officers towards you, and I am sure there is nothing they would not do to please you. Hitherto I have invited them with regularity to dinner—Fitzjames daily—and I shall continue to do so until we get to the ice, or in a situation when neither I nor they may be able to spare the time for sitting down to dinner. I have got the master of the transport to spare what wine he could, sugar and coffee, which amounts to 7*l.* 2*s.* . . .

Tuesday, July 8.—Still unloading the transport. If we do not quite complete this job to-day we shall be able to do so early to-morrow, and at least to ascertain whether one if not both ships can carry all she has on board for them. Of this we are certain, that the two ships will have on board three years' supply of provisions, fuel, and clothing.

And then, with that solicitude for the mental repose of those he was leaving behind him, which was never long absent from his mind or utterances, he continues :—

I mention this the more particularly that you may not have the slightest apprehension respecting our welfare, though we should have to winter twice ; and with respect to this point let me entreat you and Eleanor not to be too anxious, for it is very possible that our pro-spects of success and the health of our officers and men might justify our passing a second winter in these regions. If we do not succeed in our attempt, we shall try in other places, and through God's bless-ing we hope to set the question at rest. Parry, Ross, and Richardson will be the best persons to consult on every occasion that you may feel anxious, each of whom will give you the result of their judgment and experience and advise you in every way. . . .

Wednesday, July 9.—I had this evening the pleasure of knowing that all our stores had been received on board from the transport ; but the difficulty now is where they are to be stowed. A very large portion of them will have to be secured on deck, but, as we have very little sea in these high northern parts, that will not matter.

Friday, July 11.—Another lovely day, in which we are fully occu-pied in filling up every hole and corner of the ship with stores. The transport will soon remove from alongside to make her own prepara-tions for sailing, and in order to leave us room to swing the ships and find the deviations of the needle on each point of the compass—as was done at Greenhithe. I have written to Sabine and Parry, to each of my sisters, to Sophy, your sister Mary and your aunt, and I think every other letter which appears to me of importance to write. . . . The transport has removed from us and will sail to-morrow.

Saturday, July 12.—This is another lovely and clear day, which makes me desirous of getting away, which I think we shall do to-night, for both ships are now busy in swinging to obtain the dip and deviation of the compass, which is our last operation in harbour.

I have just written the sketch of my official letter to the Admiralty for Mr. Osmer to copy. Fitzjames has seen the draft and approves of it. It is short, and only gives those points the Admiralty wish to receive. . . . Mr. Osmer has begged me to present the kind remem-brances of all the officers to you. Be assured that you have their best wishes, and I feel confident of having their cordial co-operation. This observation may also be applied to Crozier and the officers of the Terror. I hope Crozier has written to you, and I have no doubt that he was desirous of doing it.

I trust that I have not omitted any point that you wished to be informed upon. If so, exercise your own excellent judgment if it relates to any of our personal matters. This also I particularly wish you to do with regard to my dear Eleanor and Gell, if the latter should come home and get settled before my return. They will both prove blessings and comforts to you and to me. I have written to each of my dearest friends to comfort and assist you with their best counsel. To the Almighty care I commit you and dear Eleanor. I trust He will shield you under His wings and grant the continual aid of His Holy Spirit. Again, that God may bless and support you both is and will be the constant prayer of your most affectionate husband,

JOHN FRANKLIN.

And with this last message of benediction to those nearest and dearest to him, the voyager set sail for the Eternal Shore.

CHAPTER XXI

'TOWARDS NO EARTHLY POLE

1845–1848

ONE more glimpse of the two vessels and of their devoted crews was yet to be given to the world. They were seen and spoken with by a whaler twelve days after their departure from their anchorage in Disco Bay, and Captain Dannet's record of the fact was duly published in England three months later. A London newspaper of October 27 printed the subjoined extract from the log of the whaling ship in question :—

Sir John Franklin's Expedition—Prince of Wales, Davis Straits.

Melville Bay : July 26, 1845.

At 8 P.M. received on board ten of the chief officers of the expedition under the command of Captain Sir John Franklin, of the Terror and Erebus. Both ships' crews are all well, and in remarkable spirits, expecting to finish the operation in good time. They are made fast to a large iceberg, with a temporary observatory fixed upon it. They were in latitude 74° 48', longitude 66° 13' W.

It was to be many years before any human hand should lift the veil of mystery which descended between the explorers and their countrymen when the Erebus and Terror faded from the view of the whaler as she sailed southward through Baffin's Bay. Nor, indeed, was that veil ever to be completely raised at all. Such certain, or at any rate such historic, knowledge as we possess of the movements and fortunes of the two ill-fated vessels is scanty in the extreme. The only evidence under the hands of the crews themselves consists of the manuscript entries and marginal inscriptions on an Admiralty 'bottle paper,' not found till fourteen years later ; and by a curious mischance this solitary and fragmentary record actually contains a demonstrably mistaken assignment of the date of a year. For the rest, the particulars of the tragic story have had to be filled in from the more or less probable conjectures founded by other Arctic explorers on this narrow basis of ascertained fact.

At the very outset of the narrative we are met by the necessity of furnishing a hypothetical explanation for an ascertained but unexpected fact. It is known from the document above mentioned that the route already taken by the expedition during the summer of 1845 was other than that contemplated by Franklin except in the last resort. And this, too, although there was not only nothing to foreshadow the necessity of this change of route, but, on the contrary, there was substantive ground for anticipating that the original plan would be found practicable. Writing from Whale-fish Island on July 11, Fitzjames reports under date of the 6th of that month: 'A man just come over from Lievely, a Dane who has married an Eskimo, says that they believe it to be one of the mildest seasons and earliest summers ever known, and that the ice is clear away from this to Lancaster Sound. Keep this to yourself, for Sir John is naturally very anxious that people in England should not be too sanguine about the season. Besides, the papers would have all sorts of stories not true. I do believe that we have a good chance of getting through this season if it is to be done at all.' The information thus quoted must have been welcome hearing to Fitzjames, for in his diary a few days before we find the entry : 'In talking to Sir John Franklin, whose memory is as good as his judgment appears to be correct, it appears that one great difficulty is to get from where we are to Lancaster Sound ; Parry was fortunate enough in his first voyage to sail right across in nine or ten days, a thing unheard of before or since. In his next voyage he was fifty-four days toiling through fields of ice, and did not get in till September, yet Lancaster Sound is the point we look to as the beginning of work. If we are fortunate we shall be there by August 1, which will be time enough ; sooner would probably put us among the clearing ice.'

Nevertheless, it seems certain that their Danish informant

must have been mistaken, and that this reputedly 'mildest of seasons and earliest of summers' turned out, in fact, to be specially unfavourable to Arctic navigation. On July 26, three weeks after this was written, and only five days before the date when Fitzjames hoped to be at the mouth of Lancaster Sound, we find the Erebus and Terror moored, as has been seen, to an iceberg in Melville Bay—that is to say, still on the Greenland coast, and with all the breadth of Baffin's Bay between them and the point which they looked to as 'the beginning of their work.' The only possible inference is that the ice had proved to be unusually late in clearing, and that the start to cross had had to be deferred till several weeks after the normal period of the year.

What sort of a passage they made of it is not known, nor at what date they reached Lancaster Sound ; but their experiences after entering that waterway were presumably disappointing. It is not stated in the record to which reference has been made that they found it impossible to proceed further westward than Wellington Channel, but it is difficult to imagine any other cause for Franklin's turning to the northward instead of holding on his course through Barrow Strait. His instructions from the Admiralty were to traverse that strait and then bear to the south-westward, and he himself, in a letter already quoted, declared in the most distinct manner that he should only enter Wellington Channel in the event of finding westward or south-westward navigation impracticable.

The point is of so much importance, and the course taken by the ships during their first season—which, so far as regards the search for a north-west passage, was a season lost—may have so momentously affected the ultimate fate of the expedition, that it is desirable to recapitulate as briefly as possible the plans and resolutions discussed in the last chapter. In Franklin's original proposal to Lord Haddington, it was observed, it may be remembered, that 'the discoveries of Parry and Ross have narrowed the parts in which the passage should be sought' to 'that space between Cape Walker and Banks's Land of Parry where I should recommend the trial first to be made, and in case of the passage not being forced in that direction, then to the north-ward by the Wellington Channel.' But, as we afterwards saw from his letter to Mr. Elliot, he had, after further considera-tion and inquiry, modified his original proposal. To have kept a straight course from Cape Walker to Banks Land would have led them to the channel afterwards discovered by McClure, if indeed the route to it had been traversable ; but the difficulties likely to be met with in these waters had evidently occurred or been represented to him, and his thoughts were now turned in a more south-westerly direction. He spoke of endeavouring to proceed as directly as possible to Behring Strait by taking a course to the south-westward after passing Cape Walker. The space to the south of Banks Land and the islands which are close to the main coast of America is, he wrote, 'entirely unknown.' ' We are as yet ignorant whether it is occupied by detached islands or by a large extent of land stretching north from the coast of America. This in itself is a geographical question desirable to be settled. We hope, however, to find it in that state which will admit of a passage to the westward.' The former of these two hypotheses was of course the correct one. Banks Land, as we know, is divided from the American con-tinent not by a group of detached islands, but by a large extent of land stretching north from the coast of America— to wit, that vast rhomboidal mass, to the northern, the south-western, and the south-eastern parts of which the names of Prince Albert Land, Wollaston Land, and Victoria Land have been respectively given. In this direction, again, if they had been able to take it, it is conceivable that success might have awaited them ; for they would perhaps have struck Prince of Wales's Strait, into which McClure penetrated some years later in his eastward voyage from Behring Strait, and so have reversed the course of the first actual navigator of a north-west passage.

The question, however, is not as to what would or might have been the results of taking a south-westerly-to-southerly course, but as to what were the expectations based by

Franklin on the selection of such a route. And it is clear that these expectations were so strong as to make it pretty certain that nothing short of positive necessity would have induced him to abandon a plan thus hopefully regarded, and to exchange it for one which he had consistently spoken of as the less eligible alternative. In short, the whole probabilities of the case appear to favour the view, since generally accepted by Arctic authorities, that it was the absolute compulsion of the impassable, encountering him in Barrow Strait, which deflected Franklin's course to the north-westward in the season of 1845. He had, in fact, to choose between exploring Wellington Channel and going into winter quarters even before the autumn had set in.

What their experiences were during the few weeks of the season still remaining to them we have fairly sufficient means of judging. They must have sailed northward until what is now known as Grinnell Land rose ahead of them, and must then have turned to the westward into Penny Strait. No doubt their idea was, as suggested by Admiral Sherard Osborn, to try for a north-about passage round the Parry Islands, and they continued to pass up the strait as far as progress was possible in the hope of reaching an open or navigable sea. But they doubtless found, as (writes Admiral Osborn) 'we found in 1852, a wide expanse of water much choked up with ice extending from the head of Wellington Channel to the westward for hundreds of miles.' Thus, again baffled, the ships' heads were turned southward, and, holding on this course, the explorers found that the land to the west of Wellington Channel was insular, and that the strait which they had now entered divided it from what has since been known as Cornwallis Island. Through this waterway they continued to pursue their course, and eventually found themselves once more in Barrow Strait at a distance of about one hundred miles west of the point at which they had quitted it, thus effecting the first of those contributions to geographical knowledge which the various expeditions afterwards despatched in search of the missing vessels were so largely to increase.

It is probable that by the time they issued from Corn-

wallis Strait it was too late in the year for further operations.
They accordingly retraced their course to the eastward in
search of eligible winter quarters, which they found at
Beechey Island, in a bay near the mouth of the Wellington
Channel, on the south coast of the much larger insular mass
known as North Devon. Here they made such preparations
for the long and dreary season which lay before them as the
experience of their commander suggested and as their means
allowed. No doubt the winter was spent, under the circumstances, comfortably enough. They had well-found ships, a
beloved and trusted leader, and the unabated inspiration of
their hopes. A few eager spirits might have been disappointed by the comparatively slight progress which had been
made; but the more experienced among the party could
hardly have shared the exaggerated expectations of their too
sanguine shipmates, and the time had been far too short to
have raised any presumption, even in the least hopeful minds,
against their future success. At the worst, they had had a
bad exploring season, and better luck was to be looked for in
the coming year. Moreover, their labours even thus far had
not been altogether fruitless. In their passage up Wellington
Channel and down the new strait to the west of Cornwallis
Island they had explored and mapped out 300 miles of new
coast-line; and, above all, they had already reached a point
divided from the southern line of exploration by no more
than 250 miles of hitherto untraversed water. For it was but
this distance which separated them from that portion of the
American coast along which Dease and his companions had
made their eastward way some dozen years before; and the
crews of the Erebus and Terror had already, it may be, in
imagination, traversed this intervening belt of the unknown
and reached that point on the chart to which Franklin had
once pointed, with the words, ' If I can but get down there,
my work is done; thence it's plain sailing to the westward.'

In the course of the winter of 1845–6 the explorers lost
three of their number, two seamen who died in January, and
a marine, whose death followed a few months later. They
were buried on the island, and the discovery of their graves

five years later supplied the first clue—not, however, to be successfully followed till long after—to the course taken by the lost expedition.

As soon as the season of 1846 was sufficiently advanced, which would not be, it is thought, until July or August, the ships resumed their voyage to the westward, but were not now to proceed so far in that direction as Franklin had thought they might be compelled to do. It was not necessary for them, as in the plan he had sketched out for Lord Haddington, to make for 'the space between Cape Walker and Banks's Land of Parry.' The event shows that Franklin only suggested this south-westward route because at that time no passage leading more directly southward was known. It was due southward, as has been said, that his gaze was perpetually turned, for, the straighter the course he could take towards the north coast of the American continent, the sooner would he reach the already explored waterway which led to Behring Strait. He had not much westing to do in the summer of 1846 before coming upon the southward-leading channel of which he was in search. He came upon it before reaching Cape Walker, or indeed before attaining the longitude of the northward-leading channel from which he had emerged in the autumn of the previous year. This new and welcome avenue to the south divided North Somerset, which had been hitherto supposed to extend at least as far as Cape Walker, from what is now known as Prince of Wales's Island, and its entrance has since received the name of Peel Sound, while that of Franklin Strait has been given to its southerly portion.

Down this channel, then, they shaped their course, full, no doubt, of exultation at having found a passage which seemed to lead so directly to their wished-for goal. The weather, however, and the conditions of navigation generally must have been highly unfavourable, judging from the small progress made by them, or rather from the short period during which, as was afterwards learnt from their only discovered record, they were able to advance. For it appears from this document that their voyaging of 1846, and indeed their earthly voyaging altogether, was brought to a close on September 12 in that year, so that, according to all calculations, they could not have had more, and may have had considerably less, than two clear months of travel. During this period they succeeded in accomplishing only between two and three hundred miles of southing from the entrance of Peel Sound, though every mile of the coast-line on either hand represented so much addition to geographical knowledge. Emerging from the mouth of Franklin Channel into the wider—one fears that they could hardly be called the open— waters to the southward and skirting the western shores of Boothia Felix, the Erebus and Terror held on their toilsome way until the early days of September. But on the 12th of that month the gallant struggle of the two vessels came to an end for ever. The ice closed immovably round them in lat. 70° 5' N. and long. 98° 23', and from that day forward its deadly embrace was never for a moment relaxed. For the awful period of 587 days from early September in 1846 until late April in 1848, the hapless crews were held fast in an icy prison, from which at last the desperate remnant of them broke out only to die.

To winter in the pack is, of course, no very uncommon experience in Arctic travel. Nay, to be inextricably beset for more than one winter was not unheard of. It happened, as we know, to the Rosses in their extraordinary Arctic adventures of 1829–33. For three years the Victory was frozen up in her first winter quarters on the east coast of Boothia Felix, although every attempt was made to release her, till in 1832 she had to be abandoned, when her crew, making their way northward up Prince Regent Inlet in the vain hope of falling in with some stray whaler, would in all probability have perished of starvation had they not been supported through their fourth winter by the stores and provisions which had been landed by Parry at a point on the eastern shore of North Somerset from the wreck of the Fury in those waters eight years before. The escape, however, of the Rosses and their return to England in 1833 amazed their friends like a resurrection from the grave. It was without precedent in the history of Polar exploration, nor has anything like it ever since occurred. The Victory, again, was a small vessel, carrying not many mouths to feed and victualled for four years. The stores of the Erebus and Terror could only last for three winters, and to have their movements thus arrested in the autumn of 1846 would throw the whole of their remaining work on the short exploring season of the following year. Unless by the end of 1847 they had either found their way through into the Pacific or had reached some point on the Arctic coast of America at which they could winter in the comfortable certainty of being able to make Behring Strait in the following spring, they would have, they knew, to return home, if they ever returned at all, defeated in their search for a north-west passage.

Their anxieties, however, were not confined to the future alone ; for their present situation must, to men familiar with the aspects of Arctic icefields, have given rise to grave misgivings. The ice-stream in which they had found themselves after passing the southern point of Prince of Wales's Island is one of the most powerful and dangerous in all the Polar regions, as more than one of the search expeditions were afterwards to find. Admiral Sherard Osborn writes, in his ' Narrative of the Last Voyage of Franklin : '—

If we open a chart of the Arctic Regions, it will be observed that westward of the Parry Islands and Baring Island there is a wide sea whose limits are as yet unknown, and the ice which encumbers it has never yet been traversed by ship or sledge. All those navigators, Collinson and McClure in their ship, and McClintock and Mecham with their sledges, who have with much difficulty and danger skirted along the southern and eastern edge of this truly frozen sea, mention in terms of wonderment the stupendous thickness and massive proportions of the vast floes with which it is closely packed. It was between this truly polar ice and the steep cliffs of Banks Land that Sir Robert McClure fairly fought his way in the memorable voyage of the Investigator. It was in the narrow and tortuous lane of water left between the low beach line of North America and the wall of ice formed by the grounded masses of this fearful pack that the gallant Collinson carried, in 1852 and 1853, the Enterprise, by way of Behring Strait, to and from the further shores of Victoria Land ; and it was in the far north-west of the Parry group that McClintock and Mecham, with their sledges, in 1853 gazed, as Parry had done five-and-thirty years before, on that pack ice to which all that they had seen in the sea between Prince Patrick Land and the Atlantic was a mere bagatelle.

The vastness of these ice masses is not due to any special intensity of cold in these latitudes, but to the want of any large direct communication between that portion of the Polar Sea and the warmer waters of the Pacific and Atlantic Oceans. The channels connecting it with the latter are exceedingly tortuous and much barred with islands ; its only connection with the former is by Behring Strait, the waters of which are ' so shallow that the Polar ice, which has been found to draw as much as sixty and eighty feet of water and to have hummocks upon it of a hundred feet in height, generally grounds in it until thawed away by the action of the Pacific Gulf Stream.'

Still, of course, this ice-sea sullenly obeys the law by which the Polar waters are ever drifting towards the torrid zone, and although the accumulation of ice every winter exceeds its dissolution, its masses are ever slowly moving towards the south. The march, however, is so slow as to resemble rather the movement of a land glacier than of a Polar pack. Its frozen billows are seldom if ever broken by lanes of water, still less by clear spaces of sea ; indeed, so compact and impenetrable is it that as yet no navigator has ever succeeded in crossing any of the ice-streams issuing from this ocean of desolation. ' One of these impenetrable ice-streams flows down between Melville Island and Banks Land, impinging with fearful force upon the exposed shores of Prince of Wales's Land and the islands across Barrow Strait, curves down what is now called McClintock Channel, until it is fairly blocked at the strait between King William and Victoria Land.' Here the southern edge of the ice-stream comes in contact with the warm waters flowing northward from the rivers of the continent of America, and undergoes a constant and rapid disintegration, the rear of the ice-stream ever pressing forward, while its vanward masses are being constantly melted away.

It was in the grip of this slow-moving but unrelenting enemy that the ships of the expedition were caught fast.

Had the geography of the region in which they first came within its clutch been as accurately known in those days as it is now, they could have avoided it. For to the south-eastward, between Boothia Felix and King William Land, lay a clear and promising path of exit from the ice, a channel which would have led them to the American shore, whence they could have resumed their westward course through Simpson's Strait. But in that day the only known passage to the coast of America lay to the south-westward, through the hopeless-looking ice-stream above described, and there was no alternative to entering it. The explorers had already traversed more than 200 of the 300 miles which separated Barrow Strait from the mainland of the American continent, and they might hope with good fortune to accomplish the remainder of the journey before the winter overtook them. But it was not to be. On the date and at the point above mentioned, the pressure of the pack became too strong for further progress, and just as King William Land hove in sight—that is to say, some twelve miles north of Cape Felix, its most northerly point—the Erebus and Terror were immovably beset.

Helpless as were the vessels in that Titanic ice-stream, they had not even the most limited choice of halting place ; and winter quarters more cruelly inhospitable could hardly have fallen to their lot.

Sixteen years previously Sir James Ross had stood upon Cape Felix. He travelled on foot in the early spring of 1830 from Victoria Harbour in the Gulf of Boothia, and explored the northern coast of King William's Land, and, standing on the 29th of May on this very Cape Felix, remarked with astonishment the fearful nature of the oceanic ice which was pressed upon the shores, and he mentions that in some places the pressure had driven the floes inland half a mile beyond the highest tide-mark. Such were the terrible winter quarters of these lone barks and their gallant crews ; and if that season of monotony and hardship was trying to them at Beechey Island, where they could in some measure change the scene by travelling in one direction or another, how infinitely more so it must have been with nothing round them but ice-hummock and floe-piece, with the ships constantly subjected to pressure and ice-nip, and the crews often threatened during the depth of winter with the probability of having their ships swallowed up in an Arctic tempest,

H. M. S.hips *Erebus and Terror*
{ Wintered in the Ice in

28 of May 1847 { Lat. 70° 5' N. Long. 98° 23' W

Having wintered in 1846—7 at Beechey Island

in Lat 74° 43' 28" N. Long 91° 39' 15" W After having

ascended Wellington channel to Lat 77° and returned

by the West side of Cornwallis Island

Commander.

Sir John Franklin commanding the Expedition.

All well

WHOEVER finds this paper is requested to forward it to the Secretary of
the Admiralty, London, *with a note of the time and place at which it was
found*: or, if more convenient, to deliver it for that purpose to the British
Consul at the nearest Port.

QUINCONQUE trouvera ce papier est prié d'y marquer le tems et lieu ou
il l'aura trouvé, et de le faire parvenir au phitot au Secretaire de l'Amirauté
Britannique à Londres.

CUALQUIERA que hallare este Papel, se le suplica de enviarlo al Secretario
del Almirantazgo, en Londrés, con una nota del tiempo y del lugar en
donde se halló.

EEN ieder die dit Papier mogt vinden, wordt hiermede verzogt, om het
zelve, ten spoedigste, te willen zenden aan den Heer Minister van de
Marine der Nederlanden in 's Gravenhage, of wel aan den Secretaris der
Britsche Admiraliteit, te London, en daar by te voegen eene Nota,
inhoudende de tyd en de plaats alwaar dit Papier is gevonden geworden.

FINDEREN af dette Papiir ombedes, naar Leilighed gives, at sende
samme til Admiralitets Secretairen i London, eller nærmeste Embedsmand
i Danmark, Norge, eller Sverrig. Tiden og Stœdet hvor dette er fundet
önskes venskabeligt paategnet.

WER diesen Zettel findet, wird hier durch ersucht denselben an den
Secretair des Admiralitets in London einzusenden, mit gefälliger angabe
an welchen ort und zu welcher zeit er gefunden worden ist.

Party consisting of 2 Officers and 6 Men
left the Ships on Monday 24th May 1847

when the icefields would rear and crush them down one against the other under the influence of the awful pressure from the north-west.

From this supreme danger, however, they were preserved, and the winter of 1846–47 seems to have run its course without casualty. With the arrival of the spring, and, of course, long before the season of navigation to which the imprisoned men looked forward had commenced, a land exploring party was organised, and on May 24 Lieutenant Graham Gore and Mr. Des Vœux, mate, both of the Erebus, left the ships, and with a party of six men started in sledges for the shore of King William Land. After a four days' journey they reached Point Victory, so named after his gallant vessel by Sir James Ross, who was the first to explore King William Land, and who here reached his furthest westward. Under the cairn raised on the spot by that distinguished navigator, Lieutenant Gore deposited the record which has been so often referred to and was for more than ten years to lie undiscovered. It was in these terms :—

28 of May, 1847. { H.M. ships Erebus and Terror wintered in the ice in lat. 70° 05° N. and long. 98° 23' W., having wintered in 1846-7 [a mistake, as has been remarked, for 1845–6] at Beechey Island in lat. 74° 43' 28" N., long. 91° 39' 15" W., after having ascended Wellington Channel to lat. 77°, and returned by the west side of Cornwallis Island.

Sir John Franklin commanding the expedition.

All well.

Party consisting of two officers and six men left the ships on Monday, May 24, 1847.

Gм. Gore, Lieut.
Chas. F. Des Vœux, Mate.

Thence it is to be presumed the party pushed onward in the direction of Cape Herschel, which or its vicinity there is no reason to doubt that they succeeded in reaching. Here they could have sighted the American coast, and would indeed have been surveying, in the intervening waterway, that very point on the chart which Franklin had touched with his finger while uttering the memorable words already quoted, to the effect that from that point it was 'all plain sailing to the westward.'

The reader must be reminded that the doings of Gore and his party after reaching Point Victory—the extent of their advance beyond that point, their rate of travel, the date on which they turned back again, and the time which it took them to regain the ships—are all matters of which no records exist. All that can be said of them is of necessity conjectural, but conjecture can, as in this case, happily base itself on so broad and firm a foundation of probability that we are warranted in treating its conclusions as virtually certain. We know, for instance, that the despatch of Gore and his comrades could have had no other object than that of ascertaining by ocular evidence that the American coast, and with it that line of navigable water-way which led, as past explorers had shown them, along the northern shore of the continent to Behring Strait, was actually within the calculated distance from those ice-locked ships which it was hoped that the coming summer would set free. We know, further, that they could have reached a point of land on King William Island from which this goal was visible, and that thence it would be possible for them to return to the ships before, and well before, a certain day which was thenceforward to become sacred in the calendar of Arctic adventure. We may be sure that, having fulfilled the object of their mission, they would make their way back with all practicable speed to bear the eagerly awaited tidings to Sir John Franklin. Surely, therefore, we have ample warrant for presuming that possibilities which could so readily be realised, and which there was every inducement to endeavour to realise, were realised in fact.

The journey from the ships to Cape Victory had occupied four days, but it must be borne in mind that the party were then travelling over rough hummocky ice, across which it would of course be impossible for them to make rapid progress. On reaching the shore they would have the smooth land to travel over, and could easily accomplish the distance to Cape Herschel in another three days, or, in other words, by May 31. 'Their return journey,' writes Admiral Markham in a private letter, which he kindly permits me to quote, 'with a lightened sledge and over a road known to them would not

probably occupy them more than half the time of the outward
journey, say four days, so that they could easily get back to
the ships by about June 4 or 5.'

The importance of ascertaining these dates is very great,
because at the date last mentioned the honoured and beloved
leader of the expedition had but a week to live. The nature
of the malady of which he died is not stated in the subsequent
brief record of his death, but the sad event is unfortunately
but too easy to account for by what may almost be called
natural causes. Sir John Richardson was no doubt amply
justified two years before in testifying professionally to his
old comrade's bodily vigour and capacity for resisting cold ;
but a doctor of course can only bear witness to present conditions and appearances, and found upon them one of those
medical forecasts which unforeseen events may often falsify.
It is easy to believe that there may have been some deep-
seated element of weakness in Franklin's constitution which
escaped his friend's discovery. He had led a life of almost
unbroken activity and exposure since the age of fifteen, and
he was now in his sixty-second year. It appears, too, from
the correspondence of some of his officers, that certain traces
of that natural infirmity which comes with advancing age
were visible even in the earlier days of the voyage ; and these
had presumably become more noticeable as time went on.
Two Arctic winters in succession are trying to the health
and spirits even of men in the prime of life ; and the second
of the two in Franklin's case must have been spent in circumstances exceptionally calculated to increase the severity
of the ordeal. For although the commander of the expedition may not latterly have shared—nay, certainly did not
share—the over-sanguine hopes of his younger officers, and
in all probability was quite prepared to find his south-westward route impassably obstructed in the first year (he must
indeed have had a presage of it soon after entering Lancaster
Sound, if not before crossing Baffin's Bay), it could hardly
have been other than a keen disappointment to him to meet
with a repetition of these experiences in the following year.
The winter of 1845–46 may have passed cheerfully enough at

Beechey Island, but the winter of 1846–47, spent in the pack off Cape Felix after weeks of laborious and baffled effort, with some two-thirds of their food supply exhausted, and the prospect of ultimate success growing ever more uncertain, must have moved with a much slower and heavier step. Whether it depressed that unconquerably buoyant spirit which a quarter of a century before had sustained his fainting fellow-travellers on the Barren Lands, we do not know ; but if it did, one can only say that years must have effected a total and indeed an abrupt revolution in Franklin's temperament. Such sudden changes are not indeed unknown in advancing years ; but we have no warrant for supposing this to have been the case here. Ample explanation of the sad event which was to follow is to be found in the advanced age—advanced, at any rate, for Arctic exploration—of the commander, and in the hardships necessarily undergone by him during a sojourn of some three-and-twenty months in Arctic latitudes.

Anyway, the end had come at last ; the long day's work was over, and the worker's rest was drawing nigh. The hour was near when those most moving words of the Shakspearian lyric, too reposeful to be sad, would be fitly addressed to this strenuous toiler through all the weathers of life :—

> Fear no more the heat o' the sun,
>   Nor the furious winter's rages ;
> Thou thy worldly task hast done,
>   Home art gone, and ta'en thy wages.

But a part, the dearest part, of Franklin's wages, next to that which was to be denied him—the ' wages of going on, and not to die '—would have been the knowledge that the most cherished object of his life had been accomplished, and that the North-West Passage had been discovered. This knowledge we have every reason to believe was vouchsafed to him. The sledge party under Graham Gore had ample time, as has been already pointed out, to reach the neighbourhood of Cape Herschel, and, having thence sighted those shores and waters which, once seen, would have assured them of the virtual success of their mission, to make their way back to the ships a full week before their leader's death.

We have reasonable ground of assurance, therefore, that Franklin's dying hours were cheered by the welcome tidings of which Graham Gore was the bearer, and that he passed away in the calm and happy consciousness that the toils and sufferings undergone by himself and his gallant companions had not been endured in vain.

On June 11 he died, and was laid to rest beneath the ice-boulders of his Arctic prison. Like that of another leader who perished in a less gloomy wilderness, and on the borders of a fairer Promised Land, his sepulchre no man knoweth to this day. That 'vast and wandering grave,' the Polar pack, received the wanderer's remains, to be slowly carried with the breaking up of the winter towards those shores which, in the prime of his manhood, he had been the first to conquer from the unknown. Distressing as are such deaths and burials to the contemporaries of the dead, they are clothed for the men of a later generation with a dignity of tragic fitness which rebukes regret. Having lived as he had lived, it is well that Franklin should so have died and so been buried. England has given ungrudgingly of her bravest sons to the most distant and desolate regions of the globe, nor has any race a better title to repeat, and in a more literal sense, that lofty utterance of the Athenian orator, 'The whole earth is the sepulchre of famous men.'

Even to a biographer of Franklin whose direct concern with the ill-fated expedition comes, of course, to an end with the death of its heroic commander, it is impossible to part company at this point with his gallant band of surviving comrades. Years were to pass before the story of their fate could be laboriously built up on a basis of more or less plausible conjecture. But, on the whole, we are able to trace with sufficient certainty all its material details.

The crews, then, of the two imprisoned vessels, the command of which had, by the death of Franklin, devolved upon Captain Crozier, must have watched with intense anxiety the slow and halting advance of the Arctic summer, during which their utmost exertions would have to be put forth to release themselves. And desperate, doubtless, were their efforts to effect their liberation when at last the navigating season arrived. 'We may be sure,' writes Admiral Markham, 'that everything was done with this end in view that could possibly be accomplished. Ice-saws, we may reasonably suppose, were in constant use; powder was doubtless employed in futile endeavours to break the frozen bonds that held their ships so securely, and every expedient, we may be certain, was resorted to that science or human ingenuity could devise; but all were fruitless; the ships remained fixed and immovable.'

It is true that, though the ships were stationary, their prison itself was moving. With the advance of summer the usual thaw set in on the southern edge of this frozen sea, and they felt themselves drifting southward with the whole body of the pack. Hope for a time revived in their despairing hearts; for should this movement continue long enough they would be carried down to the American continent, where their chances of rescue and succour would be materially increased. But their rate of progress was terribly slow. For all prospect of extrication which it held out, the drift of this Arctic ice-stream might as well have been the secular crawl of the Alpine glacier. From a comparison of the bearings of the Erebus and Terror between the beginning of their besetment in the ice and their ultimate abandonment by their crews, the movement of this frozen stream has been computed at a rate of about a mile and a half per month!

Throughout the weeks of alternating hope and fear during which the vessels thus drifted slowly southward from 70° 5' N. to 69" 46' N., every man among their crews must have borne about with him the haunting thought that this was for them their last year of attempted navigation, and that should the present summer fail them, there would be nothing for it but enforced abandonment of their trusty ships, and an exchange of the at least familiar danger of the ocean for the unknown perils of the shore. Upon Crozier and Fitzjames the weight of their responsibility must have borne heavily.

Both were trained and experienced seamen, and one at least had faced similar dangers in the seas both of the Northern and the Southern Poles. But nothing could make amends to them for the loss of a leader who had been battling with the perils and privations of the Arctic voyager when they themselves were in the nursery, and who, above all, had possessed a knowledge of the northern coast of America, and a hard-won experience of the dangers and difficulties of land travel in those regions, with which his comrades, if driven, as they threatened to be, to the abandonment of their vessels, could ill dispense. Another winter in the pack and Franklin's lieutenant would be forced to stake the lives of his crews in a desperate attempt to make his way to some place of safety and succour by an overland journey through one of the most savage and forbidding tracts of country on the face of the earth.

Anxiously indeed must they have watched the moving ice-stream in the late summer and autumn of 1847, counting the hours ere the winter should set in, and praying for but one narrow lane of water through which the ships might hope to make their way into the open sea. Ten, twenty miles are passed over with the drifting ice, and still they are beset. But now there are only sixty frozen miles between them and the open sea off the American coast ; nay, less, for could they but once succeed in rounding that western point of King William Land which is seen projecting into the ice-stream, they would find clear water under their keels. September 1847 came in, and found them still captive. The new ice was forming fast, the drift of the ice-stream slackened, grew slower and slower—stopped. They were fast for another winter, the third since they had left their homes !

And now their situation must have appeared to them de-sperate indeed. It was too late in the season to think of quitting their ships and attempting to reach the American coast in the hope of being able to make their way by the Great Fish River to the nearest of the Hudson's Bay posts. They knew from Franklin's awful experience of a quarter of a century before that game was not to be obtained during the

B B

winter months in the Barren Lands of the continent, and were, therefore, well aware that in the event of their being unable to reach one or other of these posts starvation must be their inevitable fate. Nothing, however, remained for them but to wait out another dreary winter and to take to the land in the spring. Slowly and painfully the months of darkness wore away, and the sun of 1848 rose upon a party weakened in numbers as well as in strength. Cold, privation, and disease had done their work, and no fewer than nine officers and twelve men, besides those who died on Beechey Island, had now succumbed. Among them was Lieutenant Graham Gore, the gallant young officer who had traced the first entry on that record which was to be found years afterwards under its lonely cairn. He had been promoted at home to the rank of commander, a barren honour but too soon to be carried with him to the grave. The survivors now numbered 105, but many of them must have been reduced by weakness and disease, and some, it is only too sadly probable, were in a helpless condition. Nevertheless, the start must be made. The choice between a lingering death by famine and this almost desperate enterprise of escape was peremptory. By the month of July or August in the year now dawning upon them their stores would be exhausted, and, even if a warmer summer should now at last loosen the pack and render navigation once more possible, the relief would come too late. Accordingly on April 22, 1848, the crews of the Erebus and Terror, having prepared and packed their sledges, bade adieu to the two gallant and ill-fated vessels which had for three years sheltered them, and set out upon their journey towards the American coast.

Near at hand as was now the time when their provisions would be exhausted, it has yet been a cause of some surprise to Arctic travellers that they should not have delayed their departure a little longer. 'It is estimated,' according to Admiral Markham, 'that they were not able to carry away with them provisions for more than about forty days, so that, even had they succeeded in reaching the continent of America, they would have been without food for some considerable time, as their provisions would have been expended long before they could possibly hope to find game in sufficient quantity to supply their party with food, for, as a rule, the animals do not begin to frequent the Barren Lands of the continent before the latter end of the summer. It would therefore, it seems, have been better for them to have deferred the abandonment of their ships until the month of May, when they would have had warmer weather for travelling,' and when the period at which the party might hope to have been self-supporting would have been nearer at hand. To the reasons for their actual decision, however, no clue will ever now be discoverable. It may have been that they found their food supplies waning even faster than they had expected, or it may have been that men whose nerves had been overstrung by months of weary waiting, and whose hearts were sick with hope deferred, had become impatient to exchange the slow torture of suspense for the relief of action, even though action should end only in death.

In addition to the provisions and stores with which their sledges were laden, they carried also, each secured on a separate sledge, a couple of whale boats. That they must have found themselves too heavily weighted, at any rate for their then physical condition, is made evident by the fact, long afterwards discovered, that at Point Victory, a distance of only fifteen miles from the ships, they lightened their sledges by abandoning everything that could possibly be spared, or that might be considered superfluous, carrying with them but those articles that were absolutely and essentially necessary for their sustenance. Years later McClintock and Hobson found the spot strewn with a heterogeneous mass of articles— ' clothing in great quantities, stores of various descriptions, blocks, shovels, pickaxes, red, white, and blue ensigns, and even the brass ornaments of a marine's shako, the fragment of a copper lightning conductor, and a brass curtain-rod.' That so many useless articles should have been packed on the already heavily laden sledges seems explicable only on the assumption that they were taken for the purpose of barter with the natives, and only abandoned through the fear that the weight of these encumbrances might prevent the party from reaching the territory frequented by the Eskimo at all.

Their halt at Point Victory was further signalised by an act of vast importance to their countrymen and to the history of Arctic travel. Lieutenant Irving, of the Terror, here found the record which Graham Gore had left on the spot nearly a year before, and to the precise whereabouts of which he had, no doubt, taken care to leave directions behind him at his death. Removing it from the cairn in which it had been placed by their late comrade, Crozier and Fitzjames unrolled it and wrote on its margin as follows :—

April 25, 1848.—H.M. ships Terror and Erebus were deserted on April 22, five leagues NNW. of this, having been beset since September 1846. The officers and crews, consisting of 105 souls, under the command of Captain F. R. M. Crozier, landed here in latitude 69° 37' 42'' N., longitude 98° 41' W. A paper was found by Lieutenant Irving under the cairn supposed to have been built by Sir James Ross in 1831, four miles to the northward, where it had been deposited by the late Commander Gore in June 1847. Sir James Ross's pillar has not, however, been found, and the paper has been transferred to this position, which is that on which Sir James Ross's pillar was erected. Sir John Franklin died on June 11, 1847, and the total loss by death in the expedition has been, up to this date, nine officers and fifteen men. Start on to-morrow, 26th, for Back's Fish River.

The curious fatality of error which seems to have attended the entries on this record was illustrated in this instance by the elision of the word 'May,' originally and rightly assigned as the date of the deposit of the paper by Graham Gore, and the substitution of the word 'June.' The mistake, however, *is fortunately of no importance, because its correction appears* at the foot of the record itself, where, as we have seen, May 24 is entered in Gore's own handwriting as the date of his quitting the ships. And that he did not inadvertently write May for June can again be proved from the document itself, which shows by Gore's entry that Franklin was alive and well at the time he left the ships, and by Crozier's entry that ten days before June 24 their commander had passed away. Why Gore's record was transferred from Ross's cairn to the site of Ross's pillar four miles to the south-ward there is nothing to show. But by a strange and pathetic coincidence the point on the western shore of King William Island, on which this record of the abandonment of the ships and of the death of their commander was deposited, had nearly twenty years earlier received the name of Franklin Point from Sir James Ross, its discoverer, and it was actually within sight of this and the adjoining headland, named by the same explorer Cape Jane Franklin, that his old friend and comrade breathed his last.

Disencumbered of their superfluities, the crews started afresh with a lightened load, but hardly, it is feared, with lighter hearts. From Victory Point to Cape Herschel would be about fifty or sixty miles as the crow flies, but to make their journey thither round the deeply indented coast line of King William Island, as the sombre relics of their wanderings afterwards proved them to have done, was to triple its length. If we look at their route in that sketch-map, 'showing the line of retreat,' which years of patient and heroic endeavour at last rendered it possible to draw, we see a sinuous and serrated littoral, covered with familiar names since bestowed upon it by pious followers in the track of the lost—by such names as Crozier Bay, Fitzjames Island, Terror Bay, Graham Gore Peninsula, and marked here and there with the grim word 'skeleton.' The long-delayed discovery of these remains will be more appropriately recounted in another chapter. Here one can only endeavour to piece together the more or less conjectural story which these scattered remnants of mortality have rendered it possible to construct.

The helplessness of a certain number of the crews is proved by the fact, which these melancholy evidences only too clearly establish, that before the expedition had proceeded many miles in their toilsome march it was compelled to separate into two parties. We must suppose it to have become apparent to all that if the abler bodied of the travellers were obliged to accommodate their rate of progress to that of the sick and feeble, all alike must inevitably perish, and that the only hope of salvation for any of them was

that the weakest should return to the ships while the strongest
pushed on in the hope of finding and bringing back succour
to the rest. Better it was thought that those who could hold
out no longer should take refuge on board their vessels, where
at least was some shelter for them from the rigours of the
Arctic climate, than that they should die of cold on the bleak
shores of King William Island. The few days' prolongation
of their lives might just afford the chance of assistance
reaching them, and, if not, they would at least perish by what
seemed to the imagination, though perhaps the very reverse
was true in reality, a less appalling death. Probably the cold
would have despatched the unhappy men more swiftly and
painlessly on the plains than starvation on board their
beleaguered ships ; but men in their position do not reason
thus, or at any rate not for others, and probably, if the
weaker members of the party had lost all hope for themselves,
their stronger comrades hoped for them.

We know, at any rate, that this separation of the party
did take place, and that one division of it did make an effort
to return to the Erebus and Terror. That was proved beyond
doubt by the tragic discovery which will be related in another
chapter. The other detachment pushed on probably in much
diminished, and, we may be only too sure, in continually
diminishing numbers. Many of them must have failed to
get even as far as Cape Herschel. Those who did reach
that point may have left some record of their having done so
which never reached civilised hands. They would have been
close to the cairn erected by Simpson in 1839, and it is natural
to suppose that if they had the wherewithal to record the fact
they would have done so. But nothing of the kind was
found here or anywhere else, either on King William Island
or the mainland, on the route to the Great Fish River. It is
conjectured that some of them did succeed in crossing
Simpson Strait and gaining Adelaide Peninsula, but, if so, it
could only have been a miserable remnant, soon themselves
to perish. Not one of them is known to have gained the
estuary of the river for which they were making. The points
reached by individual members of the band have here and

there been ascertained by the subsequent discovery of their
bleaching skeletons, and, for the rest, the sad story had to be
fitted together years afterwards from the statements, partly no
doubt historic, but more than half legendary, of the natives.

Six, eleven, twenty-one, and thirty-two years afterwards,
information which by the last of these dates at any rate must
have become mere tradition, was collected from these people.
According to them, a party of about forty white men were
seen during the spring (as we must suppose) of the year 1848
travelling southward, dragging sledges and a boat. They
were very thin and appeared to be in want of provisions.
None could speak the Eskimo language, but by signs they
gave the natives to understand that their ship or ships had
been destroyed by the ice, and that they were journeying to
where they hoped to get deer or other food. From the
same source came all the tidings, if that word be not too
definite, that were ever obtained of the two lost vessels.
Eskimos told of a ship that was 'crushed by the ice off the
north shore of King William Island; but all her people
landed safely, and went away to the Great Fish River, where
they died.' They spoke also of a second ship, which 'had
been seen off King William Island,' and had 'drifted on
shore at the fall of the same year.' Their account of this
vessel was curiously circumstantial. They described her as
apparently intact when first seen by them, with one boat on
her deck and four others outside; and they further declared
that on board one of the ships was the body of 'a tall man
with long teeth and large bones.' But no vestige of either
ship was discovered by any of the search parties, and the only
possible inference is that the pressure of the pack gathering,
winter after winter, on that iron coast became at last too
tremendous for their vessels to hold out against, that they
were broken up, and their fragments swept southward by the
ice-stream towards the American coast.

In 1869 'Captain Hall was informed by the natives he
met in King William Island that the graves of two white
men were found in the vicinity of the Pfeiffer River, and that
there was another white man's grave on a long low point

jutting out into the sea some five or six miles to the eastward. The remains of five white men were also discovered on a small island called Todd Islet, about two or three miles off this point. He was further informed that in a bay to the west of Point Richardson, which has subsequently been named Starvation Cove, a boat covered with an awning and containing the remains of thirty or thirty-five men was found. It was also reported that a tent had been seen in the vicinity of Terror Bay, "the floor of which was completely covered with the bodies of white men."' Point Richardson is on the mainland of the American continent, and Starvation Cove could have been reached in a boat from Todd Islet, on the southern shore of King William Island, and about twenty miles off. Terror Bay is on the island, and full sixty miles to the west of Starvation Cove. If dead were found in considerable numbers at both places, it would seem as if the southward party had again divided and that the weaker had again been left behind. Then the last and toughest of the travellers, the thirty or thirty-five, dragged themselves painfully round the southern coast of King William Island to Todd Islet, left five of their number dead there, struggled across in their boat to Starvation Cove, where they themselves at last succumbed to famine.

These details, however, though possessing unhappily but too much plausibility, rest, it must be remembered, on hearsay alone. The discoveries in 1859 of Graham Gore's record, a boat with two skeleton occupants, and another skeleton many miles distant from it, and, twenty years later, of the grave and remains (identified by a medal) of Lieutenant Irving, constitute all the material proofs of these tragic deaths that have ever been brought to light. For all other knowledge of the fate of our unfortunate fellow-countrymen we have to fall back on the fragmentary statements of the natives, and to reconstruct in imagination that shadowy and wavering line of wanderers, 'very thin and appearing to be in want of provisions,' who were seen by the nomad Eskimos as they dragged their boat and sledges slowly southward in the summer of 1848, and who, in the piteous words of an old Eskimo woman, 'fell down and died as they walked along.'

CHAPTER XXII

THE SEARCHES FOR THE LOST

1848–1854

TIDINGS of the explorers were no doubt hopefully looked for by their friends and families during the year 1846, but the unbroken silence gave rise, we may presume, to disappointment rather than anxiety. The history of Arctic expeditions is very various, and the dates at which communications may be expected from them are of necessity incapable of being even approximately determined. News of them might quite conceivably come to hand within a few months of their entering the Arctic circle, or, on the other hand, a delay of a year or more in hearing from the absent voyagers need not of itself give rise to serious apprehensions. In this case, moreover, there was a special cause in operation to mitigate uneasiness. It will be remembered with what earnestness in his last letters to his wife and his sisters Franklin had entreated them not to give way to premature alarms. Again and again, as we have seen, he endeavoured to familiarise them with the possibility of a two years' absence, and had bade them not to expect him, or not with any anxiety, until a second winter had come and gone. All depended, he constantly told them, on the amount of progress made by the expedition in the seasons of 1845 and 1846. If their work were not accomplished by the end of the summer season of the latter year, but there should nevertheless seem to be a fair prospect of completing it in a third season, and the officers and crew should be continuing in good health, such a state of matters, he had impressed upon them, 'might justify our passing a second winter in these regions. If we do not succeed in our attempt, we shall try other places.' Indeed, in his farewell letter to Mr. Robert

Brown, he had put the matter even more strongly still. He begs his friends to remind his wife that 'we may be so circumstanced at the end of the first winter and even of the second, as to wish to try some other part;' and he adds that Lady Franklin and his daughter 'should be encouraged not to look for our arrival earnestly till our provision gets short.'

Now they were, as we know, provisioned for three years when they left England in May 1845, so that, strictly construed, these words of Franklin would have amounted to an injunction to those he had left behind him to await the expiration not of a second merely, but of a third winter before allowing themselves to feel anxious as to his fate. Such a literal construction of his language, however, was of course inadmissible. Even though provided with supplies of food to last until the early summer of 1848, no exploring expedition would voluntarily have passed the winter of 1847–48 in Arctic latitudes, for the obvious reason that their provisions would be exhausted before the opening of the navigation season of the following year. Hence, their non-appearance in temperate latitudes at some time or other before the third winter would amount to a virtually certain indication that their ships were either lost or immovably beset in the ice. In the latter case it would have become a question with them of the possibility, not of extricating their vessels in time to resume and complete their work of exploration by a homeward journey through a discovered north-west passage, but of effecting their escape from their icy prison to save their lives. For before midsummer their stores would have been exhausted, and usually it is not till several weeks later that the ice-floes begin to move and the grip of the pack relaxes.

When, therefore, the second twelvemonth was approaching its completion, when the spring of 1847 was ripening into summer, yet no word reached England from the adventurers who had sailed in May 1845, and who were known to be supplied with only stores and provisions enough to last them another year, even men not given to alarm began to feel anxious. Pressure was brought to bear on the Government to procure the despatch of supplies to various parts of the

North American continent, wherever there seemed any probability of falling in with the missing men, and the prompt organisation of a search for them was also urged. The Admiralty, as is the way of public departments, elected to do the easier thing first, and to put off the other; and arrangements were made with the Hudson's Bay Company for the stocking of their most northern stations with a large supply of provisions—seventy-four days' rations for 120 men—in readiness for the explorers in the event of their having abandoned their ships for an attempted retreat by land. The Company's officers at their various posts were also instructed to warn the Indians to look out for and assist any surviving members of the party that they might happen upon. Large rewards were offered by the Government to the masters and crews of all ships employed in the whale fishery in Baffin's Bay if they should 'succeed in obtaining any information or record of the progress of the Erebus and Terror through Lancaster Sound, and to the westward;' to which was added a reward of 2,000l. offered by Lady Franklin herself for information as to her husband's fate.

Thus passed the year 1847. In the following spring the Government proceeded to organise the first of the many expeditions which were despatched in search of the illustrious navigator and his crews. It consisted of two vessels, the Enterprise, of 471 tons, and the Investigator, of 420 tons burden, with Captain Sir James Clark Ross in chief command and Captain Bird in command of the second ship. The former officer's Arctic record has often been referred to in these pages; the latter had taken part in Parry's memorable attempt to reach the North Pole in 1827. A second expedition, under the command of Franklin's old comrade Sir John Richardson, accompanied by Mr. John Rae, an officer of the Hudson's Bay Company, of whom more hereafter, was despatched with directions to proceed overland through the Hudson's Bay Territory, to descend the Mackenzie River and examine the coast thence to the Coppermine River, as also the southern and western shores of Wollaston Land. And yet a third expedition, consisting of the Herald, under Captain

Kellett, and the Plover, under Commander Moore, was sent to Behring Strait, with instructions to proceed as far as possible to the eastward, and to endeavour to communicate with the party under the command of Sir John Richardson.

But a word must here be said about Richardson's second in command, a man of remarkable gifts as a traveller, and one whose indefatigable labours have given him, apart from his services in connection with the search for Franklin, a foremost place among explorers of the Arctic coasts. John Rae, by birth an Orkney man and educated at Edinburgh University for the medical profession, had, at the age of barely twenty, obtained the post of surgeon to a ship of the Hudson's Bay Company, in whose service he had been for twelve years, when, in 1845, he was placed by them in command of an expedition in two small boats to the Arctic seas, to endeavour to complete the survey of some 700 miles of coast, forming the shores of a large bay left unexplored by Parry in 1822–23. Setting out from York Factory in 1846 with this modest equipment, a party of ten men, and only four months' provisions, Rae accomplished a voyage of 900 miles, during which much dangerous obstruction by ice was met with, and, reaching latitude 66° 32' N., in Repulse Bay, which was intended to be the starting point of the survey, spent there a very severe winter, during which the temperature often fell to 35° and 40° below zero. Early in April foot journeys were commenced and carried out to the extent of over 1,300 miles, whereby 700 miles of new coast line were surveyed, thus practically uniting the surveys of Ross on Boothia with Parry's explorations at Hecla-and-Fury Strait. Such a record as this was naturally calculated to catch the eye, and arouse the admiration, of an old Arctic traveller like Sir John Richardson, and Rae had not long reached London in 1847 when he received from him an offer of the post of second in command of the expedition which Sir John was personally organising for the search after his missing comrade and friend. The offer was accepted, and, the boats and crews having been sent out to York Factory in 1847, Richardson and Rae left England in the early spring of 1848, and in the course of the season the two explorers made a thorough examination of the Arctic shores of America, from the Mackenzie River eastward to the Coppermine, without finding any clue to the missing expedition. They wintered at Fort Confidence, on Great Bear Lake, and in the spring of 1849 Richardson returned to England, while Rae remained behind for the purpose of returning to the sea by the Coppermine River, and crossing thence over the strait which divides the continent from Wollaston Land, and which had been rendered impassable the previous season. In 1851 Rae was appointed to the command of another search expedition to the Arctic coast, with no other instructions than to take the route he thought best. In the course of this expedition Rae, accompanied by two other men, made a sledge journey of over 1,000 miles, searching every corner along the shore of Wollaston Land. The whole coast eastward of the Coppermine River, as also that of Victoria Land, was also examined, and the Victoria Strait, the actual channel in which the Erebus and Terror had been finally beset four years before, was discovered and named. Rae and his companions attained indeed to about the latitude at which the ships were icebound, though, coasting along the shore of Victoria Land, he was of course divided from that of King William Island, off which they were finally abandoned, by a distance of some four or five degrees of longitude. Rae returned by way of the Lakes and Fort Winnipeg, having covered either by boat, sledge, or snowshoes, a distance of 5,380 miles during his eight months of continuous travel. For this and for his survey of 1847 he was rewarded in 1852 with the Founders' gold medal of the Royal Geographical Society.

From 1848 onward, for a period of some six years without intermission, and intermittently for some eleven years, the search for Franklin was prosecuted—at first officially, afterwards by private enterprise, at last by Lady Franklin alone. From first to last the number of search expeditions despatched from this country and America amounted to as many as thirteen, without reckoning overland journeys, and the Arctic Ocean was entered by no fewer than twenty-four different vessels (including repeated voyages of the same vessel) in the course of this long and fruitless quest. The wide range of hitherto unexplored land and water which their crews traversed and the immense value of their contributions to geographical science will appear in the course of this narrative; but an examination of the area of their travels only makes their prolonged failure to raise the veil of obscurity which shrouded Franklin's fate the more remarkable. It would be an almost pardonable exaggeration to say that they discovered nearly everything except what they sought.

That they missed it for so long was partly due to sheer perversity of luck, but in some measure also to perversity of official instructions. In the case of the first three expeditions, the former agency was alone at work. No one could have known that the Erebus and Terror might not in this, the third year of their absence, be nearing the end of their journey from the Atlantic to the Pacific, and in that case either Kellett or Richardson might very well have fallen in with them at some point on the North American coast between Behring Strait and the mouth of the Mackenzie or even of the Coppermine River, and have been able, no doubt, to render them valuable assistance. As to Sir James Ross, who left England with his two ships on July 12, 1848, he was not, indeed, able to make much progress in the course of that year, being compelled by the ice which he encountered in Barrow Strait to seek winter quarters in Port Leopold, on the north-east coast of North Somerset. But in the following spring the eastern and western coasts of Prince Regent Inlet were thoroughly explored by the expedition, and in particular a certain point on the western coast was reached by them, at which there was some reason to think that they might fall in with the missing crews, and to which, indeed, it is by no means improbable that their commander seriously considered the question of directing his course after the abandonment of the ships. The point in question was Fury Beach, the scene of the wreck of Parry's ship of that name in 1825. It must have been known to Crozier, who had served in Parry's expedition, that there was here a large store of provisions which had been landed from the Fury at the time of her loss. Fury Beach, however, was seventy or eighty miles north of the point at which the Erebus and Terror were beset. To have made for it would have involved something like an actual retracing of the course of the expedition, and, having regard to the possibility that the provisions might have been discovered and appropriated by the Eskimos,[1] one can hardly wonder that Crozier declined the responsibility of such a return upon his footsteps, and decided to push on towards the south.

Even as it was, however, Ross really hit upon the right track, and, had he been able to follow it up, he would have solved that problem which had to wait nearly another ten years for its solution. For in this same spring of 1849 he sledged along the eastern coast of Peel Strait as far south as latitude 72° 38' N., or but little more than two degrees from the point at which the Erebus and Terror wintered in 1846–47, and less than three from the spot at which, after their slow drift of some twenty miles with the moving ice-pack in the summer of 1847, they had in the following spring been abandoned. Had Ross, then, and his companion McClintock been able to make their way but two hundred miles further— a trifle to that indefatigable sledger who afterwards covered thousands of miles by this mode of travel in repeated search expeditions—the latter would have anticipated his discoveries of 1859. For in lat. 69° 46' or thereabouts lay the two derelict vessels, and on the coast of King William Island, a few miles to the SSE. of that point, was the cairn and the record which would have cleared up the mystery as to the fate of their crews. That any of them could then have been rescued is no doubt extremely improbable. Franklin had been dead two years, and it was more than a year since the vessels were abandoned. That thin and straggling line of famine-stricken men which has left sombre traces of itself along the route to the American coast, must ere this have

---

[1] As a matter of fact, these stores and provisions were found by Admiral Markham 'in a perfect state of preservation' in 1873, nearly fifty years after their original deposit.

ceased its march for ever. The last of those heroic fighters with death in the most terrible of his shapes must have 'fallen down and died as he walked along.' But the ships were probably still there, or not far off, even if the ice-pack should have carried them a little further south, and the discovery of the ships would have guided them to the cairn. England and the lost men's families would have known in 1849 instead of 1859 the whole sad truth, and the toil, the expenditure, and, above all, the vain yearnings of years would have been spared. But it was not to be. Ross and McClintock had nearly exhausted their store of provisions, and were forced to return to Cape Leopold without discovering any traces of what they sought. Nor must we forget to reckon on the other side of the account that, had they then and there succeeded in clearing up the mystery, our Arctic explorers would have lost that stimulus to adventure which was for the next seven or eight years to impel them upon enterprises redounding to the maritime glory of their country and extending the dominion of geographical science over vast tracts of land and ocean hitherto unexplored.

The return of Sir James Ross and Sir John Richardson unsuccessful from their respective missions in the autumn of 1849 was rightly and laudably regarded by the Government of the day as a summons to fresh exertions. In the year 1850 no fewer than six separate expeditions were despatched in quest of the lost explorers—two of them of a fully official character, and manned by officers of the British Navy; a third subsidised by the Government; and the other three privately organised. The Enterprise was again sent out, this time under Captain Collinson, while Commander McClure, who had served in it as a first lieutenant under Ross in its late expedition, was appointed to the command of the Investigator. The route of the two vessels was, however, on the second occasion reversed. They were to approach the field of search from the west instead of from the east; and they sailed from England for Behring Strait in January 1850, with orders to enter the Arctic Ocean through that channel, and thence to proceed with all speed to the eastward, examining Melville Island, Banks Land, Wollaston Land, Victoria Land, or otherwise according to the discretion of Captain Collinson. Their voyage was a famous one in Arctic history, but its details must for the present be reserved.

Less important in its geographical results, but far more so in its relation to the primary object of these undertakings, was the expedition despatched four months later under Captain Austin, in command of the Resolute, and Captain Erasmus Ommanney, commanding the Assistance, whose instructions were to carry out an exhaustive search through Lancaster Sound in the direction of Melville and the Parry Islands. It was to this expedition, assisted by the efforts of two whaling brigs, under the command of Captains Penny and Stewart, which had been despatched by the Government with orders to undertake the examination of Jones Sound and Wellington Channel, that the first discovery of any traces of their lost countrymen was due. The three other search parties, however, though but one of them rendered any service, and that merely as a bearer of intelligence, must not pass unnoticed. One of them was fitted out by an American citizen, Mr. Henry Grinnell, and was manned by officers and men of the United States Navy; Lady Franklin at her own expense equipped another, the Prince Albert, a schooner of ninety tons, captained by Commander Forsyth, and instructed to explore the shores of Prince Regent Inlet; and, finally, the veteran Sir John Ross, then in his seventy-fourth year, started off for Baffin's Bay and Lancaster Sound in a small vessel called the Felix, accompanied by a still smaller one, a yacht of twelve tons, the two equipped and fitted out partly at the cost of the Hudson's Bay Company and partly by private subscription.

The expedition under Captain Austin's command was not long in meeting with its good fortune. His ships wintered at Griffith Island in Barrow Strait, but before seeking their winter quarters they made the first discovery which had as yet rewarded these manifold and extensive investigations. It is to the Assistance and its commander that the honour of this welcome 'find' belongs. At Point Riley, the headland

C C

on the south shore of North Devon which forms the eastward
arm of the natural harbour completed by Beechey Island on
the west, Captain Ommanney lighted upon conspicuous and
unmistakable traces of a winter encampment, and soon afterwards, on Beechey Island itself, Captain Penny found, each
marked with simple headstone and epitaph, the graves already
referred to of the three lost members of the expedition—the
two seamen and the marine.   Further examination revealed
the exact spot at which the ships had been laid up, and even
yielded evidences of the manful and cheerful fashion in which
the crews had whiled away the monotony of the winter.
'The ruins and traces which they left behind them,' wrote
Admiral Sherard Osborn, himself a member of the expedition, 'all attest it.'

The observatory, with its double embankment of earth and stones,
its neat finish and the lavish expenditure of labour in pavement and
pathway ; the shooting gallery under the cliff ; the seats formed of
stones ; the remains of pleasant picnics in the form of empty bottles
and meat tins strewed about ; the elaborate cairn on the north point
of Beechey, a pyramid of eight feet high and at least six feet long on
each side of the base, constructed of old meat-tins filled with gravel,
all tell the same tale of manful anxiety for physical employment to
distract the mind from suffering and solitude.   On board the ships
we picture to ourselves the Arctic school and theatre ; the scholars
and dramatists exerting themselves to kill monotony and amuse or
instruct their comrades.   There are not wanting traces at Cape Riley
to show how earnestly the naturalists Goodsir and Stanley laboured
to collect specimens ; now was there time to arrange and note their
labours.   There is more than one site still visible of tents in which
the magnetical observations were obtained ; now was the time to
record and compare such observations.   And in addition to the
charming novelty of a first winter in the frozen sea, the officers in so
scientific an expedition had abundance of employment in noting the
various phenomena which were daily and hourly occurring round
them.

A word here in further reference to the meat-tins above
mentioned, which were labelled 'Goldner's Patent,' for on
them hangs a scandalous and hideous tale.   Seven hundred
of these articles were counted, and must have contained, it is
calculated, a considerably larger quantity of such food than

the crews could possibly have consumed during their first
winter; and from the fact that an enormous number of these
tins supplied to the Navy were subsequently found to contain
putrid meat, it is inferred that many or most of those tins
discovered on Beechey Island had been condemned on the
same ground. If this inference be well-founded, the loss of
so large a proportion of what would be considered fresh in
contradistinction to salt provisions would be most serious, and
might ' so cripple their resources as to lead in all probability
to the disastrous fate of the expedition.' Such, at least, is
Admiral Markham's belief; his brother-officer, Admiral
Osborn, contents himself with the less circumstantial but
no less significant observation : ' Sad it is to record it, but
nearly all their preserved meats were those of the miscreant
Goldner.' And though the renown of contractors for exploits
of this kind is historic, the man who supplied putrid meat to
the crews of an Arctic expedition certainly seems to merit an
infamy as lasting in human memory as the fame of the victims
whom he supplied with poison because it was more profitable
than supplying them with food. He is, at any rate, welcome
to the humble effort here made to ' plead against oblivion for
his name.'

It must, however, be admitted that the relics discovered
at Beechey Island gave evidence of other elements of weakness than that created by the villany of a contractor. Exploring parties had evidently been despatched by Franklin in a
northward direction along the eastern shore of Wellington
Channel, where the marks of encampments and the trails of
sledges were frequent. But in Admiral Osborn's view they
told a somewhat disquieting tale :—

It was sad to remark, from the form of their cooking-places and
the deep ruts left by their sledges over the edge of the terraces which
abound in Beechey Island, how little Franklin's people were impressed with the importance of rendering their travelling equipment
light and portable, both as a means of exploration while their ships
were imprisoned and to enable them to escape if their ships were
destroyed. The anxiety for their fate expressed by many in Captain
Austin's expedition when remarking upon the fearful expenditure of
labour which must have been entailed on Franklin's men in dragging

about such sledges as they evidently had with them, has been [1860] only too fully verified. The longest journey made by sledge parties from the Erebus and Terror at Beechey Island, so far as we know, did not exceed *twenty* miles. Franklin's experience of travelling in the Hudson Bay Territory was evidently at fault in the rugged and desert region in which he was now sojourning, and he had no McClintock at his side to show him how by mechanical skill and careful attention to weights and equipment sledges ought to be constructed, on which men might carry boats, tents, clothing, food, and fuel, and travel with impunity from February to August, and explore, as he himself had done in that time, 1,400 miles of ground or frozen sea. However, no anxieties then pressed on the minds of those gallant men ; 'large water' was all they thought of ; give them that, and Behring's Strait in their ships was still their destination.

Immediately on the discovery of Franklin's first winter quarters, the Prince Albert, the vessel equipped by Lady Franklin, hastened home with the intelligence. The other ships remained to winter, as has been said, in Barrow Strait, but not before a thorough, though futile, search had been made in every nook and corner of Beechey Island for some record or document from which a clue to the intended course of the Erebus and Terror in the summer of 1846 might be obtained.

Nor, it may be imagined, with their recent discoveries to encourage them, were they likely to remit their efforts during the following year. The spring and summer of 1851 were spent in the industrious exploration of the surrounding territory in every direction, both by sea and land. Captain Penny sailed up Wellington Channel to the northward, and no fewer than five sledge expeditions were despatched by Captain Austin to the south and west. One of these, under Lieutenant McClintock, explored to the westward as far as Melville Island ; two others, under Ommanney and Sherard Osborn respectively, prosecuted a south-westward search from Cape Walker along the south and west coasts of Prince of Wales Land. A fourth, travelling in the same direction, namely, by way of Cape Walker, ascertained the insularity of the land from which that headland projects, and which is now known as Russell Island. And, finally, an expedition again unconsciously hitting off, like that of Sir James Ross, the route taken by the missing ships, pursued a course along the western shore of Peel Sound as far south as 72° 49', or within 150 miles of the spot at which the Erebus and Terror were abandoned.

It will be observed, however, that while for the second time the track of the explorers had been struck by a sledging party which, as it happened, had not the best chance of following up its clue to the wished-for goal, the maritime operations of the expedition, which alone could have brought them within sight of the deserted vessels—if, indeed, their timbers still held together—were again mis-directed. It is true that both Wellington Channel and a route to the southward and westward of Cape Walker were mentioned in Franklin's instructions, but both in those instructions, and still more distinctly in Franklin's own letters from which quotations have already been made, the former of these two routes is treated as the 'second best' of two alternatives. The Erebus and Terror, it is repeatedly insisted upon, were only to make for Wellington Channel in the event of their finding their westward progress obstructed in Barrow Strait. Yet both now and afterwards we find search parties invariably shaping a northward or north-westward course after entrance into Barrow Strait, instead of, as one would have expected, holding on in a westerly direction with the hope of finding an opening to the south. It may be that the despatch of sledging parties along the shore of Peel Sound was regarded as sufficient provision against the possibility of Franklin's ships having found and threaded this southward-leading channel, since it was perhaps assumed that they would in that case find the route of the missing vessels indicated by cairns; and, indeed, the total absence of this familiar form of Arctic beacon has always puzzled the most experienced inquirers. Cairns are easily constructed from material always at hand. They form conspicuous landmarks, and their importance as such, writes Admiral Markham, 'was well known to Franklin and his officers. If they had been erected, the direction for the search would have been indicated, and an enormous amount of labour would have been saved, while a successful issue of the search would possibly have been the result. The only reason that can be advanced for this apparent neglect of what has always been regarded as one of the most important duties of an Arctic explorer is the supposition that the channels were comparatively clear of ice when the Erebus and Terror passed through, and that it was in consequence deemed inexpedient to delay the progress of the vessels by stopping to build cairns—a serious omission, however, for their absence necessitated the expenditure of much invaluable time besides a great waste of money in the prosecution of a long and fruitless search.'

On the return of the Prince Albert in 1850 with the news of the discoveries on Beechey Island, Lady Franklin's hopes of ascertaining her husband's fate were naturally quickened. The vessel was again despatched in the following year, under the command of Mr. Kennedy, and numbering, it is pleasant to record, the veteran John Hepburn among its crew. The voyage led to the discovery of Bellot Strait, the channel separating Boothia Felix from North Somerset; and by traversing which Mr. Kennedy of course found himself in Franklin Strait, and therefore on Franklin's track. Had he turned to the southward, another 510 miles' sail would have brought him to the fatal spot. But no ; the same invincible determination to set the face to the northward governed the movements of Kennedy as it had those of the searchers who had preceded, and of some who were to follow him. Issuing from Bellot Strait—so named after the gallant and unfortunate young officer of the French Navy who had volunteered for this service, in the course of which he lost his life by drowning—the Prince Albert's course was directed up Franklin Strait to the north-east point of Prince of Wales Land, which the lost explorers had only skirted and never touched at, and where, therefore, no traces of them could possibly be discoverable. Mr. Kennedy returned to England in 1852, and in the course of the same year Lady Franklin fitted out a screw steamer, the Isabel, which also returned unsuccessful after an (apparently) somewhat aimless three months' cruise in Baffin's Bay.

In 1852, moreover, another attempt was made by Government on the larger scale. The four ships of Captain Austin's squadron, the Assistance and Resolute, with the two steam tenders Intrepid and Pioneer, were again refitted and sent out under Captain Sir Edward Belcher, flying his pennant in the Assistance, in chief command, and with Captains Kellett, McClintock, and Sherard Osborn in command of the three other vessels of the squadron. Here, again, the instructions given to the commander were to sail anywhere except in the direction which Franklin might have been known to have taken. He was to despatch one of the vessels with its steam tender up Wellington Channel, which it was perfectly understood that Franklin was not to enter save in the last resort ; while the other vessel and its steamer were to push westward towards Melville Island, a route which Franklin had been specially warned to avoid in consequence of the obstructing ice masses which had been met with and reported upon by Parry in those waters, and which, as we have already seen, he had fully determined to avoid.

There was, however, a better reason for prescribing this course to Sir Edward Belcher than there had been for the instructions given to the commanders of previous expeditions, for in truth it was not in search of Franklin alone that he had been sent out. That earlier search-party, the expedition of Collinson and McClure, in the Investigator and the Enterprise, of whose memorable adventures I have hitherto delayed to speak, had now been absent more than two years, and fears for their safety had begun to be entertained. Sir Edward Belcher's movement to the westward was therefore no doubt prescribed to him, in part at least, with the view of rendering assistance to these vessels, which it was supposed might have reached positions on Melville Island.

One of them, as it turned out, was sorely enough in need of aid, and the course of this narrative must be arrested for a moment to trace the history, so famous in our Arctic annals, of the Investigator's great cruise. Sailing from

England on January 20, 1850, the Enterprise and her consort
passed through the Straits of Magellan, and, touching at the
Sandwich Islands, proceeded at once to Behring Strait; but
shortly after entering the Pacific the two vessels accidentally
parted company, never to sight each other again during the
whole remainder of the voyage.   Passing through the Strait,
the Investigator sailed along the north coast of America as
far as longitude 130° W., when McClure shaped his course to
the north-eastward and discovered a channel between Banks
Land and Prince Albert Land now known as Prince of
Wales Strait.   This, leading as it does to waters which had
been already entered by other explorers from the eastward,
may be regarded as the last link of the North-West Passage.
McClure, however, was to discover not one but two such
passages during his three years' sojourn in the Polar Seas.
Having wintered in Prince of Wales Strait, the Investigator
retraced her course to the southern point of Banks Land,
and in the course of the next season her captain succeeded in
completely circumnavigating this island (as it proved to be)
and discovering a path of re-entry into known waters by a new
channel, now called McClure Strait, between Banks Land and
Melville Island, which is in fact a second north-west passage.

The gallant Investigator was not fated to complete the
course herself; for in 1851 she was frozen up hard and fast
in the Bay of God's Mercy, on the north coast of Banks
Land, where she remained immovably fixed for two entire
winters.   In the summer of 1853, had relief not reached them,
McClure had resolved to abandon his ship and attempt a
retreat on the Mackenzie or Coppermine Rivers; but, fortunately, that desperate and in all probability fatal undertaking
was not actually forced upon them.   They had happily taken
the precaution to deposit at Winter Harbour, on Melville
Island, a record of their plight, and the providential discovery of this by McClintock in 1852, during a sledging
expedition over Melville Island, led to the institution of a
successful search for the imprisoned ship in the following
year.   The Investigator, still ice-beset in the Bay of God's
Mercy, had to be abandoned where she lay.   Her captain and

crew were transferred to the Resolute, and, after a fourth winter spent in the Arctic Regions, they were conveyed to England *via* Lancaster Sound and Baffin's Bay, the first navigators who had ever crossed from the Pacific to the Atlantic Ocean by way of the north coast of America. In recognition of this great achievement the sum of 10,000*l.* was awarded by the English Government to McClure and his crew.

Their rescue, however, was the only success achieved by the expedition under Sir Edward Belcher. Occupied as they were in industriously scouring land and sea to the north of Barrow Strait in search of a party of explorers who had been specially directed to take a course to the south-west of that channel, their efforts were not likely to be very fruitful, and it is scarcely necessary to describe them in detail. Suffice it to say that their whole voyage, besides being one of useless toil, was specially marked out for misfortune. The Assistance and Pioneer got frozen up in Wellington Channel in 1853, and had there to spend their second winter; and the Resolute and Intrepid, also caught by the ice, were compelled to winter in the pack in Melville Sound. In the following year, Sir Edward Belcher, for some unexplained reason, ordered the abandonment of all four ships, the officers and crews of which were conveyed to England in other vessels. A court-martial was in due course held upon the officers concerned, and resulted in their acquittal; but Sir Edward Belcher's sword was returned to him without comment, and the evidence revealed painful dissensions between the commander and some of his captains.

The discouragement caused by this failure would, in any case, no doubt have considerably cooled the Ministerial ardour for the search; but, as it happened, the return of Sir Edward Belcher coincided with the arrival of a highly important piece of intelligence, which had the effect of reducing the temperature of the official mind to zero. In the year 1853, Dr. Rae, whose share in the earlier searches has already been recorded, proposed to the Hudson's Bay Company to fit out a boat expedition for the purpose of tracing the west coast of Boothia as far north as Bellot Strait, and thus uniting the surveys of Sir James Ross with those of Dease and Simpson. The proposal having been accepted, Rae left England early in 1853, and in the course of that and the following year accomplished the object of his mission. The two surveys were united, and King William Land was proved to be an island instead of being, as had been supposed, an integral portion of the American continent. But in the course of effecting this addition to geographical knowledge Rae made another discovery of far more popular interest. An ironic destiny had decreed that, after all the years that had been spent in fruitless attempts to discover the fate of the Franklin expedition, the first authentic intelligence of its disastrous issue should have been obtained by an explorer engaged upon a different service altogether.

In April 1854, Rae's sledge party, then in Pelly Bay, on the coast of King William Land, happened upon some Eskimos, and from these he obtained the first information detailed in the previous chapter as to the fate of the Franklin expedition. Nor do the particulars thus gleaned by him rest solely upon the memory or veracity of his native informants. They were supported by evidence of incontestable character in the shape of actual relics of the missing men.

Justly considering that the information he had lighted upon greatly outweighed the importance of the survey on which he had been engaged, Dr. Rae hastened home to England, where he arrived on October 22, 1854, and immediately proceeded to the Admiralty with his report, the full text of which was also forwarded to the 'Times,' and appeared in its columns on the following day. It commences by a statement of the circumstances under which Rae had lighted on his discoveries during the journey undertaken by him over the ice and snow that spring, with the view of completing the survey of the west shore of Boothia. In the course of this journey 'I met,' he says, 'with Eskimos in Pelly Bay, from one of whom I learnt that a party of white men had perished from want of food some distance to the westward, and not far beyond a large river containing many falls and rapids. Subsequently, further particulars were received, and a number of articles purchased, which place the fate of a portion if not all of the then survivors of the Franklin long-lost party beyond a doubt.'

Rae then went on to give the substance of the information obtained by him at various times and from various sources, and which was as follows :—

In the spring four winters past (spring 1850) a party of white men amounting to about forty were seen dragging a boat with them by some Eskimos who were killing seal near the north shore of King William Land, which is a large island. None of the party could speak the Eskimo language intelligibly, but by signs the natives were made to understand that their ship or ships had been crushed by ice, and that they were now going where they expected to find deer to shoot. From the appearance of the men, all of whom, except one officer, looked thin,[1] they were then supposed to be getting short of provisions, and they purchased a small seal from the natives. At a later date the same season, but previously to the breaking up of the ice, the bodies of some thirty persons were discovered on the continent and five on an island near it, about a long day's journey to the NW. of a large stream which can be no other than Back's Great Fish River, as its description and that of the low shore in the neighbourhood of Point Ogle and Montreal Island agree exactly with that of Sir George Back. Some of the bodies had been buried (probably those of the first victims of famine) ; some were in a tent or tents ; others under the boat, which had been turned over to form a shelter, and several lay scattered about in different directions. Of those found on the island, one was supposed to have been an officer, as he had a telescope strapped over his shoulders and his double-barrelled gun lay underneath him.

There must, Rae thought, ' have been a number of watches, compasses, telescopes, guns (several double-barrelled), &c., all of which appear to have been broken up, as I saw pieces of these different articles with the Eskimos, and, together with

---

[1] Owing no doubt to the haste in which this statement had necessarily to be prepared for publication, a mistake has here crept in. I am kindly permitted by Mrs. Rae, the widow of the distinguished explorer, to quote the following correction of it from her late husband's Journal : ' From the appearance of the men, *all of whom looked thin*, and with the exception of an officer (chief) were hauling on the dragropes of the sledges, they were supposed to be short of provisions.'

some silver spoons and forks, purchased as many as I could
get.' These latter, of course, were by far the most important
of all the explorers' melancholy 'finds,' for their armorial
bearings and initials stamped them as coming from the possession of the perished officers of the expedition. Among
them was 'one round silver plate, engraved "Sir John
Franklin, K.C.B." (a mistake of the engraver for K.C.H.),
and 'a star or order with motto, "*Nec aspera terrent.*
G. R. III. MDCCCXV."'

The only point at which the accuracy of this information
can be questioned is that of the year in which the survivors
of the expedition were seen by the Eskimos. 'In the spring
four winters past,' is an assignment of date which is in itself
ambiguous; but on no construction of it does it seem possible
to accept it as correct. Rae, as we have seen, interpreted it
'spring 1850,' but further consideration satisfied him that his
informants had mistaken the date; and it is indeed incredible
that any members of a party which had abandoned their
ships in such extremities in April 1848 could have been
still alive two years afterwards.

There is, however, not much difficulty in supposing that
the Eskimo recollections of the precise year were at fault.
Dr. Rae, indeed, records a curious instance of their defective
memory for dates; for they declared that an interview which
he had had with them in 1847 had taken place 'five' instead
of seven years before. But, in any case, no difficulty of
this description could detract from the value of the silent
testimony above described. In whatever year the explorers
had perished, there could be no longer any doubt as to
their fate. Proof of it had come at a moment when almost
every one regarded such proof as impossible. Fate, indeed,
remained ironical to the last. A leading article in the
'Times' of Saturday, October 21, 1854, contained the following
sentence:—'It would have been well-nigh as reasonable to
look for the discovery of La Pérouse' (lost seventy years
before) 'as for any traces of poor Franklin and his followers.'
Within forty-eight hours from the publication of these words
Dr. Rae's 'copy' was in the 'Times' office, and in the next
issue of the paper his statement was given to the world.

CHAPTER XXIII

THE 'RECORD' FOUND

1854-1859

THE effect upon the Government of this important change in the situation was such as those acquainted with Governments would have expected. A reward of 10,000*l.* had been already offered by them to any one bringing the first information of the fate of the Franklin expedition ; and Rae, who had made his discoveries and returned to England in complete ignorance of the fact, derived his first knowledge of it—together, significantly enough, with a suggestion that he should apply for the reward—from the First Lord of the Admiralty himself. He and *his* party, *said* Sir James Graham, were entitled to it, and ' he would stand in his own light if he did not put in a claim for it.'

Beyond all doubt it had been fairly earned. The intelligence which Rae had brought home with him, attested as it was by the mute evidence of the relics in his possession, undeniably answered the description of authentic ' first information of the fate of the Franklin expedition.' But the question whether Rae was entitled to the reward promised for it was quite distinct from the question whether the Government were entitled to interpret ' first ' as equivalent to ' final and complete ' information, and justified in abandoning all further efforts to supplement it. But the Admiralty was in want not so much of a justification as of a plausible excuse. The failure of Sir Edward Belcher's costly expedition, and the abandonment of four fine ships of the Navy—one of which, however, the Resolute, was later on, after an almost miraculous drift in the ice-pack into Baffin's Bay, recovered by the American Government, and presented to our own—had been 'a heavy blow and sore discouragement' to the hopes and expectations not only of the Government but of the public at large. The country was engaged in a European war, the cost of which was accumulating in rapidly mounting millions; and on the whole we cannot wonder that the Ministerial mind should have been quick to seize on what must have seemed an unexpectedly happy chance of getting quit of a troublesome business. The ten thousand pounds reward had been so fully and fairly earned by Dr. Rae, that they felt they would have a good answer to Parliamentary and other critics; and to pay it over to him promptly would be purchasing their relief from further calls upon the Exchequer at a comparatively cheap rate.

To Lady Franklin this view of their duty was far from commending itself. To her it seemed that 'information as to the fate' of her husband and his companions, or such information as the country ought alone to be satisfied with, should be of a more definite character than a story gathered from the lips of wandering Eskimos, even supported, as no doubt this was, by morally conclusive proof of the fact—which, indeed, hardly needed proving nine years after the departure of the explorers—that they had all perished. Some light on the causes which led to the loss of the ships, and on the time and manner of the deaths of their gallant commander and their crews—it was this for which Lady Franklin craved, and for which in her devotion to her husband's memory, and her pride in his achievements, she firmly believed and maintained that her countrymen were craving also. She had already fitted out four ships almost entirely at her own expense, and, as the event proved, she had no thought of shrinking from further sacrifices in the same cause. But she held, as, indeed, did the naval and scientific world in general, that only an expedition furnished with the appliances and supported by the resources at the command of the Government had any chance of attaining the desired end. Protesting, therefore, against the payment of the reward to Dr. Rae—at any rate, as definitively exhausting Ministerial responsibility in the matter—she laboured untiringly during the next two years to bring the Government to a sense of their duty to the nation.

She was not without warm support from the leading scientific men of the day, and from naval officers who had distinguished themselves in Arctic service. On June 5, 1856, a memorial, signed by many names of the highest weight in the world of science and of exploring adventure, was presented to Lord Palmerston, new at that time in the office of Prime Minister, urging the necessity of further research 'to satisfy the honour of our country and to clear up a mystery which has excited the sympathy of the civilised world.' And some months later the prayer of this memorial was further emphasised by the following dignified and touching letter to the Prime Minister from Lady Franklin herself:—

60 Pall Mall: Dec. 2, 1856.

My Lord,—I trust I may be permitted, as the widow of Sir John Franklin, to draw the attention of Her Majesty's Government to the unsettled state of a question which a few weeks ago was under their consideration, and to express a well-grounded hope that a final effort may be made to ascertain the fate and recover the remains of my husband's expedition.

Your Lordship will allow me to remind you that a memorial with this object in view (of which I enclose a printed copy) was early in June last presented to and kindly received by you. It had been signed within forty-eight hours by all the leading men of science then in London who had an opportunity of seeing it, and might have received an indefinite augmentation of worthy names, had not the urgency of the question forbidden delay. To the above names were appended those of the Arctic officers who had been personally engaged in the search, and who, though absent, were known to be favourable to another effort for its completion. And though that united application obtained no immediate result, it was felt, and by no one more strongly than myself, that it never could be utterly wasted.

I venture also to allude to a letter of my own, addressed to the Lords Commissioners of the Admiralty in April last, and a copy of which accompanied, I believe, the memorial to your Lordship, wherein I earnestly deprecated the premature adjudication of the reward claimed by Dr. Rae, on the ground that the fate of my husband's expedition was not yet ascertained, and that it was due both to the living and the dead to complete a search which had hitherto been pursued under the greatest disadvantage for want of the clue which was now for the first time in our hands. . . . The memorialists had, as yet, received no reply, and accordingly the President of the Royal Society put a question respecting the memorial in the House of Lords at the close of the session, which drew from one of Her Majesty's Ministers (Lord Stanley), after some preliminary observations, the assurance that Her Majesty's Government would give the subject their serious consideration during the recess. I may be permitted to add that, in the conversation which followed, Lord Stanley expressed himself very favourably disposed towards the proposition made to him by Lord Wrottesley, that in the event of there being no Government expedition, I should be assisted in fitting out my own expedition ; an assurance which Lord Wrottesley had the kindness to communicate to me by letter. . . . I have cherished the hope, in common with others, that we are not waiting in vain. Should, however, the decision of the Government unfortunately throw upon me the responsibility and the cost of sending out a vessel myself, I beg to assure your Lordship that I shall not shrink either from that weighty responsibility or from the sacrifice of my entire available fortune for the purpose, supported as I am in my convictions by such high authorities as those whose opinions are on record in your Lordship's hands, and by the hearty sympathy of many more.

But before I take upon myself so heavy an obligation, it is my bounden duty to entreat Her Majesty's Government not to disregard the arguments which have led so many competent and honourable men to feel that our country's honour is not satisfied while a mystery which has excited the sympathy of the civilised world remains uncleared. Nor less would I entreat you to consider what must be the unsatisfactory consequences if any endeavour should be made to quench all further efforts for this object.

It cannot be that the long-vexed question would thereby be set at rest, for it would still be true that, in a certain circumscribed area of the Arctic circle, approachable alike from the east and from the west, and sure to be attained by a combination of both movements, lies the solution of our unhappy countrymen's fate. While such is the case, the question will never die. I believe that again and again efforts would be made to reach the spot, and that the Government could not look on as unconcerned spectators, nor be relieved, in public opinion, of the responsibility they had prematurely cast off. . . .

It would be a waste of words to attempt to refute again the main objections that have been urged against a renewed search as involving extraordinary dangers and risking life. The safe return of our officers and men cannot be denied, neither will it be disputed that each succeeding year diminishes the risk of casualty ; and, indeed, I feel it would be especially superfluous and unseasonable to argue against this particular objection, or against the financial one which generally accompanies it, at a moment when new expeditions for the glorious interests of science, and which every true lover of science and of his country must rejoice in, are contemplated for the interior of Africa and other parts which are less favourable to human life than the icy regions of the North. . . . Even were the expenditure greater than can reasonably be expected, I submit to your Lordship that this is a case of no ordinary exigency. These 135 men of the Erebus and Terror (or, perhaps, I should rather say the greater part of them, since we do not yet know that there are no survivors) have laid down their lives, after sufferings doubtless of unexampled severity, in the service of their country as truly as if they had perished by the rifle, the cannon ball, or the bayonet. Nay, more ; by attaining the northern and already surveyed coasts of America, it is clear that they solved the problem which was the object of their labour, or, in the beautiful words of Sir John Richardson, that 'they forged the last link of the North-west Passage with their lives.'

Surely, then, I may plead for such men that a careful search be made for any possible survivor, that the bones of the dead be sought for and gathered together, that their buried records be unearthed or recovered from the hands of the Eskimos, and, above all, that their last written words, so precious to their bereaved families and friends, be saved from destruction. A mission so sacred is worthy of a Government which has grudged and spared nothing for its heroic soldiers and sailors in other fields of warfare, and will surely be approved by our gracious Queen, who overlooks none of her loyal subjects suffering and dying for their country's honour.

The final and exhaustive search is all I seek on behalf of the first and only martyrs to Arctic discovery in modern times, and it is all I ever intend to ask.

But if, notwithstanding all I have presumed to urge, Her Majesty's Government decline to complete the work they have carried on up to this critical moment, but leave it to private hands to finish, I must then respectfully request that measure of assistance which I have been led to expect on the authority of Lord Stanley as communicated to me by Lord Wrottesley, and on that of the first Lord of the Admiralty as communicated to Colonel Phipps in a letter in my possession.

It is with no desire to avert from myself the sacrifice of my own funds, which I devote without reserve to the object in view, that I plead for a liberal interpretation of those communications ; but I owe it to the conscientious and high-minded Arctic officers who have generously offered me their services that my expedition should be made as efficient as possible, however restricted it may be in extent. The Admiralty, I feel sure, will not deny me what may be necessary for the purpose, since, if I do all I can with my own means, any deficiencies and shortcomings of a private expedition cannot, I think, be laid to my charge. . . .

I commit the prayer of this letter, for the length of which I must beg much to apologise, to your Lordship's patient and kind consideration, feeling assured that, however the words of it may fall upon the ear of some who apparently judge of it neither by the heart nor by the head, you will not on that, or on any light ground, hastily dismiss it. Rather may you be impelled to feel that the shortest and surest way to set the unfortunate question at rest is to submit it to that final investigation which will satisfy the yearnings of surviving relatives and friends and, what is justly of higher import to your Lordship, the credit and honour of the country.

I have the honour to be, &c.,

JANE FRANKLIN.

The Right Hon. Viscount Palmerston, K.G.

No final answer was given to this eloquent appeal for another three months; but in April, 1857, Sir Charles Wood, the First Lord of the Admiralty, wrote informing Lady Franklin that the members of Her Majesty's Government 'having come with great regret to the conclusion that there was no prospect of saving life, would not be justified, for any objects which, in their opinion, could be obtained by an expedition to the Arctic seas, in exposing the lives of officers and men to the risks inseparable from such an enterprise.'

On receipt of this answer the devoted widow lost not a moment in taking independent action. She immediately entered into negotiations for the purchase of a screw steam-yacht. By the middle of the month she had written to Captain McClintock to take command of the expedition, and in less than a week she was able to telegraph to him, 'Your leave is granted; the Fox is mine; the refit will commence immediately.' The Fox was immediately placed in the hands of her builders to be strengthened and adapted to Arctic service, with the intention of getting her ready to sail by July 1. Provisions for twenty-eight months were embarked, including preserved vegetables, lemon juice, and pickles for daily consumption, and preserved meats for every third day; also as much of the 'stoutest ale' as room could be found for. The Government, to do them justice, did their best to atone for their refusal to despatch another expedition of their own by 'contributing liberally,' wrote Captain McClintock, 'to our supplies. All our arms, powder, shot, powder for ice-blasting, rockets, maroons, and signal-mortars were furnished by the Board of Ordnance. The Admiralty caused 6,682 lbs. of pemmican to be prepared for our use.' They 'supplied us with all the requisite ice gear, such as saws from ten to eighteen feet in length, ice-anchors and ice-claws ; also with our winter housing, medicines, seamen's library, hydrographical instruments, charts, chronometers, and an ample supply of Arctic clothing, which had remained in store from former expeditions. The Board of Trade contributed a variety of meteorological and nautical instruments and journals, and I found that I had but to ask of these departments for what was required, and if in store it was at once granted.' The President of the Royal Society voted 50*l.* from their donation fund for the purchase of magnetic and other scientific instruments. The expenses of fitting out the expedition, including the original purchase-cost of the yacht, 2,000*l.*, amounted to some 6,000*l.*, of which, however, about half was met by private subscription, the list of subscribers containing many well-known and interesting names. Thackeray figures in it as a contributor. Dickens had energetically supported Lady Franklin's appeal to the Government through his then newly founded periodical, *Household Words.* The crew, all told, numbered only twenty-six souls. Captain McClintock's second in command was Lieutenant Hobson, R.N., and with him was associated Captain (now Sir Allen) Young, then of the mercantile marine, who was an enthusiast for Arctic exploration, and who had not only subscribed handsomely to the expedition, but had actually abandoned a lucrative appointment to accept a subordinate post in it. Thus manned and provisioned this little yacht of 170 tons went forth to achieve a work which had baffled the efforts of many powerful ships of the navy, with all the resources of a great maritime department at their backs.

The Fox was punctually got ready for sea by the day fixed, and two days before that date Lady Franklin wrote to her captain what he described as 'the only written instruction he could ever prevail upon her to give him,' in the following admirable letter :—

My dear Captain McClintock,—You have kindly invited me to give you 'Instructions,' but I cannot bring myself to feel that it would be right in any way to influence your judgment in the conduct of your noble undertaking ; and, indeed, I have no temptation to do so, since it appears to me that your views are almost identical with those which I had independently formed before I became thoroughly possessed of yours. But had this been otherwise, I trust you would have found me ready to prove the implicit confidence I place in you by yielding my own views to your more enlightened judgment ; knowing, too, as I do, that your whole heart also is in the cause, even as my own is. As to the objects of the expedition and their relative importance, I am sure you know that the rescue of any possible survivor of the Erebus and Terror would be to me, as it would be to you, the noblest result of our efforts.

To this object I would wish every other to be subordinate ; and next to it in importance is the recovery of the unspeakably precious documents of the expedition, public and private, and the personal relics of my dear husband and his companions.

And, lastly, I trust it may be in your power to confirm directly or inferentially the claim of my husband's expedition to the earliest discovery of the passage which, if Dr. Rae's report be true (and the Government of our country has already accepted and rewarded it as such), these martyrs in a noble cause achieved at their last extremity after five long years of labour and suffering, if not at an earlier period.

I am sure you will do all that man can do for the attainment of all these objects ; my only fear is that you may spend yourselves too much in the effort, and you must, therefore, let me tell you how much dearer to me even than them is the preservation of the valuable lives of the little band of heroes who are your companions and followers.

May God in His great mercy preserve you all from harm amid the labours and perils which await you, and restore you to us in health and safety as well as in honour ! As to the honour, I can have *no* misgiving. It will be yours as much if you fail (since you *may* fail in spite of every effort) as if you succeed ; and be assured that under *any and all circumstances whatever*, such is my unbounded confidence in you, you will possess and be entitled to the enduring gratitude of your sincere and attached friend,

JANE FRANKLIN.

The first year's voyage of the gallant little yacht was unfortunate. All went well till she reached Melville Bay ;

but, in attempting to cross it, she found her way blocked by large masses of ice, though it was still but mid-August, and in a few days she was fast beset—and McClintock had to face the grim prospect of passing the very first winter of the expedition in the pack. For no less a period than 242 days the Fox was frozen fast, and drifted helplessly to the southward for nearly 1,200 geographical miles. It was not till April 25, 1858, that she was released from the grasp of the ice, and, again pushing northward, succeeded this time in crossing the bay and effecting an entrance into Lancaster Sound.

Beechey Island was their first destination, and this they reached in the month of August, bringing with them a marble tablet, which had been sent out by Lady Franklin with an American search party for erection at the first winter quarters of her husband's expedition, but which the Americans, prevented by circumstances from executing their mission, had been obliged to bring back with them and deposit at Godhavn in Disco. The inscription is as follows :—

TO THE MEMORY OF
FRANKLIN
CROZIER, FITZJAMES
AND ALL THEIR
GALLANT BROTHER OFFICERS AND FAITHFUL
COMPANIONS WHO HAVE SUFFERED AND PERISHED
IN THE CAUSE OF SCIENCE AND
THE SERVICE OF THEIR COUNTRY
THIS TABLET
IS ERECTED NEAR THE SPOT WHERE
THEY PASSED THEIR FIRST ARCTIC
WINTER, AND WHENCE THEY ISSUED
FORTH, TO CONQUER DIFFICULTIES OR
TO DIE
TO COMMEMORATE THE GRIEF OF THEIR
ADMIRING COUNTRYMEN AND FRIENDS
AND THE ANGUISH SUBDUED BY FAITH
OF HER WHO HAS LOST, IN THE HEROIC
LEADER OF THE EXPEDITION, THE MOST
DEVOTED AND AFFECTIONATE OF
HUSBANDS

'And so He bringeth them unto the
Haven where they would be'
1855

This tablet Captain McClintock duly erected 'upon the raised flagged square in the centre of which stands the cenotaph recording the names of those who perished in the Government expedition under Sir Edward Belcher.'

Quitting Beechey Island in the middle of August, McClintock entered Peel Sound, but only to find, after steaming down it for some five-and-twenty miles, that his way was impassably blocked by ice. He was accordingly forced to retrace his course to Barrow Strait, and to try a southward route by Prince Regent Inlet instead of that by way of Peel Sound. Down this new channel they accordingly proceeded, and, after a perilous adventure in the floating ice, which came near to dashing her on the rocks, the little yacht succeeded in making her way westward through Bellot Strait, and was, at the end of September, 1858, laid up snugly enough in winter quarters at Port Kennedy—a haven lighted upon by McClintock at the eastern end of the strait, and named by him after the original discoverers of the waterway.

The winter was spent in making arrangements for the thorough exploration of the coast of Boothia as the first work of the following spring. It was a winter of extraordinary severity, the thermometer ranging on Christmas Day from 76° to 80° below freezing-point, and the mean temperature for the month of December being as low as −33°—only 6° above the freezing-point of mercury. In January and February the weather still continued abnormally cold, even for these regions; but on the 17th of the latter month it was thought to have sufficiently moderated to allow of the expedition's starting out, and on that day McClintock and his sledge party set out for Cape Victoria.

Early in March they reached an Eskimo village, from the inhabitants of which they obtained some news and several relics of the lost expedition. Among the latter were some spoons and forks, a silver medal, part of a gold chain, several buttons, and knives made of the iron and wood of the wreck, as well as bows and arrows fashioned out of material obtained from the same source.

None of the Eskimo had seen any of the expedition, though one averred that he had 'seen their bones upon the island where they died.' He was understood to say that the boat was crushed by the ice. On the following day, however, more definite information was obtained. An Eskimo from whom they bought a spear told their interpreter distinctly that 'a ship having three masts had been crushed by the ice out in the sea to the west of King William Island; but that all the people landed safely; he was not one of those who were eyewitnesses of it; the ship sank, so nothing was obtained by the natives from her; all that they have got,' he said, 'came from an island in the river.' The spear staff appeared to have been made from the gunwale of a light boat. This information substantially bore out the reports of Dr. Rae, and accounted for the disappearance of one of the ships; but it gave no clue to the whereabouts of the other, nor to the direction whence they came. One thing, however, it rendered tolerably certain, namely, that the crews did not at any time land on the shore of Boothia.

McClintock now returned to the yacht, having in his twenty-five days' journey travelled 420 English miles and completed the discovery of the coast line of continental America, adding thereby 120 miles to our charts. On reaching the Fox he assembled his little crew and acquainted them with the results of his expedition, went on to point out that there still remained one of the ships unaccounted for, and that, therefore, it was necessary to carry out all the projected lines of search.

On April 2 McClintock and Lieutenant Hobson started off again, upon what, in the case of the latter officer, was to be the eventful journey of the expedition. King William Island, practically the only land not yet examined in which search seemed at all likely to be rewarded, was the object in view. By the end of the month they had reached Cape Victoria, where they separated, Hobson marching direct for Cape Felix, while McClintock kept on a more southerly course. Though less important as regards its 'finds' than that of his comrade (to whom, indeed, he is understood to have generously yielded the most promising field of search with a view to procuring him his promotion), McClintock's journey was far from being fruitless. In the course of it he succeeded in acquiring many relics of the Franklin party, and covering, as he did, the whole of the west shore of King William Island, and making his way thence to the ice at the entrance of the Great Fish River, he had the satisfaction of knowing that he had traversed the whole route taken by Franklin's unfortunate followers, and that, had they left behind them any cairn or other record of their passage, he could not have failed to discover them. Montreal Island having been carefully examined, McClintock crossed over to the mainland in the neighbourhood of Point Duncan, and on May 19 set out on his return journey.

It seemed then as though it were vain to hope for the discovery of any traces of the missing men themselves. McClintock had already satisfied himself, from his interrogation of the Eskimos, that the wreck of one of the ships, or rather its last fragments, might still be seen at a point off the west coast of King William Island, but nearly all of it had been carried off by the natives, and it was probable that the five days' journey necessary to reach it would not be adequately repaid. Still, it was evident that nothing was to be gained by pushing further to the south, and the only course open to McClintock was to retrace his steps. Regaining the shore of Simpson Strait some miles to the west of Point Richardson, the party crossed over to King William Island, and took their way along the south coast, making for Cape Herschel. Here their first grim discovery awaited them.

We were now upon the shore, along which the retreating crews must have marched. My sledges, of course, travelled upon the sea-ice close along the shore; and although the depth of snow which covered the beach deprived us of almost every hope, yet we kept a very sharp look-out for traces, nor were we unsuccessful. Shortly after midnight of May 25, when slowly walking along a gravel ridge near the beach which the winds kept partially bare of snow, I came upon a human skeleton, partly exposed, with here and there a few fragments of clothing appearing through the snow. The skeleton—now perfectly bleached—was lying upon its face, the limbs and smaller bones either dissevered or gnawed away by small animals.

A most careful examination of the spot was, of course, made, the snow removed and every scrap of clothing gathered up. A pocket-book afforded strong grounds for hope that some information might be subsequently obtained respecting the unfortunate crews and the calamitous march of the lost crews, but at the time it was frozen hard.

It was brought home to England and every effort made to decipher the letters found in it ; but only a few detached sentences could be made out, and these not referring to the proceedings of the expedition.

The victim was a young man, slightly built and perhaps above the common height ; the dress appeared to be that of a steward or officer's servant, the loose bow-knot in which his neck handkerchief was tied not being used by seamen or officers. In every particular the dress confirmed our conjectures as to his rank or office in the late expedition—the blue jacket with slashed sleeves and braided edging, and the pilot cloth greatcoat with plain covered buttons. We also found a clothes brush near and a horn pocket-comb. This poor man seems to have selected the bare ridge top as affording the least tiresome walking, and to have fallen upon his face in the position in which we found him.

A melancholy commentary on the words of the old Eskimo woman, 'They fell down and died as they walked along.' The cairn erected by Simpson in 1839 at Cape Herschel was then inspected ; but though McClintock was then and afterwards convinced that the doomed men had left some record, he found nothing, and he believes—a belief confirmed by the displacement noticeable in the stones of the cairn—that the deposit, whatever it was, had been removed by the Eskimos. Twelve miles beyond Cape Herschel he was met by the joyful intelligence that, thanks to the keen eyes and good fortune of his comrade, their mission had attained its end—the discovery of a written record under the hand of the lost. Beneath a cairn which Hobson had erected as its depository, McClintock found a paper left for him by his comrade, informing him of the discovery of Graham Gore's record at Point Victory, the contents of which have already been set out. Its importance, of course, could hardly be overestimated ; for not only did it virtually confirm the reports received from the Eskimos as to the fate of the expedition, but it fixed the precise date and place of Sir John Franklin's death, and conveyed to his widow the melancholy consolation of the assurance that he had been mercifully spared the long-drawn agony which his surviving comrades must have endured.

Lieutenant Hobson's note contained the further information that he had found quantities of clothing and articles of all kinds lying about the cairn, as if the unhappy men, aware that they were retreating for their lives, had there abandoned everything which they considered superfluous.

On May 29 McClintock and his party reached the westernmost point of King William Island, which he named after Captain Crozier. Thence the coast line was found to turn sharply away to the eastward, and, following it, the party encamped early on the morning of May 30 alongside a large boat, another sad relic of the expedition, which Hobson had found and examined a few days before ; but he had failed to discover record, journal, pocket-book, or memorandum of any description. This boat, which was mounted on a sledge of unusual weight and strength, McClintock afterwards carefully examined, but for the moment they were in no mood for minute observation, 'for there was that in the boat which transfixed us with awe.' It contained portions of two human skeletons.

One was that of a slight young person, the other of a large, strongly made, middle-aged man. The former was found in the bow of the boat, but in too disturbed a state to enable Hobson to judge whether the sufferer had died there. Large and powerful animals, probably wolves, had destroyed much of the skeleton, which may have been that of an officer. Near it we found the fragment of a pair of worked slippers . . . the lines white with a red margin ; the spaces red, white, and yellow. They had originally been eleven inches long, lined with calfskin with the hair left on, and the edges bound with red silk ribbon. Besides these slippers there were a pair of small, strong shooting half-boots. The other skeleton was in a more perfect state, and was enveloped with clothes and furs ; it lay across the boat under the after thwart. Close beside it were found five watches, two double-barrelled guns, one barrel in each loaded and cocked, standing muzzle upwards towards the boat's side. It may be imagined with what deep interest these sad relics were scrutinised, and how anxiously every fragment of clothing was turned over in search of pockets and pocket-books, journals, or even names. Five or six small books were found, all of them scriptural or devotional works, except the 'Vicar of Wakefield.' One little book, 'Christian Melodies,' bore an inscription on the title-page, from the donor to G. G. (Graham Gore?). A small Bible contained numerous marginal notes, and whole passages underlined. Besides these books, the covers of a New Testament and Prayer Book were found.

Unhappily, too, the boat contained ominous evidences of that terrible overloading of the sledges, which Sherard Osborn had had cause to suspect from the signs discovered by him at Beechey Island. Among an amazing quantity of clothing and toilet articles, McClintock found 'twine, nails, saws, files, bristles, waxends, sailmakers' palms, powder, bullets, shot, cartridges, wads, leather cartridge-cases, knives —clasp and dinner ones—needle and thread cases, slow match, several bayonet scabbards cut down into knife sheaths, two rolls of sheet lead, and, in short, a quantity of articles of one description and another truly astonishing in variety, and such as, for the most part, modern sledge travellers in these regions would consider a mere accumulation of dead weight, but slightly useful and very likely to break down the strength of the sledge crews.'

The only provisions found in the boat were a small quantity of tea and nearly forty pounds of chocolate. These articles alone would, of course, have been insufficient to support life in an Arctic temperature ; but neither biscuit nor meat of any kind was found. There was, however, no lack of fuel, for a drift tree was lying on the beach close at hand, where it had probably lain for twenty or thirty years. In the after part of the boat were discovered a number of spoons and forks marked with the initials or crests of various officers of the expedition, eight of them bearing the crest of Sir John Franklin, and having been probably, McClintock conjectures, issued to the men, as the only means of saving them, as relics of the lost commander. No doubt, indeed, the other officers did the same with their own plate, as not a single iron spoon such as sailors always use was found.

The most surprising thing to the discoverers was the position of the sledge on which the boat was cradled. It was turned towards the N.E., or in the reverse direction to the line of retreat. The spot at which it was discovered was about 50 miles as a sledge would travel from Point Victory, and therefore 65 miles from the position of the abandoned ships. On the other hand, it was 70 miles from the skeleton of the steward and 150 miles from Montreal Island, the limit of McClintock's southward search. Moreover, it was in the depth of a wide bay, where, by crossing over 10 or 12 miles of very low land, instead of following the indentation of the coast, a saving of some 40 miles would be effected.

A little reflection led me to satisfy my own mind, at least, that the boat was returning to the ship ; and in no other way can I account for two men having been left in her, than by supposing the party were unable to drag the boat further, and that these two men, not being able to keep pace with their shipmates, were therefore left by them, supplied with such provisions as could be spared to last until the return of the others from the ship with a fresh stock.

Whether it was the intention of the retroceding party to await the result of another season in the ships, or to follow the track of the main body to the Great Fish River, is more a matter of conjecture. It seems highly probable that they had purposed revisiting the boat, not only on account of the two men left in charge of it, but also to obtain the chocolate, the five watches, and many other articles which would otherwise scarcely have been left in her.

The same reasons which may be assigned for the return of the detachment from the main body will also serve to account for their not having come back to their boat. In both instances they appear to have greatly overrated their strength and the distance they could travel in a given time.

Whether all or any of the remainder of this detached party ever reached their ships is uncertain. It seems clear, at any rate, that none of them returned to the boat, or other skeletons would have been discovered in the neighbourhood ; and if the Eskimos spoke the truth in declaring that but one human body was found on board the ship that drifted on shore, the inference is that the remainder of the sledge party, probably some twenty or thirty men, must have perished in the attempt to traverse those fifty miles of land

which lay between them and the ships, and that the Arctic
wolves had left no trace of their remains.

A duplicate of Gore's record, deposited in 1847, was found
by Lieutenant Hobson on the south side of Back Bay ; that is,
on the opposite shore of the inlet to that in which the former
—for, being at a point somewhat nearer the place in which
the ships were beset, we may suppose it to have been the
earlier deposit of the two—was discovered. It of course adds
nothing to our information, and is only interesting as showing
the same mistake as its companion paper with reference to
the year in which the Erebus and Terror wintered at Beechey
Island.   Both papers had evidently been filled in and sealed
up at the same time, and that this was before Graham Gore
left the ships is to be inferred from the fact that neither
seems to have originally borne any entry of the date at
which they were *deposited*. When, the year afterward, the
record was opened by the retreating party, this date, May
28, was filled in by Captain Fitzjames, as may be gathered
from the colour of the ink, which resembles that of Fitzjames's marginal additions and not that of Graham Gore's
original entries.   The ascertainment of this point has an
importance which McClintock hardly seems to have attached
to it when he composed his narrative ; for, incidentally, it
proves that Graham Gore's party, or some of them, made
their way back safely to the ships with the news, as we may
fairly assume, of their having sighted the wished-for shores
and waters.   This would not have been proved by the mere
circumstance that Crozier and Fitzjames seem to have known
the whereabouts of Gore's record, for it might have been
arranged before he started that a cairn should be erected
and a record left on the first point of land which he reached
after traversing the ice-pack.   But it would have been impossible for the shipmates whom Gore and his party left
behind them to have known the exact date at which they
reached Point Victory, unless some of them had returned
with a full report of their journey and its results.

The two papers had been soldered up in tin cylinders, but
when discovered they were already much damaged by rust,

and in a very few years would have been illegible. The
cylinder opened by Fitzjames to get at the paper within and
add to it the information which gives it its principal value,
had not been soldered up again. Probably the retreating
party had not the means of doing so. It was found on the
ground among some loose stones which had evidently fallen
from the top of the cairn. Its preservation under the circumstances was providential. Indeed, its very existence is
a matter for congratulation, for it does not seem to have
been intended, in McClintock's opinion, that any record at all
should be deposited after the abandonment of the ships ; and
our gratitude to the men who left it 'ought,' he adds, 'to be
all the greater when we remember that the ink had to be
thawed, and that writing in a tent during an April day in the
Arctic regions is by no means an easy task.'

A great quantity and variety of things lay strewn about
the cairn, in further lamentable testimony to the disastrous
overloading of the party—articles such as it had evidently
been found impossible to carry further than the short distance
of fifteen miles, which was all that the party had then covered.
'Among these were four heavy sets of boat's cooking stoves,
pickaxes, shovels, iron hoops, old canvas, a large single block,
about four feet of a copper lightning rod, long pieces of
hollow brass curtain rods, a small case of selected medicines
containing about twenty-four phials, the contents in a wonderful state of preservation,' and certain nautical and magnetic instruments. The clothing left by the party formed
'a huge heap four feet high ; every article was searched, but
the pockets were empty and not one of all these articles was
marked.'

Two other cairns and many relics were found by Hobson
to the north of this position, and though throwing no further
direct light on the fate of the expedition, they were indirectly
valuable as showing that no part of the coast between Cape
Felix and Cape Crozier had been visited by Eskimos since
the landing of the crews in 1848. None of the cairns had
been disturbed, nor had any of the numerous articles strewn
about, which would be invaluable to the natives, been touched.

Hence it may be confidently inferred that the evidence
of the Eskimos as to 'the white men falling and dying as
they walked along' applies only to the shore line southward and eastward from Cape Crozier, where, of course, no
traces of them were permitted by these eyewitnesses of their
death to remain. 'It is not probable that such fearful
mortality would have overtaken them so early in their march
as within eighty miles by sledge route from the abandoned
ships—such being their distance from Cape Crozier ; nor is it
probable that we could have passed the wreck had she existed
there, as there are no off-lying islands to prevent a ship
drifting in upon the beach, while to the southward they are
very numerous, so much so that a drifting ship could hardly
run the gauntlet between them so as to reach the shore.'

McClintock's mission was now fully accomplished. He
had set at rest all doubts as to the fate of the expedition ; he
had obtained for the widow of its gallant commander the
conclusive evidence so long sought, so passionately yet
patiently striven for, of the time and manner of her husband's
death ; and, finally, he had brought back with him what she
hardly less valued, definitive proof that Franklin and his
companions were actually the first to discover, though not to
accomplish in their ships, the passage from the Atlantic to
the Pacific Ocean. The bows of the gallant little Fox might
now be turned homeward ; her two years' battle with the
Arctic seas was over, and she would winter in more hospitable
waters.

By the end of July they had reached Godhavn on their
southward journey, where letters from England reached
them. Lady Franklin and Miss Cracroft had both written
to Captain McClintock in the previous March. They had
travelled, as he remarks, even 'more than we have, having
visited almost all the countries bordering the Mediterranean
and Black Seas, posted through the Crimea, and steamed up
the Danube.' Nineteen days later McClintock landed at
Portsmouth and reported himself to the Admiralty. The
Arctic medal was presented to such of the crew as had not

already received it for Arctic service. A month later the
commander of the expedition received the official acknowledgment from the Admiralty of 'the important services'
performed by him 'in bringing home the only authentic
intelligence of the death of the late Sir John Franklin, and
of the fate of the crews of the Erebus and Terror.' And in
the year following, Her Majesty, by conferring upon Captain
McClintock the honour of knighthood, which the gallant
officer still lives to enjoy, expressed her just appreciation of
what was not the least brilliant of those Arctic exploits which
have added lustre to her reign.

CHAPTER XXIV

A DEVOTED WIDOWHOOD

1859-1875

LADY FRANKLIN'S task was done. The self-imposed duty to which she had devoted so many long years of yearning, and of the heart-sickness of hope deferred, was at last accomplished. Few, save herself, had been found to believe, during the latter part of the period, that it was possible. There was proof enough, thought the world in general, that her gallant husband and his companions were all dead. Had not authentic and unmistakable relics of the ill-fated band been brought home by Dr. Rae, including some at least, such as Franklin's own decorations of honour, which it was certain that their owner would never have parted with while life remained. What more was needed? Was it proof of the time and manner of that death of which only the bare fact had been established? But such proof might never have existed at all. Circumstances might have prevented the lost explorers from leaving behind them any record of their adventures, or of the deaths by which their party had been thinned. Even if they had done so, how shadowy was the hope that that record was still in existence! Why should not the wandering Eskimos, into whose hands all the other relics had fallen, have obtained possession of this also? And if they had, was it not certain that they would have destroyed it or thrown it away as worthless? Was there any use in spending more and more money and risking more and more valuable lives in so visionary a chase?

So spoke, of course, the world of 'common-sense,' and in tones which naturally gained in decision and emphasis with

E E

every year that passed, especially after Dr. Rae's discoveries
had satisfied every one of the fact of death.   There was
nothing to oppose to it but the love, the devotion, the unquenchable faith of one solitary woman. She had clung long
after others had abandoned it to the belief that her husband
was still living ; and when this hope was abandoned, and she
had, as we have seen, to appeal to the Government in the
avowed character of Sir John Franklin's ' widow,' she was
then to cling with equal tenacity to the conviction, long re-
linquished by others, that somewhere, beneath some undiscovered cairn on the frozen coasts of Arctic America, lay the
precious record of the lost.

The passionate embrace in which she clasped and held to
her heart the faith that her husband was still living, when few
doubted that he was dead, *is most pathetically illustrated in*
the letters she has left behind. The commander of every
search expedition which left our shores between 1848 and
1853, carried one or other of these letters with him, sometimes containing an enclosure from her niece, Miss Cracroft,
always bearing messages of love and hope from her step-
daughter. Time after time they were returned to her, even
as the north wind might have blown back the forlorn cry of
the bereaved ; but they were preserved with sacred care.
The same original was often re-copied and sent out in substantially identical terms a second and a third time, and the
very reiteration of the same utterances of love, and longing,
and resignation is unspeakably sad. The first of these letters,
dated May 8 and 9, 1848, lies now before me, the wrapper
which originally enclosed it bearing the superscription, to
' Captain Sir John Franklin, R.N. : H.M.S. Erebus. To the
care of Sir James Ross.' This went with the first search
expedition that was sent out, and, written at a *time* when, of
course, there was still good ground for hope that Franklin
might be still living, its dominant note is one of pain at the
thought of the suffering which he might then, it was thought,
be actually enduring, but from which, as we know, he had
been released eleven months before. ' May it,' writes the
unconscious widow—

may it be the will of God, if you are not restored to us earlier, that you should open this letter, and that it may give you comfort in all your trials. I feel sure that you must all have suffered much, and perhaps, when you are met with, it may be in a state of great exhaustion, and your numbers even may be diminished, and many a bitter trial you may have had to bear. May you have found your refuge and strength in Him whose mercies you have so often experienced when every human aid was gone. If the prayers of all who love you have availed with that merciful God whose ear is ever open to the cry of all who trust to Him, you will yet be spared to us. But we know that His ways are not always such as we can adore without the subjection of many human feelings to the exercise of the humblest and deepest faith. I try to prepare myself for every trial which may be in store for me ; but, dearest, if you ever open this, it will be, I trust, because I have been spared the greatest of all. Next to you I think of dear Captain Crozier. I trust you have never been forced to separate, and that you have been a mutual comfort to each other. . . . We have not had any serious uneasiness about you till lately. I felt sure you *meant* to have returned last autumn, though your letter to me from Disco contemplated the possibility—at least the words were capable of this interpretation—of staying out a third winter, and everybody thinks you would not return till forced by the want of provisions. Sir James Ross thinks you have been sent by your instructions to a part where you could hardly fail of being inextricably entangled in the ice, somewhere about 73° N. and 105° W. Indeed, I believe he thinks you can never unassisted get out of it.

Here, it should be noted, are traces of that singular misconception of Franklin's intended route which for so long led the search parties astray, and through which so much invaluable time was lost. Longitude 105° W. is some seven or eight degrees west of the point at which Franklin turned to the southward, and is thus far nearer to Melville Island and that part of the Arctic Ocean which Franklin— it must, or should, have been well known to Ross and all other commanders of searching parties—had been expressly counselled to avoid.

Lady Franklin goes on to speak of her stepdaughter Eleanor's approaching marriage to Mr. Gell; of Sir John Richardson, then about to marry a third wife; of the preparations for Sir James Ross's departure on the search expedition, and many matters relating to friends and family which she thought would interest her long absent husband. She concludes :—

God bless you, my own dearest love. How ardently we pray for you you will not doubt. It was settled between us and the Bishop of Tasmania, who has lately left us, that on July 16 next prayers should be put up in Van Diemen's Land in every church and chapel for you and all the expedition. It would have been a less trial to me to come after you, as I was at one time tempted to do, but I thought it my duty and my interest to remain ; for might I not have missed you, and would it have been right to leave Eleanor ? Yet, if I had thought you to be ill, nothing should have stopped me. God bless you again. You will be welcomed back with joy and honour by your friends and family and country, most of all by your affectionate and devoted wife.

In May 1850 the substance of the letter went out a second time to the Arctic seas by the hand of the veteran Sir John Ross, who had, as he put it, 'given his word,' and had 'publicly stated that he would come to look for Franklin' if he was absent longer than three years. By this time even Lady Franklin could no longer believe that the explorers were still on board their ships.

We are all prepared to hear that you have been forced to abandon them, or that one of them is lost. If you are only restored to us in any way, enfeebled as you may be, I shall bless God for the mercy. If you live to read this and receive my fondest blessing, I will thank Him still. I desire nothing but to cherish the remainder of your days, however injured and broken your health may be, but in all cases I will strive to bow to the Almighty will and trust in His mercy for reunion in a better world.

The letter came back to the writer in the following year ; but ere it reached her the expiring flame of hope had been rekindled in her bosom by the discoveries at Beechey Island, and she despatched it again in 1851 under cover with the following :—

The enclosed letter was brought back to me this autumn by Sir John Ross on his return from Lancaster Sound. To our extreme disappointment all the ships sent out in search of you by the Government returned also. These included four under Captain Austen, and two, called the Lady Franklin and the Sophia, under Captain Penny, the whaling captain. Captain Austen during last spring sent off travelling parties to Melville Island (where *I* felt sure you would not be found, at least on the south side) and also south-west of Cape Walker, where they judged no ship could ever have passed.   Captain Penny took another direction and went up Wellington [Channel] with sledges, and convinced himself you had gone that way in open water.   They all had previously found your winter quarters in 1845-6 at Beechey Island.   Penny had not materials to pursue his search another year, so returned home this autumn as well as the rest, and now another expedition is to start in the spring to pursue the course through Wellington Channel.   The little 'Prince Albert' private expedition is attempting to reach James Ross Strait and Simpson Strait to search for you in that direction.

This was the expedition under Mr. Kennedy, which resulted in the discovery of Bellot Strait.

On the other, the Behring Strait, side, Captain Collinson and Captain McClure have passed through Behring Strait eastward towards Melville Island, but I fear in too low a latitude to fall in with you and too near the coast of America to be able to get along.

Lastly, the bearer of this letter, Lieutenant Pim, R.N., has gone out alone, supported by the Russian authorities, to seek for you on the north and east coasts of Siberia and the islands to the north, where, if God in His great mercy should bless his endeavours, you may open this letter full of consolation and joy to your broken-down and suffering heart.   I hope you have never for a moment thought that your country had forgotten you or left you to your fate.   You have felt sure that *I* could never rest till we had some tidings of you.   It is my mission upon earth, my heart's sole thought, the one only object and occupation of all my faculties and energies.   Dearest husband, I live only for you.

Eleanor and her husband are going on well in the same position in London. . . .

Sophy lives almost constantly with me and is to me as a daughter; without her aid I should never have been able to get through the work which God has assigned me, that of striving for your rescue.

Again in 1852, and yet again in 1853, this pathetic letter from the living to the dead went forth upon its fruitless quest, to return again and yet again to its writer.   In 1854 Dr. Rae came back with the relics obtained from the Eskimo, and then at last Lady Franklin ceased to write.   That brave and stubborn faith, the nobler through its very unreason, with which for eight long years she had clung to the belief in her husband's survival, had broken down at last.   Thenceforward

she seems to have spoken of herself as the 'widow,' and no
longer as the 'wife' of the illustrious explorer; but the
energies which had been so untiringly exerted heretofore in
the attempt to rescue were not relaxed, but simply diverted
into another channel, and she strove, as has been seen, with
a no less heroic resolution to obtain proof of the time and
manner of her husband's death. The story of her faithful and
unresting labours has an eloquence of its own, to which these
letters can add but little; and if, therefore, though almost
too sacred for the public eye, they are for the first time
printed here, it is much more on account of their pro-
foundly touching interest than with any idea that their
publication is necessary to put the tongue of malignant gossip
to shame and silence.

In this connection, and as evidence of the feeling with
which Lady Franklin was regarded by that kinswoman of
her husband's, who was her constant companion and confidante,
and had better opportunities than any other human being of
correctly estimating the depth of her conjugal affection, the
following letter from Miss Cracroft should here be added. It
was written for consignment to the search party sent out in
1850 by Mr. Grinnell.

My dearest Uncle,—If this reaches you it will be given by our
American friends, for friends we must call any who aid in restoring
you to us in safety. It is believed to be without a precedent that a
nation should send forth an expedition to rescue from danger
and from death the people of another, and that this noble instance of liberality, this glorious example is afforded, is due to my
dearest aunt. You will find that she is spoken of with great
enthusiasm by the Americans, and well may it be so, for she has moved
them to do great things. Last year she wrote a letter to the
President, and received a reply calculated to excite not only admiration but the strongest hopes that the Government would immediately
send out an expedition to seek for you. This letter and the reply
was republished from the American papers into our own and it (my
aunt's) was spoken of in the House of Commons by Sir Robert
Inglis as the most admirable letter ever addressed by man or woman
to man or woman. It has everywhere excited the deepest sympathy
and admiration. Unhappily, last year the American Government
were unable to fulfil their benevolent intentions, Congress was not

then sitting and it was besides (in April) too late to begin preparations, no vessels fitted for the service being obtainable.

Meanwhile my aunt kept up frequent communications with the United States, and particularly with a Mr. Silas Burrows, who formed our acquaintance in England last summer. Her letters to himself were seen by Mr. Henry Grinnell, of New York, one of the merchant princes of that city, and so strongly influenced his mind that he proposed heading a subscription for fitting out a private expedition with 5,000 dollars. Soon after he raised it to 10,000 dollars, and, upon seeing my aunt's next following letter, within a fortnight after the first I have alluded to, he made his contribution 15,000 dollars. Upon hearing of his first donation my aunt wrote to thank him for it, and when he read this letter he immediately augmented her contribution to the splendid gift of 30,000 dollars, selected his vessel and his officers who belong to the United States navy, and, with probably some assistance, will send them off early in May in search of you.

You must not suppose that my aunt has attained this wonderful result by using entreaties or by beseeching help. It has been accomplished by the force of dignity, simplicity, and earnestness, united to a most extraordinary extent in herself.

And to these qualities may in very great degree be attributed the universal sympathy now experienced in England, for there is not a woman in the kingdom so universally honoured and esteemed as your wife. I cannot express to you how entirely I honour and love her, and to be permitted to endeavour to comfort her and share her sorrow is a privilege which I value above every other. Her devotedness, her perseverance, and entire acquaintance with every part of the question of search for you, combined with her extraordinary mental endowments, have given her an influence which is really wonderful, and of which people in general see only the results. It is only for one who, like myself, has witnessed her efforts, to recognise and appreciate them, though there are some who do so nearly to the utmost, and these are your nearest and dearest friends. Full and complete indeed will be her reward if you are restored to her in safety, compensation even for all she has suffered.

Not much more remains to be written of this brave and devoted life, despite the length of years from this date to which it was yet to run. For it was one long dedication to Franklin's memory, and its history would resolve itself, so far as the purposes of this narrative are concerned, into a record of daily solicitude and effort for the preservation of that memory to the world. Assisted in this task by Miss Cracroft, the attached and faithful companion of her closing years, whose love and admiration for her found such eloquent expression in the letter given above, Lady Franklin spent the remainder of her life in the diligent collection of those materials for a memoir of her husband which have been employed for the purposes of this volume. In this mass of epistolary and other matter, numbering more than two thousand documents of various descriptions, is included all the correspondence, not only of, but with, her husband of which Lady Franklin could obtain originals or copies. Every scrap of written paper which had felt the touch of his hand, and which bore, even in the remotest degree, on the incidents or interests of his life, was carefully treasured up, often, it is evident, as a relic rather than a document. His various commissions in the navy, the official instruments attesting the successive honours conferred upon him, the roughest drafts of his memoranda as commander of ships or leader of expeditions, the maps and plans employed by him on his voyages and journeyings, the note-books, diaries, letter-books, and what not, to which he, the most regular and laborious of chroniclers, committed a record of the discharged duties or the encountered dangers of the day—everything, down even to his ' reader's ticket ' at the British Museum, and, as we have seen, the card of invitation to the ball on board that ship in which he was to die, has been religiously preserved. The papers relating to his midshipman days on board the Polyphemus and the Bellerophon are, of course, the fewest in number, and equally of course belong in most instances to the class of relics, rather than of _mémoires pour servir_, but their human interest is often none the less for that, and the tender light which is thrown on the nature of her who preserved them by (for instance) the worn and faded, but carefully arranged and labelled, packet of papers which now lies before me inscribed with the words, ' Sir John Franklin's French Exercises,' gives them a value of their own.

Nor was the diligent collector of these records less solicitous for the perpetuation of her husband's memory in other ways. Everything which appeared in any public form about him was regularly read and became the subject of her comment or correction. She was especially interested in the biographical accounts of her husband which appeared from time to time in various publications, one of which was contributed by his old friend Sir John Richardson to the eighth edition of the 'Encyclopædia Britannica,' and she interested herself earnestly in the proposal of Franklin's Lincolnshire fellow-citizens to erect a statue in his honour.

'I read with deep emotion of the disinterested honour proposed to be paid by the City of Lincoln,' she writes, addressing the town clerk of that municipality, 'to the memory of my dear husband, and I hope I may be permitted, without intruding myself too much on your attention, to express the gratitude I feel at the generous expression of your esteem for your departed countryman. Had that humble-minded but heroic man ever contemplated any higher reward in his hard career of service than the consciousness of having fulfilled his duty to the utmost, he would have desired no higher honour than the tribute you dedicate to him and to those beloved companions of his toil and danger whose honour and interests he ever identified with his own.

I strive to think that, though these martyrs in their country's service knew not of the fraternal hands that were stretched out to save them, they yet must have felt assured, living and dying, that their memories would be embalmed in the hearts of their country-men, and that whether the discovery which they sealed in death were ever revealed to the world or not, yet that their name would be inscribed among those which will never be forgotten.

Again I thank you for thus realising, and more than realising, the dreams which perhaps helped to fill their dying hours. It will be to the lasting honour of the county of my beloved husband's birth that it originated the generous movement which I trust will spread as widely as you kindly contemplate. May I beg the favour of you to convey to those gentlemen who, with you, have originated or are co-operating in it, my grateful sentiments?

Yet how her sorrow for her husband was tempered by pride in his achievements, and in what a spirit, worthy of ancient times, she could still bring herself to look upon that national work which had cost her all that was dearest to her in the world, is well seen from the letter she wrote to Sir Roderick Murchison, when projects of Polar exploration were again afoot in 1865.

Although I have little doubt you know from some of our friends that they have written to me on the subject of the expedition, yet I cannot leave it to them alone to tell you how very deeply I sympathise with the proposed effort, and how earnestly I wish it may be realised. For the credit and honour of England the exploration of the North Pole should not be left to any other country. . . .

I am sending you these lines because I do not wish you to think it possible that my interest can flag in anything connected with Arctic enterprise ; and though at first sad memories of the past made me feel some sickness of heart at the revival of the question, I have struggled against that weakness and overcome it. . . . It would indeed be unreasonable and much to be deplored if the fate of my dear husband and his companions were to be made an official objection to Arctic exploration. *They* met with the unhappy end which has often befallen the pioneers of tentative and dangerous enterprises, but they rest alone in their awful calamity. Every succeeding expedition sailed with better ships, better equipments, better charts, better supports, and with ever-increasing knowledge ; and thus it has happened that no naval service on the face of the globe exhibits on the average so few casualties as that in the Polar Seas. You have justly said that ' in the proposed expedition no such calamity can be dreaded, *for it has no analogy to the case of Franklin.*'

The project of erecting a memorial to the great explorer in his native county was not unfittingly modified by the substitution of his actual birthplace for the City of Lincoln as the site of the proposed statue ; and in the market square of Spilsby it was duly erected, and now stands. A local tribute of honour, however, would have been a wholly inadequate recognition of a fame which was world-wide, and it would have been a shame to England if one who had added lustre to her name had been left without any token of her gratitude visible among the monuments of her capital.

This national duty was at last fulfilled. A sum of 2,000*l.* was voted by Parliament for the erection of that monument which now stands in Waterloo Place to the memory of ' the great navigator and his brave companions who sacrificed their lives in completing the discovery of the North-West Passage, A.D. 1847–1848.'

Lady Franklin felt, however, that the fame and services of her husband were entitled to record in that national shrine in which it has always been the ambition of the noblest Englishmen to obtain a resting-place for their ashes, or a perpetuation of their names. One of the last, if not the very

last, of her labours on behalf of her husband's memory was
the erection of a marble monument of Sir John Franklin in
Westminster Abbey, which was unveiled in July 1875, only a
fortnight before she herself passed away at the age of eighty-
three.   She had wished to write the epitaph itself, but she
died before she had time to perform that final work, and it
was her husband's nephew by marriage, the late Poet Laureate,
who afterwards, as all the world knows, added to it that
inscription which has given a second immortality to the
hero whom it celebrates :

> Not here ! the white North hath thy bones, and thou,
>   Heroic sailor soul,
> Art passing on thy happier voyage now
>   Towards no earthly pole.

Hardly less beautiful were the words appended to it by
Dean Stanley in record of the event so pathetically close in
sequence to it—Lady Franklin's death.   The monument to
Franklin was, it runs, 'erected by his widow, who, after long
waiting and sending many in search of him, herself departed
to seek and to find him in the realms of light.'

CHAPTER XXV

CHARACTER AND CAREER

1786-1847

PERSONAL reminiscences of Franklin have become rare and difficult to obtain. Born fourteen years before the close of the last century, he has naturally left no surviving contemporaries in the strict sense of the word, and nearly all even of those who ever came into contact with him after they themselves had reached years of maturity have now sunk into the grave. The companions of his adventures and sufferings, some of whom were considerably younger than himself and outlived him many years, have all long since passed away. Sir John Richardson, the one man, perhaps, who knew him best and was the most closely attached to him by ties both of friendship and affinity, is no more. Sir George Back has been dead nearly twenty years and Sir James Clark Ross more than thirty. Sir Edward Parry, the object of Franklin's lifelong regard and generous admiration, did not even live to witness the discovery of the last record of his friend.

Of his relatives, the children and grandchildren of his brothers and sisters, many still survive, but even to the elder of the two generations of boys and girls their sailor uncle was but a mysterious and heroic figure, seldom, and then only for very brief periods, revealed to them in the flesh. Hence their recollections of him, though often interesting and touching, are necessarily among the memories of the very young. They remember him, that is to say, from a day when the oldest among them was not much over ten or twelve years of age and he himself not much under fifty. Those relatives of blood or affinity who had reached adult years before he left England for the last time, and who might have preserved the impressions left by him upon mature minds, had been, with a single exception, separated from him by many thousand miles of sea during the time when such impressions might have been formed. The one exception is that of the Rev. Philip Gell, who, then a young man fresh from the University, made Franklin's acquaintance within the last ten years of the explorer's life, and lived for four or five of those years in close and sympathetic intercourse with his future father-in-law. Mr. Gell has, at the request of the writer, been good enough to supply the following vivid and interesting reminiscences of Franklin during his Australasian career.

' It is fifty years since Franklin bade me his last farewell, and the few letters I had from him afterwards were on family matters. But I wish I could send you some photographs as they are still imprinted on my memory of his manner and actions. I first felt his attraction on the day I found myself (a boy) kneeling by his side in Rugby Chapel to take the Communion at Arnold's hands. And only seven years later, in a sequestered anchorage of Tasmania, that sorrowful face, so kind and true, looked on me for the last time as he was leaving for England.

' I remember sharing a small tent with him on one of his expeditions, and being much impressed, as I was falling asleep in the deep darkness of the primæval forest, by hearing his devotions before he lay down on his bed of ferns. Forgetful, apparently (he was deaf), of any one's presence, he spoke aloud and softly at the Throne of Grace with affecting intercessions for those dear to him ; and his prayers were those of a child.

' His mode of handling infants was delightful. He was a very strong man, and the little ones seemed to revel in his arms ; and he, on his part, seemed to " follow their innocency."

' When, in 1840–41, the Antarctic expedition put into winter quarters, under his congenial care, his grave delight at their presence, and his interest in their ways and doings, made them twice the men they were before, and nerved them for their grand discoveries. He would sit up all night with the young officers at their magnetic observatory, taking his turn at the instruments, and in the three-minute intervals of observation trying to read Shakespeare, mingled with jokes and stories of the sea.

'A miniature Vice-regal Court was in those times a curious appendage of a Crown colony. On high days and holidays his way was worth observing. Humour would sparkle in his eye as certain of his grandees rendered their ungainly homage. Yet he " honoured all men ; " and all honoured him. And when the outside multitude drew him home in his carriage, he took it like a sailor in a breeze of wind, and they liked him all the more. No one ever heard that they did so to other Governors. His presence seemed to satisfy a want.

'When attending him on board a newly arrived convict ship from England, I heard him speak to the prisoners with such candour, firmness, and kindness, that it really seemed as if he felt more than they—which perhaps he did. Certainly they liked him for it, and began, some of them, to love him.

'Chicanery he could not away with ; it made him ill, and so paralysed him that when he had to deal with it he was scarcely himself.

'More than once his health was shaken under the burden of three thousand convicts, annually thrown upon his hands from England. There were elements of violence and corruption to be controlled, fierce, dangerous, and foul. And truly it was sickening work.

'Almost as paralysing, to a man of his temper, were the vagaries of sundry weak and wilful officials, who had made their way into the service of the Crown.

'And he found another source of hopeless sorrow in the fate of the perishing Aborigines. One evening his reception rooms at Government House were filled by local magnates, and showy uniforms, and bright daughters of the colony, with music and singing, when a man in livery came up to his Excellency, bearing a sheet of gum-tree bark, half as large as himself. It had been brought that night from the depths of the forest, a hundred miles away ; the forest which it was hoped and believed had been long since cleared of blacks.

The bark bore the charcoal picture of a kangaroo, freshly made by a native. An anxious future of bloodshed and reprisals rose before the company. The word on every lip was, "Catch them." But the Governor remained sorrowful and silent; as one who dealt with an insoluble problem.

'There was a wild girl taken in the woods, where her father and mother had perished; and when she was brought before Sir John he pointed to her, saying, "What name?" She wore nothing but a necklace of small bright shells, strung on a sinew. Thinking that he asked after that, she said, "Methinna"—native for necklace. So he gave her the name, and entrusted her to the care of his own daughter. Soon a scarlet tunic was provided; and the little one proved a good girl, though her tempestuous passions sometimes shook the order of the schoolroom at Government House.

'His comfort in the darkest days was his early walk with his daughter in the beautiful Government garden. She much resembled him in the nobler points of his character; his devotion, fortitude, and self-sacrifice; his endurance, his generosity, and care for his followers and dependents; and she shared his heavenward aspirations. As they walked together, Methinna would be darting about, or climbing the trees with hand and toe, native fashion, peering down with wild bright eyes out of the lofty foliage upon the two best friends she had in the world.

'Like his old friend, Sir Edward Parry, he was an impressive reader. When his last ship was in commission, the Bishop (Stanley) of Norwich would come on board on a Sunday to "hear" the captain. And what the Bishop liked, the officers and men liked too. Here is a last letter home from one of his men:

Erebus, May 25, 1845.

We had church this morning, and Sir John Franklin read to us a very beautiful sermon. Sir John took his text from the xviith chapter, 1 Kings, 16th verse, 'And the barrel of meal wasted not, neither did the cruse of oil fail, according to the word of the Lord.' Sir John called the ship's company's attention to that part of the sermon: and the whole of the ship's company were very much pleased with Sir John's appropriate text, and united in this point of view with Sir John, to accomplish our object which we have in view. And that with the help of the Almighty, I verily believe [we shall]. I have just received orders to pass the word for all that wish to attend divine service to go aft into Sir John's cabin at 3 o'clock this evening. And, my dearest Anne, I shall always go as long as I am able. I could remain for hours to hear him.'

One or two anecdotes derived from the recollections of the Rev. Canon Wright, the son of Sir John Franklin's youngest sister, Henrietta, have already appeared in the text. Their narrator has now kindly enabled me to supplement them with the contribution following :—

' In reply to your letter asking for any personal reminiscences I might have of Sir John Franklin I am sorry to say that these are necessarily very few. I have a dim recollection of his coming to my father's house at Wrangle just before he went out to Van Diemen's Land in 1836, and, though I was then the merest child, I can see him now in imagination standing before the fire in the dining-room, rather deaf but engaged in earnest conversation with my father and mother about other members of the family, in whom he manifested the greatest interest. The next and only other time I saw him was at Boston, at the house of Mr. Millington (my father's brother-in-law), who kindly invited Sir John's relatives in Lincolnshire to meet him there, a few days before he left England, in May 1845. Just then I was fired with the English boy's idea of becoming a sailor, and so, in my simplicity, I begged my mother to ask him whether he could take me with him on the approaching expedition. I expressed my readiness to go even as a *powder-monkey*, though exactly what the duties of a powder-monkey were I had no very definite knowledge, except that they were of an inferior description. I remember very distinctly his reply ; placing his hand on my shoulder he said, " No, my boy, I cannot take you. We must have in this service no cats that can't catch mice. Do your duty and what your mother tells you, and when I come back I will see what can be done for you." The dear old sea captain has never returned ; but on my part, God helping me, I have tried to follow out his last instruc-

tions, and to my doing so I owe whatever of success in life I
may have attained.

'I have, not unfrequently, heard my mother speak of Sir
John Franklin in earlier days. They were nearly of the same
age, and as children often together. When he was a small
boy he used to make it his practice to attend all the weddings
and funerals that occurred in Spilsby Church, and hence it
may be, as well as from the religious tone of his character, that
it was thought that he would be favourably disposed to taking
Holy Orders, and the living of Holton Beckering, near Wragby,
was obtained for him under that expectation. On one occasion he and his playmates were competing with one another
as to the position of future distinction which each should aim
at. This one would be content with the occupation of a
country squire, with carriages and horses, etc., that one with
some great military achievement against the French; but
John, as the discussion went on, perceiving that the whole
field of earthly ambition was rapidly being swept from his
grasp, impatiently exclaimed, " And *I'll* get a ladder and *climb
to Heaven !* " Verily it would seem that even at that early
age he had caught the spirit of Glaucus, when he tells Diomede
in the 6th Book of the Iliad that he had learnt

$$Αἰὲν ἀριστεύειν, καὶ ὑπείροχον ἔμμεναι ἄλλων.$$

'The boys of the Franklin family were generally considered
to be the "defenders of the right" at Spilsby, and some
amusing stories have been told of their prowess in this respect

'Mrs. Drummond Rawnsley, a daughter of his brother,
Sir Willingham Franklin, Judge of the Supreme Court of
Judicature at Madras, told me shortly before she died that
after her confirmation she met with Sir John Franklin in
London, who asked her whether she had ever attended the
Holy Communion, and on her replying in the negative, he said,
with the air of one who considered that a most important
standing order had been broken, " Why, my dear, this is all
wrong ; you must be prepared to go with me on Sunday
morning next. I shall come for you." And he came, and
with him she made her first Communion.

F F

'I have asked my cousin, Lady Tennyson (who was also my godmother, and therefore older than myself), whether she has any interesting recollections, but like my own they are not many. She replies : " I am sorry I can contribute nothing which seems to me worthy of Mr. Traill's Biography. My uncle was a great deal with my father during my mother's lifetime, but, of course, I remember nothing of this, since I lost my mother when I was only three years old. My first recollection of him is that, when carried in my nurse's arms to her funeral, I touched his shoulder and asked, ' What are they doing ? ' My last is when, just before his latest Arctic expedition, I saw him at Somerset House, and, if my memory fail not, he said, ' Remember, Emily, if I do not return when I am expected, I have made for the open sea at the Pole."

'Personally I have always had the warmest admiration of Sir John Franklin's character, based not only on what I have heard from those who knew him well, but also on a large correspondence of his which has come into my possession. He seems to have been always so brave and generous, so able, unselfish, and affectionate, so unshrinkingly true in his duty to God and man.'

Mrs. G. B. A. Lefroy, a surviving sister of Miss Sophia Cracroft, so often referred to in the foregoing pages, writes as follows :

'With respect to the suggestion that I may be able to supply some personal reminiscences of my uncle, Sir John Franklin, I regret very much that I can add but little worth publishing. He was so seldom on shore, and for such short intervals, and although my mother, Mrs. Thomas Cracroft (who was left a widow at an early age), and her children were always objects of his interest and most affectionate care, I cannot remember his ever staying with us except for a few weeks at Castle Hedingham, Essex, soon after his return from Tasmania and shortly before he obtained the command of the Erebus and Terror. Although he was very fond of the companionship of children and young people, I recollect that his usually grave and serious manner rather awed us, although he liked a joke and had a most loving and affectionate nature.

He was quick in reproving faults of habit and manner, and would not hesitate to try to correct them by good advice, which I suppose is not always palatable to children. Some of my sisters had the very objectionable habit of biting their nails, which he could not endure, and when taking a walk with him round the garden and into the country, in which he delighted, they avoided, if possible, taking his hand, that they might escape the detection of a bitten nail which would bring down a reproof.

' He was a devourer of books of every kind, and nothing pleased him more than to be let alone. When thus employed and oblivious of all around him, he would pass many a happy hour undisturbed.

' He disliked notoriety and never sought it. He was never so happy as when afloat. Soon after his return from one of his early Arctic voyages, my mother told me he joined her at Brighton. The Court was then resident there at the Pavilion, and the place crowded. My uncle attracted a good deal of observation when out of doors, and this he avoided as much as possible. On one occasion, however, from the midst of a crowd who recognised him, a voice called out, "That's the man who ate his shoes," much to his amusement.

' To illustrate his determination of character, a few weeks before he left England on his last voyage he took a house in Brook Street, Grosvenor Square, for the purpose of taking leave of his friends and of making acquaintance with the officers selected to accompany him. He was there attacked by a severe influenza cold, the first illness, I believe, he ever had, although he never took to his bed but went about as usual, and was much occupied in preparations for final departure. His medical attendant recommended him to leave off his lifelong habit of taking snuff. He undertook to do this, and, although I suppose he could scarcely have realised the great strain such a sudden abandonment of the habit would entail, he never wavered in his determination or shrank from the self-denial. He used to endeavour to supply the loss of the stimulant with strong smelling salts and harts-horn, and so he persevered and never resumed the old-fashioned habit of those days. Would an habitual smoker of these days show as much self-denial and determination?

'I heard from my sister that a few days before he sailed on his last voyage his wife, the late Lady Franklin, was putting a finishing touch to a union-jack he was to take with him, and, as he lay on the sofa, she threw it over him, which distressed him, and he exclaimed, "Oh Jane! what have you done?" alluding, of course, to the popular superstition which has arisen from the use of the union-jack as a shroud for the bodies of those who are buried at sea.' [1]

Among those still spared to us who knew Franklin well in the later years of his life was, it may be remembered, the distinguished diplomatist Sir Henry Elliot. In an article contributed by him to a monthly review a few years ago, on the subject of Admiral Markham's then recent monograph on the great explorer, Sir Henry speaks of himself as ' having, as a very young man, lived for three years as one of the family in the home of Sir John Franklin, for whom,' he adds, he had ' the affection of a son for his father.' How true a description of the feeling with which his sometime private secretary regarded Franklin, the correspondence which passed between them after the former's quitting Tasmania to enter the diplomatic service amply proves, and Franklin's reciprocation of this filial sentiment no less fully deserves to be described as paternal. No breath of disagreement ever seems to have ruffled the tranquillity of relations which only good nature, good sense, and tact on both sides could have maintained for three years in unbroken smoothness. Not many more men are angels to their private secretaries than are heroes to their valets; and that the youth of twenty, necessarily inexperienced in his duties, should have lived to look back on his

---

[1] Mrs. Lefroy adds this curious little anecdote in illustration of the manners of the forties : ' A large party of relations and friends went down to Greenhithe, to see the last of the Erebus and Terror, and to share in the final farewells and the sanguine hopes for a speedy return. On their way home the party passed through Greenwich Park during the notorious Greenwich Fair, and one of the party, a great friend and admirer of my uncle, the late Bishop of Norwich (Stanley), was knocked down and had his pockets emptied, and all were glad to escape.'

intercourse with the busied and worried, not to say 'badgered,' governor of a not easily governable colony with the feelings which animate Sir Henry Elliot's retrospect, speaks highly for the qualities both of the secretary and of the chief. ' Franklin's great characteristic,' he writes, ' was his thoughtfulness for others and his complete absence of thought for himself ; deeply religious, his duty to God and man was at all times his sole and only guide ; and when he had once decided what that duty was, no earthly consideration could turn him a hair's breadth from it. Of a singularly simple and affectionate nature, identifying himself with the interests and welfare of those over whom he was placed, he won their love in an extraordinary degree, and although of highly sensitive feelings, he was never known to be provoked to use a harsh or hasty word ; and with such a combination of kindness and resolution Captain Fitzjames might well describe him as " of all men the most fitted " to command an expedition such as that in which they both lost their lives.'

The universal sentiments of respect and affection with which he inspired the people of that colony, his administration of which had so untoward a close, have been already noted in the account of his departure ; and the enthusiasm with which the colonists bade farewell to him was no momentary emotion. It may be doubted whether any colonial governor has ever left behind him more enduring memories of regard. The generous contribution which was so readily made by the people of Tasmania to the search expeditions was only one of many and various testimonies to their grateful recollection of their former ruler. Nearly ten years after his departure the historian of the colony, whose work has been so frequently quoted in the foregoing pages, paid a tribute to his character and services which is all the more valuable from the candour with which the writer dwells upon Franklin's inability, as he considers it, to cope with the difficulties of an office ' for which his former pursuits had not prepared him.' ' His manner (says Mr. West) was often embarrassed and hesitating, and presented a contrast to the quiet vigour of his more able but not more amiable predecessor.' But 'the administration of the former was eminently disinterested. He had no private speculations or secret agents, and his measures were free from both the taint and the reproach of corruption. His expenditure greatly exceeded his official income, and while the plainness of his establishment and entertainments was the topic of thoughtless censure, the charities of his family were scattered with a liberal hand.' The writer might have added that Franklin declined an increase of salary voted him by the colonial Legislature.

Another witness, of the same profession as this writer, the Rev. T. L. Ewing, writing from Newtown Parsonage, assures Lady Franklin that her 'husband's name is never mentioned here without an endearing epithet. So true is it that people only value their blessings rightly when they have lost them.' And how his memory lived in the hearts of the humblest and most despised class of the community, the following most interesting letter from Commander Pasco to Lady Franklin in 1858 will show :—

The circumstance which has induced me to write direct to you instead of to Miss Cracroft as usual, is that of meeting an old man yesterday as I was travelling through the bush about ten miles from this place down the Murray.

Overtaking a weary traveller on foot, with his bundle of bedding on his back, and learning on enquiry that he had *walked* up from the Darling, a distance of at least 200 miles, I could not help offering to dismount and give him a lift for a few miles ; which he declined for himself but accepted for his *swag*, as he termed his bedding. We jogged along talking of his long journey, which he made light of.

I soon ascertained that he had been a prisoner, and in reply to my question, how long he had been free, he said, 'Oh, that dear old gentleman Sir John gave me my free pardon for going to Macquarie Harbour with him.' I did not at once discover to him that I had any knowledge of that event, but let him relate to me the details of the journey. I cannot tell you how my heart warmed towards the old man as he enlarged on your and our beloved and revered absent one. Especially was I struck with the vivid impression left on the man's mind by the aptness of his chief to encourage and support those of the party who might appear to despond. 'Oh sir !' he said, 'you should have seen him cheering us up when smothered in snow under the "Frenchman's cap." "Come, come, my boys !" he would say,

" this is nothing at all, you should laugh at this ! " And when we got on short tucker (to use old Smith's own phrase for provisions) there was a doctor chap who wanted to cut us short and keep a full allowance for the gentry and Lady Franklin (for she was there too), but Sir John said, " No, no ; let us go short, if you like, and give it to the men who do the work," for,' said Smith, 'there was one gentleman with a hammer who used to load us with big stones [doubtless some ardent geologist of the party], but Sir John was always our friend.'

I could fill a quire with his anecdotes, including some of yourself being borne in a sort of sedan they rigged up for you ; but sometimes you let your maid have a spell.   I let him run on with his tale, and I cannot describe his astonishment on hearing how near I was to the party when it quitted Macquarie Harbour.   Smith has been many years shepherding in the neighbourhood, and is on his way to a new station.

It is satisfactory to find that he made such good use of the liberty obtained for him fourteen years before.   He was, of course, one of the men whose release had been maliciously commented upon by the Tasmanian press, and in his account of the ' rigged-up sedan ' we find the germ of the calumnious legend which represented Franklin as dispensing the royal favour, as a sort of Oriental satrap, to the bearers of his wife's ' palanquin.'

The honour in which his name was so long held in this distant part of the globe is in some sort typical of his general fame.   In the enduring vitality of their affection for Franklin the people of Tasmania were only supplying, as his countrymen at home had supplied, an impressive illustration of the grand truth that it is not in what men do but in what they are that their greatness lies.   Franklin's government of the colony had been marred by contentions and had closed in storm ; but the instinct of its people told them that the man was greater than his work.   And so, in a certain sense, he had shown himself in every undertaking of his life.   Mr. A. H. Beesly has justly remarked in his interesting monograph on the famous explorer, published some years ago, that the whole history of his explorations is a record, if not exactly of failure, yet always and everywhere of imperfect success.   In 1819–22 he accomplished a maritime journey of great scientific value under extraordinary difficulties, and fought his way home by land through appalling privations ; but he did not succeed, as he had hoped, in completing the survey of the coast of Arctic America eastward from the mouth of the Coppermine River.   In 1825-27 he made another large addition to the sum of geographical knowledge to the west of the Mackenzie ; but he failed to effect the desired junction with the voyagers from Behring Strait.   In 1845 he set forth in quest of a north-west passage, and succeeded only in discovering a route which he did not live to traverse.   Yet the fame which he won for himself could not have been brighter of lustre or more assured of perpetuity if he had explored the whole coastline of Arctic America to the eastward in 1821 and to the westward in 1826, and had sailed from the Atlantic to the Pacific in 1845.   His countrymen, and the entire civilised world, have recognised that the great though imperfect exploits of the traveller were outshone by the heroic qualities of the man, and out of the wealth of their own admiration they have made good his 'inheritance of unfulfilled renown.'

He was moreover endowed, and in a pre-eminent degree, with a quality which does not always accompany greatness— the quality of charm.   To the abundant evidences of his many endearing characteristics which have been cited in the course of this narrative it would be superfluous to add.   No leader ever lived who commanded a more enthusiastic devotion from his followers.   From the comrades whom he sustained with his indomitable spirit in the frozen wilds of Arctic America to the convicts who responded so heartily to his cheery encouragement in the Tasmanian bush, the attraction of his personality seems to have been felt alike by all.   The fervent piety of his deeply religious nature was never obtruded by him, never became, as it has too often become with men of a less genial and humane temperament, a repellent influence upon those who were not in sympathy with his devout spirit. There was no touch of self-righteousness or spiritual vanity about him.   In this respect he differed as widely as possible from that peculiar type of officer, well-meaning of motive, but injudicious of method, who used to be known in the army as a 'preaching colonel.'   Though far from being ashamed of his

religion or unwilling to testify in its behalf before the world—
an old messmate of his told his sister that he always considered that Franklin 'first introduced religion into the gun-
room' of the Bedford—his piety was throughout his life
of the sober and practical order natural to an Englishman
born and brought up in the Church of England during
that long period of what certain excitable persons would
call 'stagnation,' which divided the two great 'revivals' of
the mid-eighteenth and mid-nineteenth century from each
other. It had no affinities with either the ecstatic or the
ascetic form of the religious emotion, and it was certainly free
from any tendency to give undue prominence to faith over
works. It was emphatically the piety of a man of action and
endeavour, of him to whom, though the evening never fails to
bring the hour of spiritual self-communing and meditation,
the day seems best spent in untiring struggle with the hostile
forces of Nature, best dedicated to that labour which itself is
prayer. In a word, it was the piety which supported Have-
lock in his swift and splendid march over the burning plains
of India, and Gordon in his lonely vigil at Khartoum ; the
piety which, through generations of our history, has carried so
many strenuous English workers by land and sea through a
life of perils to an heroic death.

And in Franklin's case, as in theirs, it was fused and
interpenetrated with that patriotism which to Englishmen is
itself a religion, and to too many among them the only one
they have. Cradled in the traditions of the most glorious era
of our naval history, it seemed as natural a thing to him that
English sailors should lead the van of maritime exploration
as that English ships of war should command the seas. He
was devoted, as we have seen, from his midshipman days to
the duties, scientific as well as practical, of his calling, and as
for the sea itself, the ardour of his passion for it never abated.
That 'love at first sight' was also a love for life ; the spell
which was thrown over the schoolboy on the beach at Saltfleet remained unbroken to the end. 'He was never so
happy,' says Mrs. Lefroy, 'as when afloat.' It is almost
amusing to note how soon at all periods of his career the

landsman's life began to pall upon him—how little of it he really wanted, and how long a way that little went. Next to 'active employment,' the one perpetual need of his nature, the sea and the seaman's life were the objects of his strongest craving. Rather than remain idle he would govern a colony willingly enough; but far rather than govern a colony would he have taken command of a ship for some adventurous voyage. All the sailor in his nature came out in the eager enthusiasm with which he welcomed Ross and Crozier to Hobart Town, the almost boyish delight with which he threw himself into their work, the wistfulness with which he watched the fading of their sails in those mists of the unknown Antarctic into which he would so fain have followed them.

With these instincts, moreover, he united the whole traditional character of the sailor—that character which is dearer than all others to the national heart. Never has it been represented in a more typical example. The bluff, straightforward honesty, the hearty kindliness, the invincible buoyancy of temperament, the quick impetuosity—they were all there in Franklin; and we somehow seem to recognise their latent presence under whatever uncongenial conditions of circumstance and environment. One is certainly conscious of their suppression during much of the history of his Tasmanian governorship. That Franklin's intellectual gifts were by no means inconsiderable, his official correspondence shows. His shrewd mother wit and sound judgment, his spirit of healthy contempt for the mawkish, restrained as that spirit was by genuine goodness of heart from running into harshness, would have made him, under happier conditions, the ideal ruler of a penal settlement; for convicts, like children, know well enough how to distinguish the firm kindness which wins their respect as well as their love from the weak amiability which, while they practise on it, they despise. And Franklin, with a freer hand, would have been an excellent and successful administrator all round. As a benevolent despot of the early Anglo-Indian type, he would have been admirably well placed; as, indeed, he would have been in any other post entailing a maximum of practical activity with a minimum of consultation and debate.

He was a governor born to govern, as has been said, 'from the saddle' rather than from the council room ; and even his ablest and most carefully drafted memoranda on transportation, trade, local government, and other colonial matters, leave the impression that the writer would far rather be illustrating his views in practice than explaining them on paper. Among the variety of untoward causes which led to his later administrative troubles, one may perhaps include a touch of impatience with an uncongenial situation and its distasteful duties.

Foremost, however, and most conspicuous among his qualities was his extraordinary fortitude. Richardson, himself a man with immense powers of endurance, was wont to the end of his days to speak of it with wondering admiration as without parallel among the hardy race of Arctic explorers to which they both belonged. It was so much the more marvellous, he was in the habit of saying, because Franklin owed least of all men to any peculiar advantages of bodily constitution. The capacity to resist extreme cold is very unequally distributed among natives of the milder regions of the earth, and Franklin had not more, but less, than the normal share. His circulation was slow and his vitality, therefore, easily lowered. He suffered all his life, and even in England, from cold hands and feet. Temperament had in his case to be called in at an unusually early stage to supply the lack of temperature, and long before his comrades had exhausted their physical powers of resistance to the rigours of the Arctic climate, Franklin had been drawing upon moral resources alone. Yet this was the man, this 'chilly mortal,' of the sluggish blood and benumbed extremities, who, from the deadliest of all his struggles with frost and famine, brought home so untamed a courage and so unshaken a resolve that ere a year had passed he was longing to renew the battle, nay, eagerly soliciting the order to measure himself once more against these cruel foes.

But though he loved adventure for adventure's sake, though he revelled, as strength and daring always revel, in the strife with difficulty, it was another and a rarer impulse which sent

him to his death.   His highest and truest claim to the rank
of a national hero is that he was filled with that spirit which
is even more national than the love of adventure, more English
even than the passion for the 'great waters'—the thirst for
the discovery of the unknown.   'They cannot help it, these
Arctic fellows,' said Lord Brougham, when he was told that
Franklin, on the verge of sixty, had set out in quest of the
North-west Passage ; ' they cannot help it ; it is in the blood.'
But it has been in the blood, not of 'these Arctic fellows'
alone, but of their countrymen for centuries past ; in the blood
of Drake and Hawkins, of Cook and Flinders, of Speke and
Livingstone and Stanley.   In the veins of Franklin it glowed
with an unquenchable and lifelong ardour.   Neither advancing
age nor the distractions of a new career had any power over
it.   That blank space on the map of Arctic America haunted
him incessantly for twenty years ; that unbridged gap of
300 miles between the overlapping routes of Dease and
Parry would not let him rest.   And thus it was that, in the
evening of his life, at a time when most men's thoughts would
be turning to repose, he set forth once more, another Ulysses,

> To follow knowledge like a sinking star,
> Beyond the utmost bound of human thought.

The great lines of the poet who was afterwards to write his
epitaph, might almost seem to have been inspired ten years
before by a prophetic prevision of that Homeric figure for whom
' old age had yet its honour and its toil,' and who, more
truly than any man then living, could re-echo that eternal heart-
cry of the explorer in every field of search, that

> all experience is an arch wherethro'
> Gleams that untravelled world whose margin fades
> For ever and for ever when I move.

It was at the call of this insatiable longing that he went
forth to die, and it is for his loyal obedience to that summons
that the nation has placed him unhesitatingly among its heroes.
It is the one form of romantic service—for our patriotism we
can defend as 'practical'—which Englishmen appreciate.   The

only war which they will wage ' for an idea ' is the war against the forces of nature for the prize of an undiscovered world. How purely ideal is this warfare we have shown again and again—in our indifference alike to the cost at which it is prosecuted and to the material value of its gains. That North-west Passage, on which the hearts of our Arctic voyagers were so long set, was at last discovered ; and its discovery was wholly useless to the commerce of the world. Half a century has nearly passed since then, yet this shadowy channel, varying yearly with the caprices of the seasons and the drift of the Polar pack, remains, and will remain, untried. No trader will ever pick his difficult way through those silent ice-fields from the Atlantic to the Pacific waters. For all its worth to mankind, as measured by material standards, the much-desired passage might as well have been the visionary Eldorado that seemed to beckon to our seafaring ancestors of three centuries ago. But, even as the spirit of the great Elizabethan mariners lived again in the breast of John Franklin, so his place is with them in our history, and his memory will live with theirs.

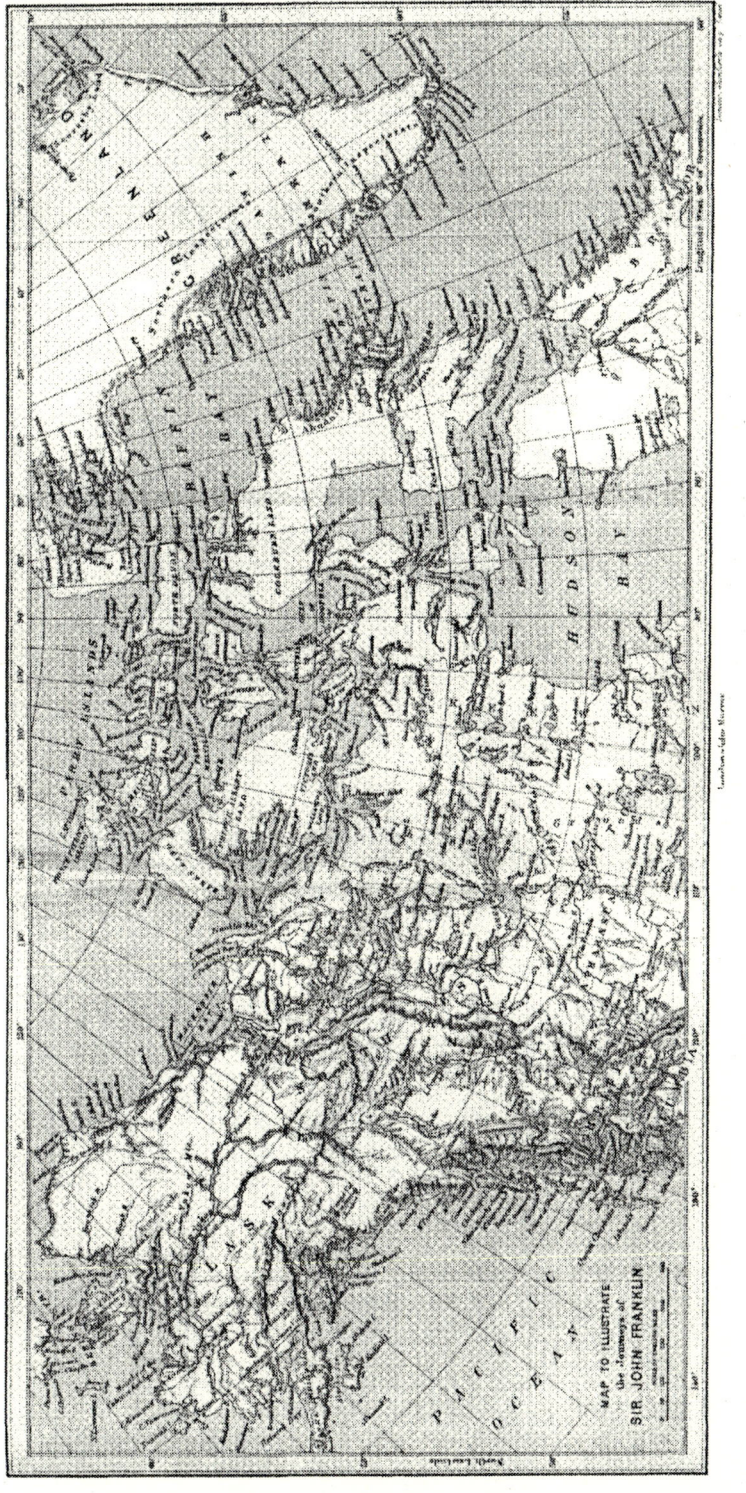

MAP TO ILLUSTRATE
the Journeys of
SIR JOHN FRANKLIN

INDEX

pointment, 237 ; complimentary dinner at Horncastle, 237 ; speeches,
238; departure, 240; enthusiastic
reception in Tasmania, 246; report
on the state of the colony, 246 ;
anxiety for peace, 247 ; letter to Capt.
Cumby on his duties, 248 ; scheme
of founding a colonial college, 250 ;
letter to Dr. Arnold, 250–253 ; his
criticism of the charter, 254–256 ; on
the system of penal discipline exercised under his administration, 259 ;
on the practice of 'assignment,' 262 ;
endeavour to work new probationary
system, 265 ; dismissal of Capt.
Mackonochie, 267 ; starts for Macquarrie harbour, 272 ; lost in the
bush, 272–274 ; relief parties, 275 ;
letter from Mr. Disraeli, 276 ; advocates Hepburn's claim to employment,
277 ; correspondence with him, 278 ;
his youthful tricks, 280 ; the Flinders
memorial, 281, 282 ; construction of
the observatory, 283 ; account of
Capt. Ross's expedition, 285–287 ;
festivities on board the Erebus, 287 ;
difficulties of his administration, 288 ;
reasons for his failure, 289–295 ;
quarrels between the Attorney and
Solicitor-General, 295 ; the Distillation Bill, 296 ; opposition of Mr.
Gregory, 297 ; suspension, 298 ;
strained relations with Mr. Montagu,
299–305 ; decision in the Coverdale
case, 300 ; newspaper attacks, 302 ;
suspends Mr. Montagu, 304 ; error
of his recommendation, 305 ; despatch
from Lord Stanley, 309–312 ; its
publicity, 314 ; delay in its reception,
314 ; resignation, 315 ; mode of his
recall, 315–318 ; preparations for
departure, 319 ; leave-taking, 320 ;
view of his character, 321 ; interview
with Lord Stanley, 323 ; statement
of his claims for redress, 327 ; reply
to Lord Stanley, 328 ; his ' Narrative,' 329 ; projected expedition, 331 ;
reply to the Admiralty, 331 ; repu-
diates his susceptibility to cold, 333 ;
interview with Lord Haddington,
334 ; appointed to the command of
the Erebus, 336 ; proposed route,
337, 354 ; letters of farewell, 339 ;
from Stromness, 340 ; on the qualities
of his officers, 341 ; testimonies to his
powers and attractions, 342–344 ;
last letter from Whalefish Island,
345–351 ; selects the north-westward
route, 354 ; winter quarters at Beechey
Island, 357 ; discovers the southward

leading channel, 358 ; set fast in the
ice, 359 ; despatch of a land exploring
party, 363 ; illness, 365 ; death, 367 ;
monuments, 426 ; piety, 440 ; love
of the sea, 441 ; fortitude, 443
Franklin, Lady, her letters to Sir John,
167–169 ; illness of her step-
daughter, 196 ; meeting with her husband at Malta, 198 ; account of an
interview with Mahommed Ali, 201 ;
tour in the Holy Land, 201–203 ; in
Greece, 205 ; her travelling companions, 205–207 ; illness and death
of a young Englishman, 207–210 ; in
Alexandria, 216, 218 ; return home,
221 ; proposal to erect a memorial
to Captain Flinders, 281 ; her share
in the Tasmanian troubles, 293 ;
sympathy with Captain Mackonochie, 295 ; equips the schooner Prince
Albert, 385 ; fits out the screw
steamer Isabel, 390 ; her appeal to
Lord Palmerston, 399–402 ; equipment of the Fox, 402 ; contributors,
403 ; instructions to Captain McClintock, 404 ; her repeated letters to
the dead, 418–421 ; approaching
marriage of her step-daughter, 419 ;
collection of letters &c., 424 ; letter
to Sir R. Murchison, 425 ; death,
427
— Mrs., her delicate health, 112 ;
bright temperament, 114 ; birth
of daughter, 115 ; extracts from her
letters, 114–116 ; death, 119
— Miss Sarah, 3
— Thomas, 8 ; death, 32
— Willingham, 2, 3
— Strait, 358
Frome, Mr., 282

Gawler, Colonel, Governor of South
Australia, 281
Gell, Rev. J. P., Principal of Tasmania
College, 253 ; his inscription to
Captain Flinders, 282 ; reminiscences
of Franklin, 429–432
George IV., death of, 157
Germain, St., 93
Gibbs, General, 47
Gipps, Sir George, Governor of N. S.
Wales, 269, 274
Gleig, Rev. C. R., his account of the
attack on New Orleans, 39
Glenelg, Lord, Colonial Secretary,
offers the governorship of Antigua
to Franklin, 232
Gloucester, Duchess of, 213
' Goldner's Patent,' the putrid meat-
tins of, 386

PRINTED BY
SPOTTISWOODE AND CO., NEW-STREET SQUARE
LONDON

Printed in the United States
25613LVS00003B/20

9 781417 970407